P9-AFE-351

Knowing and Making
Wine

Knowing and Making Wine

EMILE PEYNAUD

Translated from the French by Alan Spencer

A Wiley-Interscience Publication
JOHN WILEY & SONS
New York · Chichester · Brisbane · Toronto · Singapore

Library of Congress Cataloging in Publication Data:

Peynaud, Emile.
 Knowing and making wine.

 Translation of: Connaissance et travail du vin.
 "A Wiley-Interscience publication."
 Includes index.
 1. Wine and wine making. I. Title.

TP548.P4513   1984   663'.22   84-11936
ISBN 0-471-88149-X

Printed in the United States of America

10 9 8 7 6 5 4 3 2 1

Preface

TO THE SECOND EDITION

The 1971 edition has been reprinted several times and the various issues have now reached a total of 12,000 copies. It has been translated into Italian and Spanish, and now finally into English.

When it first appeared, this book was merely a condensed, more accessible version of the *Traité d'oenologie* in two volumes by J. Ribéreau-Gayon and E. Peynaud which had been published a few years before. This digest was more particularly aimed at the enologist and wine technician. It had been written as an introduction to the teaching of enology and a guide adapted to the Government Continuous Training Scheme. In it were to be found both the language of the winery and the laboratory. In spite of the effort required to read it, perhaps indeed because of this effort, it has been appreciated by wine workers and informed amateurs as well. Each discovered in the book a new way of talking about wine.

The plan of the first edition and the breakdown into different lessons has not been changed in its essentials. On the other hand, the text has been rewritten in a new form and adapted in its content. Over the last 10 years, there has been considerable progress both in knowledge itself and in its practical application. Improvements in equipment and the industrialization of production have continued to go ahead, laws have been changed and brought into line throughout the European Economic Community. It was necessary to update these concepts, widen the scope of their application in the light of the latest edition of the treatise *Sciences et techniques du vin*.

A new eighth part has been added. It deals in two chapters with the conditioning of wine during bottling. This operation raises problems of stability

v

and quality control and involves the enologist more and more. It needed to be dealt with in a manual of enology which is intended to be directly related to practical problems.

EMILE PEYNAUD

Bordeaux, France
June 1984

Preface

TO THE FIRST EDITION

This book is the outcome of 40 years of study and research plus 20 years of teaching both students and professionals. It is intended to be at once theoretical and practical, explanatory and realistic. Its purpose is to help people know wine better in order to make it better, cultivate it, mature it, and appreciate it better too. A product of man's work, wine is worth, in the final analysis, only what man himself is worth and the ignoramus only makes good wine by accident.

Enology is not an abstract science. It has grown out of research into solutions to practical problems. But whereas the facts are observed during work at cellar level or in the winery, they can only be explained, rules laid down, and progress made at the higher level during study of these phenomena. In this way enology has its fundamental basis in physical chemistry, biochemistry, and microbiology.

Technical progress evolves through applied scientific research and propagation of the knowledge acquired. It is not enough to pursue the knowledge of wine in the laboratory alone, it must be spread through the wineries in order for this knowledge to become part of daily practice. Moreover, the faster scientific progress advances, the greater risk there is of widening the gap between what we know and what we do. It is necessary to narrow this gap and speed up evolution. That is the intention of this book. It responds in this respect to the need frequently expressed by professional organizations for a serious popularization of knowledge and methods for use at production level and in the wine trade.

It has been conceived as a handbook for the enology student and the enologist faced with practical problems. However, it is mainly directed towards the wine "professional": grower, wine maker, technician, cellar worker, cellar master, wine taster, shopkeeper, broker. It is for them that the author decided to avoid the usual chemical and analytical approach common to books on enology. This book should be a way of introducing the reader to an easier understanding of *Traite d'œnologie* and of *Analyse et contrôle des vins*.

The author was Professor Jean Ribéreau-Gayon's first pupil and collaborator. Although it does not bear his signature, this book is impregnated with his work and his doctrines.

EMILE PEYNAUD

Bordeaux, France
January 1971

Contents

PART 1   TASTING AND THE COMPOSITION OF WINE

1   MECHANICS AND METHODS OF TASTING   3

Definition of Tasting   3
Mechanics of Tasting   6
Practice of Tasting   8

2   GUSTATORY CHARACTERISTICS AND VOCABULARY   14

The Relationship Between the Composition of
Wines and Their Gustatory Qualities   14
Gustatory Vocabulary   17

3   TASTING EXERCISES   24

Training in Tasting   24
Theoretical Tasting Exercises   25
Exercises in Analytical Tasting   32

4   THE COMPOSITION OF WINE   35

Definition of Wine   35
Sweet-Tasting Substances   36
Sour-Tasting Substances   39

Salty-Tasting Substances   43
Bitter- and Astringent-Tasting Substances   44
Other Substances   47
Analytical Definitions   52

PART 2   THE RIPENING OF THE GRAPE AND HARVESTING

5   WHAT HAPPENS DURING THE RIPENING OF THE GRAPE   57

Description of the Grape   57
Transformations in the Grape in the Course of Ripening   58
Overripening   72

6   HARVESTING   75

Setting the Vintage Date   75
Harvest Work   79
Gray Rot   80
The Quality of Vintage Years   81

7   ADJUSTING THE VINTAGE   83

Sugaring or Chaptalization   83
Deacidification   86
Acidification   89

PART 3   MICROBIOLOGY OF WINE AND FERMENTATION

8   ALCOHOLIC FERMENTATION AND YEASTS   93

Process of Alcoholic Fermentation   93
General Characteristics of Yeasts   95
Species of Helpful Yeasts   96
Species of Noxious Yeasts   100
Use of Yeasts in Vinification   102

9 CONDITIONS FOR DEVELOPMENT OF YEASTS—
   CONDUCTING ALCOHOLIC FERMENTATION   107

   Influence of Temperature   107
   Influence of Aeration   111
   The Yeasts' Nutritional Needs   117
   Influence of Acidity   119

10 MALOLACTIC FERMENTATION AND LACTIC BACTERIA   120

   Nature of Malolactic Fermentation   121
   The Bacteria of Malolactic Fermentation   124

11 CONDITIONS FOR DEVELOPMENT OF MALOLACTIC   129
   BACTERIA—CONDUCTING MALOLACTIC FERMENTATION

   Modern Principles of Fermentation   129
   Conditions for Malolactic Fermentation   131
   Use of Malolactic Inocular Cultures   136

PART 4   VINIFICATIONS

12 VINIFYING RED WINE—WORK WITH GRAPES AND
   FERMENTING APPARATUS   143

   Mechanical Operations of Work with Grapes   144
   Fermentation Tanks   148
   Cap Management   153

13 VINIFYING RED WINE—CONDUCTING FERMENTATION   159

   Addition of Sulfite or Sulfur Dioxide   159
   Supervising Fermentation   163
   The Thermal Problem   165
   Dealing with Stuck Fermentation   169

14 VINIFYING RED WINE—CONDUCTING EXTRACTION
   DURING POMACE CONTACT   172

   Laws of Extraction   172
   Length of Pomace Contact   176

Draining   176
Pressing   179
Technical Evolution by Area   181

15 VINIFYING RED WINE—RECENT TECHNIQUES IN USE   184

Continous Fermentation   185
Vinification in Specially Equipped Tanks   187
Vinification with Maceration Carbonique   189
Thermal Vinification   192

16 VINIFYING WHITE WINE—WORK WITH GRAPES AND
    PROCESSING THE MUST   197

Diversity of Types of White Wine   197
Method of Picking   198
Mechanical Work with the White Vintage   199
Settling and Racking   205
Treating Must with Bentonite   210

17 VINIFYING WHITE WINE—PROTECTION FROM
    OXIDATION AND CONDUCTING FERMENTATION   212

Preventing the Effects of Oxidation   212
Conducting Fermentation   214
Sweet and Semisweet Wines   217

18 VINIFYING ROSÉ WINES AND SPECIAL WINES   221

Definition and Processing of Rosé Wines   221
The Wines of Champagne   222
Sparkling Wines   224
Asti Spumante   225
Natural Sweet Wines (VDN)   226
Port Wines   227
Sherry   228
Brandy   229

PART 5 STORAGE AND AGING

19 CELLAR WORK—CLEANLINESS AND HYGIENE MEASURES FOR WINE CONTAINERS **233**

Cleanliness of the Premises 233
Cleanliness of the Wine Containers 235
The Practice of Racking 238
Topping 242
Storage Under Nitrogen 243
Blending Wines 245

20 MATURING AND AGING WINES **246**

Role of Oxygen 247
Changes in the Color 250
Changes in the Bouquet 251
Conditions for Barrel Aging 252
Conditions for Bottle Aging 253
Accelerated Aging 254

21 MICROBIAL SPOILAGE **255**

Acetic Spoilage or Acescence 256
Film Yeast (Flor) 258
Lactic Spoilage 259
Tourne 259
Fermentation of Glycerol 260
Lactic Souring 261
Lactic Fermentation of Small Quantities of Sugar 261
Ropiness (Graisse) 263
Microbiological Control 263

22 THE USE OF SULFUR DIOXIDE IN THE STORAGE OF WINES **266**

Forms of Sulfur Dioxide in Wines 267
Combination Rate of Added Sulfur Dioxide 270
Doses of Sulfur Dioxide to be Used 271
Instructions for Use of Sulfur Dioxide 272
Other Preservatives Used with Sulfur Dioxide 274

PART 6   CLARIFICATION OF WINES

23   **CONCEPT OF CLARITY**   **281**

    Examining Clarity   282
    Particles in Suspension in Wine   283
    Spontaneous Clarification   285

24   **CLARIFICATION BY FINING**   **287**

    Mechanism of Fining   288
    Fining Tests   290
    Fining Agents   291
    Method of Using Fining Agents   295
    Stabilizing Effect of Fining   296

25   **CLARIFICATION BY FILTERING**   **298**

    Mechanism of Filtration   299
    Filtering Using Filter Pads   300
    Membrane Filtering   303
    Filtering Through Diatomaceous Earth   304
    The Sensory Consequences of Filtering   307
    Fining or Filtration?   307
    Clarification by Centrifugation   308

PART 7   STABILIZING PROCESSES FOR WINES

26   **BASIC PRINCIPLES OF STABILIZING PROCESSES**   **315**

    Cloudiness   315
    Rational Bases for Stabilizing Processes   317
    List of Treatments   320

27   **STABILIZATION IN REGARD TO METALLIC CASSE**   **323**

    Description of Ferric Casse   323
    Mechanism of Ferric Casse   324

Processes for Treating Ferric Casse 325
Description of Cupric Casse 329
Mechanism of Cupric Casse 330
Treatments for Cupric Casse 331

28 PHYSICAL TREATMENTS APPLIED TO WINES 332
Stabilizing Wines by Heating 333
Refrigeration of Wines 336

29 OTHER TREATMENTS APPLIED TO WINE 342
Use of Bentonite 342
Use of Gum Arabic 345
Use of Metatartaric Acid 346

PART 8 BOTTLING WINES

30 BOTTLES AND BOTTLING 351
Glass: Its Nature and Composition 351
Cleanliness of Bottles 355
Filling the Bottles 356

31 Corks and Closures 362
Technology of Cork 362
Manufacture of Corks 364
Corking Bottles 366

INDEX 371

The Baume degrees scale for densities of musts is a specifically French scale. To convert this scale to the Brix scale, which is more widely used in America, the reader can consult the following conversion table:

MUST-WEIGHT CHART

Specific Gravity	Oechsle (German)	Baume (French)	Brix (American)	% Potential Alcohol (v/v)
1.065	65	8.8	15.8	8.1
1.070	70	9.4	17.0	8.8
1.075	75	10.1	18.1	9.4
1.080	80	10.7	19.3	10.0
1.085	85	11.3	20.4	10.6
1.090	90	11.9	21.5	11.3
1.095	95	12.5	22.5	11.9
1.100	100	13.1	23.7	12.5
1.105	105	13.7	24.8	13.1
1.110	110	14.3	25.8	13.8
1.115	115	14.9	26.9	14.4
1.120	120	15.5	28.0	15.0

Note: It is common to refer to a reading corresponding to the density of 20.0 g of sucrose per 100 g of solution at 20°C as 20.0° Brix or simply as Brix 20.

Knowing and Making Wine

PART 1

Tasting and the Composition of Wine

1

Mechanics and Methods
of Tasting

DEFINITION OF TASTING

Tasting (sometimes called organoleptic examination or sensory analysis) is the appreciation by sight, taste, and smell of the sensory properties of a wine. Tasting (the word gustation is also used) is submitting a wine to our senses in order to get to know it, to determine its organoleptic characteristics, and, finally, evaluate it. In the act of tasting wine, four phases may be discerned: observing it through the senses, describing what we perceive, comparing our perceptions with known standards, and judging the wine. Many people are potential tasters; for drinking to become tasting, often it only requires a little effort of concentration and an analysis of the impressions received. The most difficult part, which at the outset is not within everyone's grasp, is undoubtedly the description of the sensations received followed by a reasoned opinion. The taster has to be able to describe what he* feels in clear terms and be capable of forming a judgment.

Complexity of the Taste of Wine

The first idea that comes to mind when you try to describe and explain the taste and odor of wine is its complexity and diversity.

* The male pronoun is used here and throughout for reasons of simplicity of styling and it is not intended to imply that all tasters are male. The pronoun he should be translated mentally into "he or she."

3

Analysts have reported more than 500 compounds and more refined research techniques are constantly discovering new ones. Nevertheless, we must admit that the most important factors from a qualitative standpoint, those that affect taste and odor, are the least well known. We know how to identify those parts that make up the structure, the main framework, but we are not so well informed about the details. These, however, give the complete edifice style. What the analyst does is anatomy, but the essential personality of the wine is not perceived.

Wine is one of the natural food products having the greatest variety of tastes. All manner of drinks made from grapes are given the name wine yet have few characteristics in common. The influence of climate, different varieties of grapes, picking the grapes at various stages of ripeness, vinification techniques, and methods of storing have all contributed to creating a considerable number of types of wine. Each has its own standards of quality; for each, there exists a scale of values. Thus you do not use the same code of reference in tasting a Champagne, a Médoc, a chianti, a sherry, a table wine, or a dessert wine. They are not judged by the same standards. One of the great difficulties in tasting is, precisely, appraising each wine within its own category.

The Senses Used in Tasting

The first sense to come into action is sight. It informs us about the wine's appearance, its color (intensity, shade)—what we call the robe. We say a wine is ruby, garnet, purplish, or brickish. This first indication, often instinctive, has a great influence on those that follow: The taster will be tempted to judge a wine more severely if it is cloudy or of abnormal color. The color intensity of a red wine is an indication of its "body" and its volume; the hue, of its age. The color of a white wine shows its state of oxidation. The eye, therefore, plays an important part in tasting and is a preparation for it. To taste without seeing considerably increases the difficulty: it is not always easy to pick out among a series of wines tasted without looking, which are the dry whites, the rosés and the reds when these have little tannin. This blind tasting exercise is very instructive.

The second sense involved is smell. You should always smell a wine, taking time over it before bringing it to the mouth. You will then be using the nasal passage. It will be seen in tasting exercises how stirring magnifies the olfactive sensation. Certain types of wine may be judged almost entirely on their odor. The sensations perceived when the wine is in the mouth do not belong solely to the sense of taste as such. Smell brings an important contribution by way of the retronasal canal (this is the gustative aroma or mouth aroma) and even the sense of touch. So when we speak of the "taste" of a certain food or drink, often we are actually referring to sensations due to smell. Specialists use the term "flavor" to designate the overall sensation of taste combined with smell.

The part played by touch is important; it groups the impressions of temperature, consistency, viscosity, unctuosity, and volume. Furthermore, certain "tastes" are rather tactile sensations, reactions from the mucous membrane. Thus with the warmth of alcohol, its causticity is due to its liposolubility and its dehydrating effect. The astringence of tannin is due to the drying of the lingual mucus and the coagulation of saliva that normally provides buccal lubrication.

Tasting and Tasters

Wine being made to be drunk and appreciated, it is only logical that tasting should be the most valid means of judging its quality. Chemical analysis, however detailed, is insufficient. It throws light on the act of tasting and supports it; it cannot replace it. A routine analysis can make no distinction between an exceptional wine and an ordinary wine; every enology laboratory is well aware of this.

In the traditional wine-growing countries, tasting is carried out by all those in the wine trade, merchants, brokers, growers, technicians, trained by long practice and constant repetition and having reached a high degree of experience. The taster trains himself by dint of tasting once he has acquired the basic knowledge.

Professional tasting may have several objectives. It may be simple and limited or else detailed and complex, as the case requires. It can be either superficial or in-depth. A wine may be tasted to determine the type of wine, to appraise its quality, to estimate its market price, to detect its origin, or as a means of comparison with different wines, to classify them, follow their development, to determine the effect of a particular treatment, to maintain a uniform standard and commercial quality by selection, blending, and so forth. You may also taste a wine simply for the pleasure of drinking it (hedonic tasting).

Senses Used in Tasting

Tasting carried out by a technician or enologist is bound to be more detailed in the analytical area and in its conclusions than a purely commercial tasting. Above all, it tries to explain the taste in relation to the wine's composition. It attempts to break it down into simple flavors, tries to link a given taste to a particular ingredient, to go back to the conditions in which the wine was

SENSES USED IN TESTING

Organ	Sense and Sensations	Characteristics Perceived		
Eye	Vision, visual sensations	Color, clarity, fluidity, effervescence	} Appearance	
Nose	Olfaction, (direct nasal passage), olfactory sensations	Aroma, bouquet } Odor		
Mouth	Olfaction (retronasal passage), olfactory sensations	Mouth aroma		Flavor
	Tasting, taste sensations	Basic tastes	} Complex taste	
	Chemical or haptic sensitivity	Astringence, causticity, spritz		
	Mouth feel Thermal sensitivity	Consistency Temperature	} Touch	

made and stored to foresee the terminal texture, the aging. It is explanatory. We call this analytical tasting.

MECHANICS OF TASTING

The Sense of Taste

The cells sensitive to taste are only to be found on the rough part of the tongue. They are called papillae. Each of these mushroom-shaped cells measures 1 mm across and is equipped with several hundred taste buds. They are spread across the tongue's surface in a very irregular manner and the central area is free of them (Fig. 1.1). The other parts of the mouth (cheek, roof of the palate, buccal floor, gums) do not have any papillae.

The tongue is kept constantly moist by the salivary secretions produced from a set of glands that open onto various parts of the buccal cavity: parietal, submaxillary, submandibular, and parotid glands. The saliva that lubricates the papillae plays a very important part in tasting just as it does in our perception of the flavor of food.

Only four basic tastes can be distinguished by the tongue's papillae: sweet, sour, salt, and bitter. The rest is tactile perception or of chemical origin. Trying to ascertain the sensitivity thresholds for the four basic tastes, applied to a

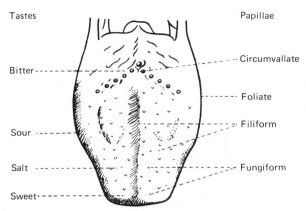

Tastes   Papillae

Bitter - Circumvallate

- - - - - - Foliate

- - - - - - Filiform

Sour - - - - - -

Salt - - - - - - - - - - - - - - - - - - Fungiform

Sweet - - - - - - - - -

Figure 1.1. Distribution across the tongue of the various papillae and perception centers of the four basic tastes.

group of tasters, is a highly recommended exercise. The thresholds are defined for each person by tasting pure solutions in diminishing strengths of substances that are sweet, sour, salt or bitter. The minimal perceived dose is then noted. From this, it will be ascertained that the level of sensitivity to sweet taste and to sour taste varies very widely. Tasters may be capable of detecting 0.5 g of sucrose per liter or again less than 0.1 gram of tartaric acid while a few rare persons are not sensitive to 5 grams of sugar per liter or to 0.3 gram of acid. The faculty for detecting a bitter taste can vary even more.

Of the four elementary tastes, only one is really agreeable: the sweet taste. The other sensations in their pure state are unpleasant and are only tolerated if compensated by sweet tastes. Wine contains all four basic tastes. The sweet taste is provided by the alcohol and, where present, its sugars; sour taste comes from the free organic acids; the salt taste from the salts; the bitter taste from the wine's phenolic components, generally called tannins. In tasting wine, these four tastes are not perceived at the same time, they become apparent one after the other. The taster should keep close track of the progressive change in sensations. There are three distinct phases in the sequence of gustative sensations: *Attack* or impact taste is perceived in the first few seconds; *evolution* is the continuing change of sensations; the *finale* or *fin de bouche* or *après-goût* is the impression felt at the end of the tasting that lingers on in the mouth after the wine has been rejected. Finally there is the *aftertaste*, which is that final sensation, different from those previously felt and generally disagreeable.

The different basic tastes are not identified at the same time because, for one thing, the relevant taste buds are situated in different areas of the tongue.

The tip of the tongue is the most sensitive spot for sweet taste, whereas sour tastes are felt on the sides and underneath. Salt taste concerns the edges and not the central surface; bitter tastes react on the back part of the tongue in an area that is only brought into contact when swallowing. There is, therefore, a lapse of several seconds between the impact of sweetness and the sensation of bitterness. When tasting a wine, the first impression (the first two or three seconds) is always agreeable. It is a mellow, sweetish sensation due mostly to the alcohol. Bit by bit the other flavors intervene, masking the sweet taste. The finish, in which sour and bitter tastes dominate, can end up leaving a less agreeable sensation after eight or ten seconds. Only wines of great quality maintain their pleasant impression to the end.

The Sense of Smell

The olfactory area is situated in the upper part of the nasal cavities. The olfactory mucous membrane is yellowish in color, covering an area of about 2 cm^2. It is bordered by the median turbinate, fine cartilaginous laminae that divide the nasal cavity and serve to filter and warm up the air being inhaled. This sensitive surface is situated behind a slit 2 mm wide. Since it is on one side of the usual passage of air being inhaled, only a slight portion of the odorous gases in the atmosphere can reach it during normal breathing. This quirk of anatomy is a fortunate conformation protecting us from many olfactory assaults.

As shown in Figure 1.2, there are two passages leading to the mucous membrane: the *direct nasal passage* via breath drawn in through the nostrils and the rhinopharynx called the *retronasal passage* via the buccal cavity to the nasal cavities. The action of swallowing tends to create a slight internal pressure that forces the vapors from the warmed wine which fills the mouth up toward the turbinates and in this way adds to the olfactory sensations.

These sensations are neither fixed nor lasting. During an olfactory cycle of four or five seconds, the time it takes to breathe in slowly, you notice a gradual increase in the sensations, followed by a decrease and a slow disappearance. This discontinuity makes olfactory comparisons difficult. They require a high degree of technical competence on the taster's part.

PRACTICE OF TASTING

Personal Nature of Tasting

Tasting is only as good as the taster. He is confronted by two primary difficulties: on the one hand, the subjectivity of the sensation (i.e., its personal interior character which is particular to each person doing the tasting) and

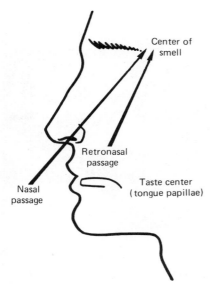

Center of
smell

Retronasal
passage

Nasal
passage

Taste center
(tongue papillae)

Figure 1.2. Perception centers and olfactory passages. Distinction is made between the nasal or external passage, which determines odor proper, and the retronasal or internal passage which determines mouth aroma.

on the other hand, the difficulty of accurately describing the impact on the palate and on the sense of smell.

It is impossible to measure a taste or a color and attempts made in this direction have hardly been successful, whereas the impressions received on our other senses can easily be quantified. We can only make comparisons and say that a particular taste is stronger than another, or that an odor is more intense, but we are incapable of saying how many times more.

At the same time, we can only define tastes and odors qualitatively in words by trying to describe them. The taster's vocabulary is difficult to codify since it is obviously full of imagery. It may be incomprehensible to the un-initiated and might even make them smile. There is no doubt for instance that terms like "suppleness," "roundness," or "nervousness" applied to a wine require some explanation. To understand the taster's vocabulary, you need to have some previous knowledge of tasting.

Gustative appraisal cannot be considered independent of the taster. It is subject to the taster's personality, mood, language, the precise meaning attributed to the words used, as well as the relative importance attributed to a particular quality or a particular defect.

Influence of Conditions on the Tasting

The time of day, whether it is just before, during, or after a meal, the environment and the company, even an unexpected shape of glass, can cause

Figure 1.3.   Room for teaching tasting at the Bordeaux Enology Institute (Photo Burdin).

the same taster to judge a wine relatively differently. The best tastings take place at the end of the morning because the taster will achieve maximum sensitivity when he has an appetite. Tastings on the spot, in the wine cellar itself, never have the discipline of those held in the tasting room (Fig. 1.3). The analysis laboratory is not suitable either. There exists an incidence of conditioning or adjustment of the sense of smell caused by tiring of the senses. If you spend all your time in a place where a certain smell persists, you do not notice it anymore. If you go on drinking a faulty wine, you reach a point where you no longer recognize its defects. During the course of a tasting, you gradually get used to the characteristics of the wines being tasted. Sometimes it is said there are fluctuating tastes and odors that vanish in the glass; actually it is more likely the tasters' senses which are getting dulled or adjusted.

Certain disagreeable tastes like acidity or bitterness or astringency quickly tire out the palate. They add up in the course of successive tasting sessions. If you compare "hard" wines with each other, the impression of hardness accentuates with each tasting. Another form of fatigue is the effect of alcohol, which during a long tasting gets absorbed into the bloodstream via the mucous membranes in the mouth. The effects of contrast, which make, for instance, a dry white wine seem more sour after tasting a sweet wine or a tannic red wine appear even harsher after tasting a soft wine, once again modify appraisal.

The temperature of the wine you are tasting is a factor to be taken into consideration. A red wine appears less tannic when its temperature is low,

18 or 20°C, but it seems more alcoholized. A white wine appears less acidic at a lower temperature.

The Importance of Suggestion

In his *Studies on Wine*, Pasteur relates a meaningful story on the influence of suggestion and imagination. During his research on the preservation of wine by heating, Pasteur asked a commission of competent tasters to make a comparison between wines having been subjected to this treatment. At their suggestion, he presented to them two glasses from the same bottle. Nevertheless each of them, believing one of the glasses to contain wine which had been heated and the other not, found a difference and preferred one to the other. It is easy enough to prove this same statement in relation to some other treatment. It should be pointed out that in a case like this, the taster who is subjected to this suggestion, does perceive a genuine difference. So it is quite possible to influence a taster and lead him or her into making a mistake. This problem is the main reproach that can be made against tasting. Many attempts have been made to limit it in various ways.

Various Methods of Tasting

The comparison between two wines can be carried out in several ways. The simplest is to present them in two glasses; the taster responds to the question "Is there a difference between these two wines?" or else "Which is the better of the two?"

The same question can be put in relation to three glasses of which two are identical and one different. The taster is given a reference for comparison. He only has to say which of the other two wines is identical to the reference wine.

The "triangular" test also involves comparing two wines presented in three glasses, but without knowing their sequence. Suppose, for instance, you want to know the effect on the taste of a small quantity of sulfuric acid added to the wine. You give the taster two glasses without any acid added and one with acid, or else two glasses with sulfuric acid and a single reference glass. There are, in fact, six possible combinations, so that it is unlikely in this case for the odds to be in favor of the operative. Therefore, he has to be more disciplined in his work. However, it should be stated that this method does not always allow tasters to discover the difference they detect perfectly well when given only two glasses.

Group Tastings

Another way of avoiding personal factors intervening is by working with a group of several tasters. Then you do not rely on the opinion of only one person but on the concerted appraisal of several. The competence of each member needs to be ascertained and the group should be uniform. In practice, good results are obtained from small groups of tasters used to working together. Still it is best if each taster works and scores independently. He should not see the others' reactions or hear their conclusions. But a group discussion after each one has given his opinion can be of interest.

Tasters are often apt to taste a whole series of rather too many samples too rapidly. Then sense fatigue intervenes more quickly. In the same way, constantly tasting the same wine should be avoided. A good odor analysis, two or three successive tests at the outside, should be enough to come to an appraisal of a wine. Tasting is delicate work, even tiring, which requires time and concentration. It is always best to insist on getting, both for yourself as well as the other tasters, a written detailed report. The necessity of setting down their conclusions and clearly describing the characteristics of a wine, forces people to carry out an analysis likely to stimulate accuracy in their observations.

Wine-Scoring Systems

There may be several motives in the tasting of a range of wines: picking out the best, which is a regular form of trade tasting; eliminating samples that are not up to standard, such as in quality-control tastings of original appellation wines; finally there is ranking a certain number of wines of the same type in order of preference, an exercise that can be quite difficult and take a fair time if there are a lot and if quality variances are narrow. According to the number of wines to be ranked, either the direct comparison method is used or else each wine is scored. A maximum of twelve to fifteen wines may be compared directly. Glasses are numbered and then shunted, putting the best each time to the left. After the third time around, the wines are checked to see if they are in descending order of quality from left to right.

When the range is greater, the wines are tasted separately and given a score. In a collective tasting, a mean score is established for each taster. It is, however, always a difficult thing to give an objective score to a subjective characteristic. Several scoring procedures have been recommended. You can score overall from 0 to 20 or according to any numerical scale. Some people total up the individual scores applied to particular characteristics such as color, clarity, intensity, the finesse of an odor, flavor, body, harmony, and so on. Sometimes coefficients are applied to these characteristics. The objection to this scoring procedure is its tendency to give fairly close scores for widely different wines. Moreover, it is based on a false premise: The quality of a wine is not the sum of its respective qualities of color, odor, and taste. A wine that is undrinkable on account of fixed acidity, for instance, may be clear and even have a delicate nose. In this case, a number including as many figures as there are characteristics being scored is more significant than a total.

A simpler overall system of scoring might be preferable based on the fact that it is easier to give a description or a ranking than a score. Below is an attempt to give equivalents to the various quantified rankings and descriptions used on the most common scales.

5-Point Scoring		20-Point Scoring	
Ranking	Score	Ranking	Score
Very good	5	Perfect	20
Good	4	Excellent	18–19
Fairly good	3	Very good	16–17
Fair	2	Good	14–15
Poor	1	Fairly good	12–13
Bad	0	Fair	10–11
		Insufficient	7–9
		Poor	4–6
		Bad	less than 4

Ranking Wines in Categories

A carefully prepared tasting allows wines ready for consumption to be ranked in different categories, determined by the Coste system, taking into account solely their agreeableness to the taste beyond any of the usual rankings based on origin and price. This ranking specifies the following groups:

First Group. The "wine-drink" swallowed without being tasted, drunk by force of habit, defined by professionals in the phrase: "without vice, or virtue."

Second Group. The "sham quality wine," which may come from grand origins and be cultivated in the best tradition and which therefore sometimes gives illusions. It usually reveals defects of a technical nature: for a red wine, hardness, astringency, high fixed or volatile acidity, ethyl acetate, and so on; for a white wine, oxidation, odor of sulfuric acid, and so on.

Third Group. The quality wine, clean, well-structured smooth, straightforward but pleasant and easy to drink, generally consumed young, fruit-flavored, sometimes with a flowery nose.

Fourth Group. The great wine, a work of art, complex, with personality, rich in sapid and aromatic substances, defying description and therefore that much more fascinating to taste.

2

Gustatory Characteristics and Vocabulary

THE RELATIONSHIP BETWEEN THE COMPOSITION OF WINES AND THEIR GUSTATORY QUALITIES

The odor and taste of a wine depend on its chemical composition. Wine may be identified with an aqueous, alcoholic solution containing sugar, acids, salts, phenolic components, volatile substances, and many others. Each of these components has its own taste and its own smell, which contribute to the overall effect. But these tastes and odors interact with each other, are superimposed or interpenetrate. Consequently, the appeal of a wine is not related to the proportionate content of a single substance, but to the harmonious symmetry of its construction.

Balance of Flavors

The organoleptic qualities of a wine may be looked upon as the result of a series of balances between odorous substances and between the components that regulate the harmony of odor and savor. The gustatory pleasure is conditioned mainly by the balance that exists between the sweet tastes, generally considered to be agreeable, and the sour and bitter flavors, in themselves unappetizing. The quality of a wine depends on the overall harmony of these different tastes. One should not override another. This is true for wines that have reducing sugars, but it is also true for wines that are completely dry since at the forefront of those wine components giving a sweet taste, you should place alcohol. It can be demonstrated that a solution of alcohol at 32 g/L (4%) gives just as strong a taste of sweetness as a solution of glucose at

14

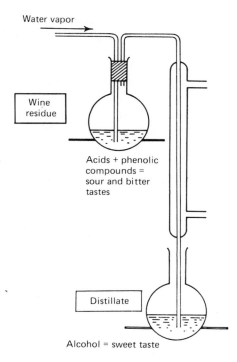

Water vapor

Wine
residue

Acids + phenolic
compounds =
sour and bitter
tastes

Distillate

Alcohol = sweet taste

Figure 2.1. Separation by distillation of a red wine into its sweet-tasting, sour-tasting, and bitter-tasting substances.

20 g/L. It is even more obvious that alcohol intensifies the sweet taste of sugar: a solution of sucrose slightly alcoholized produces an even sweeter taste. We also know that sour tastes and sweet tastes mask each other. The addition of sugar reduces sour taste, and also bitter taste. This theory is commonplace enough since people put sugar into lemon juice to provide a thirst-quenching drink. A drink that is too bitter may be sugared in the same way.

In wines the taste of the sweet substances should nicely balance the sum of flavors from the sour substances plus the bitter substances:

$$\text{sweet taste} \leftrightarrows \text{sour taste} + \text{bitter taste}$$

Demonstration of This Balance

It is possible in the laboratory to separate a red wine by means of distillation into its two opposing flavors, on the one hand, alcohol, which represents the sweet taste, and on the other, the acids and tannins, which provide the sour and bitter tastes (Fig. 2.1). In fact the distillate has a mellow taste, truly sweet, combined with the warmth and vinosity of the alcohol as well as being most insipid. As for the residue, it is highly acid and bitter, quite unpalatable. From experiment, it is clear that wine only has a pleasant taste because the taste of the alcohol (distillate) balances the taste of the acids and tannins (in the residue). This tasting exercise clearly illustrates the notion of flavor balance.

From this equation, we understand why a red wine in which the bitter taste of its tannins adds to the taste of its acids, will not sustain such a high acid content as a white, which does not normally contain bitter substances. Another consequence: a sweet white wine can better sustain a fairly high acidity.

It should be pointed out in this connection that wine is the most acid of all fermented drinks. Its strong acidity is only tolerable because it is sufficiently alcoholized. It is precisely due to its high percentage of alcohol and high acidity that it can be kept for a long time.

Suppleness Index

Attempts have been made to establish relationships capable of quantifying a wine's qualities between the elements that affect taste. The *suppleness index* calculated by the following formula represents fairly well the taste harmony of a red wine. It derives from the equilibrium previously defined.

$$\text{alcoholic strength} - (\text{total acidity} + \text{tannins}) = \text{suppleness index}$$

Total acidity is expressed in grams of sulfuric acid per liter and the tannins (phenol-based components) are calculated in grams per liter to correspond with the measure used on the polyphenol index (Folin); 1 g of tannin arbitrarily represents 20 points. Suppose there is red wine with 11% alcohol having 4.0 g of total acidity and 3.0 grams of tannin. Its suppleness index $11 - (4.0 + 3.0) = 4.0$ corresponds to a thin wine and certainly a rather hard one. On the contrary, a red wine of 12% alcohol with 3.3 g of acidity and 2.0 g of tannins with an index of $12 - (3.3 + 2.0) = 6.7$ leaves an impression of roundness and "fat." Red wines with a suppleness index of 5 are generally thin and firm. Those that have a suppleness index higher than 5 are supple. Those with an index of more than 6 or 7 are fat and full-bodied. The suppleness index can be measured just as well using acidity expressed in terms of tartaric acid or in milliequivalents. It then leads to a different scale of values.

Certain observations may be made. A wine will sustain acidity if it has sufficient alcoholic strength. The hardest red wines are those that are at the same time rich in acidity and in tannins. A strong tannin content is acceptable if acidity is weak.

Balance of Odors

The odorous complexity of wines is considerable not only because tens of substances (possibly several hundred) take a part in it, but also because the odorous interactions are varied and intermingled. The effect of additions should be noted (a mixture of fragrant substances in proportions that do not individually give any smell together may be odorous) and even the phenomenon of synergy, that is the mutual strengthening of smell. On the other hand, certain odors, dissimilar but of equal intensity, are not miscible and remain intact, side by side within the mixture. Lastly other odors mask each other or cancel each other out. It can be demonstrated, for instance, by experiment that the odor sensitivity threshold of a substance (minimum concentration for perception of its odor in a solution) is considerably lowered when mixed with other odorous substances. The following remarks concerning ethyl acetate, an ester that gives certain wines their acescent characteristics (acetic vinegariness), are examples of this.

	Odor Sensitivity Threshold to Ethyl Acetate (mg/L)
Water	25
10% alcohol solution	40
10% alcohol solution + traces of ethyl enanthate	120
Wines	160–180

The smell of alcohol itself covers up the other odors and we see by this circumstance how a high alcohol content will diminish the intensity of a wine's odor. Ethyl enanthate is a highly odorous ester that only exists in trace quantities in wines. The more complex the mixture of smells, the more intense they are and the more the special smell of ethyl acetate is masked.

GUSTATORY VOCABULARY

It is not enough for a taster to have a trained palate, he must possess a tasting vocabulary sufficiently extensive and accurate to be able to express what he feels. Anyone is capable of saying a wine is good or is not good, but the taster must explain why a wine is of high quality or, on the contrary, what its shortcomings are. Training and practice in tasting with people who have acquired a technical vocabulary makes it possible to establish a precise relation between words and sensations. It is important for tasters to be able to understand each other and to use the same terms for the same tastes. Vocabulary should be relatively extensive and include sufficient means of expression.

It is possible to gather together several hundred terms and phrases used by tasters. It is necessary to set up a codification with equivalents in different languages. We give below a certain number of epithets classed in a logical sequence. This list only contains the most current terms.

Characteristics Relating to the Body of a Wine

This concerns what the taster also calls volume or richness. We will be considering in this range sensations in increasing strength.

The following terms relate to red wines of light body but perfectly balanced, well-proportioned and therefore harmonious and agreeable: light, thin, smooth, tender, delicate, dissolved, velvety, silky.

Suppleness is the one great quality sought for in red wines. The word is frequently misconstrued. A supple wine does not shock the palate. Suppleness does not just mean low in tannin content, it also corresponds more than anything to low acidity. Above 3.6 g of total acidity, no wine can possibly be called supple. On the other hand, supple wine does not mean empty wine, thin. Anyway, suppleness is not merely lack of firmness: It is a positive quality, the result of good harmony of constitution.

An elegant, distinguished wine is a supple wine that has finesse and personality.

In a range of richer wines, still with a harmonious constitution, we speak of wines having roundness, filling the mouth well, being ample, full, mature in the sense of having a taste of ripe grapes, complete, fleshy, unctuous. Fat is the ultimate description, putting into words one of the most valued qualities. Other epithets relating to wines of strong constitution are: full-bodied, well-filled, fully structured, substantial, massive.

Characteristics Due to Fixed Acid

The following terms refer to situations in which wines have slightly excess acid, getting more and more acid.

Thinness is always caused by imbalance, due to overacidity but is not necessarily perceived as such. It is said of a wine that it is hollow, anemic, lean, fleshless, that it is short or brief as if the pleasant impressions were cut short in the mouth, as opposed to a wine that has "length" and which remains agreeable long after, in a lengthy tasting. The adjective "dry" in the sense that it has dried up, you can also say arid, describes a wine that has grown thin and lost its pristine freshness. Furthermore, you may speak of a wine that is slightly acid and say it has bite, that it is raw, aggressive, rough. Firmness or harshness may stem from different causes; excessive fixed or volatile acidity, a high proportion of tannins, or yet too much ethyl acetate. The taster should be capable of recognizing these various causes.

When excessive acidity is identified on the palate, the wine is inflexible, sharp, acidic, tart, green, it has the taste of the unripe grape.

Characteristics Due to Acetic Acid

Acetic acid, a constituent part of volatile acidity, does not just increase the acid taste. It has a particularly unpleasant bitter taste. Wines with high volatile acidity are thin and dry, their defect appears at the end of the tasting as a burning sensation, a sourness in the throat. We shall see further on the effect of acescence on odor.

Characteristics Due to Phenol Compounds

These are the final sensations. As soon as there are too many tannins upsetting the balance, the wine seems hard or firm. A highly colored wine is thick, heavy. With high tannin content, the wine is harsh. You also say it has "sting"; it is rough, rugged. It has the taste of fermentation with the stems or the taste of press-wine. It is bitter and causes the sensation of puckering of the mucous membrane known as astringence.

Characteristics in Relation to Sweet Taste

The "softness" of a red wine relates to a certain preponderance of substances having a sweet taste. It is said that such a wine is "glycerined," that it has "sugar"—not because it has a high proportion of reducing sugars or glycerol but because it gives that impression.

Flabby wine lacks acidity and tannins. It lacks freshness and shape. It is flat unless some other delicacy of character is evident. For very low acidity content and for high pH levels when a large proportion of the acids are present in the salt form, the wine leaves a salty, "alkaline" impression, of lye. Excess sugar in a liqueur wine makes it sugary, cloying, honeyed, pomaded.

Characteristics in Relation to Alcohol Content

With low alcohol content, wines are small, weak, or light. They may be agreeable at the same time if they are well-balanced, but it is more difficult to get a good balance when the degree of alcohol is low. A poor wine will show overall weakness. A light fixed acidity gives such wines freshness. In contrast, weak acidity in a wine containing little alcohol makes it appear flavorless, flat, washed-out, or watery.

Wines with a high alcohol content are "vinous," a term that should not be interpreted as merely meaning "which has the taste of wine." Vinous is akin to *viné* (fortified by adding alcohol) and to *vinage* (the operation of enriching with alcohol, authorized for wines sent from France). The vinosity of a wine is hardly apparent at less than 11.5%. Alcohol gives wine vigor providing it has a sufficiency of acids. A high degree of alcohol gives "warmth," a term that brings to mind the causticity of alcohol. A wine rich in alcohol is alcoholized, generous, heady, spirituous, and, in the final analysis, alcoholic or even fierce if there is nothing but the taste of alcohol.

Characteristics of the Odor of Wines

The first impression is that the odor of a wine, even more than taste, belongs to the realm of the ineffable, the indescribable. The taster goes to some lengths to distinguish the intensity or volume of odor and its shades and quality. By careful examination, he manages to identify in the aroma of a wine, a series of perfumes, reminiscent of a particular flower, a particular fruit, a particular wood essence, or a hint of fat, acid, aromatic substances, aldehydes, or spices. Therefore, there is in the bouquet of a wine, just as in any perfume, a dominant note. It is by the agreeable character of its odor that we recognize a good wine, but it is complexity and a multiplicity of shades in its aroma that denote a great wine. In olfactory descriptions, we must differentiate between aroma and bouquet. Aroma refers to the odor of a young wine, whereas bouquet is only acquired through aging. According to this definition, a new wine cannot yet have bouquet and a wine that has aged in the bottle has no more aroma.

We can identify two types of aroma: primary aroma with a fruity smell that comes from the grape and is characteristic of the variety of vine (Muscat, Pinot, Sauvignon, etc.) and the secondary aroma, which appears during the course of the fermentation: The yeasts when they change sugar into alcohol and the grape juice into wine produce a lot of odorous substances.

The bouquet of premium wines develops slowly during its cask life or tank life and is considerably enhanced by being sealed off from contact with air during bottle aging. On the other hand, most ordinary wines do not improve from being kept for a long time and even lose the freshness that is what makes them attractive. To describe the intensity of a wine's odor, the taster chooses among adjectives such as weak, neutral, dull, poor; or scented, aromatic, bouqueted.

The first quality required of a wine's odor is finesse, which means an agreeable odor of fruit or of a flower. Some white wines really smell of vine flowers or of lime blossom. The opposite would be an odor that is common, coarse, vegetable, herbaceous, or leafy. Some wines, rich in tannin, have an odor that is dominated by their tannic character, which gets progressively more powerful after aging and recalls wood or bark.

A wine has character, is true to type when it can easily be distinguished by its personal tone. The reverse is commonplace wine, dull. The "life" (sève) of a wine, a term used in olden times, implies finesse but also a certain class, a character related to its origins; such wine has breeding. You say a wine is fruity when it has a nose that makes you think of fruit, not necessarily grapes but perhaps apple, peach, plum, blackcurrant, strawberry, raspberry, cherry, banana, quince, lemon, or hazelnut, and so on.

The study of odors and the description of them requires an effort of olfactory analysis striving to establish a similarity or an analogy between the fragrance wines exhude and those we come across in the outside vegetable or even animal world. Among wine odors, you will find represented the nine general classifications of odors: animal, balsamic, woody, chemical, empyreumatic, spicy, floral, fruity, green.

After the odors of fruits, the odors of flowers (rose, violet, reseda, magnolia), and the odor of honey, we come across certain whiffs of vegetable perfumes: hay, ferns, mugwort. The odors of spices and of essences appear frequently as faint traces in the bouquet of great wines: clove, cinnamon, fruit stones, orris root, vanilla, kirsch, bitter almonds, and so forth. You may also sometimes detect a lightly burnt smell: caramel, wood smoke, toast, coffee, grilled almonds, or a redolence of wood (cedarwood, resin, liquorice) or of leather or of withered and dried leaves, tea, tobacco even. The smell of truffles in old wines or animal odors (musk, amber, venison, game, fur) are even more astonishing. It only requires a little imagination to find in wines the whole, rich and complex world of familiar smells. The origins of a fermented product are rediscovered in the odors of yeast and in lactic odors.

A series of adjectives relates to the sanitary state of the wine. A healthy wine will be described as frank, clean, candid tasting, true, pure. Deterioration of a wine is detected in its odor, it is questionable, impaired, sick, vinegary, acetic, sour, butyric. It has a smell of yeast or of *tourne*. A "mousy" smell is a foul aftertaste that recalls the odor of acetaldehyde, transmitted through bacterial spoilage. The smell of geraniums or pelargoniums comes from the deterioration of a wine with sorbic acid added.

Another series of descriptions concerns the aerated state and the degree of oxidation. A wine that has just been handled and aerated is tired, it is a temporary state due to the dissolving of oxygen. Longer contact with the air makes a wine deflated, worn, flat, stewed, that is to say, it has the taste of chewed or crushed fruit. These defects caused by free acetaldehyde may dissipate after sulfuring and laying down. Some young wines sensitive to exposure, showing some oxidation damage, get the cooked taste of overripe grapes or raisins; this is the taste called casse. Even longer exposure to the air makes a wine oxidized or in extreme cases, maderized or rancio. These characteristics due to aldehyde derivatives and acetol can no longer be reversed. On the contrary, certain young wines kept away from contact with the air for too long get a reduced taste and improve with a little aeration. You say they are stifled or asphyxiated. A white wine that gets too old goes into the maderized stage; if it is acid, it sometimes acquires a burnt taste. A red wine when it is too old is shabby and worn out, decrepit, overaged, decayed.

A rather high level of carbon dioxide present in certain types of white wine or even light reds, not high enough to make them fully gassy, gives them flavor and crispness. The optimal content is variable with the wine, from 300 to 600 mg/L. If it is too high the wine has a *piquant* taste. The same wines completely devoid of CO_2 would be insipid, without shape. Yet for other types of wine, carbon dioxide is undesirable, it brings out the acid taste, reduces the ambrosial flavors and accentuates the astringence and tannic hardness.

Too much gas deteriorates the flavor of an old wine and considerably hampers judgment when tasting red *vin nouveau*. Then it is useful to eliminate excess gas by the relatively easy method of pouring from one glass to another five or six times or, better still, stirring it a few seconds in the laboratory under vacuum created by a pump. The terms used to describe relative richness in carbon dioxide are well known: still wines for those that have no bubbles, then beady or pearled, frothy, *pétillant, crémant,* effervescent and sparkling.

Off Tastes

The list of accidentally disagreeable or off tastes is long, and they cannot all be enumerated. We may head the list with the odor of sulfuric acid, improperly called an odor of sulfur that depreciates a number of white wines and even some reds and is nevertheless easy to avoid by judicious dosing of this antiseptic. Its excessive use is not only critical on account of the acescent odor, which is overpowering and assaults the mucous membrane, it is just as much because it eliminates a great part of the more agreeable elements in the aroma. It weakens the character of the wine and neutralizes it.

The nauseating smell of hydrogen sulfide, lees, rotten eggs, is apparent in new wines which have not been racked but allowed to remain on their lees of yeast. If action is taken quickly, a strong aeration is enough to make the off odor evaporate. When it is older, mercaptans (thiols) will have formed that are much more stable and resistant to aeration. The wine becomes alliaceous, stagnant, rotten, putrid.

Gray rot on the grape gives rise to quite a number of unpleasant tastes, sometimes close to moldiness: iodized, phenolic, of fungus, chemical, accompanied by strong bitterness.

Certain hybrid grafts have the foxy aroma of American vines.

The most common off tastes are transmitted by faulty containers. A bad cask is the origin of dry tastes, casky or woody. A distinction should be made between the agreeable woody flavor given by sound casks of new oak that marries so well later on with the bouquet of premium red wines and the woody taste that comes, in fact, from wood which has been invaded by mold. There are several sorts of mold: mold that has a taste of fungus, mold with a taste of cork (due to a cork mold in bottled wines and which you can even come across in wines from badly maintained casks or tanks), mold with a rancid taste and mold with a vegetable odor, which is particularly disagreeable and resists any form of treatment. The common earthiness of some vineyards is often none other than a taste transferred from year to year by bad storage conditions. Earthiness, (in French, *terroir*) has here a deprecatory sense. The resiny taste, not necessarily disagreeable when not too pronounced, transmitted through contact with tiny surfaces of resinous wood, may sometimes be encountered.

We will not dwell on the tastes of petroleum or mineral oil, rubber, solvent, tar, paper, smoke, earthiness, dust, cement, cloth, and so on that arise from contact with different products or materials. Wine easily absorbs odors from the places in which it is kept and materials it comes into contact with. The grape itself is capable of absorbing and retaining certain odors. Even before the grapes have ripened, the retarring of a road alongside the vines can communicate a strange taste to wine made from that patch.

It is worth noting that the astringent aftertaste that comes from metal, particularly copper, is not uncommon to samples drawn from a bronze faucet without taking necessary precautions.

The odor of acetamide, sometimes called mousy odor, is often caused by microbes. Rather than from sniffing in the glass, it is more easily detected by dipping the thumb and index finger in the wine and letting them dry off. The off odor develops and remains stuck to the skin.

3

Tasting Exercises

TRAINING IN TASTING

An apprenticeship in tasting involves frequently tasting different types of wines under the guidance of competent tasters capable of expressing their sensory reactions and thus storing in the memory a large number of impressions. A number of different exercises exist that classify and refine sensations, putting tasting on firm foundations. This means really educating the sense of taste and of smell, which sharpens perceptions and strengthens judgment. Tasting requires an effort of memory and concentration. You are constantly comparing immediate impressions with those previously memorized. In order to analyze your sensory reactions, you need to be able to really focus your mind on it. In this sense, tasting is a veritable discipline. Too frequently, people taste without actually paying much attention to what they feel. Similarly the consumer often drinks without paying any heed to the flavor of his drink; it impinges on his mind without him really thinking about it.

A competent taster obviously needs to have normal sensitivity to different tastes and odors. Different people have different levels of perceptual acuteness, but total insensibility to taste (ageusia) or to smell (anosmia) is rare.

An apprenticeship in tasting is based on constant repeated exercise. A sufficient knowledge, either of a technical or commercial nature, is indispensable. Knowing wine well and being interested in it is of great help in this initiation. Instead of straightaway tasting commonplace wines at random, you should begin with carefully selected exercises, like a pianist practicing scales. Training starts off with advice on how to taste. The taster needs to acquire certain skills. Three categories of exercises should be undertaken each dealing with a different topic:

1. *Theoretical Tasting.*   Exercises that allow the physiological basis of tasting to be defined: study of the tasting mechanism; fixing sensory thresholds for the four basic tastes, testing different sapid and odorous substances in a water solution, conception of balance between tastes, and odors of these substances.

2. *Analytical Tasting.*   Exercises that study the influence on taste and odor of varying proportions of the basic components in wines: alcohol, acids, esters, phenolic compounds, sugars, polyalcohols, salts, and so on.

3. *Applied Tasting.*   Vocabulary Exercises consisting of describing the impressions created by the different wines in a precise, detailed fashion selecting codified epithets and relating these impressions to their composition. In this kind of exercise, you start by describing the odors (intensity, quality), then the different taste sensations: attack, evolution, finish, and the balance between them. You end by summing up the quality of the wine tasted.

THEORETICAL TASTING EXERCISES

The Four Basic Tastes

Using a little mineral water, prepare the following solutions, which present the four basic tastes:

Sugar taste	Sugar solution (sucrose) at 20 g/L
Acid taste	Tartaric acid solution at 1 g/L
Salt taste	Sodium chloride solution at 4 g/L
Bitter taste	Quinine sulfate solution at 10 mg/L

Taste them carefully trying to locate the different sensations on the tongue. Obviously everyone is familiar with these basic tastes. However, it is always instructive to go back to these pure sensations and examine one's own sensitivity. The salt flavor of the sodium chloride solution gives a rough idea of the not insignificant brackish taste of the various salts a wine contains.

At this degree of concentration, the bitter taste of quinine is perceptible to most people. Repeated tasting accentuates the impression of bitterness.

Prepare also a solution in water of a good enological "alcohol" tannin (oak-gall tannin) at 1 g/L. This solution is bitter and astringent at the same time. It gives an opportunity to examine the difference between the two sensations.

Figure 3.1. Some examples of tasting glasses.

Practical Tasting Arrangements

The shape of the glass is important. Choose a "balloon"- or "tulip"-shaped glass with a stem, that is to say, a round or oval shape cut off across the top, and of adequate capacity, say, 20 to 25 cL. Figure 3.1 illustrates some correctly shaped tasting glasses. The glass on the right is the one most recommended. In France, it is the French Standards Institute (AFNOR) standard glass.

The glasses are filled to about one-third full. This quantity or more correctly the relation between the volume of wine and the empty volume has an influence on odor. When making comparisons, glasses should be filled in the same way. More than a third makes swirling the wine in the glass inconvenient.

During a tasting the taster must make an effort to concentrate and meditate on what he is doing. That will be easier if the tasting room is quiet. He should shut himself off, mentally at least, from the other people.

Before any tasting, the taster "prepares his mouth" with a wine similar to those he is about to taste, of average quality. If possible, the wine should be one the taster already knows.

After observing the wine's appearance, the taster begins with an olfactory examination. This should be attentive and prolonged. Swirling the wine in the glass is necessary to ensure the odor is emanating properly. The following exercise demonstrates this. Sniff the wine undisturbed in the glass standing on the table and note the intensity of its odor. Then swirl it with a brisk rotary motion for several seconds and smell it again while it is still moving. The odor will have intensified considerably and you detect the finer nuances. Swirl it more vigorously still, shaking the glass and you will find the odor is even more powerful, but perhaps less agreeable. Vigorous shaking brings out the defects, the accidental off odors, the coarser acescent characteristics.

Because of the influence of greater or less shaking, making an exact comparison between the odor of two wines can be a ticklish job. It is often better to place the two glasses on the table and quickly smell them one after the other without touching them.

Next take a small quantity of wine in the mouth. The taster instinctively takes the right amount, often less than 10 mL. Too little does not provide sufficient sensory examination, whereas too much requires more time to get warm and some has to be swallowed.

The taster records successive impressions, the attack or immediate taste, then the evolution, and finally the finish. He checks persistence after having spat out the wine.

Factors of Taste and Smell

The following three exercises are intended to attempt to distinguish, within the overall gustatory sensations, those impressions due to taste as such, on the one hand, and on the other, those due to smell. Often no distinction is made. The taster cannot be satisfied with recording an overall sensory reaction, he must try to analyze his impressions. He must make a distinction between what belongs to the palate and what is strictly in the olfactory area.

1.   After having ejected the wine, exhale vigorously through the nose, breathing out several times. In this way the vapors with which the mouth is impregnated are pushed up toward the olfactory centers. You will notice at each breath what is customarily known as the "taste" of the wine.

2.   During a tasting, as soon as the wine has warmed in the mouth, draw in a little air and let it bubble across the wine. This provokes a veritable extraction of the volatile substances that considerably heightens the olfactory sensation. This tasting technique is particularly suited to detecting defects. Ethyl acetate, for instance, is much more acutely perceived in this way.

3.   Eliminate olfactory senses by pinching the nose. The process is well known: you only need to block the air through the nostrils in order to swallow a nasty medicine without unpleasantness. This avoids the passage of vapors from the mouth across the olfactory turbinates to the center of smell. Tasting wine in these conditions means reducing impressions felt to a vague acidulous impression. Only at the moment the nasal passages are released, do you discover what is generally called the "taste" of wine and which is, in fact, its odor.

Acid and Bitter Tastes Reinforce Each Other. Prepare three solutions of 0.75 g of tartaric acid per liter using ordinary water. Add 10 mg of quinine sulfate to the first, 1 g of tannin to the second, the third acts as a reference sample of acid taste. Compare the taste of these solutions.

The taste of tartaric acid masks the bitterness of the quinine at first. This reappears, however, at the finish. The disagreeable character of acidity is reinforced by the bitterness.

When bitterness is due to tannin, sour and bitter tastes accumulate, and the acidity reinforces the astringence.

Alcohol Has a Sweet Taste. Prepare solutions with neutral ethyl alcohol at 4% (32 g/L) and at 10% (80 g/L).

At 4% alcohol has a sweetish taste, slightly sugary, which appears distinctly compared with water yet without the special taste of alcohol being recognizable. This taste is distinct from the sweet savor of sugar, but it belongs to the same family. At 10% alcohol, the sugary taste comes out again very strongly together with a sensation of warmth. This solution demonstrates clearly the complex taste of alcohol, at once flavor and tactile reaction.

Moreover, alcohol considerably strengthens the sweet taste of sugar. Prepare solutions of sucrose at 20 g/L with different alcohol strengths: 0.4% and 10%. This tasting is more demonstrative than the previous one since the presence of alcohol considerably enhances the impression of sweetness. On the other hand, at this strength the sugar does not mask the warm flavor of the alcohol.

Sweet Tastes Change Acid Tastes. Prepare the following three solutions:

1. Sweet solution: 20 g of sucrose per liter.
2. Acid solution: 1 gram of tartaric acid per liter.
3. Simultaneous sweet and acid solution: 20 g of sucrose plus 1 g of tartaric acid per liter.

Compare the sweet and acid taste of solution 3 with the respective tastes of solutions 1 and 2.

The sweet taste and the acid taste of solution 3 are perceived at the same time, practically side by side. You can concentrate your attention when tasting on the sweet taste alone or on the acid taste alone. Yet the relative intensities are changed. Tartaric acid distinctly reduces the sweet taste of the sugar. On the other hand, at these strengths the effect of sugar on the acid taste is less obvious. The solution appears more acid than sweet. It would take 30 g of sugar per liter to attenuate it. The interference of these flavors and the point of equilibrium varies with different people.

Prepare solutions of tartaric acid at 1 g/L with different alcoholic strengths: 0, 4%, 7%, 10%. At 4% alcohol, the acid taste is hardly attenuated; at 7%, it very clearly is. At 10%, the reaction is more complex; you get a sensation of hardness, the acidity reinforcing the burning sensation due to the alcohol.

Sweet Tastes Change Bitter Tastes. This is a fairly common notion: sugar masks the bitterness of coffee and tea; the more bitter the various types of vermouth are, the more sugar used in their preparation.

Prepare two series of bitter solutions, one with 10 mg of sulfate of quinine per liter and the other with 1 g of tannin. Each series should consist of the following variants:

Reference sample
20 g of sugar per liter
40 g of sugar per liter
4% alcohol
10% alcohol

Compare the tastes of these solutions.

The taste of sugar obliterates the disagreeable character of bitterness in the quinine which takes longer to be perceived; it even gives flavor to the solution sugared at 40 g/L.

In the same way sugar delays the moment when the bitter and astringent taste of tannin appears. The tannic taste in the reference sample is perceived rapidly. It is delayed by 2 or 3 seconds for 20 g of sugar and by 5 or 6 seconds for 40 g.

The taste of alcohol masks the flavor of quinine. The effect on the tannic taste is more complex, since the burning flavor of alcohol at 10% tends to accentuate the disagreeable impression at the finish.

Balance Between Sweet, Acid and Bitter Tastes in Wine. Distill 200 mL of a fairly supple red wine that leaves an impression of good balance in the mouth (more than 5 on the suppleness index). Retrieve 100 mL of the distillate and bring the volume up to 200 mL with water. Next retrieve the residue, cool it, and bring it to 200 mL as well. The distillate contains wine alcohol and no fixed acids or phenolic compounds. The residue or *vinasse* is alcohol-free but does contain the acids and phenolic compounds.

Taste these two liquids separately, comparing them with the original wine. The distillate represents the sweet taste in wine (incompletely, however, since glycerol and reducing sugars will have remained in the residue). The residue represents the acid and bitter tastes (except for volatile acidity). In wine, the sweet taste of the alcohol counterbalances the taste of the acids and phenolic compounds.

We will next compare the preceding wine, which served as a reference sample with a wine having a much lower suppleness index, in the region of 4, as well as dominant acid and bitter tastes. This wine will have, to some extent, the taste of the "residue."

In the same way, comparison could be made with a wine having a high suppleness index, say 8 or more, and strong alcoholic strength with a certain weakness in acidity. In this wine, the taste of the "distillate" dominates.

Tasting Constituents of a Wine Having a Sweet Taste. Prepare the following five solutions:

Alcohol at 4% (32 g/L)
Glycerol at 20 g/L
Glucose at 20 g/L
Sucrose at 20 g/L
Fructose at 20 g/L

Alcohol, glycerol and glucose, with slight differences in their sweet taste, show similar intensities of flavor. The sucrose is considerably sweeter, 20 g of sucrose being equivalent to 30 or 35 g of glucose. Fructose is sweeter still, 20 g of fructose being equivalent to 40 or 45 g of glucose.

We could also compare a solution of inositol, a normal constituent of wine, or of mannitol, not normally a constituent, both of which are as sweet as glucose.

Tasting Constituents of Wine Having an Acid Taste. Prepare the following six solutions:

Tartaric acid at 1 g/L
Malic acid at 1 g/L
Citric acid at 1 g/L
Lactic acid at 1 g/L
Acetic acid at 1 g/L
Succinic acid at 0.5 g/L

Tartaric, malic, and citric acids, being grape acids, have the same pure acid flavor. It is understood that tartaric acid is the hardest, malic acid the greenest, and citric acid the freshest. These slight variances are better perceived in partially buffered solutions with the same pH.

Lactic, acetic, and succinic acids, being fermentation acids, have a more complex taste reminiscent of their origin. They have a lower acid intensity. Lactic acid has a weak acid taste, rather sourish. Acetic acid has an unpleasant bitterness. As for succinic acid, at this level of strength it does not show a proper acid taste but rather a strong salt and bitter taste at the same time, not very agreeable at this intensity, making the mouth water. This is the wine acid that gives the richest flavor.

Determining Individual Thresholds for Sweet, Acid, and Bitter Tastes

Tasters are presented with a series of three glasses one of which, placed at random, contains a sweet solution (triangular tasting). The other two contain water. Solutions of sucrose in diminishing strengths are presented for 5, 3, 2, 1, and 0.5 g/L. The minimal amount correctly indicated is recorded for each taster. This is the sensitivity threshold for sweet taste.

Mean results taken from a large number of tests:

Sensitivity Threshold per 100 Persons	Sugar (g/L)
18	0.5
31	1
35	2
12	3
4	5

Similar tests can be arranged for acid taste (0.05–0.2 g of tartaric acid per liter), for salt taste (0.1–1 g of sodium chloride per liter), or for bitter taste (0.5–2 mg of quinine per liter in sulfate form).

Olfactory Measuring

Determining the olfactory sensitivity threshold of an odorous substance in solution is practiced in the following fashion. Aqueous or slightly alcoholized solutions of the odorous substance to be examined, in varying degrees of concentration, are presented to a group of persons to be smelled in the glass under standardized conditions. The absolute olfactory threshold retained is the weakest mixture that half the population manages to detect and is expressed in milligrams per liter. Here, for example, are the approximate olfactory thresholds for a few odorous substances to be found in wine: isoamyl alcohol, 7.0; butyric acid, 4.0; isoamyl acetate, 0.2; linalool 0.1.

EXERCISES IN ANALYTICAL TASTING

Effect on the Taste of Wine of a Change in Alcoholic Strength

This trial involves using a white wine and a red wine. The taste of white wine being less complex (absence of polyphenolic compounds), changes in its composition are generally more perceptible. The first exercise consists of strengthening the wines by adding 0.7 and 1.4% totally neutral vinous spirits. You could always diminish the wine's strength in the course of a similar test by watering it down and readjusting the acidity. The change in the taste is then directly related to the reduction in alcohol and also in the "volume" of flavor.

A variance of 0.7% is not always perceived by untrained persons. In fact the exercise is difficult because alcohol does not have a direct influence by its own taste which is quite complex, but acts in an indirect way, changing the balance of other tastes. The taster must direct his or her attention particularly to the length of the agreeable sensation in the attack and to the moment when the acidity becomes apparent, rather than to the finish, which is not usually improved by the increase in strength. The first tasting is carried out knowing the alcohol content of the samples. This allows the part played by the alcohol to be measured exactly. Next the tasting will be made blind. The glasses will be set out in any order, and the taster will rearrange them in ascending order according to the strength of alcohol.

This exercise repeated over several weeks, progressively diminishing the variances, improves the taster's sensitivity so that he finally manages to detect variances of 0.3%.

This tasting of "vinous" wines gives a clear idea of the indirect part played by alcohol on account of its dual flavor, sweet and warm. Variances in strength of the same range between fortified wines would be more easily perceived since the other elements in the wine, thanks to better grape maturity, follow the alcohol content.

Other exercises, easy enough to carry out, consist in tasting a series of wines of the same type and ranking them according to their alcoholic strength or else just giving an estimate of their alcoholic content.

Adding Glycerol

Add experimentally 2–5 g of glycerol per liter to samples of a red wine that has for preference a suppleness index of less than 5. Compare them to the reference sample in a blind tasting; then, if necessary, knowing their respective order. The glycerol reinforces the instant sweet taste, slightly increases the gustatory volume, improves evolution by masking the acid flavors but has little influence on the tannic aftertaste. The glycerol acts through its own sugar taste and not through its viscosity.

This trial demonstrates the part played by sweet-tasting substances in wine in modifying the sour taste. (It should be made clear that this addition to wine constitutes a fraudulent practice, easy to detect by quantitative analysis of the glycerol).

Adding Sugar

The subject of this test is to train tasters to recognize the presence of small quantities of reducing sugars in wines that are supposed to be totally dry. For instance, 2 and 4 g of sugar per liter are added to a wine and attempts made to distinguish the sweetened samples from the reference sample. You may also try to rank young wines that show naturally different reducing sugar contents.

The trial is carried out on red wine and dry white wine. Ranking sweet and semisweet dessert white wines in relation to their sugar content is generally easier.

Ranking According to Acidity and the Addition of Different Acids

In a first series of exercises, the same wine is presented with three different acidities, obtained in the laboratory by acidifying with tartaric acid or by deacidifying, the variances being 0.5 g/L, for instance. The difference can be increased or diminished depending on performance. This operation is practiced on red wine, dry white wine, or semisweet white wine. As has already been observed, differences are better perceived in white wines than in red wines, which have a more complex taste due to the tannin. It will be seen that a higher acidity masks the sweet flavor of a semisweet wine.

The samples are tasted in a known or unknown order. The exercise teaches how to understand the part played by acidity, which is vital to the taste of wine but is not always recognized due to insufficient sensory analysis.

In other exercises, different wines could be compared and ranked in relation to the acid sensation they give. Attempts could even be made to estimate their total acidity.

The addition of different constitutive organic acids to wine gives the taster a clear idea of their share in the taste of wine. The same red wine is acidified by 0.5 g/L of the various organic acids. The addition of tartaric acid hardens it, citric acid gives it an acid freshness, lactic acid is hardly perceptible, malic acid amplifies the harshness, and succinic acid participates in the vinosity.

Acescence

The same wine is given added acetic acid (0.25, 0.5, 0.75, 1.00 g/L) or ethyl acetate (50, 100, 200 mg). The acetic acid is strongly felt at the finish (sour) and hardly smelt at all. Ethyl acetate has in its odor that specific character of vinegariness. It is perceptible from 160 to 180 mg/L. Below these levels, it already begins to have an effect on taste and hardens the wine in a disagreeable way. The gustatory role of these substances is commented in Chapter 21 under Formation of Ethyl Acetate.

The Gustatory Role of Sulfur Dioxide

Comparison is made by means of tasting, paying particular attention to its olfactory character, of several samples of the same red wine or the same dry white wine, raised earlier to different levels of free sulfur dioxide: 0, 10, 20, 30, 50 mg/L. In the same way, sweet white wines could be compared at, for instance, 30, 60, 90, mg/L.

The disagreeable vinegar odor of sulfur dioxide is perceived by strong inhalation, the nose being placed in the glass very close to the surface of the wine. It appears as an irritation around the olfactory turbinates. Furthermore, the sulfur dioxide, to a large extent, neutralizes the fruity aroma, obliterates the finesse, and levels down the character of wines.

The Bitter Taste of Polyphenolic Compounds

Certain substances (leucoanthocyans or tannins) possess tastes that are more or less bitter and astringent according to their degree of polymerization, that is to say, the size of their molecule. It is instructive to compare red wines showing different levels of phenolic compounds, determined by measuring the permanganate or Folin's index, or, better, by quantitative analysis of the different groups of these substances. Wines that are more or less astringent can be obtained by diluting samples with press wine. It may be noted that a polyphenolic index of 30 generally corresponds to supple wines, a 40 rating to a full-bodied wine, and a 50 rating or over means hard, astringent wines likely to keep a very long time. These ratings may vary considerably according to the grape variety and the type and balance of the wine.

It will be seen that tannic hardness is different from acid hardness (fixed acidity) and from acetic hardness (acetic acid and ethyl acetate).

The tannin level in white wines, which commonly fluctuates between 0 and 400 g/L, is an important factor in their flavor. The oak tannin in the casks or enological tannin hardens them.

Using analogous procedures, these exercises in analytical tasting can be extended to other saporous or odorous constituents.

4

The Composition of Wine

DEFINITION OF WINE

"Wine is the product obtained exclusively from total or partial alcoholic fermentation of fresh grapes, crushed or not, or of grape-must." This is the definition adopted by the European Economic Community (EEC). This definition is made more explicit and completed by a whole set of decrees relevant to the approved methods of production, operations and treatments authorized, the limits of chemical composition and additives. Each wine-producing country has its own official texts and methods of control.

A more enological definition would be as follows: "Wine is the drink resulting from the fermentation by the yeast-cells, and also in certain cases by the cells of lactic bacteria, of the juice from the crushing or maceration of grape-cells."

Wine is a product of the transformation by microorganisms of the vegetable tissues in a fruit. Its composition and evolution are directly linked to biochemical phenomena. This definition gives a better understanding of its extremely complex composition and therefore the particular interest involved in its study due to the great diversity of subjects touched on. It defines, moreover, the nutritional value of wine. Developed from living cells, it contains, in a diluted state it is true, all that is necessary for life.

One of the enologist's tasks is to study the composition of wine in as complete a way as possible. The technician should also know the composition of wine if he expects to understand the events which take place during the course of the maturation of grapes, the elaboration of the wine, during its

SAMPLE DETAILED ANALYSIS OF A RED WINE:
SAINT-ESTÈPHE 1976

Alcohol	12%	Tartaric acid	2.21 g/L
Density at 20°C	0.9977	Malic acid	0
Density of wine without alcohol	1.0107	Lactic acid	2.02 g/L
Reducing sugars	1.9 g/L	Succinic acid	1.02 g/L
Reduced dry extract	27.0 g/L	Glycerol	11.7 g/L
Ash	2.92 g/L	Butylene glycol	0.75 g/L
Total acidity	3.52 g/L	Total nitrate	0.40 g/L
Volatile acidity	0.45 g/L	Polyphenol index	43 meq/L
Ethyl acetate	0.12 g/L	Anthocyans	165 mg/L
Free SO_2	6 mg/L	Tannins	2.30 g/L
Total SO_2	64 mg/L	Carbon dioxide	0.24 g/L

cellar life and during treatment. We have adopted a classification of the constituents of wine based on their share in its gustatory characteristics.

SWEET-TASTING SUBSTANCES

These are the elements that give softness, fat, and mellowness to wines.

Sweet taste does not belong only to those bodies commonly called sugars. Many substances have a sweet taste without being sugars, for example, saccharin, which is 500 times sweeter than ordinary sugar, and chloroform, which is 40 times sweeter. Chemically these bodies have no relationship to sugar.

Sweet substances in wine fall into three groups: (1) sugars as such, which exist in the grape and remain partly unfermented in sweet white wines but which are also present in dry white wines and red wines in minute quantities; (2) polyalcohols, which also come from the grapes at a few hundred milligrams per liter of must and which are to be found in the wine in proportions changed more or less by fermentation; and (3) certain substances having one or several alcoholic functions, formed by the alcoholic fermentation.

Sugars

The grape contains 15–25% sugar made up of glucose and fructose. These two sugars have the same basic chemical formula. Glucose is a right (D-

PRINCIPLE SWEET-TASTING SUBSTANCES FOUND IN WINES

Sugars (originating in the grapes)	Hexoses	Glucose
		Fructose
	Pentoses	Arabinose
		Xylose
Polyalcohols (originating in the grapes)	Inositol Mannitol Arabitol Erythritol Sorbitol	
Alcohols (of fermentation origin)	Ethyl alcohol Glycerol Butylene glycol	

configuration) sugar with an aldehyde function; fructose is a left (L-configuration) sugar with a ketone function.

In a perfectly ripe grape, these two sugars are to be found in very similar quantities. However, there is always slightly more fructose than glucose. The glucose/fructose ratio is close to 0.95. During fermentation, this ratio declines, the large majority of the yeasts causing the glucose to ferment first. Below is an example of the evolution of sugars during the fermentation of grape must.

		Glucose (g/L)	Fructose (g/L)	Glucose/Fructose Ratio
Must before fermentation		123	126	0.97
Alcohol formed during	0.7%	111	125	0.88
fermentation	5.3%	57	103	0.55
	12.4%	8	32	0.25

The sugar that is present in the largest quantity toward the end of the fermentation is fructose. However, as has already been mentioned, fructose has a taste that is twice as sweet as glucose. Therefore, it is easy to understand that, given equal amounts, the semisweet and sweet wines with the most fructose appear the sweetest. For this reason, white wines sweetened with grape must, sulfured with sulfur dioxide, or concentrated by heating (a practice authorized within certain limits) seem less sweet than sweet wines obtained by arresting fermentation. They are, in fact, proportionally less rich in fructose than the latter.

The P/x ratio, where P is the weight of sugar and x the saccharimetric deviation measured by means of a polarimeter, is another expression of the glucose/fructose ratio. It is used in the control laboratory to investigate sugar addition. In normal wines the P/x ratio is below 4. A ratio of 5.26 is the equivalent of equal quantities of glucose and fructose. Above this level, glucose is dominant or there may be some sucrose. The P/x ratio is a test that allows differentiation between fortified wines with alcohol added during fermentation and *mistelles*, which are musts alcoholized before fermentation.

In completely fermented wines, there still remains a fraction of a gram of fructose. A little glucose also remains. In red wines, glucose also comes from the hydrolysis of certain glucosides during storage. The grape contains only traces of sucrose, which disappear during fermentation. Wine, therefore, can only contain this sugar if it has been introduced. The sugaring of must or the harvested grapes, authorized under certain conditions, leaves no sucrose in the wine since this sugar is only fermented after inversion by the yeasts, that is to say, hydrolysis into equal quantities of glucose and fructose. The presence of sucrose in a wine is a sure sign of fraudulent chaptalizing.

The grape also contains a small quantity of nonfermentable sugars, made up of pentoses and pentosans partly condensed, around a gram per liter. Of course, these are also found in the wine. Their principal constituent is arabinose; xylose may be present. Because of these sugars and other substances capable of reducing the sugar reagents, you never find a zero proportion of the "reducing sugars" in a totally dry wine and the amounts currently found vary between 1 and 2 g/L.

Traces of certain other sugars found in the grapes, such as raffinose, stachyose, melibiose, maltose, galactose, are of little enological importance. A little trehalose is formed by the yeasts in all fermentation.

Alcohols

After water, of course, which represents 85–90% of the volume in wine, ethanol is the most plentiful ingredient. If we allow that the alcoholic strength of wines varies between 9 and 15%, alcohol represents 72 to 120 g/L. 0.5% of this quantity relates to alcohols other than ethylic alcohol. These will be mentioned later under Volatile and Odorous Substances.

In addition to its complex taste, alcohol possesses an odor that is the vehicle, the carrier, for aroma and bouquet in wines. At the base of a wine's odor, there is a distinct alcoholized odor.

Glycerol (a modern term for glycerine) is, after alcohol, a wine's most important ingredient by weight: 5–10 g/L. Glycerol possesses three alcohol functions; it is a polyalcohol. Due to its sweet flavor, almost equal to that of glucose, glycerol contributes to a wine's softness, but is far from being the main factor. It was thought that the viscosity of glycerol was a vital contributing factor in fatness. In fact, it only plays a small part compared to alcohol. In the proportions found in wine, its presence does not increase viscosity.

Glycerol is a product of alcoholic fermentation. In normal circumstances, it represents a tenth or even a fifteenth of the alcoholic weight. It is formed chiefly at the beginning of the fermentation process from the first 50 g of fermented sugars. Its proportion depends on the initial sugar content, the type of yeasts and the fermentation conditions: temperature, aeration, acidity, sulfiting, and so on.

In addition, glycerol is formed during the noble rot on the grape. Dessert wines obtained from botrytized grapes are particularly rich in glycerol (up to 15 g/L).

The butylene glycol, another polyalcohol, is also a constituent of all the fermentation media. Amounts to be found in wines vary between 0.3 and 1.5 g/L. Its sweet flavor comes close to bitterness.

Inositol, a cyclic alcohol with a sweet taste and vitaminous properties, exists in the proportion of 0.5 g/kg in the grapes and in the wine. Belonging to the same chemical family, mannitol, which can be created from fructose through lactic acescence, sorbitol at less than 0.1 g/L, and a series of various polyalcohols exist.

SOUR-TASTING SUBSTANCES

Acidity in wine is made up of several organic acids:

PRINCIPAL INGREDIENTS OF ACIDITY IN WINES

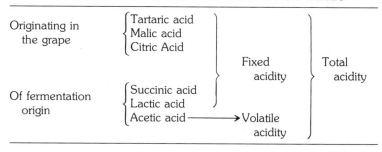

Other acids present in small quantities are: galacturonic, glucuronic, gluconic, oxalic, mucic, citramilic, dimethylglyceric, pyruvic, and ketoglutaric.

Acids are to be found in wines in two forms: most of the acid occurs in a free form and constitutes the total acidity, the rest is in salt form. It is determined by the alkalinity of the ash (see Ash under ANALYTICAL DEFINITIONS later in this chapter).

**EXAMPLE OF AN ACIDIMETRIC
ANALYSIS[a] OF A WHITE WINE[b]**

Total acidity	83
Alkalinity of ash	20.8
Ammonia cation	0.6
Sum of cations	104.4
Tartaric acid	27.5
Malic acid	14.8
Citric acid	4.1
Acetic acid	14.4
Succinic acid	15.7
Lactic acid	11.9
Phosphoric acid	3.3
Sulfuric acid	3.9
Sum of anions	95.6

[a] Missing from this quantitative analysis are a few acids present in very slight quantities.
[b] Amounts expressed in milliequivalents per liter.

A wine's mineral acids are mostly present in the form of neutral salts.

Tartaric Acid

This is the acid specific to the grape and to wine. In temperate regions, it is rarely found in nature other than in the vine. It represents a third or a quarter of the acids in wines. It is also the strongest acid (the one that liberates the most H^+ ions) and the pH of wine depends to a large extent on its richness in tartaric acid. Of the three grape acids, it is the most resistant to the decomposing action of bacteria.

Its concentration diminishes through precipitation in the form of potassium bitartrate crystals and neutral calcium tartrate caused by an increase in alcohol and reduction in temperature. The finished wine contains two or three times less tartaric acid than the must it was made from.

The precipitation of the tartar crystals, particularly that of the calcium salts, is slow. The colloidal substances and the particles in suspension in the wine impede it. Filtration or centrifugation speed it up. It is made much easier by chilling or cooling the wine.

It can happen that the tartaric acid in the wine is attacked by certain lactic bacteria that make it decompose, forming lactic acid and volatile acidity. The wine loses fixed acidity and goes flat; its color turns pale. This is the sickness known as *La Tourne*. Nowadays rare, such accidents would be frequent and almost regular if wines were vinified and stored without using sulfuric anhydrides.

The addition of tartaric acid to the harvest is permitted and useful only in certain areas and under certain conditions (see Chapter 7, ACIDIFICATION).

Malic Acid

This is one of the most widespread acids to be found in the vegetable realm. You find it in the leaves and the fruit. In contrast to tartaric acid, it is a fragile acid, easily metabolized, that is to say, subject to degradation.

In enology, it may be considered the key acid, the one that it is most important to consider during ripening of the grape and the elaboration of wines.

Found in large quantities in the green grape to which it gives that sharp tang, malic acid disappears gradually during maturation. The ripe grape, according to the variety and according to the year, will contain a greater or lesser amount in relation to its state of ripeness, say from 1 to 8 grams per liter of must, for instance. During alcoholic fermentation these amounts shrink by 20–30% due to action by the yeasts.

After that, there is another transformation, one of prime interest. In red wines and dry white wines made with small quantities of sulfuric anhydride, malic acid is fermented in its entirety by the lactic bacteria, which transform it into lactic acid and carbon dioxide. This gas is given off and in this way the total acidity of the wine is reduced by half the fermented malic acid. This reaction, called malolactic fermentation, produces a considerable improvement in the wine's quality, causing it to become more supple and lose the acid character of new wine.

We can measure the scope of these malic acid transformations. From the green grape to the finished wine, its level gets lower and lower until it reaches zero, in three stages: ripening of the grape, alcoholic fermentation, malolactic fermentation. In this way, the amount of malic acid in the ripe grape decides the final acidity of the wine.

Efforts are made to maintain the malic acid and avoid malolactic fermentation for certain types of dry white wine or again for rosé wines or sweet white wines obtained by sulfuring with sulfuric anhydride.

Citric Acid

This acid is not very plentiful in grapes: 150–300 mg per liter of juice. It undergoes the same fate during vinification as the malic acid. Fermented by the lactic bacteria, it disappears.

The use of citric acid in limited doses is allowed depending on the country and its acidification requirements. One advantage is that it is a solvent for iron in its ferric state and therefore it provides protection against ferric damage. Its use in young red wines is not advisable because of the bacterial instability and the increased volatile acidity which its lactic fermentation causes.

Succinic Acid

This acid is formed by the yeasts and always accompanies the sugar fermentation. You find 0.5–1.0 g of it per liter of wine.

Very stable as regards bacterial fermentation, succinic acid does not develop during storage of the wine. Its flavor is a mixture of acid, salt, and bitter tastes, It gives fermented drinks the special taste they all have in common.

Lactic Acid

This acid also has a fermentative origin. It does not exist in the grape and is a normal constituent of wine. Although it is more abundant in sick wines, its presence is not necessarily a sign of deterioration. Lactic acid can in fact be formed in three ways:

1. Formation by the yeasts during alcoholic fermentation of the sugars. The healthiest fermentation tends to produce 0.2–0.4 g/L.
2. Formation by bacteria during malolactic fermentation at the expense of malic acid. In wines having undergone this fermentation, 1–2.5 g/L are usually found.
3. Finally, in deteriorated wines, formation by lactic fermentation of the sugars, the glycerol, tartaric acid, or other constituents of wine. The level of lactic acid may reach several grams.

In point of fact, there exists in wine a mixture of right lactic acid (L+) and left lactic acid (D−). The yeasts give mainly a left acid. On the other hand, the malolactic bacteria only form right acids from the malic acid. An enzymatic dosage of the right lactic acid is the most sensitive process for detecting bacterial intervention.

Acetic Acid (or Volatile Acidity)

The preceding acids are the fixed acids in wine. In the course of distillation, they do not pass into the wine spirits, but remain in the residue. Acetic acid, however, is volatile and is found in the distillate. Hence the distinction made between fixed acidity and volatile acidity.

Acetic acid is formed in the same two ways as lactic acid, plus by means of the acetic bacteria.

1. *Alcoholic Fermentation.* All wines have volatile acidity because acetic acid is a normal byproduct of alcoholic fermentation. The amount formed by pure fermentation of the must is always small: 0.15–0.30 g/L expressed as sulfuric acid. It depends a lot on the types of yeast and their association but also on the composition of the must (acidity, richness in sugars and nitrates) and on the fermentation conditions (temperature, aeration).

2. *Malolactic Fermentation.* This is always accompanied by a slight formation of volatile acidity, from 0.1 to 0.2 g, actually arising mostly from the fermentation of the citric acid and the pentoses. Volatile acidities possibly reaching 0.40 g are for this reason inevitable in well-finished young wines and are not necessarily indicative of nascent deterioration. To always demand volatile acidities below this level in wines that no longer contain malic acid would reveal a lack of enological knowledge.

3. *Bacterial Spoilage.* Above this level suspicion may be directed to disease bacteria. The acetic bacteria in contact with the air are capable of oxidizing alcohol, giving high rates of acetic acid. Another cause of a rise in volatile acidity is an attack by lactic bacteria, shut off from contact with the air, on certain constituents of musts and of wines.

As long as volatile acidity does not exceed 0.55–0.60 g, the taste of the wine generally does not depreciate although wines are still better when their volatile acidity is less. It is not correct to say that a high rate of volatile acidity enhances the bouquet; only poor tasters make such an assertion.

In any case, long before the legal limit of 18–20 meq. (0.92–0.98) chosen rather generously by the EEC, deterioration in taste due to acetic acid is perceived as a hardness, a final bitterness. The vinegary odor is due not to acetic acid, but to ethyl acetate.

SALTY-TASTING SUBSTANCES

Wine contains 2–4 g of these substances per liter. These are the salts of the mineral acids and a few organic acids. The ash of wine, resulting from incineration of the extract, roughly represents them. They participate in the flavor of the wine and give it freshness. For instance, potassium bitartrate has both an acid and salt taste. Nevertheless, adding salts, chlorides, or sulfates to wine generally leads to a decrease in gustatory enjoyment.

In 1 L of wine there is about 1 g of potassium, 100 mg of magnesium and calcium, and several tens of milligrams of sodium. A higher level of

PRINCIPLE CONSTITUENTS OF
SALTS IN WINE

	Anions	Cations
Mineral	Phosphate	Potassium
	Sulfate	Sodium
	Chloride	Magnesium
	Sulfite	Calcium
Organic	Tartrate	Iron
	Malate	Aluminum
	Lactate	Copper

sodium generally indicates fraudulent additions of alkaline salts (deacidification).

To complete this list we should really include certain other mineral substances existing as traces (oligo elements): fluorine, silicone, iodine, bromine, boron, zinc, manganese, lead, cobalt, chromium, nickel, and so on (Fig. 4.1).

BITTER- AND ASTRINGENT-TASTING SUBSTANCES

These are the phenolic compounds formerly referred to as coloring matter, tannoid matter, or enotannin. These substances perform a vital organoleptic and technological function. They give wines their color and a large part of

Figure 4.1. Atomic absorption flame-spectrophotometer used for quantity determination of numerous cations (Varian).

EXAMPLE OF ANALYSIS[a] BY WEIGHT
OF A RED WINE'S ASH

Weight of Ash	Amounts (mg/L) 2500
Potassium	698
Sodium	41
Calcium	80
Magnesium	156
Iron	30
Alkalinity (CO_3)	542
Phosphate anion	245
Sulfate anion	559
Chloride anion	28
Total	2379

[a] This analysis would be completed with the numerous oligo elements present

their flavor. They explain their evolution. The taste of red wines, more precisely, what makes the difference between the taste of white wines and that of red wines, is due to the polyphenolic compounds. They have the additional property of coagulating proteins and are used in the clarification of wines by fining. Finally, a certain number of them have an effect on the nutritional qualities of red wines, especially through their vitamin P properties (resistance of capillary blood vessels) and their bactericide powers.

Two methods of overall measurement of these substances are available: volumetric measure of the permanganate index and colorimetric determination on Folin's index (which is preferable). To simplify matters, the figure thus determined is sometimes called the polyphenolic index.

The phenolic compounds belong to several closely related chemical groups.

1. Anthocyanins, which are the red pigment, represent 200–500 mg/L in young red wines. Several substances of this kind exist in black grapes and in the wines, different for different varieties. These are the glucosides: Each molecule contains one or two molecules of glucose. It has been demonstrated that during aging the anthocyanin molecule gradually releases its glucose. The monoglucoside of malvidol is the main coloring matter in the grapes from European vines (*Vitis vinifera*), whereas the diglucoside of malvidol is particular to certain American vines and their hybrid cross-breeds. On account

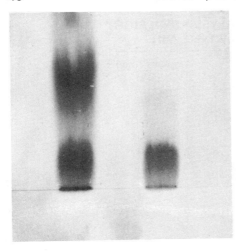

Figure 4.2. Chromatograms of the anthocyanin in a Vitis Vinifera wine (*right*) and a hybrid wine (*left*). The hybrid wines are characterized by the presence of diglucoside of malvidol (upper stain fluorescent in ultraviolet light).

of this, you can recognize certain wines from hybrids in a Vitis vinifera wine, even in minute proportions, by chromatography on paper (Fig. 4.2). Anthocyanins, or more exactly the tannins-anthocyanins combinations are partially polymerized in wines, that is to say, condensed by association with numerous molecules until they reach a colloidal condition which can be precipitated in the cold state or carried away by a fining agent. The level of free anthocyanins drops after several years to a few dozen milligrams per liter.

2.   Flavones, of yellow coloring, only exist in minute quantities (glycosides of quercitin, myricetin, and camphor oil). The color of white wine is incorrectly attributed to them.

3.   Certain acid phenols are also present in the form of esters (cinnamic acids, benzoic acids).

4.   Condensed tannins located in the seeds and skins and abundant in the stems, are composed of leucoanthocyanins. In red wine, there exists 1–3 grams of these substances and a few tens of milligrams per liter in white wines. The astringency of these compounds is linked to their degree of polymerization. There is not always an exact relation between the total tannin content apprehended by determination of the index and the astringent taste of the wine. Analyzing by quantity the condensed forms gives a better idea of the astringent flavors. Certain aged wines, rich in tannins, have lost their astringency and become more supple. In old red wines, these substances take on a brickish red color that replaces the livelier younger color of the free anthocyanins.

5.   Pyrogallic tannins do not exist in the grape. They may be derived from commercial tannins or from wood in the casks.

The table below gives examples of the composition of phenolic substances.

PHENOLIC COMPOUNDS OF RED WINES[a]

	2 Years	4 Years	7 Years
Optic density[b] per 420 μm	0.352	0.321	0.374
Optic density[b] for 520 μm	0.420	0.355	0.385
Intensity (420 + 520)[c]	0.772	0.676	0.759
Hue (420/520)[c,d]	0.836	0.904	0.971
Anthocyanins (mg/L)[d]	188	130	95
Tannins (mg/L)[e]	2590	3080	4120
Polyphenol index	43	48	60

[a] Analysis of three wines of different ages from the same growth in the Graves (district of Bordeaux).

[b] The optic densities for wavelengths 420 and 520 μm represent the coloring intensity brownish yellow and the coloring intensity red, respectively.

[c] The total color of the wine is defined by the sum of these two values, whereas the hue is specified by their ratios.

[d] Note the rise in color hue and the progressive decrease in the anthocyanins (red color) during aging.

[e] The proportion of tannins depends on the vintage.

OTHER SUBSTANCES

Nitrate Substances

There exists in wines 1–3 g/L of nitrate substances. They have little effect on taste, but are important nutritional substances indispensable to the yeasts and the bacteria. Some become insoluble and make bottled white wines go cloudy during storage.

In addition to being present in the form of ammonia, nitrate may be found in musts and wines in different forms that can be ranked according to the size of their molecules and, for simplification, divided into the following groups:

1. Proteins are called "albuminous material" with high molecular weight, over 10,000. They are found in a micromolecular state and have a colloidal character. The proteins precipitate due to the effects of heat and the tannin. They are an obstacle to the stabilization of clarity in white wines and special treatment is necessary to eliminate them. The organic finings used in the clarification of wines are also proteins.

2. Polypeptides are the grouping of the amino acids more or less condensed but they have smaller molecules than proteins. These bodies constitute the most abundant form of nitrogen in wines.

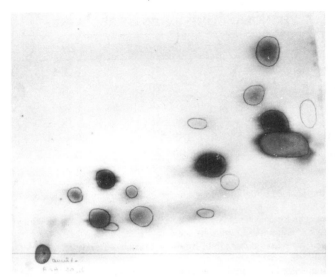

Figure 4.3. Chromatogram in two dimensions of the amino acids of a wine. Each stain corresponds to a different amino acid.

3.   Amino acids are the basic links of the micromolecules of the proteins and of the polypeptides (see Fig. 4.3). The table on the following page gives the most important by weight. It is possible that the special flavor of glutamic acid participates in the taste of wine.

Pectins, Gums, and Mucilage

When a little alcohol is added to grape must or an acidified wine in a test tube, the mixture becomes cloudy and is resorbed into a gelatinous deposit. This deposit, which represents a few grams of colloidal substances per liter, is made up of polysaccharides of pectins, gums, and mucilages.

The pectins are concatenations of galacturonic acid partially esterified by the methyl alcohol. They exist in all fruit. They form part of the composition of the walls of vegetable cells. Pectins are hydrolized during fermentation, freeing methanol and pectic acid, which precipitates. Hardly any pectins are found in a wine a few months old.

Gums are polysaccharides composed of galactins, arabines, xylines, and fructosines more or less polymerized. These are the colloidal protectors that come into action during the fining processes. Wine may contain from 0.1–3 g of them per liter. They play the most important part in the colloidal phase of the wine.

MEAN LEVELS OF CERTAIN FREE AMINO ACIDS

	mg/L		mg/L
Arginine	50	Lysine	50
Aspartic acid	30	Proline	100–500
Glutamic acid	200	Serine	50
Leucine	20	Threonine	200
Isoleucine	20	Valine	40

We know that *Botrytis cinerea*, the agent that causes rot on grapes, produces a mucilage precipitable in alcohol at 25°C in the form of characteristic filaments. It consists of a glucose mixture of high molecular weight (900,000), formerly known by the name of dextran, with other polysaccharides of a lower molecular weight (around 20,000) containing rhamnose, galactose, glucose, and mannose. The dextran or glucose polymer of *Botrytis cinerea*, although in small doses, prevents clarifying by means of gravitation or fining since it quickly clogs the filtration surfaces.

Volatile and Odorous Substances

Up until the turn of the century, the odor of wine was attributed to a small number of substances, sometimes only one, an "enanthic acid." Not long

NITRATE COMPOSITION OF MUSTS AND WINES[a]

	Must	Wine
Total nitrogen	390	350
Ammonia nitrate	44	14
Amino nitrate	75	73
Polypeptide nitrate	81	148
Protein nitrate	51	42
Oseamino nitrate[b]	23	14
Nucleic nitrate[c]		23

[a] Cordonnier has calculated the mean values (mg/L).
[b] Oseamino nitrate (glucosamine) is in a heteroside state.
[c] Nucleic nitrate comes from the nucleus of the grape cells or yeasts.

Figure 4.4.   Gas chromatography apparatus for the study of volatile substances in wine (Perkin-Elmer).

ago we began to recognize the complexity of a wine's makeup. As of about 1952, some fifty substances had been identified as being components of a wine's odor.

The progress which has been made since then has been due to the use of gas chromatography. This method has made it possible to distinguish several hundred volatile substances present in wines. For all that, (see Figs. 4.4 and 4.5) our knowledge is still not sufficient to enable us to draw up a kind of identity-card characteristic of a type of wine. The olfactory senses have, what is more, greater sensitivity than the detectors on chromatographic instruments. We may assume that the agreeable odor of a wine is due to a harmonious whole to which a large number of substances, present as trace elements, contribute. The volatile substances in wine, of which many are odorous, belong to different chemical families: alcohols, carbonyl components, acids, esters, terpineol, and others.

Vitamins

The list on the following page shows wine's average vitamin richness. Even if the contribution in vitamin content made by this drink appears low in relation to the food ration, we may nevertheless ascertain that wine, the essence of grape cells transformed and completed by action of the yeast cells, contains practically all the biotic elements. In this way, vitamins play their part as indispensable growth factors for the yeasts and bacteria. They ensure the proper functioning of the fermentation.

SOME OF THE VOLATILE SUBSTANCES IN WINE

Alcohols
Methanol
Ethanol
1-Propanol
2-Propanol
1-Butanol
2-Methyl 2-propanol
2-Butanol
3-Methyl 1-butanol
2-Methyl 1-butanol
Hexanol
Heptanol
Phenylethanol

Carbonyl Components
Ethanal
Propanal
Butanal
Pentanal
Hexanal
Acetone
Acetine
Diacetyl
Acetyl

Acids
Formic
Acetic
Propionic
Butyric
Valeric
Caproic
Enanthic
Caprylic
lauric

Esters
Ethyl formate
Ethyl acetate
Isopropyl acetate
Isobutyl acetate
Isoamyl acetate
Phenylethyl acetate
Ethyl propionate
Ethyl butyrate
Ethyl valerianate
Ethyl caproate
Ethyl enanthate
Ethyl caprylate
Ethyl Caprate
Ethyl undecanate
Ethyl laurate
Ethyl lactate
Ethyl succinate

Terpenes and Other Components
Geraniol
Terpineol
Limonene
Linalool
Nerol
Citronellol
Ionone
Farnesol
Vanillin
Methyl anthranilate
Ethyl salicylate
Tyrosol
Tryptophol

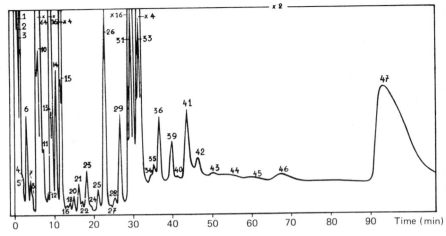

Figure 4.5. Chromatogram of volatile substances of a wine obtained by gas chromatography apparatus. Each number shown at the tops of the peaks corresponds to a different substance. The position of the peak allows the nature of the substance to be identified. The height of each peak is representative of the quantity of substance present.

AVERAGE VITAMIN CONTENT OF RED WINES

Thiamine B1	0.10 mg	Pyridoxine	0.47 mg
Riboflavin B2	0.18 mg	Mesoinositol	334 mg
Pantothenic acid	0.98 mg	Biotin	2.1 μg
Nicotinamide PP	1.89 mg	Cobalamine B12	0.06 μg

ANALYTICAL DEFINITIONS

Specific Gravity and Relative Density

The voluminal mass is the quotient of the mass of a certain volume of wine or must at 20°C divided by the volume. It is expressed in grams per milliliter.

The relative density 20/20 is the ratio expressed as a decimal number of the voluminal mass of the wine or must at 20°C to the voluminal mass of water at the same temperature.

Degree of Alcohol

The volumetric degree of alcohol or voluminal alcoholometric strength is the proportion of ethylic alcohol the wine contains. Usually the concentrations of the wine's constituents are calculated in grams per liter. Alcohol is the only constituent expressed in volume.

Alcohol represents, depending upon the wine, from 8 to 16% of the volume. It is said that wine weighs so many degrees. The proportion of alcohol contained in a wine is expressed in alcoholic degrees according to the principle of Gay-Lussac.

Pure alcohol has a strength equal to 100 degrees. A degree corresponds to 1 ml of pure alcohol contained in 100 mL of mixture, these two volumes being considered at the same temperature of 20°C. The alcoholic degree is the percentage of alcohol present in the wine expressed in terms of volume.

So when it is said that a wine weighs 11 degrees for instance, that means it contains 11% of its volume in alcohol or that in 100 mL of the wine under consideration, there are 11 mL of pure alcohol, that is 110 mL/L or else 11 L/hL. We also see that 0.1 degree corresponds to 1 mL of pure alcohol per liter of wine. The official definition is as follows: "The voluminal alcoholometric strength is equal to the number of liters of ethylic alcohol contained in 100 liters of wine, these volumes being both measured at a temperature of 20°C."

Alcohol is expressed in grams per liter in an approximate way by multiplying the alcoholic degree by 8. Example: an 11 degree wine contains roughly 88 g of alcohol per liter.

Dry Extract

The total dry extract or total of dry matter comprises all those substances which, under given physical conditions, do not volatilize. These physical conditions have to be fixed in such a way that the substances making up this extract undergo minimum change.

The nonreducing extract is the total extract reduced by the total sugars.

The reduced extract is the total dry extract reduced by the total sugars in excess of 1 g/L, by the potassium sulfate in excess of 1 g/L, by the mannitol (if there is any), and by any chemical substances that may have been added to the wine.

Ash

We call ash the entire sum of the products of the incineration of the wine's dry extract, carried out between 500 and 500°C up to complete combustion of the carbon. The ash is composed of carbonates and other anhydrous mineral salts.

The alkalinity of ash is the sum of the cations, other than ammonium, combined with the organic acids of the wine. Increased by the ammonium cation, it represents the buffered organic acids.

Definition of Acidities

Total acidity is the sum of the titratable acids when the wine is brought to pH 7.0 neutrality by the addition of a base. Another way of expressing it is titratable acidity. Carbonic acid and sulfur anhydride, both free and combined, are not included in total acidity. Total acidity is expressed in milliequivalents (meq. or mL of normal solution) per liter. This is determined to the nearest milliequivalent. It can be expressed also in grams of tartaric acid, as in most countries, or in grams of sulfuric acid, as in France.

Volatile acidity is constituted by that part of the fatty acids belonging to the acetic series which are found either in a free state, in the wines, or in a buffered state. Carbon dioxide needs to be eliminated. The acidity of free and combined distilled sulfur anhydride along with that of any sorbic acid that may be present, should be removed from the acidity of the distillate. Volatile acidity is expressed in milliequivalents per liter and determined to the nearest 0.5 meq. In practice, it is stated in terms of acetic acid and, in France, in sulfuric acid.

Fixed acidity is determined by the difference between total acidity and volatile acidity.

pH

Many of a wine's properties and a lot of the various phenomena that take place in it, depend on its acidity. However, a wine's total acidity only gives the sum of the free acids without taking their strength into account; it does not sufficiently define acidity. On the contrary, actual acidity or the concentration of hydrogen ions, represented by the pH, relates not only to the quantity but also to the strength of the acids. There are strong acids and weak acids. The strength of the acids is represented by their dissociation constant, that is to say, the proportion in which they are dissociated, in which they liberate H^+ ions. In direct value, the concentration of H^+ ions in wines is around 0.001–0.0001 g/L. For reasons of convenience, this concentration is expressed not in direct values, but as a logarithmic value. The pH is exactly the cologarithm of the concentration of H^+ ions. Practically, it is a convenient representation of the acid strength of the wine. pH 7.0 indicates neutrality. pH values from 1 to 7 correspond to the acid medium; pH values from 7 to 14 to the alkaline medium.

The pH of wine, which depends on the nature of the acids, their concentration, and the proportions in which they are saturated by the bases, varies roughly from 2.9 to 3.9 in logarithmic value; that is actual acidity of wines varies in ratio from 1 to 10, whereas total acidity differs by only 1 to 2.

There are numerous examples in enology of reactions that depend on pH rather than on total acidity.

PART 2

The Ripening of the Grape and Harvesting

5

What Happens During the Ripening of the Grape

The state of maturity of the grape conditions the quality and even the type of wine. Therefore, it is one of the principal factors in winemaking. In most wine-growing regions, good wine is only achieved with fully ripe grapes and good vintages correspond invariably with hot summers, which give grapes optimum maturity. But in hot regions, since ripening is accelerated, the thing to avoid is excess maturity, which gives unbalanced wines lacking freshness. There are other regions where, depending on the vintage season, the wine maker can produce a dry white wine sufficiently acid, vigorous, and fruity, or else a wine with low acidity, weaker, rounder, and more fleshy, or again, with a basic must that is very rich in saccharin, a wine that has retained a certain quantity of sugars.

Thus it is important for the winemaker to know what goes on during the ripening of the grape, and it is obvious that the enologist will be interested in all these transformations. The enologist's work begins with maturity control.

DESCRIPTION OF THE GRAPE

The bunch of grapes includes two completely distinct parts: the wood of the grapes, or stems, and the berries themselves. Each berry is made up of the pellicle or skin, pips or seeds, and pulp, the fragile tissue with large swollen cells which when burst gives the juice or must (see Fig. 5.1). The must, which is separated mechanically by draining or pressing the grapes under pressure, is cloudy because it contains suspended sediment formed by the cellulose and pectic matter from the cell walls, the coagulation of protoplasm, protein

57

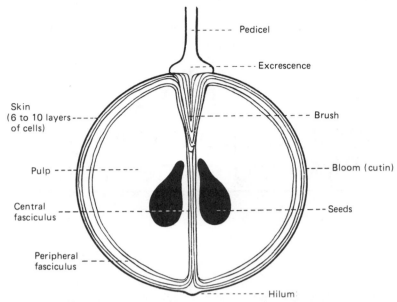

Figure 5.1. Diagrammatic cross section of a grape berry.

flocculation and also the remnants of the skins. The pomace obtained after pressing represents the solid part of the grapes, skins, and seeds and, unless destemming is practiced, the stems.

TRANSFORMATIONS IN THE GRAPE IN THE COURSE OF RIPENING

It is convenient from the description point of view to divide the transformation of the grape on the vinestock into four periods.

1. *The vegetative period* extends from the time the tiny berry forms (called the *nouaison*) up until ripening starts (called the *véraison*), signified by a change of color. During this period, the grape is green, colored by the chlorophyll, and its consistency is hard. It only contains 20 g of sugar per kilogram and almost as much acidity.

2. The *véraison* is the start of the ripening period and is related physiologically to the coloration of the grape. At the same time, the berry swells and becomes elastic. The white grape changes from green to yellow and the black grape from green to light red, then to dark red. The change is abrupt, a grape berry taking on its tint in one day. Under ideal conditions, a whole

AVERAGE COMPOSITION IN FIGURES FOR TWO
VARIETIES OF A GRAPE BUNCH

	Cabernet-Sauvignon	Sémillon
Composition of the bunch		
Stems (%)	2.9	3.1
Berries (%)	97.1	96.9
Composition of the berry		
Mean weight (g)	1.32	1.83
Pulp (%)	74	76
Skin (%)	20	21
Seeds (%)	6	3

vineyard will turn color in a fortnight. The sugar in the grapes increases suddenly.

3.   The period of *maturation* stretches from the ripening point to the final stage of maturity. During the 40 or 50 days it lasts, the grape goes on swelling, gathers sugar and loses acidity. A distinction should be made between the physiological maturity, which is the time when the grape reaches its largest diameter and maximum sugar content per berry, and technological maturity, which defines the picking time in relation to its ultimate utilization. The dates of these two maturity conditions do not always coincide.

4.   In a few cases, when the grape is left on the vine, *overripening* follows maturation. The fruit lives on its reserves, loses water, and its juice gets concentrated. Noble rot, which benefits from infection by *Botrytis cinerea*, is a special case of overripening (see Pectins, Gums, and Mucilage).

The main things that happen during ripening of the grape and that concern us here are as follows:

The grape berry swells
Sugars accumulate
Acids diminish
Tannins are formed and the skin changes color
Aromas are formed

The Grape Berry Swells

The berry continues to get bigger and heavier from the time it first forms up to maturity. Its growth is irregular and takes place in stages. At maturity, its size is subject to outside conditions in relation to the circulation of water in the plant.

For instance, the mean weight of 100 berries, which at the halfway stage before color change is 97 g for Merlot and 77 g for Cabernet-Sauvignon (average figures over a large number of readings) have by the maturity stage reached 138 and 114 g, respectively (i.e., an increase of around 50%). (Fig. 5.2).

The size of the ripe grape varies from year to year, particularly in relation to rainfall as the mean weights of 100 berries of Merlot shows.

Dry summers	1961	118 g
	1959	120 g
Wet summers	1960	160 g
	1965	165 g

The variations in size from one year to another may, for a similar crop tonnage, be 25 or 30% up or down, which makes vintage volume control difficult to forecast. Heavy rain during ripening makes the berry swell up suddenly and the skin may burst (Fig. 5.2).

A less known factor concerning the size of the berries is the number of seeds. Here is an example of the inference to be drawn from the development of the berry by its seeds, for the Malbec variety, as also its sugar content and acidity (in g/L) for berries having from one to four seeds.

	Weight of a Berry (g)	Sugars	Acidity
1 seed	1.91	188	6.7
2 seeds	2.52	160	7.1
3 seeds	2.96	153	7.7
4 seeds	3.25	145	8.0

The substances accumulated in the pulp, in particular the sugars, represent in a certain way the surplus nutrition of the seeds.

The Storing of Sugars in the Grape

This is the most obvious thing that happens. The grape merely needs to be tasted to realize that as it ripens it becomes sweet. The sugars which, in glucose or fructose form, are stored in the grape, come from several sources, but it has not yet been clearly elucidated how much comes from each. It is thought that when the fruit begins to ripen it draws sugar from reserves stored in the vinestock. Later, sugars are mostly produced by photosynthesis in the leaves.

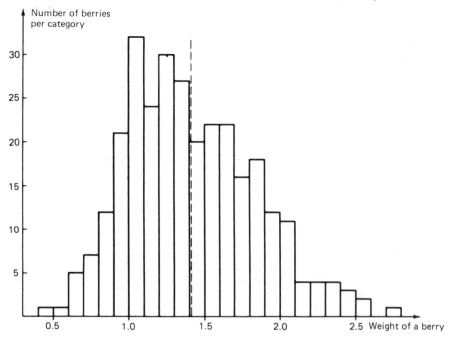

Figure 5.2. This histogram illustrates distribution according to weight in 100 mg steps for 300 berries of Merlot grapes randomly selected at maturity. It gives an idea of the considerable irregularity of the size of berries. The weight of a berry varies from 0.4 to 2.8 g. Each block represents the number of berries for a given weight. An irregular distribution is to be seen, showing three groups of berries of different sizes. The dotted line indicates the mean weight.

In addition, the plant has many ways of forming sugars: The grape can transform malic acid into glucose. Similarly it uses a complex system of migration that has not yet been thoroughly explained.

The wood (roots, trunk, and shoots) contains reducing sugars and sucrose (10–25 grams per kilogram of fresh weight) and starch (40–60 grams per kilogram). The abrupt nature of the ripening is explained by the sudden migration toward the grape of a fraction of these reserves of sugar and starch.

Because of this, it is easily understood that the history of a vineyard as well as the age and healthy condition of the vinestock play their part in the quality of a vintage. The care taken and treatment carried out on the vine as well as improvements and regular upkeep constitute a capital that pays interest in the form of quality in the wine. It is well known that old vines, richer in reserves, give more regular maturity and a better and more consistent quality. Some years with cool damp summers, drawing on the reserves from the previous year, can achieve suitable richness in sugar.

SOURCES OF SUGAR IN THE GRAPE[a]

	Total Sugar in grams per kilogram of Fresh Weight					
	31 August at 2 P.M.	1 September at 5 A.M.	Difference	28 September at 2 P.M.	29 September at 5 A.M.	Difference
Leaves	21.3	18.6	−8.7	19.3	13.3	−6.0
Branches	9.6	7.5	−2.1	8.0	8.0	+1.5
Stems	16.0	13.4	−2.6	8.0	9.0	+1.0

[a] These analyses, done by Marteau, show the migration of the sugars from the different components of the vine. At the beginning of ripening (end of August), the grape is fed by the leaves, the wood of the shoots, and the stems. At the end of September, only feeding through the leaves continues.

However, sometimes the importance of these events has been minimized by certain authors who consider that the sugars in the grapes come from the daily photosynthesis more than anywhere else. A common image is to symbolize the leaf as the "laboratory" of the plant. Photosynthesis indeed, thanks to the chlorophyll in the leaves and under the influence of solar energy, manufactures all the constituents of the vegetable cells: sugars, organic acids, amino acids, and so on from the carbon dioxide in the air (0.3 mL/L) and the water and mineral salts that the roots draw from the soil. It is easy to follow by analysis the formation of sugars in the leaf during the course of a sunny day. Certain techniques utilizing radioactive carbon even manage to measure the speed at which the photosynthesis products are formed.

The distribution of sugar in a bunch of grapes or in those bunches growing on the same stem is not regular. It is easy to ascertain with a pocket refractometer, which allows you to calculate the amount of sugar in a drop of juice, that the berries situated at the top of the bunch nearest the trunk have the highest sugar content. These are the first to receive sugar through migration. Moreover, the internal composition of the grape berry is not regular. The pulp from the outside just under the skin where juice is pressed out first when the berry is squeezed between thumb and index finger has a high sugar count with very little acid. The intermediary area is more acid and sometimes more sugary. Finally, the pulp in the center of the berry nearest the seeds has a much lower sugar count and much more acid.

The quantity of sugars formed through photosynthesis and accumulated by the grape depends on the duration and intensity of the sunshine during the ripening period (see Fig. 5.3). Generally the warmest climates, that is, the sunniest and, within the same region, the hottest summers give grapes

PHOTOSYNTHESIS IN THE VINE LEAF: SUBSTANCES FORMED IN 45 SECONDS OF EXPOSURE TO THE SUN[a]

Sugars	Acids	Amino acids
Fructose	Malic	Alanine
Glucose	Pyruvic	Serine
Sucrose	Phosphopyruvic	Glycine
Raffinose		Aspartic acid
Stachyose		Glutamic acid

[a] These observations were made by G. Ribéreau-Gayon. As for tartaric acid, it is not a direct product of the photosynthesis. It only appears after two hours of illumination of the young vine leaf.

with the highest concentration of sugars and the most alcoholized wines. The quality of a vintange is above all related to the number of sunshine hours during August and September. However, excess heat and severe drought block photosynthesis and prevent normal development of the ripening process (see Figs. 5.4 and 5.5).

Acid Development

This is a common enough concept: Grape acidity diminishes during ripening. The juice of the unripe grape contains 20 or so grams of acidity expressed as sulfuric acid per liter. After a few weeks, the acidity of the juice in the ripe

EVOLUTION OF SUGARS IN THE VINE LEAF DURING THE COURSE OF AN AUGUST DAY[a]

	Reducing Sugars	Sucrose
	(in grams per kilogram of fresh weight)	
9 A.M.	5.8	9.3
1 P.M.	6.3	13.2
8 P.M.	5.2	16.8

[a] A rise is to be seen in the sucrose level of the leaf during the course of a sunny day. The migration of the sucrose toward other parts of the vine takes place during the night.

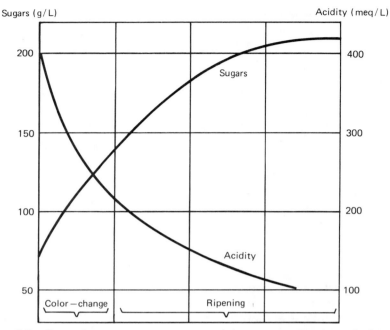

Figure 5.3.   Figure showing increase in sugars and decrease in acidity during the last eight weeks of ripening (Cabernet-Sauvignon in Bordeaux climate). The curves represent the development of the average composition of the grape population of a vineyard. What happens in a single grape is actually much more rapid.

grape drops to 8 or 6 or 4 g. This gradual reduction in acidity is explained by the behavior of the grape's two organic acids: tartaric acid and malic acid (see Fig. 5.6). In fact, it is generally admitted that the acids are "burnt up" by the respiration of the grape. Every vegetable cell consumes oxygen and rejects carbon dioxide. In the grape, the organic acids contribute most to this combustion. But there are other causes for the drop in acids. For instance, malic acid, toward the end of the ripening period, is transformed into sugar. It is not an important cause of sugar increase, but it is one of the contributory reasons for the reduction of this acid.

The acidity level of the ripening grape, at any given moment, depends on the action of migrations, which bring the grape its acids, and respiration, which prevents them from giving off carbon dioxide. There are, in fact, other transformations going on as well.

Tartaric acid and malic acid do not evolve in the same way. Also they are synthesized in the plant in different ways. They are not degraded at the same rate. Malic acid disappears more rapidly than tartaric acid (see Fig. 5.7).

Sugars	Organic acids	Amino acids	Mineral matter
originating in the wood and leaves	originating in the roots and leaves	originating in the leaves (and created in the fruit)	originating in the soil via the roots

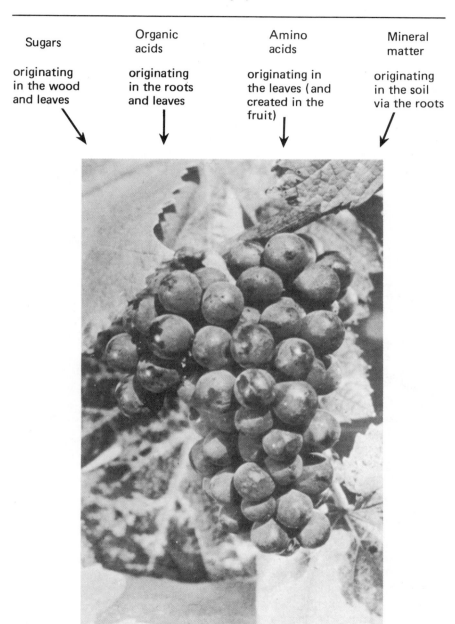

Figure 5.4. The anthocyanins of the pigmentation as well as the aroma substances appear to be synthesized on the spot in the grape. The tannins are more plentiful in the stems and the seeds than in the skin.

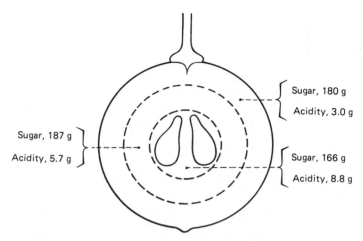

Sugar, 180 g
Acidity, 3.0 g

Sugar, 187 g
Acidity, 5.7 g

Sugar, 166 g
Acidity, 8.8 g

Figure 5.5. Distribution of the sugars and the acidity (in sulfuric acid) in different parts of the berry showing its irregular composition.

When analysis is used to follow the development of tartaric acid in relation to one grape berry, it is observed that the proportion varies within very narrow limits. It may happen that the ripe grape contains the same absolute quantity of tartaric acid as the unripe grape. But during a period of drought, the tartaric acid level goes down. It rises after a rainfall following the water circulation in the plant.

On the contrary, the malic acid level never stops decreasing, at first very quickly then more slowly as maturity approaches. Its degradation explains the loss of acidity in the ripening grape being different from one year to the next. The hotter the summer, the greater the number of very hot days there are (maximum temperature equal or greater than 30°C), the more the malic acid level diminishes, without, however, ever reaching zero. Conversely, if the summer is relatively cool, the grape retains more malic acid.

The harvested crop is very irregular in terms of both acidity and sugar levels. When the composition of the grapes is studied berry by berry the day before gathering, it will be ascertained that a larger or smaller proportion (e.g., 10–30%) of berries exist with less sugar and more acid than the others. That is to say, these berries are not yet ripe. It is because of this depreciatory portion that wine makers in many regions recommend delaying the vintage to give these late-ripening berries time to improve.

Different grape varieties have distinctive acid characters because of different malic acid levels. This is one characteristic of a particular grape found to be the same every year under different climates. Some varieties are rich

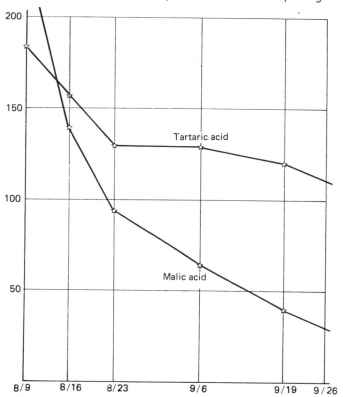

Figure 5.6. Development of acids during ripening (example relates to Cabernet-Sauvignon). Levels shown in milliequivalents per liter of must. These graphs follow the development of the composition of the must, which is of direct practical interest. These values depend at the same time on physiological changes (migration, combustion) and on the evolution of the proportion of water in the grapes.

in malic acid, with sour fruit, and other varieties have little malic acid and therefore low acidity. The acid character of a grape is one of the factors taken into account when selecting the variety for planting vinestock. In certain regions, a better regularity of composition in the wines is obtained by a blend of various types.

The Incidence of Water

Among the numerous factors that influence the composition of the grape and the quality of the wine, one of the more important is the supply of water to

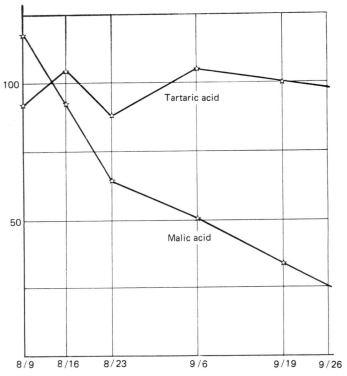

Figure 5.7. Development of acids during ripening (example relates to Cabernet-Sauvignon). Levels in milliequivalents for 1000 berries. This graph represents physiological changes, independently of dilution, that is, the balance between acid intake (migration) and outflow (transformation and combustion) in the grape berry.

the vine. The best vintages are those when rainfall is sparse. However, if heavy rains are unfavorable to the ripening, a prolonged drought is equally so. It is rare that rains are spread in a regular fashion or that their arrival coincides exactly with the plant's needs. The soil, because of its power of retention, can store up water. The best vineyards are those where the soil can provide water to the vine during its growth period and is fairly dry at the time of ripening.

There exists a relationship between the presence of water in the subsoil and acidity in the grapes. In ground that retains humidity, ripening is delayed and the grape's tartaric acid and malic acid are more plentiful. Conversely in permeable ground, which is fairly deep, the grape ripens more quickly and

EVOLUTION IN THE COMPOSITION OF A GRAPE DURING RIPENING CABERNET-SAUVIGNON STOCK, PAUILLAC (MÉDOC, FRANCE), YEAR 1978

Dates	Weight per 100 Berries (g)	Levels (g/L)			
		Reducing Sugars	Acidity	Tartaric Acid	Malic Acid
August 28	82	88	17.4	9.7	16.7
September 4	93	124	13.4	9.4	11.6
September 11	107	136	10.0	7.5	8.7
September 18	114	166	8.8	7.5	6.6
September 25	113	188	7.0	7.3	5.2
October 2	111	196	5.9	7.2	4.6
October 11	124	204	5.4	6.8	3.9

is less acid. The underground water level decides the depth of the soil the roots will use and also influences the grape's susceptibility to rot.

Maturity Index

Attempts have been made to express the state of maturity of the grape using certain ratios between the different ingredients. The sugar/acidity ratio is the simplest and most meaningful. Since sugar levels rise while acidity diminishes during ripening, the sugar/acidity ratio rises sharply and develops more

MALIC ACID LEVELS FOR DIFFERENT VARIETIES[a]

White Grapes	g/L	Red Grapes	g/L
Sauvignon	2.9	Malbec	3.3
Sémillon	1.3	Merlot	1.6
Muscatel	2.0	Cabernet franc	2.5
Ugni blanc (Trebbiano)	5.5	Cabernet-Sauvignon	3.0
		Petit Verdot	4.7
		Verdot-colon	5.0
		Saint-Macaire	5.1

[a] Varieties grown on the same soil, grapes picked at maturity. Certain varieties have three times more malic acid than others.

MALIC ACID LEVELS FOR DIFFERENT CROPS[a]

	Merlot (g/L)	Cabernet-Sauvignon (g/L)
1968	4.8	5.2
1969	3.4	3.9
1970	2.0	2.6
1971	2.0	3.1
1972	5.3	5.9
1973	3.0	3.8
1974	1.9	2.9
1975	2.1	2.7
1976	2.0	2.7
1977	4.7	6.9
1978	4.6	3.7

[a] Grapes picked at maturity always from the same plot of vines. The malic acid levels may more than double from one year to another.

quickly that its two factors. Although the accumulation of sugars and the combustion of acids not being subject to the same factors, take place independently in the grape, this index is a fairly accurate expression of the state of ripeness. Its value depends on the variety.

Grape Pigmentation

As ripening begins (at *véraison*) the green berries lose their chlorophyll and start to turn color. Their shade deepens throughout the ripening period. The cells in the skin of the black grape accumulate anthocyanins. The skin is colored through in depth, and in grapes that are heavily pigmented, the underlying cells themselves contain anthocyanins. Maturity can therefore be judged by the color of the must, by the ease with which the anthocyanins in the skins are distributed through the juice. In the same way, white grape skins deepen in hue and some varieties turn golden.

The pigmentation of black grapes requires a lot of sunshine, a good dose of solar energy. Away from light, fruit does not take on color. It can often be observed that the side of a bunch of grapes facing the shade is less colored or that a tightly knit bunch will have paler berries on the inside, where they are covered. Generally black grapes only acquire sufficient color in fairly hot

EVOLUTION OF THE SUGARS/ACIDITY MATURITY INDEX[a]

	Merlot	Cabernet-Sauvignon
August 30, 1976	33	43
September 6, 1976	41	45
September 14, 1976	44	50
September 18, 1976	47	53
September 21, 1976	48	55

[a] For calculation purposes, acidity has here been calculted in sulfuric acid.

climates. For this reason, it will be seen that red varieties must be grown in lower latitudes than white varieties. The use of fertilizers and an increase in yield lead to grapes with less color and less tannin.

Even before the anthocyanins, which are the visual elements, other polyphenols accumulate: the leucoanthocyanins or tannins. The tannin is plentiful in the seeds which contain 65% of the polyphenols of the grape. The stems contain 22%; the skin, 12%; and the pulp only 1%. The production of the polyphenols is closely linked to climatic conditions. It is the years with hot summers, everything else being equal, that produce wines with greater tannin. However, in the course of ripening, the proportion of soluble polyphenols rises to a maximum, then diminishes.

Many other substances that add to the flavor of wine later are prepared in the course of ripening periods. Good conditions during this ripening period give grapes rich in all the elements.

ACCUMULATION OF ANTHOCYANINS IN THE GRAPE DURING RIPENING

Levels in mg for 1000 berries of Merlot (1.3 kilograms of ripe grapes)[a]

September 9	300
September 16	600
September 23	720
September 30	1000
October 14	1300
October 28	1600

[a] These quantities by P. Ribéreau-Gayon translate in figures the common observation that ripening fruit increases in coloration visually.

Formation of Aromas

The aromas are variously distributed in the grape berry. The internal cells of the skin are the ones that contain most of what could be called the essence characteristic of the variety concerned. With certain exceptions, the must is generally low in odors. The sediment resulting from the solid parts of the pulp may communicate herbaceous aromas in which case racking the must is essential. It is easy to collect the aromas by steeping the skins in diluted alcohol. This is carried out in the following way: 200 grape berries are crushed and pressed in a handpress. The skins are separated from the seeds, washed quickly to remove the remaining pulp, dried and placed in 200 mL of alcohol at 16°C, and acidified at 3 pH with partly neutralized tartaric acid. This is sealed in airtight bottles and a week later the colored liquid poured off. The amount of color intensity reveals the skin's richness in anthocyanins, the polyphenol index is defined. Smelling the liquid in a glass gives an indication of the kind of odor and its odorous intensity. White varieties yield a characteristic, more or less flowery odor with a tinge of "fruit-stone," recalling too the infusion. The characteristic varietal nature of the scent is magnified by a little sulfiting. Red varieties treated in the same way have in common the odor of fruit, of cherries, or of fruitstones and also tannic odors of pomace or of tea. It is easy to compare degrees of finesse and in regions where fine wines are produced, considerable differences appear among the extracts of skins from one vineyard to another.

The same technique may be used to note that aroma is prepared during fermentation. In a test, the aroma obtained in a maceration of skins from Merlot grapes on September 14 had a leafy odor, on September 21 an odor of fruit mixed with a note of greenness, on September 28 a refined, more powerful fruity odor, and finally on October 5, the maceration of skins had changed decisively and had an extremely fine intense odor. The proportion of essences from the skins and particularly the quality of these essences goes on improving as the grape ripens. However, it is more than likely that overripening or too rapid a ripening in a climate that is too tropical diminishes the intensity and agreeableness of certain aromas, bringing out particularly that part of the phenolic compounds and the tannic nature, which is called bark taste or woody taste.

OVERRIPENING

Overripening starts the moment when, the grape having achieved maximum size and sugar content, the action of consumption by respiration is no longer compensated by translocation and at the same time the grape begins to lose

OVERRIPENING GRAPES BY HEATING[a]

	Nonheated Grapes	Heated Grapes
Potential strength (alcohol)	10.4%	11.5%
Total acidity	5.94	5.71
Tartaric acid	4.77	4.44
Malic acid	6.00	5.50
Anthocyanins (in mg)	86	135
Tannins (in mg)	169	557
Pigmentation intensity (optical density)	0.385	1.064
To be noted are the concentration of the sugars, combustion of the acids, and diffusion of the polyphenols.		

[a] Cabernet-Sauvignon grapes are heated for 24 hours at 40°C. The analyses indicate the composition of the musts.

water. In fact once overripening starts the grape may be considered to no longer receive anything from the plant.

· Certain wine-making techniques are based on a method known as *passerilage*, which consists of leaving the grapes on the vine, sometimes even twisting the stem of the bunch of grapes to cut off sap. The berries shrivel slightly (raisined grapes) and their juice gets concentrated.

In preparing certain special types of wine, the *passerilage* is carried out after the grapes have been picked by laying them out in the sun or spread on straw; sometimes they are hung up indoors for several weeks.

Artificial overripening can be obtained by heating grapes for a few hours at 40°C in an apparatus using hot-air circulation. This heating promotes combustion of the malic acid and a slight concentration by evaporation of water. The grape's acidity decreases, and the must becomes richer. The pigments become more soluble.

Noble Rot

The production of sweet white wines based on overripening of the grapes obtained by infection of noble rot is without doubt a very ancient vinification process. Its success, however, is linked to exceptional climatic conditions.

Noble rot is due to the infection of *Botrytis cinerea*, a mold capable of attacking and digesting the grape skin. The development of this microscopic fungus requires alternating humidity and sunshine, which promotes the con-

COMPARISON BETWEEN THE MUSTS OF
HEALTHY AND OF "NOBLE ROTTED" GRAPES

	Levels (g/L) of Must	
	Healthy Grapes	Rotted Grapes
Baumé degree	13.6	20.5
Reducing sugars	238	360
Total acidity	3.92	4.02
Tartaric acid	5.1	4.3
Malic acid	2.0	4.0
Gluconic acid	0	1.8
Acetic acid	0	1.1
Glycerol	0	10.5

centration of the berry of the grapes that are attacked. These conditions are generally only met with in river valleys.

There is a distinction to be made, depending on the evolution of the noble rot, between "rotted" full berries, which are not dehydrated and have a smooth brown-colored almost violet, skin, and "roasted" berries, which are shriveled, wrinkled, and covered with gray tufts of mold. To be beneficial, the action of *Botrytis cinerea* should only intervene when the grape is properly ripe. The harvester only picks those berries, portions of bunches, or bunches that have reached a satisfactory degree of evolution.

The must from rotted grapes is richer in sugar and in all elements, than the must from healthy grapes but acidity does not increase in proportion to the concentration. Noble rot is therefore a process that enriches and improves must. However, the gain in quality is in fact only achieved with considerable loss in volume and in the absolute quantity of sugar.

Botrytis cinerea attacks above all the tartaric acid. It forms glycerol and gluconic acid and also secretes other substances that give sweet wines their special aroma. The bacterial microflora of the botrytized grapes may form acetic acid, which is found in the must.

The fermentation difficulties are explained by exhaustion of the nutritive substances and the presence of antibiotic substances (botryticine).

6

Harvesting

SETTING THE VINTAGE DATE

One of the first questions the viticulturist needs to ask concerns the starting date for the vintage. He often needs to plan this a long time ahead in order to get the work organized but this date is not always easy to settle. Each type of wine, according to the climate, corresponds to a particular picking time, for instance, to make a dessert wine the grapes will be left on the vine for a longer time than for a dry wine. Each variety responds differently to climatic conditions. Its sanitary state is decisive and yet it cannot be known in advance. Weather forecasts are not yet really accurate enough to be useful. Finally, the vintage lasts several days or indeed in certain vineyards several weeks, so that you need to start a little early not to finish too late. A big crop prolongs the vintage.

In many regions, there is a tendency to harvest too early. Every writer has been saying this for quite some time. However, in certain years or in certain regions there is also a fair risk of gathering too late. The success of a wine is related to the weather conditions at the time of picking and inevitably implies a certain element of luck. It has been said that half a wine's quality is decided by the kind of weather prevailing at harvest time. This is only a saying, but rain on the ripe crop does jeopardize quality even before promoting mold.

These days vintage dates should never need to be fixed by guesswork. Nobody can be satisfied any longer with just examining the grape's appearance and consistency, its acidity to the taste, or the color of its stem. The ripening process needs to be followed through by accurate measurement. If certain risks are undertaken in expectation of a better state of maturity, these will be calculated risks. The beginning of the vintage can be forecast in two ways: at long range based on the length of the vegetative cycle or most

75

MATURITY PERIODS FOR A FEW VARIETIES

	Red Varieties	White Varieties
First period (at the same time as Chasselas)	Gamay Pinot noir	Chardonnay Melon Traminer
Second period (12–15 days after Chasselas)	Cabernet-Franc Cabernet-Sauvignon Cinsaut Malbec Merlot Syrah	Altesse Chenin Muscadel Riesling Roussane Sauvignon Sémillon Sylvaner
Third period (24–30 days after Chasselas)	Aramon Carignane Grenache	Clairette Folle Blanche Maccabeo Trebbiano (Ugni-Blanc)

important by following at short intervals the progress of the grape's composition during ripening.

Long-range Forecasting

This is built on a certain consistency in the vegetative cycle given average weather conditions and takes account of the length of time that elapses between flowering and maturity or else between *véraison* when the berry begins to change color and maturity. The length of the vegetative cycle varies according to both the variety and to the wine region. Good forecasting must be based on experience acquired in a given vineyard by comparison with observed data over preceding years.

In certain regions, the vintage date is in fact calculated at least approximately by this method, three months ahead. In Burgundy, for instance, they count 102 days from full blossom to harvest for the Gamay variety, 107 days for Chardonnay or Pinot or again 45 to 50 days from mid-*véraison* (color change) to maturity. By August therefore the probable vintage date can be determined. In fact varieties do differ a little, Merlot is ripe eight days before Cabernet-Sauvignon although their *véraison* takes place almost at the same

PHENOLOGICAL OBSERVATIONS IN BURGUNDY FOR PINOT NOIR[a,b]

	Mid-flowering a	Mid-*véraison* b	Maturity c	Length (in days)[c]		
				a to b	b to c	a to c
1977	20 June	19 August	5 October	60	47	107
1976	8 June	25 July	5 September	47	42	89
1975	16 June	7 August	23 September	52	47	99
1974	17 June	5 August	2 October	49	58	107
1973	18 June	10 August	23 September	53	44	97
1972	28 June	16 August	6 October	49	51	100
1971	7 June	4 August	16 September	58	43	101
1970	23 June	20 August	28 September	58	39	97
1969	30 June	18 August	9 October	49	52	101
1968	21 June	14 August	10 October	54	49	103

[a] Data assembled by Lobreau and Borde.
[b] From one year to another, the utmost variations in these phenological dates can be a month.
[c] The evolutionary cycle of the grape varied from 89 to 107 days.

time. Cabernet-Franc changes color later and is picked before Cabernet-Sauvignon. Each region needs to establish its own phenological calendar drawn from the above examples.

Often the harvest is begun earlier than the theoretical date in late years and in wet years on account of mold, sometimes too in very hot years for fear of overripening and in years with heavy crops because of the length of time needed to pick it.

Picking needs to be done variety by variety. Whenever possible, it is better to allow maximum delay starting the vintage and then speed up the picking.

Keeping a Check on the Development of Ripening

Periodical controls use rational means, each adapted to a particular case. It is very instructive for the winemaker to follow the progress of ripening in the vineyard, even by means of summary findings with the help of a mustimeter or refractometer, and by checking acidity levels. This examination is the basis for correctly setting the vintage date. It informs the winemaker in advance on the composition of the must and also, within certain limits, determines the method of vinification to be adopted.

For each crop, in most wine-growing regions, documents are compiled from periodic analysis of the grapes. This is a practice that should be put into general use everywhere. In France, numerous organizations take part: en-

**CLIMATOLOGICAL CONDITIONS FOR THE MONTHS APRIL–
SEPTEMBER[a] IN VARIOUS WINE REGIONS**

	Total Temperatures	Sunshine Hours	Rainfall (mm)
Alicante, Spain	4064°C	1847	147
Palermo, Italy	4005	1619	138
Oran, Algeria	3908	1784	79
Jerez, Spain	3880	1930	117
Mendoza, Argentina	3909	1688	136
Patras, Greece	3811	1778	132
Perpignan, France	3691	1619	247
Florence, Italy	3659	1697	339
Adelaide, Australia	3622	1544	177
Nîmes, France	3592	1731	345
Montpellier, France	3420	1771	295
Bordeaux, France	3165	1252	358
Dijon, France	2984	1433	403
Reims, France	2782	1226	318

[a] or for months October–March for the Southern Hemisphere.

ological stations, the INAO (National Institute for Original Appellations), county agricultural boards, chambers of agriculture, viticultural syndicates, and so on. From the twentieth day after the *véraison* (color change), samples of the different varieties are taken twice a week in a great many vineyards. These controls allow the progress of ripening to be closely followed and give those responsible the means of providing wine growers with the best information possible on vintage date.

Grape-Sampling Techniques

To follow the progress of ripening it is not enough to just collect a few bunches of grapes from time to time, picked from the biggest and best exposed. Results obtained in this way are not at all representative of the crop's overall average condition. It is in fact the average concentrations of sugar and acidity which are important to know.

Grapes from the same vineyard, at a given point in time, have compositions that are very dissimilar. In one bunch, different berries and, on the same plant, different bunches are never at the same stage of ripeness This is even more evident when considering different varieties.

The most accurate sampling technique requires selecting exactly 250 berries from 250 plants within one uniform plot, breaking off one berry per plant, varying the exposure of the sample taken from each side of a row and taking care not to select deliberately but letting chance guide the operator's hand. The juice from the 250 berries culled in this way will be fairly representative of the grapes from that plot of vines and if the same operation is carried out several times, you may be sure of getting roughly the same results.

The 250 berries are weighed, which allows their increase in size to be followed. Then they are crushed and pressed in a small handpress. Very simple sugar and acidity level ratings, completed by notes on the color and their sanitary state, allow the various aspects of the development in their ripeness to be followed. This constitutes a document, which can be filed and usefully referred to each year.

HARVEST WORK

Winemaking will always keep its empiric character on account of the practical impossibility of choosing the maturity date of the clusters to be picked. The ideal would be to pick the grapes as and when they reach the desired degree of ripeness, which is obviously impossible.

Grape picking as such need not be described and the tools used by the pickers and carriers are well enough known. Moreover this nonspecialized labor force is not very open to improvement in terms of quality. It is difficult enough to get people to pick off individual grapes from an overripe crop yet it often happens that sorting is imperative to reject spoiled clusters or sour grapes, white mold or green rot. Picking the tiny clusters may be advisable or not according to the acidity of the crop. The grower ought to insist on the grapes not being soiled with lumps of earth or with branches and leaves mixed in with the vintage. In areas where grapes are botrytised, picking is done in successive "selections" and only those clusters or portions of clusters which show a sufficient degree of overripeness are picked each time.

For carrying grapes, each area has its traditional equipment: baskets, buckets, hods, *mannequins*, *comportes*, *bastes*, *douils*, *pastierès*, which are local variations in the form of tubs or vats, or else tip-bins. Containers using a wormscrew to simplify off-loading must have the correct standards at the reception bay, screw of a sufficient diameter, and adjustable rotation speed. Picking and trucking using wooden or plastic sorting containers with only a shallow layer of grapes is developing in areas where quality white wines are made. The important thing in point of fact is to make sure the grapes are not crushed or squeezed down in the vineyard, in the deep-rooted tradition, or even bruised on the way to the winery. Oxidation and maceration before the grapes reach the winery seriously jeopardize quality. The longer the time lapse between picking and crushing or the higher the temperature, the more damaging this premature fermentation may be. Sulfiting the grapes in this instance does not give the protection hoped for and may even emphasize deterioration caused by maceration.

For social reasons more than any other, mechanization of the vintage is becoming more developed in the bulk vineyards. For red grapes, crushing and destemming in the vineyard is also being practiced, tank-trailers being used to truck the crushed and sulfited crop to the fermentation vats. The arguments in favor of using machines to harvest a quality vineyard are not nearly so convincing. If the enologist is being forced to accept the use of harvesting machines, he should at least insist that manufacturers respect enological requirements. The quality of work done by the machine depends not only on its mechanical design and the way it is set but also on the condition of the vines and the grapes which in themselves are extremely variable. The main technological drawbacks with mechanical harvesting are these: increased oxidation of the must, maceration of the grapes in their juice, presence of extraneous trash like green or dried or torn leaves, stems, fragments of shoots and stalks, etc. It needed two full decades to manage to get people to avoid detrimental crushing of the grapes in the vineyard. It would be quite illogical to adopt systems now which go against the progress already achieved with such difficulty. Mechanization of the vintage could not in any circumstances be a factor in favor of quality. At best we can only hope it will not appreciably diminish it.

GRAY ROT

The sanitary state of the grapes also controls the harvest date for the same reasons as the degree of ripeness. Indeed, picking has to be done more quickly when there is danger of rot setting in. Rot is due to the development on the grape of various fungi or molds, the most common being *Botrytis cinerea* (gray rot).(Fig. 6.1) The situation becomes much more serious if at the same time *Penicillium* and *Aspergillus* start to develop. When gray rot is very advanced or the rotted part has dried, the wine made from it exhibits disagreeable tastes of mold or fungus, a "phenol" taste.

Between gray or common rot, which depreciates wines, and noble rot, which improves it, the only distinctive factor may be the influence of the climate. However, rot will always be pernicious on red grapes or white grapes

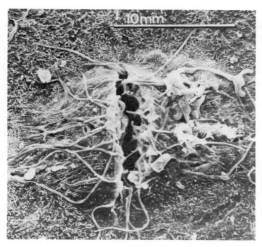

Figure 6.1. Primitive development of *Botrytis cinerea* fibers erupting from a microlesion in the grape skin (Department of Electronic Microscopy, University of Bordeaux I).

that have been split or been damaged by insects. Certain varieties with thin skins and close-packed clusters are more susceptible to it.

In addition to the loss of volume it incurs, gray rot is detrimental for four main reasons: it destroys the anthocyanins and consequently the color of the grape, it causes oxidative spoilage later in the wine, the aromatic substances contained in the skins disappear, and lastly it communicates off tastes. The use of insecticides and cupric mixtures to avoid injury to the berry delays the development of rot but is not enough to prevent it. There exist antifungal products that are more effective. The late application of certain among them may have the drawback of making the musts less fermentable. But other preventive measures should be taken. When "bad rot" is left on the vine or thrown down on the ground, it increases the danger of infection of the next crop.

THE QUALITY OF VINTAGE YEARS

Somewhat paradoxically, quality wine areas are not necessarily those most favorable to the growth and production of the vine. A Mediterranean plant, it does not give the best wines in a climate that is too hot. The quality regions are rather marginal areas more subject to irregular annual climates and equally more sensitive to microclimates. In hot areas, the less aromatic varieties or ones with a less agreeable tannin content are grown. One year is like another and all the slopes equally valid so that the notion of vintage years and of specific growths on privileged sites is lost. Special or "made" wines are produced there more than anything else.

In Europe, vineyards that are not along the Mediterranean seaboard are subject to variable summer conditions which stamp the wine each year with a different character. The same wine is never made two years running and two vintages are never exactly similar. This is a very general remark. In California the best wines come from cool areas along the coast, in the Napa and Sonoma valleys and not from the central valley, which is too hot. In Argentine, wines are finer in San Rafael than in San Juan 600 miles further north. Many other examples could be given. Numerous factors enter into consideration in the assessment granted in favor of a year's vintage, not only the overall quality, but also the volume of the crop and even the state of the market. In point of fact, the quality of a harvest always corresponds very closely to the climatic conditions during the summer.

Generally the good years are those when August and September are dry and hot. Often enough they are early years reaping the benefit of more extended daylight to ripen the grapes. Only rarely are late years great vintage years. But still if it rains in September, an early year can sometimes end up short on quality.

Yield and quality are not necessarily incompatible. Certain good years are also years of plenty but generally speaking fine wines are a product of soil relatively poor in fertilizing materials. If there exists the possibility for this style of vineyard to increase yield by moderate manuring without compromising quality, the optimum limit is soon reached. The greatest danger in fine-wine production is heedlessly increasing yield.

7

Adjusting the Vintage

Because of the wide variability of situations and climates, it does happen that the state of maturity of the grapes is insufficient to produce a well-constituted wine. To put right these variations in quality, the winemaker has license to make a few additions, under certain conditions and within well-defined limits, with the object of mitigating the deficiencies of the vintage. He or she can strengthen the alcohol by adding sugar or must concentrate, or lower the acidity by deacidification. Conversely in cases where the grape shows insufficient acidity, the winemaker may improve balance by adding tartaric acid. Also the addition of tannin is still occasionally practiced.

It is important to emphasize that these adjustment procedures never completely compensate for insufficiencies due to unsatisfactory maturity. Thus the possibility of improvement should not tempt people to harvest earlier or carelessly.

SUGARING OR CHAPTALIZATION

Adding sugar to the vintage or the must is often called chaptalizing. It was in fact Chaptal who suggested it in 1801 in his book *Art de faire les vins* (Art of making wines). Chaptal was trying to increase in this way the "force" of the wine and make sure it was converted by exhausting a hypothetical "ferment." The fermentation, he said, resulted from the action of the "ferment" on the sugar from the grape and these two elements mutually destroyed each other. If after fermentation, the wine still contained some "ferment," it might turn bad. On the other hand, if sugar were added, the "ferment" would be exhausted and the wine was likely to keep better. This reasoning of Chaptal's was a reflection of the ideas in his time. Half a century later Pasteur was to discover the true nature of fermentation.

The regulations concerning sugaring are complex and vary for different countries. They are adapted to circumstances and the economic situation.

European wine-growing areas are ranked according to latitudes into five different categories by the regulations fixed in the EEC. Thus for each zone are defined: the natural minimum alcoholic strength which the must should have for that type of wine, the total maximum alcoholic strength after being sugared, and the limits of this enrichment. The northern zones may benefit from sugaring every year. In the more southerly zones, certain areas may only sugar in unfavorable years. Finally the other warmer areas are not permitted to use enrichment.

In France, the winemaker needs to fill in a written declaration of his intent to add sugar and address it to the local indirect tax office covering the district where it is going to be carried out at least three days before. This extensive notice is occasionally a hindrance to sensible sugaring practices.

Crystalline white sugar (sucrose) is used. For red vintages, no distinction is made between cane sugar and beet sugar. Cane sugar is used exclusively for white wines, especially in the preparation of syrup for the *tirage* and *dosage* operations used in making sparkling wines. The use of brown sugar with its taste of muscovado should be avoided. Sugar ought to be kept in impervious paper bags; jute sacks impart an off-flavor.

To raise the alcoholic strength by 1%, theoretically 17 grams of sugar per liter needs to be added, that is to say, 1.7 kg/hL or 3.8 kg per 225-liter (50-gal) cask. In making red wines, which is generally done at a higher temperature, 2 kg/hL need to be used because of loss of alcohol by evaporation during pumping-over operations. Indeed, it is the free-run wine that is most enriched; the press wine more or less keeps its initial strength.

Sugaring should always be done in moderation without attempting to reach the maximum authorized level. Inconsiderate chaptalization always involves a risk of fermentation accident and upsets the gustatory balance of the wine, excessive vinosity masking the fruity taste and increasing the wine's meagerness. Within reasonable limits, anything from 1 to 1.5%, chaptalization constitutes an excellent ameliorative process maintaining the wine's character and increasing body and roundness.

The sugar should be dissolved before adding it. Never add sugar in powder form directly in the fermentation vat, it would drop to the bottom and a sweet layer would be found when running off. The making up of a syrup with water is generally forbidden, it encourages disguised watering of the wine. Dissolving is done in the must, more easily so when it is already warm due to the start of fermentation. To treat a vat, the weight of sugar needed is poured little by little into a small container fed by must from the main tank. The liquid is stirred continuously and pumped up to the top of the tank or under the pomace while a circuit is created by opening the lower faucet. This is the pumping-over technique.

Chaptalization should be done at the beginning of fermentation at the moment when the fermenting must is starting to get warm and when the cap of pomace is forming. It is better to sugar in one step before half the sugar in the must has been transformed, that is to say, during the rapid fermentation phase. Sugar added during the second phase of fermentation is introduced into a medium already depleted of the nutritive elements the yeasts need and fermentation is more difficult to complete.

When the grapes are high acid with short pomace contact time, two or three days for example, interrupted before fermentation has completely finished, chaptalization is sometimes carried out after draining. Some people think they can by this means avoid any sugar supposedly retained by the pomace. Although generally speaking fermentation continues with more regularity after separation from the pomace, this practice is not always advisable. The danger of late sugaring consists in the possible beginnings of malolactic fermentation, which might give rise to lactic souring before the yeasts have transformed all the added sugar.

Allowance must be made for the fact that chaptalization always gives rise to increased calorie output and makes fermentation cooling systems even more essential.

Sucrose cannot be fermented directly and needs to be hydrolyzed into glucose and fructose. Previously, it was recommended that this inversion be carried out before introducing the sugar into the vintage by heating it in acidified must. However the grape juice itself has this property of inverting sucrose to a high degree and the yeasts too decompose it more quickly and more completely than acid hydrolysis ever would. What is more, acidification is not permitted when sugaring is done.

Adding Must-Concentrate

Concentrated musts are prepared from muted musts (musts kept under heavy sulfite dosing) by eliminating a large part of their water through heat, generally under a light vacuum. Concentrated commercial musts have densities between 1.240 (28 degrees Baumé under the old measure) to 1.330 (about 36 degrees Baumé). Heating must concentrates all the elements, organic and mineral constituents. Acidity is concentrated in almost the same proportions as the sugar as only a part of the tartaric acid precipitates after concentration in the form of potassium bitartrate. To avoid acidification, which the addition of concentrated must is likely to cause, the base must may be deacidified

EXAMPLES OF ENRICHMENT OF A RED VINTAGE[a]

	Sample	Chaptalized	Enriched with Concentrated Must
Alcoholic strength	10.3%	12.3%	12.4%
Fixed acidity	5.81	5.54	6.48
Reduced extract	18.6	17.0	19.5
Alcohol/extract ratio[b]	4.40	5.82	5.10

[a] Wine composition obtained after chaptalization or after addition of concentrated must. Chaptalization slightly lowers acidity: addition of must-concentrate raises it.
[b] The alcohol/extract ratio is higher in the case of chaptalization than when concentrate is used.

before concentration. The concentrated musts are high in potassium, calcium, iron, copper, and so on.

The addition of must concentrate is permitted by EEC regulations within the same limits as sugaring. Wines that in France obtain the appellation *"vins de qualité produits dans une région déterminée,"* better than ordinary table wines but not Appellation Controlled, can only be enriched with must-concentrate from the same region. Certain French Appellation Controlled areas forbid this form of enrichment in their control regulations.

DEACIDIFICATION

In temperate regions, winemaking generally includes a process for reducing acidity in the grapes. Normally alcoholic fermentation is the first thing to bring about a drop in acidity. A more advanced biological deacidification could be obtained by the action of special yeasts (*Schizosaccharomyces*) or else under special grape-processing conditions (maceration carbonique) and, in a much more general way, by malolactic fermentation. These natural deacidification processes may not be enough, or they may be difficult to implement.

In years of inadequate maturity or in northern vineyards, chemical deacidification may be used. This consists of neutralizing the excess acidity in the musts by plastering and consequently produces less acid wines. The EEC regulations allow possible deacidification in practically all the wine-growing areas of Europe except for the extreme southern French Mediterranean vineyards and in Italy those south of Rome and on the islands.

The agents utilized are neutral potassium tartrate, potassium bicarbonate, and precipitated calcium carbonate. In normal conditions of usage, these agents only act on the tartaric acid, making it insoluble. The first one works slowly, the second takes effect more quickly, and both set off a precipitation of potassium bitartrate with an acid reaction. The calcium carbonate brings on a precipitation of neutral calcium tartrate.

To reduce the acidity of the must by 1 gram (in sulfuric acid), it needs 1 g of calcium carbonate per liter or 2 g of potassium bicarbonate or 2.5–3 g of neutral potassium tartrate. The drawback with calcium carbonate, particularly if used at the end of fermentation, is increasing the calcium in the wine and setting up tartaric precipitations later in the bottle. It is kept only for light deacidification of the vintage or the nonfermented must. Potassium bicarbonate, on the other hand, can be used in new wine just finishing fermentation. According to the text of the regulations, deacidification must be done in one operation. However, particularly in the case of significantly large adjustment, it would be more sensible to do it in two parts, finishing off at the end of fermentation the first deacidification of the original vintage.

An official text considers deacidification as a means of "bringing the acidity of over-acid musts back to the average acidity in musts in the same wine region in a normal year." In this form of arithmetical adjustment, the operation would not be justifiable from an enological viewpoint. In fact, a heavy drop in acidity in a must, applied only to the tartaric acid, can remove it almost completely. The amount left might be too low to ensure gustatory balance and storage of the wine. Besides, the minimum level of tartaric acid is fixed by the regulations (in France, it stands at 1 g/L). The effect of deacidification on taste is proportionately far more important than its effect on the expression of total acidity.

In fact, deacidifying a vintage should not be considered as a chemical adjustment, but simply a way of starting the natural deacidification chain in the wine by raising the pH: precipitation of the tartaric acid salts first, then malolactic fermentation followed by further tartaric precipitations. Chemical processes for deacidification ought to be considered as critical in their application and are best left to the enologist.

In cases where the vintage is excessively acidic, it is recommended to use a deacidification technique of precipitation of a double calcium salt consisting of equal parts of tartrate and malate. The neutralization of a grape must of up to 4.2–4.5 pH with calcium carbonate containing small quantities of double calcium salt of tartaric and malic acid does not in fact just promote the precipitation of the tartrate alone, but an equimolecular mixture of calcium tartrate and malate. A fraction of the must to be vinified is treated in this way, the crystallized deposit is separated by racking or better still by filtering, then the must, greatly deacidified by this process, having also lost some malic acid, is mixed with the rest of the acidic must.

Below are some examples of the rules for deacidification recommended
in the Bordeaux area.

Deacidification of White Musts and Red Vintages

The deacidification of white must is done after settling the must, at the same
time as bentonite is added. Deacidification of red vintage can be practiced
when wine is first pumped over.

Acidity Before Fermentation Equal To or Over: (grams of SO_4H_2 per liter)	Deacidification Agent To Be Added (g/hL)	
	Ca Carbonate	K Bicarbonate
6.0	50	100
7.0	75	150
8.0	100	200

Deacidification may be applied on the same scale to red wine at the time of
racking.

Deacidification with Different Agents

The must is deacidified with 1.0 g of calcium carbonate per hectoliter or by
1.5 g of potassium bicarbonate. The following analyses are expressed in grams
per liter of wine.

	Sample	Ca Carbonate	K Bicarbonate
Fixed acidity	5.86	4.96	5.07
pH	2.94	3.20	3.17
Tartaric acid	4.37	3.11	2.97
Potassium	0.86	1.00	1.03
Calcium	0.08	0.12	0.08

The reduction in the amount of tartaric acid corresponds exactly to the reduction in fixed acidity. Note the increase in potassium and calcium in the
deacidified wines.

ACIDIFICATION

The shortage of acidity in very ripe grapes can be rectified by adding tartaric acid. The EEC regulations provide for this contingency, allowing acidification of grapes, musts, and new wines during fermentation, in relation to the different wine-growing zones. Acidification is forbidden when the musts have been sugared or when the wine is finished. However, it is not unusual after malolactic fermentation to discover a lack of acidity that is unexpected when related to the acidity of the vintage.

Certainly in hot regions, the use of tartaric acid is often necessary to obtain a balanced wine with a bright color that is pleasant to the taste and will keep well. For temperate climates, the utility of acidification is much more rare, even exceptional where quality red wines are concerned. Indeed, if acidification makes it easier to keep wines during storage, this safety margin can only be obtained to the detriment of quality. Acidification gives wines hardness or, in any case, it reduces their softness. In these regions, methods other than acidification should be used to ensure safe storage. Great red wines that show well are always supple, fat wines with low acidity, which is precisely what makes it difficult to produce them successfully. In working with wine, you are always coming across this conflict between security and quality. The conditions that make for great quality are also ones that make vinification and storage more critical. The years of full maturity are those when the wine is most difficult to make with success. Acidification is often just a way for the winemaker to save himself trouble and not have to worry.

Although it is difficult to give a general rule for this operation, it is admitted that slight acidification may be resorted to for crops showing an overall must acidity of less than 4 g/L. The pH gives another indication: acidification is warranted when this is over, say, 3.6. Taking into account the fraction precipitated, it is considered that about 200 g of tartaric acid per hectoliter is required to raise the fixed acidity of the wine after fermentation by 1.5 g in tartaric acid or by 1 g in sulfuric acid. But the quantity of tartaric acid to be added should not be calculated in a way that would bring acidity back to that of a normal must. The levels of tartaric acid used are much lower, in the region of 100 g/hL, which besides, by making the potassium insoluble, have a greater effect on taste and on real acidity than on the proportionate acidity. The aim is in effect to slightly lower the pH without raising the proportionate acidity too much. Often picking a part of the crop before it is fully ripe or utilizing the smaller green clusters, constitutes a better natural means of acidification.

The use of citric acid in making red wine, which is occasionally recommended, calls for the very greatest reserve since this acid is not stable and can decompose under the influence of malolactic bacteria with formation of diacetyl, which gives an odor of butter or else a rise in volatile acidity.

Adding Tannin

The addition of enological tannins (tannins from chestnuts or from oak galls) to the vintage or the must has occasionally been recommended and certain vinification products, fermentation activators, in powder or liquid form contain, besides metabisulfite or sulfur dioxide and ammonium phosphate, a certain percentage of tannin, the use of which is much more debatable.

The tannins added to the red vintage with a composition very different from grape tannins, in no way facilitate the dissolving of pigmentation and do not make it any more stable. It does not prevent oxidative spoilage when the vintage has rot. For red vintages low in tannins, the adjustment achieved by more prolonged skin contact and dissolving the tannins from the pips and in particular by fermentation with the stems is far more efficient in giving more body than adding tannin. Similarly when the vintage has rot, addition of tannin does not have the same effectiveness on color stability as vinification with a vintage that has not been destemmed.

Adding tannin at 5 g/hL is commonly used for protein-rich white grape must in order to make clarification by sedimentation easier, in champagne, for example. The use of bentonite is much more efficient.

As a general rule, the vinification of the great majority of vintages and musts does not gain anything by the addition of tannin.

PART 3

Microbiology of Wine and Fermentation

ENOLOGY IS A MICROBIOLOGICAL SCIENCE

It can be said that the basis of enology was established by the first micro-biologist, Pasteur. Scientific enology thus dates from the very advent of microbiology.

It is microorganisms, the yeasts, that make wine. Besides these, under certain conditions, useful bacteria transform the wine. But it is also bacteria, noxious ones, which in other circumstances can destroy it.

Microorganisms, which take part in the vinification, act more or less in-depth on the composition of wine and through their action are largely responsible for its taste and its aroma.

Vinification and storage of wines are dominated by problems concerning microbiology. Rational transformation from grapes into wine implies good knowledge and good utilization of yeasts and lactic bacteria. Success in winemaking is always subordinated to a reasoned means of conducting microbiological phenomena.

On the other hand, the storage of wine, a perishable product, is a constant battle against action by microorganisms that cause deterioration.

Therefore, the science of wine is to a large extent, applied microbiology. We certainly have not yet exhausted all the possibilities that the microbial world offers in the problems of winemaking.

8

Alcoholic Fermentation
and Yeasts

PROCESS OF ALCOHOLIC FERMENTATION

The fermentation of crushed grapes or of their juice is a fairly everyday occurrence unlikely to surprise the professional. The must goes cloudy, gets
hot, and bubbles rise causing seething. Fermentation has always been compared to boiling and the word comes from the Latin *fervere*, which means
to boil. At the same time, the liquid loses its sweet taste and becomes vinous.

This tranformation which seems spontaneous has always intrigued ob-
servers. The most enlightened people have become absorbed in its study.
Lavoisier showed that sugar is transformed into alcohol and carbon dioxide,
which is given off. As a matter of fact, it was with regard to fermentation that
he defined the primary chemical principle: "Matter cannot be created or
destroyed." Of fermentation, he said: "It is one of the most startling and most
extraordinary operations of all those that chemistry presents us with." Later
Gay-Lussac gave a chemical formula to explain the reaction:

$$\text{sugar} = \text{alcohol} + \text{carbon dioxide}$$
$$100 \qquad 51.34 \qquad 48.66$$

In reality, the phenomenon is more complex, like all reactions with living
cells. Pasteur established that the Gay-Lussac equation is only valid for 90%
of the sugar transformed, the rest gives other substances: glycerol, succinic
acid, acetic acid. Since then, other by-products have been discovered: lactic
acid, butyleneglycol, acetaldehyde, pyruvic acid, higher alcohols, and a large
number of various substances present in minute quantities. A little over a

PRODUCTS FORMED BY THE FERMENTATION OF 170 G OF SUGAR

Mean rates in mg/L

Alcohol	80,000	Higher alcohols	300
Carbon dioxide	76,000	Citramalic acid	80
Glycerol	6,000	Acetalhyde	80
Succinic acid	800	Pyruvic acid	60
Butylene glycol	400	x-ketoglutaric acid	40
Acetic acid	300	Ethyl acetate	40
Lactic acid	300	Acetoïn	10
		Etc. including 2 g of dry yeasts	

century ago, Pasteur showed that fermentation is generated by yeasts anaerobically. Previously it was attributed to a kind of spontaneous decomposition of organic matter. However, people knew how to make wine. Man was capable of utilizing these phenomena long before he was able to understand them. Obviously wine can be made without comprehending all the mechanisms involved in fermentation. However, when a process becomes known, it is easier to follow it, to reproduce it, and to direct it. So it was only after the work done by Pasteur which taught us what alcoholic fermentation really is that we were able to establish a doctrine for winemaking and avoid a lot of setbacks. Before his time, good wine was merely the result of a succession of lucky accidents.

Pasteur did not discover yeasts themselves, but the relation between the presence of these living ferments and the transformation of sugar. There is a correlation between fermentation and life and it is yeasts, unicellular microscopic fungi that decompose sugar into alcohol and carbon dioxide.

As a general rule, cells find the energy they need in two phenomena of katabolism, that is to say two means by which organic matter is dissipated: breathing, which takes oxygen from the air, and fermentation which takes place in the absence of oxygen. Breathing produces very advanced molecular fission and releases a lot of energy. On the contrary, fermentation relates to a bad use of energy because the dissipation of matter that it promotes is incomplete. Therefore, yeasts have to transform a great deal of sugar into alcohol to satisfy their energy needs. The chemical mechanism of sugar fermentation is incredibly complex. The diagram of the most important transformations comprises no less than 30 or so successive reactions, bringing into play a great many enzymes. You might say enzymes are the tools of the yeasts adapted to one stage of the transformation. Each reaction necessitates a specific tool, a different enzyme. The by-products that have already been mentioned are somewhat like the remnants of these multiple reactions.

Figure 8.1. Various shapes of wine yeasts. From left to right: elliptic yeast of the genus *Saccharomyces;* sporulated elliptic yeast; round yeast, previously known as *Torula;* tiny elongated yeast, *Torulopsis stellata;* apiculate yeast, *Hanseniaspora;* large apiculate yeast, *Saccharomycodes ludwigii.*

GENERAL CHARACTERISTICS OF YEASTS

Yeasts, then, are the fermentation agents. They can be cultivated as tiny microscopic plants. By putting a trace quantity of yeasts into sterile grape must, the cells can be observed under the microscope as they start to bud and reproduce. At the end of fermentation, 2–3 g/L will be recovered.

There exist a considerable number of yeast species differentiated by their shape, their properties, their mode of reproduction, and by the way they transform sugar. Wine yeasts belong to a dozen genera each divided into species. In botanical classification, yeasts are designated by a double name in Latin, the first corresponds to the genus and the second to the species. For instance: *Saccharomyces ellipsoideus,* here the genus is *Saccharomyces* (literally the sugar fungus, which transforms the sugar) and the species *ellipsoideus* (elliptic-shaped).

Yeasts found in vinification may present one of the four following shapes: elliptical or ovoid; elongated, in the shape of a sausage; spherical; or apiculate, that is to say, having a bulb at each end like a lemon (Fig. 8.1). The majority of wine yeasts show two possible methods of reproduction according to prevailing conditions: vegetative reproduction by budding, and reproduction by the formation of spores, which after germination give more yeasts. The nonsporogenous yeasts, scarce in wines, are only reproduced by the vegetative process.

As soon as a yeast cell is to be found in a nutritive medium, a swelling can soon be seen appearing on its circumference that gradually gets bigger at the same time that the shape of the little cell begins to be defined. When the two cells are the same size, they separate and the budding of the two cells continues. This multiplication can be followed under a microscope. Under ideal conditions, only two hours are needed to double the yeast population.

When the medium is unfavorable, for instance when yeasts have exhausted all the sugar from the nutritive medium, they cease multiplying by budding and some produce asci, which cover the spores. These constitute a form of seed whose reduced life state and resistance tolerate survival under conditions (dehydration, heat, contact with chemical agents) that properly speaking, would be fatal to yeasts. Sporulation requires special conditions and it is exceptional in wine. Yeasts filled with granulations observed in the lees are dead yeasts whose protoplasm has coagulated and rarely sporulated yeasts. When conditions again become favorable, the spores germinate and give birth to new yeast cells.

The size of yeasts varies according to the species. Their diameter can vary from 2 to 10 μm (thousandths of a millimeter). To examine them correctly under the microscope, an enlargement of 600 or 900 diameters is needed.

One astounding fact is the number of yeasts to be found in must in full fermentation. The yeast populations are extremely dense, in the region of 80,000–120,000 per cubic millimeter, or 80 million–120 million per milliliter. In one drop of fermenting grape juice, there may be 5 million yeasts.

Yeasts are to be found on the ripe grape at the time of the harvest and are brought to the tank and the wine press with the grapes. Another part proliferate in the winery itself. It is principally the upper layer of the soil that is their winter habitat. In the summer they are carried onto the grapes for the most part by insects. Midges convey yeasts in this way together with other microorganisms which they pick up in the centers of fermentation which exist in nature at this time of year. Hardly any yeasts are to be found on green grapes and it is only after ripening has started, when insects begin to visit the small clusters, that their presence can be observed in great quantity. The distribution of the yeasts is governed by pure chance. There are no yeasts specific to grapes in general or to a particular grape variety. Microorganisms retained on the outer surface of the grape are varied and numerous. They are not retained by the bloom, waxlike scaly matter that covers the skin, but by secretions of indeterminate origin. Beside the good yeasts are found my-codermic yeasts or flower ferment, molds, lactic bacteria, and acetic bacteria. On the grapes, there is a mixture of microorganisms that help the vinification and those that cause spoilage.

SPECIES OF HELPFUL YEASTS

The yeast microflora in the majority of wine regions are known. Everywhere they show a certain similarity. In vineyards in different parts of the world, the same species of yeast are to be found with a few differences in detail due to the local climate.

DISTRIBUTION OF YEASTS AFTER A
FEW DAYS OF HARVESTING

Number of yeasts per cubic millimeter of must, determined on:	
Grapes picked on the vine	1–160
Vintage arriving at the winery	2–280
Must after crushing	460–6400

There are many species: 70 species belonging to 15 genera have been named. The yeast microflora on grapes are, therefore, complex. A first observation is important: Grape yeasts are not quite the same as those on musts in fermentation.

The number of fermentary yeasts obtained from a bunch of grapes picked from the vine is small and irregular. When a few very sound grapes are cut and crushed, taking all necessary aseptic precautions, it may happen that, due to absence of yeasts, fermentation does not start up. When grapes that have been handled by the pickers are taken from the picking tub, the yeasts that are isolated are already far more numerous.

After crushing and pumping through, however, yeasts are plentiful. The crusher and the stemmer act, as it were, like contaminators as do the crushers, drainers, and presses used in making white wine. This equipment is permanently covered with grape juice amply exposed to the air and the first yeasts brought by the grapes develop there with great speed. The study of the microflora from the musts after crushing, has in consequence much greater practical importance.

Numerous experiments have shown that certain products with antifungal properties used for treating vineyards have an influence on the natural microflora of the yeasts and change the course of fermentation. The inhibitory threshold for yeasts has been fixed per liter of must at 2 mg for Difolatan, 5 mg for captan, 10 mg for dichlofluanide, folpe, or manebe. Certain antifungides give preference to apiculate yeasts that are more resistant, to the detriment of the *Saccharomyces* genus.

Variety of Vinification Yeasts

The species may be divided into three groups: principal yeasts, auxiliary yeasts of special nature, and the rare and accidental yeasts. The most widespread of all the yeasts that are found in combination in almost all the musts are *Saccharomyces ellipsoideus*, the common elliptical yeast, and *Kloeckera apiculata* or *Hanseniaspora uvarum*, the tiny apiculate yeasts, spore-forming or

PRINCIPAL SPECIES FOUND IN VINIFICATION

Brettanomyces intermedius.

Candida intermedia, krusei, parapsilosis, rugosa, sake, solani, vini, zeylanoides.

Hanseniaspora osmophila, uvarum, valbyensis.

Hansenula anomala, subpelliculosa.

Kloeckera apiculata, africana, corticis, javanica.

Kluyveromyces veronae.

Metschnikowia pulcherrima.

Pichia fermentans, membranaefaciens, vini.

Saccharomyces aceti, bailii, bayanus, capensis, chevalieri, coreanus, delbroeckii, ellipsoideus, exiguus, fermentati, florentinus, globosus, heterogenicus, inconspicuus, italicus, oviformis, prostoserdovii, rosei, rouxii, uvarum.

Saccharomyces ludwigii.

Schizosaccharomyces pombe, malidevorans.

Torulopsis stellata.

not. These three species alone represent at least 90% of the strains responsible for fermentation.

In order of frequency, after that come *Saccharomyces chevalieri* for red vintages, a yeast whose fermentary attributes are no different from those of *Saccharomyces ellipsoideus* and for white musts, *Torulopsis stellata* and *Saccharomyces oviformis*. *Torulopsis stellata*, a small elongated yeast, is specific to grapes attacked by noble rot. The microflora of rotted grapes is different from that of sound grapes. *Saccharomyces oviformis* is a yeast capable of reaching a high alcoholic percentage. *Saccharomyces rosei* is an almost round yeast that does not create measurable quantities of volatile acidity.

The names of the yeast species are often subject to revision. Not all the changes are justified. *Saccharomyces ellipsoideus* is still called *Saccharomyces cerevisiae* or *vini* and *Saccharomyces bayanus* has become synonymous with *Saccharomyces oviformis*.

The other species are not often encountered. They can, however, intervene in particular circumstances. Exceptional fermentations have been observed involving *Schizosaccharomyces pombe*, which has the property of making malic acid vanish and of deacidifying the must. Vinification microflora are widely varied but enology centers its interest on a very small number of species.

Succession of Yeast Species

The different species take over from each other during the course of fermentation of the must. In sulfited musts the apiculate yeasts provide the start

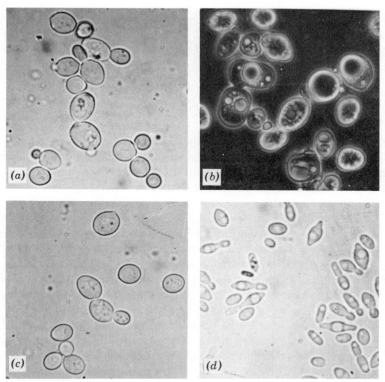

Figure 8.2. (a) *Saccharomyces ellipsoideus*, elliptical yeast; (b) *Saccharomyces ellipsoideus* with a few cells in a sporulated condition; (c) *Saccharomyces oviformis* (*bayanus*), yeast with high alcohol-generating powers; (d) *Hanseniaspora uvarum*, apiculate yeast.

and the first phase of fermentation. The first degree of alcohol is their work. For grapes with rot, fermentation starts through the action of *Torulopsis stellata*. The apiculate yeasts can only tolerate 3 or 4% of alcohol, *Torulopsis stellata* will ferment to 7 or 10%. Sensitive to sulfur dioxide, the more the vintage is sulfited, the less their participation. Then very quickly the *Saccharomyces* invade the medium and by mid-fermentation the yeasts from the beginning have disappeared. Among the elliptical yeasts certain strains are encountered with varied alcohol-generating powers, stretching from 8 to 16%. The constant predominance of *Saccharomyces ellipsoideus* is not so much dependent upon a greater resistance to alcohol, but to a greater fermentary intensity (quantity of sugar transformed per unit of time). Toward the end of fermentation of those musts rich in sugars, the dominant species in its turn is *Saccharomyces oviformis*, less sensitive to alcohol (see Fig. 8.2). Some of these strains are capable of taking production over 17–18% of alcohol. It is not unusual to reach these strengths in certain areas of Spain, for instance. Some strains even attain 20% during fermentations carried out in the laboratory. These yeasts are very helpful for finishing off wines with high percentages.

SPECIES OF NOXIOUS YEASTS

These are the yeasts causing spoilage. They contaminate containers and equipment. Resistant to alcohol, to sulfur dioxide, and to anaerobic conditions, they remain alive in the wine in a latent state for months. They are generally different from vinification yeasts.

In the practice of storing wines, multiplication may be observed of yeasts that disturb the clarity and form deposits. When the wines contain reducing sugars, a genuine fermentation may be set off and the wine will go gaseous. These disturbances may be observed not only during tank-life but in the cask or in the bottle too. It is important to know to what extent the various clarification treatments eliminate yeasts and which are the most dangerous species. More and more microbiological controls are being developed in practice.

Yeast Count in Wines

Under the microscope all the yeast cells present can be counted. It may be necessary to first concentrate the yeasts by centrifugation into a smaller volume.

This enumeration in the winery constitutes an indispensable control of clarification treatments. It informs the winemaker about the state of the equipment and general cleanliness. This is much more sensitive than a visual appreciation of clarity. It should be realised that a wine appears clear still, even with 3000 yeasts per milliliter.

Young wines still turbid after a few months without being disturbed may contain 200,000 (or more) yeasts per milliliter. After fining, some tens of thousands may still remain. Proper filtering across infusorial earth may bring the population down under the best conditions to 1500. Centrifugation clears yeasts better, but does not clarify so well. Filtering across ordinary pads of cellulose leaves 200 to 1000 yeasts, always per milliliter, in proportion to the porosity of the pads. To get below these figures, small pored, or what are sometimes called sterilizing pads, have to be used.

Living yeasts capable of reproduction are counted after development in petri dishes or when there are few, by the membrane filter technique. Each living yeast gives birth to a visible colony. This count gives a measure of the risks of real infection. It is a common method of determination requested of

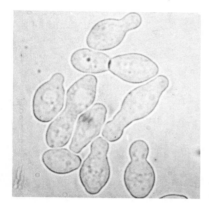

Figure 8.3. *Saccharomyces ludwigii,* a yeast strongly resistant to sulfur dioxide.

the enologist in setting up and controlling installations for winemaking, bottling, and filtering or for checking the cleansing and sterilization of equipment in the winery or in the storage cellars. Normally the proportion of living yeasts is low, 5% of the population of the wine, for example. In cases of recent contamination, it goes up to 50%.

Identification of Yeasts Causing Spoilage Contamination

These are no longer vinification yeasts but more resistant species. Refermentation accidents in dessert wines and yeast deposits in certain bottles of dry wine are not due to good yeasts from the first fermentation but to yeasts capable of surviving long storage in the presence of alcohol and free sulfur dioxide. Storage conditions do, in point of fact, select out the noxious yeasts. Most frequently, yeast spoilage in a wine is due to a single species that has been able to become in time adapted to the unfavorable medium. Certain yeasts should be catalogued among dangerous germs for the same reasons as certain bacteria.

In wines with high percent alcohol, *Saccharomyces oviformis* is the predominant species. It provokes refermentation of dessert wines, creates the film on certain wines, and often sets off the secondary fermentation in bottles of sparkling wines.

Saccharomyces bailii develops in wines with lower alcoholic percentage. It is particularly resistant to sulfur dioxide but less so than the large apiculate yeast *Saccharomycodes ludwigii* capable of surviving in unfermented sulfited juice (called *muté*) having 500 mg of free sulfur dioxide per liter (Fig. 8.3). The *Brettanomyces* can also develop in wine, sometimes on the surface and they impart disagreeable aftertastes (mousy flavor).

Contamination yeasts thrive on the equipment and in the wine containers. Cases of refermentation and yeast development are therefore due to infection. Within the winery, there exist yeast developments that are veritable contagion centers bordering on epidemics. The outside and inside of casks, the bungs and stopper systems, the cellar floors, the walls, equipment used for racking, topping, filtering and particularly in bottling, bottle-filler and corking-machine, all show the presence of yeasts, and since they are simultaneously or periodically in contact with the wine and with air, they maintain yeast infections.

A considerable number of species of contamination yeasts are to be found in the cellar. Mycodermic yeasts, which make the wine "flower" are particularly plentiful. In the film which is found on the surface of the wine or on the walls impregnated with wine, the species Candida vini is found together with Pichia or with Brettanomyces. None of the yeasts found in the winery is absolutely harmless. The causes of contamination are manifold and the present-day conception of storage and handling will have to be revised if it is hoped to do away with this. The winemaker should imagine the whole surface of the winery and equipment as being lined with yeasts. At certain times of year, their proliferation can be even more considerable than this. Therefore, it can be readily understood that the racking operation often enough does not achieve its purpose and that it reintroduces by contamination the yeasts it is supposed to eliminate with the lees. It can also be understood that, as a result of periodical reseeding, the topping operation maintains in wine kept in the cask in the "bung on top" position a large population of yeasts.

Contamination by bottling plants in very large installations is frequent and requires very special cleaning and sterilization of the equipment.

USE OF YEASTS IN VINIFICATION

In practice grape fermentation is not pure fermentation. Not only is it not conducted from beginning to end by a single species of yeast but, as will be seen, intervention by lactic bacteria to make the malic acid ferment is, in many cases, desirable. Pure fermentation obtained by sterilization and inoculation used in breweries and other fermentation industries is not advisable nor even feasible, for that matter. It has never been established in practice and wineries conceived on the idea of treating preserved grape juice all the year round have never gotten off the ground.

So things are more complicated than were imagined when it was suggested at the turn of the century to use pure yeasts, called selected yeasts, for wine making. At one time sulfiting and inoculation were considered the only operations permissible in rational winemaking! A lot of progress has been made since then.

Two main obstacles met with in the use of yeast inoculation have considerably delayed its application: failure in selection of the yeasts and difficulties in using them.

In fact, although inoculation has come into general use in the warm regions of Australia and California and South Africa, it was not practiced or at least only in exceptional circumstances in European areas. The yeasts supposedly selected were not, in reality, actually selected. It amounted to cultivated yeasts locally isolated and designated according to their origin, but the origin can never guarantee their worth. Selecting a yeast means choosing it from among a large number of others, following a detailed study bearing on its physiological characteristics: alcohol yield, alcohol-generation powers, tolerance for high temperatures, high glycerol or low acetic acid formation, its particular aroma, fermentation of malic acid, and so on.

On the other hand, bad utilization almost always made inoculation illusory. To be really efficient, seeding ought to be done after having eliminated the indigenous yeasts already existing on the grapes and in the winery. This result is not easy to get, it is not possible to sterilize the vintage, and natural yeasts, better adapted, outclass the yeasts introduced. Besides, this is what always happens in making red wine, even if sulfiting and seeding are generous. There are always parts of a vintage that do not receive any antiseptic or leaven and in which local yeasts develop. The addition of yeasts has to be massive, so a great deal of leaven has to be prepared in advance, representing no less than 5–10% of the volume to be fermented.

The elimination of indigenous yeasts is easier to carry out in white wine making, where the must is homogeneous and allows for better mixing, than in red winemaking. Sedimentation of must after sulfiting contributes in this elimination to such an extent that inoculation becomes indispensable.

Competition of Yeast Species in Associated Fermentations

This is observed between added yeasts and indigenous yeasts, or between two species inoculated at the same time. After seeding with an equal mixture of *ellipsoideus* and *oviformis* yeasts, the first species rapidly predominates. To get similar multiplication in both species, it is necessary to inoculate before fermentation starts ten times as much leaven of *Saccharomyces oviformis*. On the contrary with equal seeding, the *oviformis* yeasts will be in the majority when fermentation is over.

The utilization of the yeasts *Schizosaccharomyces*, which can cause deacidification of acidic musts by making malic acid more or less disappear, sets a practical problem which is even more difficult to solve since their devel-

DEACIDIFICATION OF A MUST BY THE *SCHIZOSACCHAROMYCES*

	Spontaneous Fermentation	Seeding with *Schizosaccharomyces*	
		Mixed Fermentation	Pure Fermentation
Alcoholic strength	9.2%	9.2%	9.4%
Total acidity	6.90	5.80	3.95
Malic acid	5.36	5.02	1.34

opment is only significant in the absence of elliptical yeasts. It only requires 10% *Saccharomyces ellipsoideus* in the leaven to reduce by one-third the *Schizosaccharomyces'* power to attack malic acid.

The Age-Old Practice of Using a Starter Culture

To mitigate irregularity in the starting and duration of fermentation, people often resorted to an old process called *pied-de-cuve*. This is the name given to a yeast starter culture prepared in advance with selected grapes, with or without yeasts added, put in the bottom of the tank of freshly picked vintage, and used to promote the start of fermentation. It is not unusual in fact for the winemaker to observe the following facts: the first tank loaded which only gets yeasts from the grapes themselves takes longer to get fermentation started while the later ones, inoculated by the harvesting equipment, get going much more quickly. Each year there are plenty of examples of medium-sized wineries where the last tanks are ready to be run off while the first have not finished fermentation. If the yeasts in the juice during fermentation are counted, the fact that the first tanks filled have more yeasts than the last is verified.

The use of the starter technique is helpful for the first tanks each time it is important to be able to regulate fermentation. This is carried out as follows: a week before the beginning of the harvest, a few of the ripest and soundest grapes are cut. They are crushed and sulfited to 10 g of sulfur dioxide per hectoliter. In this way, in proportion to the volume to be vinified, several hectoliters of leaven are prepared. When this tiny vintage is in full fermentation, it is used to seed the first vintage. The other tanks will be seeded by the equipment; otherwise, must from the first tank can be used to set their fermentation going.

**EXAMPLE TAKEN IN A VINEYARD WHERE THE VINTAGE
HAS LASTED A FORTNIGHT TO FILL 7 VATS**

	Length of Fermentation	Number of Yeasts (per milliliter of must)
First vat	18 days	48,000
Third vat	12 days	72,000
Seventh vat	7 days	108,000

Modern Inoculation Techniques

These consist of the dried yeast powders that have recently appeared on the market. They are not lyophilized yeasts (freeze-dried and containing proportionately few living cells), but yeasts vacuum-dehydrated in hot air with a protective support present. These powders, which have a yellowish-gray appearance, more or less granular and whose humidity level does not rise above 6–8%, contain, according to their preparation, 10–60% of living yeasts instantaneously regenerable, making 1–16 billion to the gram.

Several brands of German, American, and Dutch manufacture are to be found on the market today. They are prepared from pure species, generally *Saccharomyces ellipsoideus* or *oviformis* or from a mixture of strains.

Inoculation by means of these powders is recommended in numerous practical situations, every time the natural yeasts are too scant and fermentation is sluggish getting started, for known or unknown reasons: cold years when the picked grapes arrive at the winery at a temperature below 16°C, where residue from antifungal pesticides persists, vintages heavily sulfited, white musts drastically sedimented, especially when clarified by centrifugation or some other means. Also with the help of profuse seeding, defective wild microflora, such as yeasts producing ethyl acetate, hydrogen sulfide, or sulfur dioxide or having other undesirable characteristics, can be supplanted.

This convenient form of keeping yeasts which makes them available at any time of year, also applies in the case of re-inoculating wines with sugar still remaining after accidental stoppage of fermentation or to start fermentation in preserved musts, or in champagne making. In the case of white wines with fairly high acid content or sweet dessert wines, inoculation with *Saccharomyces oviformis* a finishing yeast resistant to alcohol, should be chosen.

The use of dry yeasts in the vinification process constitutes a great stride ahead in mastering fermentation and in the quest for quality. It is highly desirable that the application be further developed and that also a full range of appropriate strains (agglutinant yeasts, cryo-yeasts, etc.) become available for particular cases and special vinifications.

The dry yeasts are used in doses of 5–10 g of powder per hectoliter, which corresponds to seedings in the 50,000–1,000,000 per milliliter range, according to the preparations. Too heavy a seeding does lead to disagreeable yeast tastes.

The method of use is important in order to guarantee optimum efficiency. The powder should never be added directly to the must but the yeasts first rehydrated by mixing in a little lukewarm water. Twenty or 30 minutes later, the cells will have recovered their vitality. They are then added to the vintage or the must. This form of direct seeding after rehydration is the most common in vinification.

For other uses, in particular for inoculating media containing alcohol (refermentation of wines with sugar remaining, bottle fermentation), it is better to prepare in advance, from powders rehydrated, a culture in active fermentation in such a way as to ensure the yeasts multiply and adapt themselves to the medium.

9

Conditions for Development of Yeasts—Conducting Alcoholic Fermentation

The conditions for development of yeasts, for their growth or multiplication, are the very conditions for fermentation itself. After all, in practice there can never be sugar-fermentation, transforming it into alcohol, without the yeasts budding and multiplying. Fermentation stoppage is a sign of stoppage in the growth and the death of yeasts.

Like all living creatures, yeasts do in fact have their precise needs in terms of nutrition and environment. They are very sensitive to temperature, they need oxygen, they need to be appropriately fed with sugars, mineral elements, nitrogenous substances, and growth factors. This chapter deals with the conditions for multiplication of yeasts that are the foundations for controlling vinification. The winemaker should thoroughly understand them in order to know how to manage fermentation. Optimal conditions for multiplication of yeasts are all the more necessary to obtain when the strength of the wine being made is high. Controlling fermentation does not set too many problems for wines at 9 or 10%. It is more difficult for wines at 11 or 12% or more.

INFLUENCE OF TEMPERATURE

Temperature is a predominant factor in keeping yeasts alive. They only develop properly within a relatively limited scale covering a maximum of 20°C.

Below 13 or 14°C, the start of fermentation of a vintage is practically impossible or else it is so slow that there is a danger in waiting for spontaneous

FERMENTATION OF A GRAPE MUST AT VARIOUS TEMPERATURES[a]

	20°C	25°C	30°C	35°C
After 2 days	0	36	60	75
After 4 days	22	107	123	127
After 7 days	95	167	172	145
After 15 days	145	176	176	148

Law 1: Fermentation is quicker at a higher temperature.
(at 35°C, this is true at first, then fermentation stops.)

[a] The must had 178 grams of reducing sugars per liter. Seeding has been low. The table indicates sugar fermented at different moments in grams per liter.

starting. When a tank has not begun to ferment after five or six days, in fact molds or wild yeasts develop on the surface. To initiate fermentation, it is necessary to intervene with yeast inoculation. The tank can be warmed up, at least partially, with an electric element, or else a few hectoliters of must may be heated to 50 or 60°C and poured on top. When fermentation has been set off in one spot, the tank is stirred by pumping over.

Over 35°C, fermentation cannot be conducted correctly. If the temperature is reached gradually, the yeasts stop working and die, sometimes at temperatures as low as 30 or 32°C. On the other hand, exceptional circumstances have been seen where the fermentation of an entire vintage, warmed through, started off at very high temperature (40–45°C), with the help of special yeasts, then finished very quickly as it cooled down. Above these temperatures and in wine in the presence of alcohol, yeasts are killed in a few minutes. This is sterilization by heating, or pasteurization.

Speed of Fermentation and Temperature

"Sugar transformation speeds up with a rise in temperature" (at least up to a certain limit). That is the first law to bear in mind. Fermentation is much faster at 30°C than at 25°C and at 25°C than at 20°C and its speed doubles for each 10°C variation. A few fractions of a degree have a measurable influence. For each extra degree (centigrade) of temperature, yeasts transform 10% more sugar in the same lapse of time.

Above 30°C, if at first fermentation is faster, it stops earlier by a kind of wearing out of the yeasts.

FERMENTATION OF GRAPE
MUSTS AT VARIOUS
TEMPERATURES[a]

Temperature	Must 1	Must 2
20°C	96	105
25°C	89	98
30°C	86	78
35°C	69	68

Law 2: Yeast multiplication attains greater populations at lower temperature.

[a] Maximum yeast population achieved during the course of a fermentation with sufficient aeration in millions of yeasts per milliliter.

Limit of Fermentation and Temperature

The amount of sugar yeasts can transform or the alcoholic strength they can attain, depends on the temperature. That is the second law, important for understanding different fermentation phenomena: " The higher the temperature, the quicker fermentation starts, but the sooner it stops and the lower the alcoholic strength attained." This law may also be stated: "The maximum yeast population is lower at higher temperatures."

One of the consequences of this law is this: When a high alcoholic strength is desired, the fermentation temperature must be kept fairly low. High strengths are achieved more easily in traditional methods of storage of small capacity, Bordeaux casks or Burgundy pieces, in which fermentation temperatures remain close to the surrounding temperature.

Everything happens as if the yeasts get tired all the more quickly the faster they work, at higher temperatures. In these conditions, they do not withstand alcohol easily, they are less able to assimilate the nitrogenous substances, they lose sterols more quickly, their reproduction, then the fermentation, comes to a halt.

Critical Temperatures for Yeasts

It is above all by acting on the fermentation temperature that the winemaker can intervene effectively in the vinification process. The fact that in practice

FERMENTATION OF ONE MUST AT VARIOUS TEMPERATURES[a]

Temperature	Time Elapsed Since Start of Fermentation	Alcoholic Strength Reached
10°C	8 days	16.2%
15°C	6 days	15.8%
20°C	4 days	15.2%
25°C	3 days	14.5%
30°C	36 hours	10.2%
35°C	24 hours	6.0%

Law 1: Fermentation starts more quickly at high temperature.
Law 2: Alcoholic strength reached is higher at low temperature.

[a] Must from Sauternes rich in sugars, with equal seeding.

the temperature in the tanks gradually rises because of the caloric output from the fermentation is a handicap.

The ideal temperature for making red wine is between 26 and 30°C. It is a compromise between the need to have a sufficiently rapid fermentation with thorough maceration and at the same time avoid fermentation stoppage through overheating. For making white and rosé wines, the temperature to be preferred is lower, in the neighborhood of 18–20°C.

The notion of critical temperatures for fermentation is an important factor to consider in winemaking. Critical temperature is the temperature above which yeasts no longer reproduce, and die, making fermentation slow down, then stop. It is difficult to define a precise limit and better, therefore, to speak of a risk zone. This may vary in fact according to the aeration, richness of the must, nutritive factors for the yeasts, and the actual nature of these. In temperate regions the critical temperature is generally set above 30–32°C and in hot regions a little beyond this. This does not mean that each time a tank reaches this temperature its fermentation is in jeopardy and is bound to come to a halt, but it does mean there is a risk of stoppage. And in practice, what must be avoided is the risk. In any case, it should be no surprise if a tank that goes over 30°C only, remains sweet. Each year examples are met.

Control and regulation of the fermentation temperature will be dealt with later. The following rule must already be emphasized: The winemaker should not wait for the temperature in the tank to reach the risk zone before thinking about cooling. Cooling ought to intervene well before. What is important is to avoid crossing into this zone. The winemaker should avoid reaching this risk zone in the first place and maintain a favorable temperature, below critical temperature, to avoid destroying the yeasts.

INFLUENCE OF AERATION

Yeasts need oxygen to multiply. In a total absence of air, they only create a few generations and their growth stops. Then all it needs is to give them a little air again for budding to restart. If the state of asphyxia is prolonged, the majority of the cells die. Pasteur defined fermentation as "life without air," because one yeast cell deprived of oxygen finds the energy it needs in this transformation of sugar. But to get prolonged fermentation and obtain fermented products rich in alcohol, new generations of yeasts must constantly be forming and traces of oxygen become indispensable.

This need for oxygen is, in a way, indirect. Yeasts require oxygen to synthesize the sterols and assimilate the fatty acids with a long molecule which they need. The sterols are the organic substances with several cycles of carbon atoms and with an alcohol function, source of several hormones and vitamins whose biological importance is considerable. At the beginning of fermentation, the first generations of yeasts benefit from the reserves of sterols from the mother cells, then sterols from the natural environment. If fermentation is carried on in a shortage of air, the sterols are used up and are not renewed. Oxygen is indispensable to sterol synthesis and thus to the continuation of fermentation.

The weight of yeasts formed in the course of a fermentation depends a lot on the proportion of oxygen at their disposal. In industry when people want to produce a lot of yeast, they vigorously aerate the nutritive medium. In vinification, conducted generally in an absence of air, oxygen is the limiting factor of yeast multiplication.

All steps in which grapes are handled (crushing, destemming, pumping through, or again, for white grapes, draining off and pressing) makes sure of a first aeration, helpful in getting fermentation started. Following this, the more oxygen the yeasts manage to get, the faster the yeasts multiply. Similarly the end of fermentation of a must rich in sugars depends on how much air the yeasts have been able to get; fermentation always reaches a stage further in the presence of air. Even very slight aeration has a noticeable effect on the way fermentation functions.

Demonstration of the Yeasts' Need for Air

In a must in fermentation, the yeast population in the part in contact with air is more dense. A must is in ferment in a 225-L (50-gal) cask, allowing a 5-

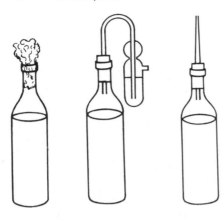

Figure 9.1. Fermentation of a grape must in the laboratory: *left*, in gradual contact with the air (absorbent wool plug); *right*, completely shut off from air (stopped with bubble system and stopped with a tapered tube).

L space needed to avoid overspill; after a few days of fermentation, a yeast count indicates 80 million yeasts per milliliter at 1 cm from the surface and only 48 million in the depth of the cask.

The following simple experiment demonstrates equally well the yeasts' need for air. A grape must is set fermenting in different bottles in the laboratory with the same seeding and at the same temperature (Fig. 9.1).

One is stoppered simply with a plug of absorbent cotton, another is sealed off by a bubble system with carbon dioxide being allowed to escape through water, and a third has a cork holding a finely tapered glass escape tube. In the first bottle, oxygen penetrates freely through the thickness of the absorbent cotton in spite of carbon dioxide being given off; the fermentation is said to be in gradual aerobiosis. In the other bottles, oxygen cannot penetrate and fermentation is said to be in anaerobiosis.

The bottle stopped with absorbent cotton begins to ferment quickly and continues right through to the end. All the fermentable sugar is easily transformed. Shut off from air, on the contrary, fermentation is much slower; it comes imperceptibly to a stop and does not terminate; the wine retains sugar. The richer the must in sugars, the more pronounced the difference between the bottles.

The first bottle indicates 80–100 million yeasts per milliliter, the others, only 50–60 million. These yeast counts are enough to explain the phenomenon: In the bottle stopped with absorbent cotton, the yeasts get a sufficient supply of oxygen to reproduce normally; in the other bottles the lack of oxygen limits the multiplication of the yeasts; being less numerous, they cannot complete the sugar transformation.

In a fourth bottle similarly fitted with a bubble system, on the second day an aeration is carried out by decanting. Under these conditions, the fermentation terminates with a yeast population that climbs back to 80–100 million per milliliter.

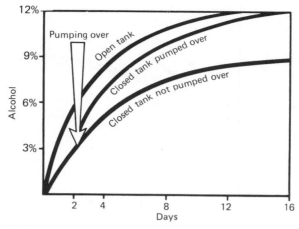

Figure 9.2. Vinification in closed or open tanks and the importance of pumping over. Fermentation in closed tank not pumped over stops and leaves wine sweet. Pumping over with aeration on the second day allows fermentation to terminate. Fermentation in open tank terminates easily.

This experiment, which can be reproduced with different volumes in an experimental cellar on an industrial scale or in practice in a large tank with crushed must or vintage, shows the importance of aeration in the course of fermentation. The aeration is achieved either by permanent contact with the air or by pumping over. To avoid fermentation stoppage through asphyxia of the yeasts, aeration is needed when working with a closed tank—even more so when the vintage is rich in sugar.

The Practice of Pumping Over

This is a practice recommended since the beginning of the century. It is also called *lessivage* (washing) or in some regions of France *ravinage* (torrenting). For closed tanks, it has replaced the sprinkling operation on the cap or punching down of the pomace used with open tanks. In open tanks with the pomace floating on top, a hole used to be made in the pomace and a little wine extracted and splashed all over the surface (Figs. 9.2 and 9.3). Or again the pomace was crushed or trampled down with the feet or sometimes turned over by tilting it and pushing it with a pitchfork.

Pumping over consists of racking fermenting must through a faucet placed at the bottom of the tank into a miniature tank or *douil* (1½ gal), letting it drop from a certain height. The pressure of the fall creates an emulsion that makes dissolving oxygen easier. It is also suggested that allowing the must to run down a plank will increase the spread in contact with the air. There are also

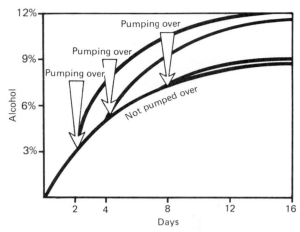

Figure 9.3. Vinification in closed tank and importance of the moment when pumping over is carried out. Pumping over at the start of fermentation is effective; it is much less so when done toward the end of fermentation.

special ajutage nozzles that fit on the faucet and create a powerful emulsion. The aerated must is forced back up with the pump onto the top of the vat where it soaks the cap of pomace. In this way, a closed circuit is set up. Rotating systems or spray nozzles of different designs effectively wash the whole surface and drench the pomace better (Fig. 9.4).

How long pumping over should last is calculated in relation to the capacity of the tank. It is admitted that pumping a third or a half of the must in the tank is a necessary and sufficient quantity. It is better to pump over several times rather than prolong it.

Efficient pumping over also means in the first instance racking a large volume of the must from the fermentation tank, then in a second stage pumping it over in such a way as to swamp the pomace.

At what moment should a tank be pumped over? The result is different depending on when it is done. However, if it is used with a view to activating the yeasts, then it should be done right at the start of fermentation, just when they are in their logarithmic growth phase which corresponds to the first hours of fermentation. In this way yeasts benefit from the oxygen they are given.

In practice the tendency is to pump over rather late. Aeration then does not appear to be very efficient because the yeasts find themselves in an environment where nutritive factors have been used up. On the other hand, if it is overaerated before fermentation has properly started the activating effect is similarly less. Oxygen needs to be supplied to the yeasts and not to the must and needs to be supplied to them when they can use it, that is,

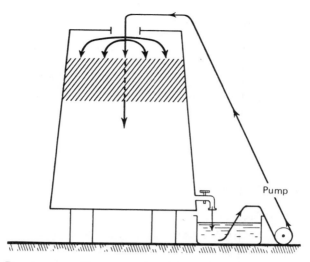

Figure 9.4. Pumping over with aeration. Arrival of aerated wine may be directed onto the cap or in depth. Inoculation, sugaring, and in some cases deacidification are done during pumping over.

when they are in reproduction. It is then that oxygen increases the yeast population and keeps their activity going.

Multiple Effects of Pumping Over

Pumping over closed tanks, just like the ancient practice of punching down or crushing the pomace in an open tank, has a certain number of repercussions for vinification. Its utility depends on several factors:

1. The effect of aeration, studied earlier.

2. Mixing together different parts of the fermenting tank. This homogenization has a bearing on the sugar content and also on the temperature, which is very uneven in different parts of the tank, particularly at the beginning of fermentation.

3. Distribution of yeasts throughout the whole mass. The yeast population does not spontaneously have a regular consistency throughout the fermenting vintage. In a tank coming to the end of fermentation 15 million yeasts per milliliter were found in the wine first run off from the bottom of the tank, 10 million halfway up, and 180 million in the wine that bathes the pomace 40 cm from the surface. Thus the greater proportion of yeasts are found in the pomace. This part of the tank is where fermentation is most vigorous, and it can be understood that the temperature here is always greater. After pumping over, the distribution of yeasts had been modified in the following way: 40 million per milliliter in the first run-off and 140 million in the pomace. Washing the pomace carries yeasts into the main part of the tank.

4.   Accentuating the extraction. Pumping over, by displacing the interstitial juice from the pomace, accentuates the dissolving of the phenolic compounds, anthocyanins, and colored tannins, as well as the other constituents of the grape skin.

These multiple consequences make pumping over, in itself a simple operation, one of the most important in making red wine. The treatment of a tank of red wine can be summed up as follows:

1.   As soon as the tank is filled, pump over with or without aeration to homogenize the lots of the vintage (which are bound to be different). By mixing them together, distribute the sulfur dioxide, the starter where necessary, and the yeasts.
2.   As soon as fermentation has started and the day after, pump over with aeration.
3.   As and when necessary and toward the end of fermentation, pump over once or several times more, with or without aeration, to homogenize the wine and wash the pomace.

These last pumpings are vital in tanks where the cap is immersed in order to shake out the pomace and give it a better wash. If fermentation slows down or gets stuck, pumping over is rarely enough to get it going again. The tank will need to be run off.

Replies to Two Objections Concerning Pumping Over Open to Air

First Objection. Aeration is dangerous in hot years. By stirring up the sugar transformation, it promotes a much faster rise in temperature, which is even more certain to make fermentation stick.

Reply. Nothing of the sort. Healthier yeasts and in greater numbers, better resist high temperatures. Indeed, the more the tank tends to overheat, the more it should be aerated.

Second Objection. Aeration is useless. Yeasts find substances (fatty long-chained acids) on the bloom of the berries that allow them full growth in aerobic conditions.

Reply. The yeasts' need of air has been established in conditions concerning the practice of crushing the vintage. Activation due to the bloom, which has been established, does not prevent fermentation stoppages often encountered in closed tanks. Aeration remains indispensable to enable the yeasts to assimilate these fatty acids and synthesize the sterols.

THE YEASTS' NUTRITIONAL NEEDS

Yeasts absolutely have to find certain foods in the must where they develop. Their needs in terms of sugar and mineral substances are easily satisfied. Musts are less well provided with assimilable nitrogenous matter.

Yeasts consist of 25–60% nitrogenous substances. To form their cells and reproduce, therefore, they need to find in their environment sufficient nitrogen in a form easy to use.

Ammoniacal nitrogen (ammonium cation) is the primary nitrogenous food consumed by elliptic yeasts, followed by certain free amino acids, such as glutamic acid. In 36 hours of fermentation, yeasts drain the must of its assimilable nitrogen and of many other nutritive elements. The rest of the fermentation goes on with starved yeasts in a state of deficiency. Toward the end of fermentation, they give the wine its amino acids back by excretion.

Now, the vintage can already, in its natural state, be poor in assimilable nitrogen. This is the case on certain soils or again when grapes are very ripe or when botrytized. The large majority are attended with a stock of nitrogen in unassimilable form (e.g., proline). Rot exhausts the grapes of these nitrogenous foods used by yeasts.

The addition of ammonium nitrate is vital in certain cases (ammonium nitrate level in the must below 25 mg/L), useful in many others (levels between 25 and 50 mg) and is never in any case contra-indicated. The EEC regulations permit the use of diammonium phosphate or ammonium sulfate at maximum dose of 0.3 g/L.

Use of Ammonium Salts

The yeast population and speed of fermentation are almost always increased by adding 10–20 g of these ammonium salts per hectoliter of vintage. In very sweet musts (Sauternes-style dessert wines), this addition allows fermentation to reach a much higher alcoholic strength. One hundred milligrams of phosphate or ammonium sulfate contain about 27 mg of ammonium nitrogen and 73 mg of phosphate or sulfate anion. Above all the ammonium cation takes the active part. The addition of phosphate, another yeast food, is less justified.

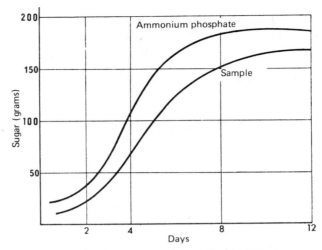

Figure 9.5. Activation of the fermentation of a must by adding 20 grams of ammonium phosphate per hectoliter.

If it is decided to enrich the vintage with ammonium nitrogen, this addition ought to be done for preference before fermentation starts (Fig. 9.5). The added nitrogen will in this way be fully used by the yeasts. It is vital to dissolve it first and mix it well. If ammonium salts are introduced on the third day of fermentation, the yeasts only use two-thirds of it, after 4 days, only half and toward the end, hardly a third. It is sometimes advisable to add ammonium salts at the termination of a sluggish fermentation or to get a stuck fermentation going again. In this case, only a little should be added, no more than 10 g/hL.

Needs in Growth Factors

For their growth, yeasts need other substances, which are none other than the vitamins vital to higher animals, in particular: biotin, pyridoxine, thiamine, pantothenic acid, mesoinositol, and nicotinamide. They also must have sterols and long-chained fatty acids present, when, in anaerobic and very high temperature conditions, they are unable to synthesize them.

Under normal conditions, the grape is sufficiently provided with growth factors to be sure of getting yeasts to multiply well. But some deficiencies (inadequate levels) can happen (molded grapes, grapes lacking maturity); certain vinification techniques outsort the richest parts of the grape. Besides, as the must ferments and one generation of yeasts succeeds another, the growth factors are used up and its facility in fermenting, which is called its fermentability, diminishes. If the same must is fermented, for experimental purposes, successively several times, boiling off the alcohol each time under vacuum and replenishing the sugar and the ammonium nitrogen, which can be done in the laboratory, at the third try a sweet liquid that will not ferment again is obtained. The yeasts have used up all they need. It is only necessary to add at that point a little natural juice containing growth factors, a little fresh must for instance, and fermentation again becomes possible.

These indispensable substances for yeasts are active in extremely small doses, a few tenths or, for some, a few hundredths of a milligram per liter. The most important one to be taken into account is vitamin B_1 or thiamine. Musts from sound grapes contain greater or smaller amounts of it (from 0.1 to 0.5 mg/L). On the contrary, sulfited musts, or musts from grapes with mold, can lack them. The addition of small quantities, lower than 60 mg/hL, that is, 0.6 mg/L, the legal amount, considerably activates fermentation of these deficient musts: The yeasts resist these inadequate conditions better and make sugar transformation go further.

Finally, by diminishing the level of the ketonic acids left by fermentation (pyruvic acid, ketoglutaric acid) thiamin allows wines to be produced with less sulfur dioxide compound. For all these reasons, it can help the wine maker. The addition of thiamin also makes it easier to get stuck wines to referment and to finish.

Other efficient activators of alcoholic fermentation have been suggested: vitamin complexes containing a mixture of growth factors necessary for yeasts (thiamin, pantothenic acid, biotin), concentrated yeast extracts, mycelium powders.

INFLUENCE OF ACIDITY

The winemaker often has false ideas about the part played by the acidity of the vintage in alcoholic fermentation. He thinks high acidity is a favorable sign, that yeasts will develop and work better, and that the more acid the must is, the more easily they will transform its entire sugar content. In point of fact, yeasts do not need acidity to multiply. They even make the sugars ferment better in a neutral or only slightly acid environment and work better at pH 4 than at pH 3. At very low pH, they create more volatile acidity.

When fermentation stops, it is not because of a lack of acidity but through excess heat or yeast asphyxia. However, low acidity can aggravate the consequences of the stoppage in that disease bacteria, conversely, develop all the more easily in an environment with lower acidity. The part played by acidity must be understood in the following way: It does not promote yeast development, but it does hinder dangerous bacterial evolution in the case of fermentation stoppage.

10

Malolactic Fermentation
and Lactic Bacteria

When the red wine is drained from the fermentation tank and pressed, more often than not it is not yet finished. After the stage of rapid transformation of sugars into alcohol and must into wine comes a phase of changes that are slower though more important and often essential for quality; this is the finishing phase. What is more, after a few days in a stationary condition, the wine usually "starts working again," as the winemaker puts it. This period relates to what has been called secondary fermentation or concluding or refining fermentation. Properly controlled, these transformations culminate in optimal quality and biological stability.

The winemaker's task is not limited to controlling the tumultuous period and does not end when the wine is drained. From the same new red wine coming out of the tank, the winemaker could, depending upon the way he conducts it, get a supple, tender wine with low acidity and a highly developed aroma, or a hard, firm wine with strong fixed acidity and a taste different from the former.

A good red wine is not, as Pasteur gave us to believe, the sole outcome of alcoholic sugar fermentation by the yeasts. This is inevitably followed by lactic fermentation of malic acid by bacteria, together with considerable reduction in fixed acidity, which makes the wine markedly more supple. This is malolactic fermentation, also called biochemical deacidification or degradation of malic acid. This transformation promotes quality, since it is the lower acidity that gives the wine its "mellow" and "fat" characteristics. For quality wines, it may be considered as the first step in improvement by aging. By the same token, it is a safeguard for stability.

NATURE OF MALOLACTIC FERMENTATION

The first time a wine was observed exhibiting extreme acidity reduction in comparison with the initial must, reduction far in excess of any relating to bitartrate precipitation, was over a century ago; at the same time the presence of lactic acid in wines was observed. However, only in the last 40 or 50 years have we begun to recognize malic acid fermentation as a useful phenomenon that must be guided and controlled.

This point of view was contested for a long time since the transformation takes place spontaneously in conditions such that it often goes unnoticed and you have to be made aware of it to perceive it.

Sometimes it happens in the tank at the end of alcoholic fermentation, before draining if skin contact time is prolonged. In these conditions, it cannot be discerned without examining the wine under a microscope or following its acidity. It was recognized by Gayon at the end of the last century that bacteria began to be visible on the sixth or seventh day of fermentation. More advanced modern techniques (bacterial cultures and L + -form enzymatic determination with lactic acid) have confirmed their presence much earlier. This initial invasion indicates, not the beginnings of a disease as used to be thought, but the appearance of malolactic bacteria, which start to develop from that moment.

At other times, this fermentation intervenes immediately after draining, as soon as the wine has been drawn off into casks or into another tank. The wine goes on bubbling, gets softer, and loses fixed acidity. This transformation was explained simply by the finishing off of the alcoholic fermentation and precipitation of the tartar. Here again malolactic fermentation can easily pass unnoticed.

Some years it carries on slowly during the winter if it is fairly mild and the wine remains gaseous for a long time. There are wines that give the impression of fermenting all winter although they no longer have any sugar. It takes place sometimes in spring or at the beginning of summer. The movement of wines at this period is well known and a parallel has been drawn with the sap rising or the vine blooming. In reality we know it is mainly a question of temperature. When the wine gets warm in the storage cellars, the malolactic fermentation bacteria start working wherever they find more malic acid. The wine goes cloudy, starts bubbling, and loses total acidity. These transformations were attributed to a secondary alcoholic fermentation transforming the remains of a few reducing sugars and this spring upsurge was given the name *pousse* ("shooting").

To sum up, without having accurate observation, malolactic fermentation could be confused with the end of alcoholic fermentation and its special character took a long time to be recognized.

Changes in the Wine's Composition

It can be understood that this phenomenon was first reported and studied in areas with less sun where the grapes retain more acid every year and give wines that are green and tart. In northern areas, wherever malolactic fermentation does not take place, some years the wine is so sour it is almost undrinkable, with 8–10 g of fixed acidity.

When the wine's composition is followed through by analysis during the course of this phenomenon, a reduction in total acidity is observed that may be as much as 1, 2, or even 3 g/L. From 5 or 6.5 g (in sulfuric acid), which new wines often have, acidity drops to 3 or 3.8 g. This reduction is not explained by tartaric precipitation but by the disappearance of malic acid. At the same time, lactic acid levels rise. The wine's composition, in its essentials, that is, its acid structure, is profoundly transformed. The overall reaction of malolactic fermentation is expressed in the following way:

$$malic\ acid \rightarrow lactic\ acid\ +\ carbon\ dioxide$$
$$1\ g \qquad 0.67\ g \qquad 0.33\ g\ or\ 165\ mL$$

The carbon dioxide formed is given off and makes the wine gaseous. It is the direct cause of reduction in acidity. Malic acid possesses two acid functions, whereas lactic acid only has one. The result of this transformation of malic acid into lactic acid is a drop in fixed acidity which corresponds to half the malic acid's acidity. In short, a part of the wine's acidity is transformed into volatile carbonic acid which is given off and disappears.

Malolactic fermentation leads to a slight rise in volatile acidity, in the region of 0.1–0.2 g. A part of this is due to the attack on any traces of sugar or citric acid by the lactic bacteria, particularly the cocci, which happens at the same time as they attack malic acid, or closely follows it. Because of this instability, it is not advisable to use citric acid in wine making.

Improving the Taste

Malolactic fermentation constitutes a genuine biological deacidification of the wine. The richer a wine is in malic acid, the more it is naturally acidic. Therefore the greater the deacidification, the greater the difference in suppleness.

The result from the gustatory point of view is a considerable amelioration. The gain in quality is the result of two things: a reduction in the amount of acids and the replacement of an acid with a pronounced taste, malic acid, by another acid that is not so aggressive on the tongue papillae, lactic acid. It is only necessary to know the respective tastes of malic acid and lactic acid

ANALYSIS OF A WINE BEFORE AND AFTER MALOLACTIC FERMENTATION[a]

	Before	After	Difference
Total acidity	100	78	−22
Volatile acidity	4.3	5.6	+ 1.3
Fixed acidity	96	73	−23
Malic acid	48	8	−40
Lactic acid	1.4	20	+19

In this case, malolactic fermentation has not been absolutely complete. Reduction in fixed acidity (23) does correspond fairly well to the difference between the loss in malic acid and the gain in lactic acid (21). According to the malolactic fermentation equation, the lactic acid formed (19) represents approximately half the malic acid lost (40).

[a] Amounts in milliequivalents (mL N) per liter.

to understand the important reduction of the acid flavor. What is more, 1 g of malic acid only gives 0.67 g of lactic acid.

In this way the young wine loses its hard, bitter character and becomes supple. With acidity getting less, its color undergoes a change toward a less vivid red. The aroma itself is transformed, moving away from a grape odor, getting richer shades and more vinosity. Red wines thus acquire that mellowness and full-bodiedness that are much appreciated elements in quality.

On the other hand, where white wines are concerned, the utility of malolactic fermentation cannot be generalized in the same way. In fact it is only looked for in a few wine-growing areas.

For dry wines, if it is possible and is regularly carried out, malolactic fermentation does not always lead to an improvement in quality. The pleasantness of a dry white wine depends a lot, after the delicacy of its aroma, on its acidity/alcohol balance. Sufficient acidity which gives freshness is necessary for certain types of these wines. A number of dry white wines at 11 or 12% can stand 4.20–4.50 g of total acidity and preserve their malic acid.

In certain areas, certain years when wines are too acid, malolactic fermentation can be helpful in managing to bring off an excellent dry wine. So people try to use it in Champagne, Burgundy, in the Mâcon area, and in Switzerland. On the contrary in Germany and Austria, chemical deacidification is generally preferred. In areas where grape acidity is low, malolactic fermentation leads to wines that are too flabby, without vivacity or freshness. It is a question of taste and also of variety. Wines from certain grape varieties tend to lose their aroma through bacterial influence and lactic tones dominate the fruity character. It is better in that case to prevent malolactic fermentation by sulfiting the must and the wine or trying to get partial transformation. On the other hand, for grapes already rich in aroma, such as a Chardonnay, malolactic fermentation adds something more to the odorous complexity.

There is on the whole, a certain unity of opinion where red wines are concerned that malolactic fermentation should take place. But this simplification does not hold good for white or rosé wines. If what is expected from these wines is the fruity flavor of the grape and the fresh acidity of a new crush, then malolactic fermentation is generally of no use. Conversely if the winemaker wants vinosity, roundness, "volume" and that character which a certain aging brings, malolactic fermentation will promote it. It is the same for rosé wines, which belong essentially to two different types: one a little more acid, fresh and fruity, obtained by avoiding malolactic fermentation, the other fleshy and with low acidity thanks to the work of the malolactic bacteria.

As far as sweet or dessert wines are concerned, they are often sulfited before malolactic fermentation can take place. However, bacterial intervention is more common than is supposed. It is dreaded because it can lead to more or less lactic acescence with a rise in volatile acidity.

THE BACTERIA OF MALOLACTIC FERMENTATION

The fermentation of malic acid is provoked by the development of lactic bacteria, little cells equipped as it were for the transformation of sugar into lactic acid whereas yeasts are equipped to transform sugar into alcohol. Lactic bacteria can be seen under the microscope (enlarge 900–1500 times) in various shapes. First the cocci, which are round or oval, and the bacilli or pellets in the shape of little dashes, long or short, thin or not so thin and sometimes sinuous (see Fig. 10.1). Cocci are 0.4–1.0 μm in diameter and bacilli can be 0.5 μm thick and 2–5 μm or more in length.

It should be realized that more often than not, the malolactic fermentation bacteria, at the beginning of their development, cannot be distinguished under the microscope from the other lactic bacteria, the wine disease agents. What is more, under certain conditions (presence of sugar for instance or high pH) malolactic bacteria themselves can cause spoilage. Simply examining them under the microscope is not enough to conclude whether they are useful bacteria or, on the contrary, whether they are dangerous.

The differentiation between lactic bacteria in wine is based on the shape of its cells and on a study of its properties. Determining physiological characteristics confirms morphological classification and identifies the genus and the species. In this way homofermentary strains that provoke pure malolactic fermentation are distinguished. That is to say, these strains form, besides the

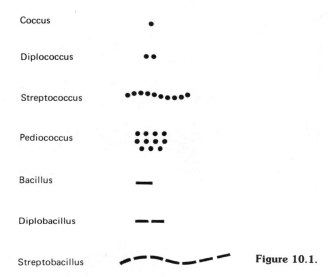

Coccus

Diplococcus

Streptococcus

Pediococcus

Bacillus

Diplobacillus

Streptobacillus   **Figure 10.1.**

lactic acid, a number of fermentation products such as alcohol, acetic acid, glycerol, mannitol and other polyalcohols, and carbon dioxide.

In cold or temperate regions, the cocci are more plentiful than the bacilli in wines during malolactic fermentation. In warm regions, the opposite is true. The proportions of these two forms of bacteria depend on the climate or initial acidity of the must, which is in fact determined by the climate.

The fermentation tests for different sugars and different constituents of wine are conclusive for the identification of bacteria. In particular, the fermentation of the pentoses constitutes a good basis for identification.

Wine bacteria belong to the genera *Leuconostoc* (heterofermentary cocci), *Pediococcus* (homofermentary cocci) and *Lactobacillus* (bacilli). This classification has a great deal of practical importance on account of the diversity of their behavior. The evolution of malolactic fermentation may give different results and afterwards, during storage, the wine may develop in one direction or another according to the nature of the lactic bacteria multiplying in it. The characterization of this microflora is a prerequisite to any examination (see Fig. 10.2). The names of these bacteria will become as familiar to the wine technician as the names of the different yeasts.

Distribution of Lactic Bacteria

Lactic bacteria are found at vintage time on the ripe grapes, mingled with the yeasts, mycoderma, and molds. The distribution and frequency of malolactic bacteria in vineyards seems fairly irregular. Malolactic fermentation is

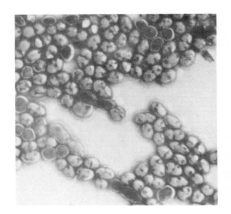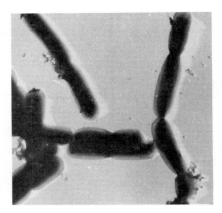

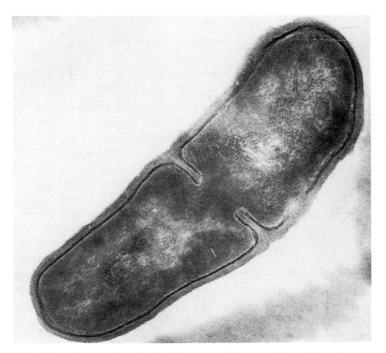

Figure 10.2. Microphotographs of isolated lactic wine bacteria taken with an electron microscope. *Above right*—heterofermentary coccus; *above left*—heterofermentary lactobacillus (according to Nonomura), enlarged approximately 5000 times. *Below,* cell of a lactobacillus in process of division, enlarged 80,000 times (according to Lonvaud).

SPECIES OF LACTIC BACTERIA FOUND IN WINES

Homofermentary cocci	*Pediococcus cerevisiae*
Heterofermentary cocci	$\left\{\begin{array}{l} \textit{Leuconostoc gracile} \\ \textit{Leuconostoc oïnos} \end{array}\right.$
Homofermentary bacilli	$\left\{\begin{array}{l} \textit{Lactobacillus plantarum} \\ \textit{Lactobacillus casei} \\ \textit{Streptobacterium} \end{array}\right.$
Heterofermentary bacilli	$\left\{\begin{array}{l} \textit{Lactobacillus hilgardii} \\ \textit{Lactobacillus fructivorans} \\ \textit{Lactobacillus desidiosus} \\ \textit{Lactobacillus brevis} \end{array}\right.$

to be seen each year operating with greater difficulty in the wines of certain vineyards than in others without the composition of the grape giving any explanation for these differences.

The existence of lactic bacteria in the equipment and wine containers is equally probable. We know danger of contamination occurs when putting a sound wine into a cask that previously contained spoiled wine. It is equally likely that in certain cases malolactic fermentation can be initiated through seeding by wine containers. Lactic bacteria probably live inside the wood or the layer of tartar. Hygienic precautions taken with the winemaking equipment and containers, necessary to prevent deterioration, tend by the same token to repel seeding by the malolactic bacteria. It is not unusual for difficulties to arise when an owner inaugurates a new fermenting room; malolactic fermentation is more difficult to obtain there.

Observations made on the crop as its arrives at the winery have shown that bacteria are generally present. However, they are not all viable, that is to say, susceptible to development at the must's natural pH or in presence of alcohol, and at the same time yeasts are in competition with them to such an extent that in practice only a small fraction of the grape bacteria has in the end a chance to multiply in the wine.

The distribution of bacteria in young wine is much more common. Almost all the samples of wines taken from the tank at the end of fermentation show bacteria capable of developing during storage, without sulfiting, and of absorbing malic acid. On the contrary, a minority of wines in storage have bacteria capable of attacking pentose, tartaric acid and glycerol or of raising volatile acidity. The frequency of lactic bacteria, greater in young wines than in musts, shows the part played in bacterial contamination, by microflora in the winery and by handling during vinification.

Useful Bacteria and Noxious Bacteria

Although in winemaking certain bacteria can, in contrast to Pasteur's ideas, have a beneficial effect, the deleterious action of contamination bacteria is much more frequent than is usually supposed. Also, when malolactic fermentation is finished, Pasteurian principles again take on their full import. Bacterial intervention does not always lead to in-depth deterioration, for instance, acescence caused by degradation of the sugars, or spoilage caused by degradation of the tartaric acid. However, it does commonly lead to increases, more or less perceptible, of volatile acidity and often too of fixed acidity. These increases have the effect of "drying" or of "thinning" the wines, which then no longer possess those qualities they ought to have, without actually being spoiled. Often the winemaker is not aware of the true cause of these changes.

Malolactic fermentation bacteria are more resistant to acidity and they transform malic acid for preference, without even touching the sugars, at least in a sufficiently acid medium. They form few volatile acids. The disease bacteria, on the contrary, work at very low acidities, they attack sugar or other essential wine ingredients more easily, and they considerably raise volatile acidity. They belong above all to the *Lactobacillus* genus.

In short, there may exist in wines two different types of lactic bacteria:

1.   Bacteria capable of decomposing malic acid in priority and, in second place, sugars, sometimes citric acid but not tartaric acid and glycerol. They are widespread. They are the normal malolactic fermentation agents but also the usual agents of deterioration of wines that have remained sweet after fermentation stoppage. These bacteria are only dangerous when they have sugars to work on in a nonsulfited medium and only if the pH is high enough.

2.   Bacteria capable of decomposing the pentoses, the tartaric acid, and the glycerol; their presence is not constant and they are the most dangerous of the two. These bacteria are the agents of a much more fundamental spoilage in wines in spite of their coming from sound vinification. Diligent care in the treatment of the wine is the best way to forestall their intervention. Only bacteria in this second category can be qualified as noxious.

The ideal lactic bacteria, useful and inoffensive, would be ones that would attack malic acid without being able to touch the other constituents. Such bacteria do not exist. But there are degrees in the danger that a bacteria exhibits relating to the properties of the species, also to the conditions, and in particular to the presence in the wine of reducing sugars.

11

Conditions for Development of Malolactic Bacteria— Conducting Malolactic Fermentation

MODERN PRINCIPLES OF FERMENTATION

From the utility of malolactic fermentation, that is to say, bacterial intervention in the wines, several conclusions may be drawn that were not recognized 40 years ago or so, and that run counter to earlier beliefs which may still be given credence in certain areas. This knowledge is of relatively recent acquisition and is the basis of modern trends in winemaking. The time it takes to get people to apply it may seem surprising yet the spread of progress in enology always comes up against strong opposition.

The presence of bacteria in fermenting must or young wine as revealed under the microscope does not signify, as has been shown, that this must or this wine necessarily exhibits the beginnings of disease and that its future is seriously jeopardized. The formula: "No microbes in the wine," which has been often enough repeated is not therefore always valid. As long as malolactic fermentation is not terminated, there are, in fact there must be, bacteria in the wine. However, as soon as this is accomplished, the words "No more bacteria" take on their full import.

Malolactic fermentation is part of the process of conducting vinification. It has to be supervised and controlled in just the same way as alcoholic fermentation. In point of fact, since this fermentation must take place, since it is of help, it might as well be done quickly, in the young wine. In this way a wine that is biologically terminated is obtained earlier. Vinification needs to be conducted in such a way that malolactic fermentation happens soon after draining, at all events before the cold sets in. This way the renewal of bacterial activity in spring is avoided and a wine is obtained that can be used earlier, having in fact already six months advance on those which only terminate in the spring.

It is a fundamental rule of modern wine making to consider that red wine is only completely finished and stable when these two fermentations are terminated. The principles in making red wine, when it is quality wines that are being looked for (and this is equally valid for white or rosé wines to the extent to which malolactic fermentation is applicable) are, therefore, as follows:

1. Make sure the sugars are fermented by the yeasts and malic acid fermented by the bacteria, without the bacteria attacking the sugars or other constituents of the wine.

2. When the sugars and malic acid have disappeared, but only then, the wine is biologically finished. All that is necessary then is to make sure the microorganisms are destroyed, a result obtained by rational sulfiting, frequent racking, filtering, fining, and in some cases, heating.

3. It is always preferable that sugars and malic acid disappear at an early stage. In fact, there is advantage in reducing the duration of the dangerous period during which, at one moment or another, either yeasts or bacteria, or yeasts and bacteria simultaneously, multiply, with the risk that the bacteria attack the residual sugars and other constituents of the wine. This risk is even greater in that the wine is deprived of free sulfuric acid. So long as a wine is not biologically finished, bacteria and yeasts can and must intervene again. This phase should take place under careful supervision to avoid any adverse outcome.

To sum up, conditions must be created that allow helpful transformations to be obtained rapidly and the length of the critical period to be as short as possible. The consequence of a delay in carrying out malolactic fermentation is not only to extend the period during which the wine is unstable, but also to increase risk of deterioration.

It is always of great help in anticipating how a wine will keep later, to know if it has been subjected to malolactic fermentation and if this has been concluded. Clarification or stabilization treatment would be premature, indeed illusory, if all the malic acid had not been absorbed. In particular, bottling could well lead to a failure. Hence the importance for the enologist to ascertain the amount of malic and lactic acids. Chromatography on paper renders in this regard considerable service since it gives visual information about the presence of malic acid.

CONDITIONS FOR MALOLACTIC FERMENTATION

Over and above the importance of natural seeding, those factors that, in practice, condition malolactic fermentation are the real acidity of the wine and the quantity of sulfuric acid used in vinification. But there are others linked to bacterial nutrition or depending on outside conditions: temperature and aeration.

Spontaneous Bacterial Growth

Bacterial multiplication during vinification generally takes place in two successive cycles separated by a phase of adjustment as shown Fig. 11.1. The first starts right from the very first hours in the vat, in parallel with the yeast development. It is interrupted by the formation of alcohol when the bacterial population suffers a strong decline. In the end, after alcoholic fermentation there only remains in the new wine, a rather variable number of live bacteria,

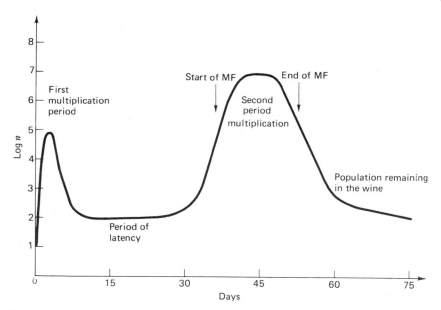

Figure 11.1. Graph showing the evolution of lactic bacteria and malolactic fermentation during the course of the vinification of red wine.

EXAMPLE OF THE DEVELOPMENT OF MALOLACTIC FERMENTATION[a]

	Total Acidity of the Tanks (in grams of sulfuric acid)	Malic Acid
October 28	5.19–6.08	2.50–3.50
November 5	4.76–5.49	2.00–3.50
November 9	3.82–5.10	0.50–3.00
November 17	3.68–4.51	0–1.50
November 25	the whole harvest 3.68	0

[a] Observations made in a property in the Médoc region of France harvesting some 20 tankfuls and running off 100–150 hL. Harvested October 4–20; run off October 19–November 6.

sometimes on the order of a few tens of thousands per milliliter. The latency period that follows is more or less prolonged. In a few rare cases, there may be overlap between alcoholic fermentation and malolactic fermentation, which is not, it should be added, desirable. More often than not the latency period is a few days or a few weeks. If a limiting factor intervenes (sulfuric acid, unfavorable temperature), it may be extended over several months.

Multiplication starts again after this period of repose, which provokes fermentation of the malic acid. Formation of lactic acid is low in the first stages. Malolactic degradation is only triggered off when growth reaches the logarithmic phase. It carries on during the stationary phase and even during the decline. When bacterial concentration is too low, there is no attack on the malic acid. It would seem that it needs more than a million cells per milliliter for fermentation to start properly. After that, depopulation is more or less rapid. When the malic acid has all gone, there remains in the wine a permanent bacterial population, larger or smaller in relation to the pH, the sulfiting, the fining processes, and the length of storage.

The Influence of pH

A factor of prime importance is the wine's pH. Real acidity has a doubly selective effect: It determines the species of bacteria and the constituents capable of being fermented. What is called the pH threshold is that pH from which development of bacteria and attack on a particular constituent become possible. For instance, different strains of bacteria are characterized, in relation to their capacity to produce pure malolactic fermentation, by the pH threshold ratings at which they attack malic acid and also sugars. For cocci, which are the agents best suited to this transformation, the former is fermented at a lower pH than the latter. The greater the difference between these ratings, the better adapted the bacteria are to malolactic fermentation. On the contrary, the bacilli attack sugars at lower pH ratings (some even from a pH 3).

In short, as the pH gets lower, new categories of bacteria are inhibited and malolactic fermentation is at once more arduous and more pure. Optimum pH for the multiplication of bacteria is situated between 4.2 and 4.5, well above the pH of wines. Between pH 3 and 4, malolactic fermentation starts all the more quickly, since the pH is higher. The absolute pH limit is about 2.9, below which malolactic fermentation may be considered no longer normally possible.

The part played by acidity means that in conditions in which malolactic fermentation is most necessary and its effects on the wine's taste likely to be most pronounced, that is, particularly when grapes lack maturity and the wines are acid, it is most difficult to get going but once started it will carry on with the least risk of deviation. Conversely, it is easiest when acidity is low and it has less impact on taste and when the risk is, after all, greatest.

Disease bacteria develop best, in fact, in wines with low acidity. These are the wines that have come out best, those that are the most supple; they are also most liable to accident. That is one of the great difficulties in storage. It is the conditions in which wine is at its best that they are most delicate and most difficult to age. In enology, therefore, there is often conflict between the techniques that allow better quality to be obtained and those that ensure maximum storage security, as we already pointed out in Chapter 7.

A slight reduction in the acidity of the vintage, considerably facilitates the triggering of malolactic fermentation. This deacidification, which moreover only needs to be practiced on a small quantity which serves afterward as a leaven, ought to be limited to an improvement in pH. It happens, for instance, that deacidification of musts with 6.5–7.0 g of acidity, with only 50 g of calcium carbonate per hectoliter, means finally ending up with wines showing, after malolactic fermentation, 3.0–3.5 g of fixed acidity. Chemical deacidification ought to be looked on only as a means of priming the natural deacidification chain reaction.

Influence of Temperature

It is well known. It has been observed that, all the conditions being equal, this transformation in wine is performed at its maximum speed between 20 and 25°C. It is slower at 15 and at 30°C. Stoppage may occur over 30°C. Tanks that go over this temperature during vinification often have greater difficulty undergoing malolactic fermentation.

People are advised to maintain the winery, where the new wines are stored before being terminated, at an adequate temperature. Fermentation of malic acid is slow below 15°C, whereas at 20°C it can be finished in a few days. It needs a few weeks to terminate at 12 or 13°C and even several months at lower temperatures. Once started, it can continue at less than 10°C. The winter cold in certain areas forms the main hindrance to the start, the evolution, and the conclusion of this phenomenon. In such instances it is advisable to heat the winery and the cellars where the new wine is kept until it is satisfactorily terminated. If not, malolactic fermentation will only start in spring when the temperature rises naturally. Nevertheless, there is an advantage in conducting it at a lower temperature, say, 18°C. The formation of volatile acidity, since other constituents are attacked more easily than the malic acid, is greater at a higher temperature.

Wines in the tank can be maintained at an adequate temperature in different ways: warming the winery, warming metal tanks directly or circulating hot water through double walls around the tank, heat exchangers via circulation outside the tanks or else sunk into the middle of the wine, screened resistances plunged into the wine, and so on. The latter are not suitable for prolonged heating.

Influence of Aeration

In practice, careful aeration often favors bacterial development. Saturating new wine with air makes malolactic fermentation appear a few days in advance. On the contrary, saturation with pure oxygen retards it without stopping it completely. In short, malolactic fermentation is possible throughout a broad range of aeration conditions, and if this factor plays some part, it is not the main one.

Moreover, the influence of air depends on the species of bacteria. Some bacteria develop better away from air: These are the optional anaerobia. On the contrary, the growth of *Leuconostoc gracile*, a common species of malolactic ferments, is favored by the presence of a little air: It is a microaerophil species.

Conditions for Nutrition of Bacteria

Malolactic bacteria have much more specific nutritional requirements than yeasts, in particular in amino acids. Generally they find in wines sufficient quantities of the various Group B vitamins, which act as growth factors, but a little extra activates them. Auxoautotrophia (that is to say, the possibility of synthesizing the growth factor, or the shortage of amino acids) does not exist among lactic wine bacteria. Contrary to yeasts, bacilli and cocci are incapable of synthesizing the matter they are short of. A nitrogen base, four vitamins and eighteen amino acids are absolutely essential to them, if not all at once, at least one or the other according to the strain. The part played by amino acids is essential in bacterial metabolism. Being at the same time growth factors and plastic elements, these acids are indispensable, and indispensable at concentrations that often must be high and well balanced. In fact, amino acids exist in musts and wines only in relatively low amounts. These deficiencies may explain why malolactic fermentation is difficult to obtain in certain cases.

Even their needs in mineral matter, in particular in manganese, magnesium, and potassium, are considerable.

Wine does not always completely satisfy these needs. It constitutes an environment that is not very favorable, imposing on the bacteria limited conditions for life, all the more so in that it contains more often than not natural inhibitors.

Influence of Alcoholic Strength

Isolated wine bacteria, especially those responsible for malolactic fermentation, are necessarily resistant to alcohol since they develop and subsist in wine. But their multiplication is nevertheless considerably impeded by the presence of alcohol, especially when strength is over 10%. At these concentrations, alcohol becomes an important limiting factor for bacterial growth and the main obstacle to the success of seeding by means of bacterial leaven.

In winemaking it is often ascertained that malolactic fermentation takes place first in the least alcoholized wines in the cellar. The greater the wine's alcoholic strength, the longer the latency period lasts, the smaller the terminal bacteria population, and the slower the degradation of malic acid.

Cocci are more sensitive to alcohol than the bacilli. Higher tolerance to alcohol has sometimes been observed in certain strains of lactobacillus, capable of developing in dessert wines of up to 18 or 20% alcohol, which therefore deteriorate by lactic acescence or souring.

Influence of Sulfiting

Another determining factor in malolactic fermentation is the use of sulfur dioxide in vinification. This antiseptic considerably hinders the lactic bacteria, much more so than the yeasts. Bacteria are extremely sensitive to it. Malolactic fermentation is more or less retarded in proportion to the amount of sulfiting of the must or the vintage. It can be even imperiled by strong doses.

The action of sulfiting depends on the pH of the vintage. In regions like the Bordeaux area of France, it can be reckoned that in making a red wine, 2 g of sulfur dioxide per hectoliter will have little effect; 5–10 g will definitely delay this fermentation, which will only take place several weeks after drain-

**INFLUENCE OF SULFITING THE MUST ON
MALOLACTIC FERMENTATION**

Sulfiting (g/hL)	Must 1[a]	Must 2[a]
Sample	40	30
+ 2.5	45	40
+ 5	70	60
+10	100	100

[a] Number of days needed to get malolactic fermentation started in two practical instances, according to the dose of SO_2 added to the must.

ing, or only in the spring; and with higher doses still, fermentation will not occur at all. In northern areas, sulfiting at 5 g may prevent it, whereas in hot regions 20 g/hL may not.

From this influence of sulfur dioxide on the development of malolactic fermentation and therefore on the fixed acidity that the wine will retain, a general rule in winemaking is derived: The extent of sulfiting depends on the acidity of the vintage. The choice of how much sulfur dioxide to use is a delicate matter since, as a throttle, it is a highly sensitive instrument, but difficult to adjust. Sulfiting should in fact be done in such a way that bacterial deviations due to over-rapid fermentation are prevented without the beneficial transformations being slowed down too much or made impossible.

It is not just the free sulfur dioxide that has these antibacterial powers, as was believed for a long time. Other species are active. Protonated sulfur dioxide is five or six times less active than free sulfur dioxide but it should be taken into account that it may be five or ten times more plentiful in the finished wine. Its practical role is so important that above 90–120 mg/L of SO_2 compound, bacterial activity (and malolactic fermentation in particular) becomes impossible in certain types of wines with a low pH.

When trying to avoid malolactic fermentation (the case with dry white wines, in particular) it should be realized that the wine's stability does not depend on the antibacterial activity of free sulfur dioxide on the must alone, but also that of the SO_2 compounds, which the wine retains after vinification. Lasting forms of sulfite combinations ensure in this way the wine's resistance and its behavior during storage.

USE OF MALOLACTIC INOCULAR CULTURES

Sometimes malolactic fermentation is not achieved in practice simply because it does not happen to have the right conditions. On the other hand, it may go wrong or not happen at all through lack of bacterial activity. Every year certain privileged vineyards in quality wine regions, due to suitable microflora, are observed undergoing malolactic fermentation very early while elsewhere it turns out to be difficult and even occasionally impossible. The fact, reported repeatedly, that malolactic fermentation takes place more easily in large bulk than in a small volume, even under equal temperature conditions, may also be explained by scarcity of bacteria and irregularity of seeding.

To propagate malolactic fermentation, good results are obtained by means of blending, for instance a wine rich in malic acid with 25 or 50% of another wine in the course of malolactic fermentation or having just finished, or else by seeding with the help of lees from racking or sediment from filtering. Promoting fermentation of a tank that has remained acid is generally successful when diluted with another tank that has spontaneously deacidified itself, so long as the temperature is maintained at the right level. Fermentation is thus finished off in a few days, after which further blending is carried out. In this manner, it is possible to deacidify a large quantity of wine in a few weeks, starting off with only small quantities of fermented wine, getting results that would, by spontaneous action, have required several months.

The question has been asked whether fermentation of malic acid can be provoked by seeding with pure cultures of bacteria in the same way that alcoholic fermentation is provoked with the help of yeast cultures. Using malolactic culture should make malolactic fermentation start quicker and clear up certain difficult cases.

Inoculating the wine with cultivated bacteria raised problems that have gradually been solved. First of all, it is easy to obtain malolactic fermentation in the laboratory, in a fairly short space of time, by seeding a must simultaneously with yeasts and cultivated bacteria. Under such conditions malolactic fermentation generally starts a little before the end of alcoholic fermentation and terminates in a few days. However, bacterial seeding of a vintage or a must cannot be advised: It presents a danger of lactic spoilage if alcoholic fermentation slows down or accidentally comes to a stop. The addition of bacteria to a finished wine, when there are only 2 g of reducing sugars left, is the only procedure that could be recommended. It is tantamount to shortening the latency period by setting up a more abundant bacterial population.

Selecting coccus strains resistant to alcohol and acidity and that present few risks because in their conditions of use they are incapable of attacking constituents other than malic acid has led to interesting practical results. Mixtures of species appear more efficient. Lactobacilli, easier to cultivate and prepare in large quantities, can be associated.

Several ways of using these bacteria are possible: suspension of centrifuged fresh cells, paste of frozen bacteria, even preserved in liquid nitrogen, powders of bacteria or of dried culture media. A phase of regeneration and of multiplication in a culture liquid is always indispensable.

One proprietary preparation suggests the following method of use. The correct dose necessary for treating 100 hectoliters of wine is composed of a small packet of dried bacteria and another with nutritive salts to be dissolved in one liter of previously boiled water. The bacteria are then poured into the nutritive medium thus constituted and allowed to incubate together at 25 or 30°C. After 48 hours, the culture is in full activity and is mixed into the volume of wine to be treated. The population obtained is on the order of a million cells per milliliter. The wine ought not to contain more than 10 mg of free SO_2 per liter; it needs to be aerated first; its pH ought to be equal to or over 3.3; the temperature is regulated between 18 and 20°C. From controls made of the process, 50% of the cases logged were positive, for which malolactic fermentation was either induced or accelerated compared to the samples not treated. In other instances, the natural bacteria population was sufficient so that the bacterial contribution served no purpose or else artificial seeding was held in check by some unknown inhibition.

Bacterial seeding applies to the first tanks run off. If necessary, malolactic fermentation is extended by mixing. As soon as it is terminated, as chromatographic quantification of the malic acid will show, without waiting, bacterial activity should be arrested by sulfiting, for instance at 3 or 4 g/hL.

PART 4

Vinifications

DEFINITION AND PHILOSOPHY OF VINIFICATION

The grapes, the vintage, and the crop are what are vinified. You do not vinify wine; wine is the result of vinification.

By vinification is understood all the operations done to transform the juice from the crushed grapes. In dictionaries, the term also includes processes like elaborating and aging, but professionals rightly use it only to describe the single phase of fermentary preparation of the wine. Many different vinification processes exist, corresponding to the various types of wine, the distinction between them being the way the different grape tissues are separated. Wine can be made just from the juice in the cell vacuoles, or else by breaking down an extraction of substances found in the skin and the seeds. Fermentation can be carried out in many ways and in vessels of various geometrical shapes. Vinification poses certain problems concerning the installation, the mechanical equipment, and the storage facilities, each of which has to be resolved according to enological requirements.

Rational vinification means applying to a particular case, in given conditions, a technique chosen in accordance with the sum of knowledge acquired about the mechanisms and the different factors related to the important vinification phenomena. For vinifying red wine, these are: mechanical preparation of the grapes, alcoholic fermentation, extraction and specifically dissolving certain constituents of the grapes, and malolactic fermentation. We know how to analyze the factors involved: temperature, aeration, pH, washing or kneading the pomace, the length of pomace contact, and the use of sulfur dioxide. For vinifying white wine, they are: extraction of the must and clarification of it, alcoholic fermentation, and protection from oxidation.

Indeed it is only in so far as these general principles are fully grasped that vinification can be truly said to have been conducted. Empiricism on its own, with so many unknown factors therefore leaving too much to chance, can never provide the means of producing every year the best wine possible.

Certainly there is, and always will be in vinification, a certain element of knack, know-how, and intuition, but everything that is done presupposes a choice and therefore knowledge and experience. The part played by guesswork must be reduced to the minimum. The winemaker does not have total mastery of the active microflora, either, but he does have ways of acting on it and giving it direction. From what he knows about it, he must calculate, anticipate, and even improvise, and he will do this all the better, the more accurate the information he bases his action on.

Vinification is at the same time an art and a science. The winemaker can stamp his own methods and his own tastes on it. It is a difficult art. Vinification has to be adapted to circumstances: You do not make wine the same way in hot years as in cool years, nor are sour grapes used in the same way as very ripe grapes or rotted grapes. Cabernet is not vinified like Gamay, nor is a wine designed for aging made like a wine designed to be drunk young. The work is not the same in Meursault as in Sauternes nor in the Rhine Valley as in the Central Valley.

Under the sanction of traditional procedures, vinification can never be left to chance. Tradition should never be an obstacle to progress, but evolve with it. Tradition is in fact progress that has achieved success, that has been ratified by time and experience. Far from being immutable, it should be in constant evolution.

As has been confirmed many times, some excellent vintners are less interested in vinification. They spend all year tending the vine with infinite care and at great cost, only in the end, all too often, to leave their highly valuable vintage in a tank without supervision, or hardly any, taking the fatalistic attitude that the transformations that take place spontaneously must necessarily be good or at least the best that could happen. In fact, the way the vinification is conducted decides to a large extent the quality of the wine and its future. Obviously in the composition of this quality, there is a liberal dose of nature's irreplaceable gifts, however the winemaker's task is not just to prevent accidents, but to achieve top quality with the vintage at his disposal.

If the owner were once convinced that good wine deserves striving for, he would already be halfway toward success.

12

Vinifying Red Wine—Work with Grapes and Fermenting Apparatus

Red wine vinification, reduced to its essentials, comprises three main classes of operation: alcoholic fermentation, extraction, and malolactic fermentation. These are generally carried out in four stages:

1. The mechanical operations of work with grapes (destemming, crushing).
2. Fermentation (alcoholic fermentation, extraction).
3. Separating the wine (draining, pressing).
4. The finishing transformations (malolactic fermentation).

However, there may exist vinification techniques that follow a different time-table, in particular those that attempt to separate the extraction phase from the alcoholic fermentation phase.

Red wine vinification makes use of many different types of building and a diversity of equipment. The winery or the vinification cellar should enable the work to be properly organized. It is the winemaker's tool. Improvements in quality are obtained every time mastery of the technical stages of vinification are refined. Still, progress is not just a question of equipment and mechanical ingenuity but also of enological know-how. People tend to think that the quest for improved quality, in vinification just as in storage, requires before all else heavy investment in equipment. Quite wrongly, enological progress and mechanical progress are confused, for it is possible to let winemaking miscarry in an up-to-date well-equipped winery and make a successful job

143

using an ancient or modestly equipped installation. The thing is, there is nothing automatic about winemaking. It is not just blindly following a series of recipes, but intelligently applying a whole sum of expertise.

MECHANICAL OPERATIONS OF WORK WITH GRAPES

The grapes are brought from the vineyards to the winery in various containers. Figure 12.1 shows several methods of transport currently in use. It is imperative to get it in as fast as possible after picking, avoiding crushing in the vineyard and even cramming it in the tubs (*comportes* or *douils*) on the way. The reception bay at the winery takes various forms, from a simple oak platform, gravity delivery onto the top of the tanks, a trough feeding the crusher-stemmer, to the continuous worm-screw feed or the delivery quays at the wine cooperatives.

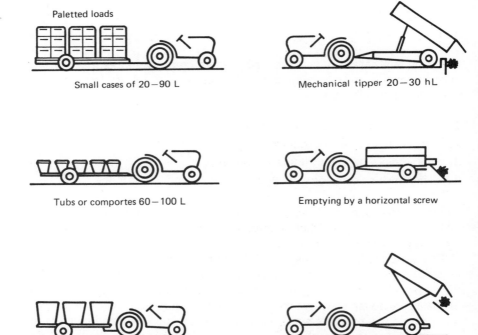

Paletted loads

Small cases of 20–90 L

Mechanical tipper 20–30 hL

Tubs or comportes 60–100 L

Emptying by a horizontal screw

Douils 600–800 L

Rising tipper

Figure 12.1. Diagrammatic illustration of various methods of transporting the crop (according to the *Bureau Commun du Machinisme et de l'Equipement Agricole*).

One of the first calculations to be made is the density of the must, which gives an estimate of the finished wine's presumed alcoholic strength, and its acidity (titratable acidity and pH), which gives a first indication of how the vinification should be conducted. Taking the must density is described further on.

Mechanical work with grapes comprises the two operations of destemming and crushing. The machines can have a direct feed or be loaded manually with forks and shovels, or else more regularly supplied by means of a worm-screw.

Destemming

This consists of separating the grape berries and taking the wood out of the bunches. In many machines, mechanical destemming is done after crushing, but there is some advantage in starting with the destemming. This way the stems are not broken between the rollers, are not soaked with juice, and do not need to be dried. This system, of more recent design, is highly recommended for quality wines.

With the old traditional methods, the stems were picked off manually in the vineyard at the end of each row and the grapes lightly crushed in the tubs, or else the traditional destemming was practiced by hand at the winery. The whole crop was poured onto an open-work table with borders round. The workers rubbed the grapes and moved them about with their hands or with little rakes on the grating. The stemmed grapes fell under the table and were hardly crushed at all before being poured into the fermentation tanks.

Mechanical stemmers are usually linked with crushers. A crusher consists of a perforated horizontal drum and a shaft with blades set spirally. The drum and the shaft turn at a low speed in opposite directions. The juice, pulp, and skins slide through the holes in the drum and are carried toward the tank-feed pump. The stems, stripped and dried, are expelled from the end of the drum. With this type of apparatus, it is possible to crush without destemming by shutting off the connection with the stemmer.

Centrifugal crusher-stemmers have a high work output but rotate too fast and handle the grapes too roughly. They should be rejected for quality wine making.

A good stemmer ought not to leave any berries unstemmed, it ought to remove the stems completely, it should not tear off the pedicels nor cut or crush the peduncles and the stems ejected ought not to be impregnated with juice. The stemmer like the crusher, should respect the tissue of the grape (see Fig. 12.2). It is better not to stem at all if the machine rips up the vintage.

The winemaker ought to choose an apparatus that simulates hand-stemming conditions. Flexible blades turn inside a cylindrical riddle and rub the

DESTEMMING

Advantages	Disadvantages
Saving space (the stems represent 3–7% of the crop in weight but 30% in volume): fewer fermentation tanks, less pomace to handle and to crush.	Destemming reinforces the difficulties of vinification. There is hardly any problem with nonstemmed grapes.
Improvement in taste: the dissolved portions of the stems have an astringent taste, leafy, herbaceous. Stemming preserves finesse.	Stems make conducting the fermentation much easier: They absorb calories, limit excess temperatures, and draw in air. Fermentation with the stems is faster and more complete.
Increase in alcoholic strength that could be as much as 0.5% if pomace contact is moderately long: stems contain water from vegetation and contain no sugar. They absorb alcohol.	Pressing the pomace with the stems is easier.
Increase in color, at least in the short term, by avoiding the fixation of pigments in the stems.	Destemming increases the acidity of the vintage, the stems not being acid and rich in potassium. The difference in acidity can reach 0.5 g/L.
	Destemming distinctly emphasizes the gravity of oxidative casse.

Conclusion.   Total destemming is advisable when the suppleness and delicacy of fragrance of quality wines are being sought.

Nevertheless in certain regions, there is an advantage in not destemming varieties with green nonligneous stems like Aramon. Other exceptions to the destemming rule are with very young wines or with rotted grapes. The stems give a little body to wines originating from vines at their third or fourth leaf. When a vintage is rotted to more than 30%, oxydative casse is to some extent avoided by not destemming.

grapes by drawing them across a grid made up of rounded components without any sharp edges. When the feed and rotation speed have been correctly adjusted, according to circumstances, the stems remain intact and the berries are detached without being bruised. They can be crushed or not as the winemaker thinks fit, by altering the space between the rollers of the crusher situated under the stemmer.

Crushing

This consists of breaking the grape's skin in such a way as to free the pulp and the juice. It can be more or less intense according to whether the skin is simply split by being compressed or whether it is crumpled and shred into pieces. The structure of the pulp can remain practically intact or, on the

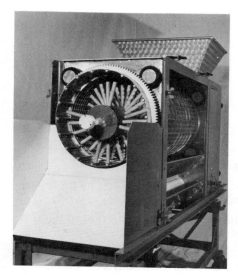

Figure 12.2. Example of an apparatus that first stems and then crushes (Amos). The clusters are first stripped of their berries, which when detached fall onto the rollers of the crusher.

contrary, the great vacuoles of the cells can surrender all their juice. Thus the crushed vintage, a heterogeneous medium, takes on various facets and the way crushing is done has an effect on the whole winemaking, on the way fermentation and extraction will be conducted, and, in the end, on the quality of the wine produced.

Two extreme instances may be quoted: the ancient technique where, the grape being treated by hand and dropping into the tank by gravity, crushing is very limited and many of the berries keep their shape, and on the other hand, the rough handling caused by a centrifugal stemmer that gradually reduces the vintage to a state of pulp. You even come across small-scale winemaking where the grape, only gently squeezed, is emptied into the tank where it gets gradually squashed under its own weight as fermentation develops.

In any case, crushing ought to be carried out without flattening the skins, squashing the seeds, or ripping the stems.

Different Types of Crusher. Five types of crusher may be described:

1. Crushers with rollers turning in opposite directions in relation to each other so that they draw up the vintage between them. The distance between the rollers determines how intense the crushing will be. The cylinders can be grooved in different ways (either straight or spiral grooving (see Fig. 12.3). They can turn at different speeds.
2. Crushers with blades that only have a single rotating cylinder crushing the grapes against a slotted plate.

Figure 12.3.   Types of roller crusher: *right*—rollers with grooves, generally spiral; *left*—grinders with interconnecting profiles.

3. Crushers using grinders with interconnecting profiles, in the form of a cross, capable of treating vast quantities.
4. Crusher-stemmers. Horizontal rotating crushers operating by projecting and crushing the grapes while destemming.
5. Vertical centrifugal crushers, turning at high speed (450–550 rpm). This last apparatus should be banished because of its rough handling

Crushers are judged by the way they work and the results they give: Every berry should be crushed but the skins ought not to be ripped and the stems and seeds ought to remain intact.

Some of the damage caused by the crushing is often made worse by the tank-feed pump. The best pump is one that takes into account the fact that the crushed vintage is a heterogeneous mass.

FERMENTATION TANKS

Types of containers and tanks are extremely varied and in constant evolution. In the days of home vinification, each area had its own way of vinifying and its local style of installation. With the development of industrial winemaking with standardization and interchange of techniques, installations have undergone considerable changes everywhere. Today, a whole swarm of different vinification methods can be seen within each area and every owner is giving vent to his individuality.

Take, for instance, the Bordeaux area, a wine-growing region in a medium latitude. Every conceivable type of fermentation installation ever invented may be seen: open tanks, closed tanks, tanks made of wood, cement or metal, in every shape and form, cylindrical, cubic, parallelepipedal, higher than wide or the other way round, built in stories in the "wall of tanks" style, underground, outside, from 25 to 500 hL, with a floating or immersed cap; you will find tanks with automatic pumping over, tanks whose specific geometrical shape makes pomace extraction easier or even automatic, controlled temperature tanks, and so on.

CRUSHING

Advantages	Disadvantages
Crushing is responsible for the first separation of the juice from the solid parts.	In cases where the vintage is more or less rotted, stirring up the grapes and aerating them are prejudicial to quality and may be enough to cause oxidative casse.
It makes transfer by pumping possible.	
It encourages the formation of the cap of pomace in the fermentation tank.	
It disperses the yeasts.	In hot areas, it gives too vigorous a start to fermentation.
It promotes aeration helpful in the multiplication of the yeasts.	Increasing extraction becomes a drawback for grapes too rich in tannins or for varieties with a "tang of the soil."
It activates the start of fermentation.	
It facilitates extraction by increasing the surface contact between the juice and the solid parts.	
It accentuates the dissolving of the color, the tannins.	It frees the seeds, which transmit astringent substances.
It allows sulfur dioxide to be used within reason.	The more vigorous it is, the more it increases the solution of astringent polyphenols. The amount of tannin increases proportionately more than the pigment.
It shortens fermentation time and makes termination easier.	
Press wine is not sweet as when a large proportion of berries remain whole.	Pressing gives a great deal of sediment and lees.

Remarks. The present-day tendency is, as far as quality wines are concerned, to crush only lightly. If extraction needs to be stressed, it can be done by longer pomace contact rather than by increasing the intensity of mechanical crushing.

A great many installations are not properly designed either for receiving and working the grapes or for actually conducting the fermentation. A winery must be clean; therefore it should be easy to keep clean, that is, washable. It should not be damp. It must be large with plenty of space and wide openings for aeration. It ought to provide the two opposing thermal conditions: cooling and ventilating the atmosphere during alcoholic fermentation, then maintaining sufficient temperature for several weeks running to facilitate malolactic fermentation. Thus overcrowding too many tanks with insufficient space round them, and intermediary floors and low ceilings should all be avoided. The equipment should be chosen to allow the crop to be treated rapidly with the vinification work well organized.

The outside architecture of a winery is of little importance; it is the inside and the way it is fitted out that matter. The cellar is built round a properly

OAK TANKS

Oak was one of the first materials used for building fermentation tanks, probably after the little tanks built of natural stone and not very deep where the grapes were crushed by trampling them underfoot in fairly thin layers during the fermentation (see Fig. 12.4).

Advantages
Oak is a very old, top quality material. New, it transmits to the wine helpful soluble elements. In a good state of cleanliness and upkeep, it is neutral.

Disadvantages
It is not tight: The wood has to swell first with water before the tank becomes tight. This prolonged soaking is attended by microbial developments on the surface and inside the wood itself. The upper part of the tank and the top chimb, the closing hatch, do not swell much and are often not jointed.

Old wood is a source of contamination and off-tastes. The wine that soaks into the wood in-depth goes bad during the 10 or 11 months the tank remains empty.

Being a bad conductor of heat, wood allows no thermal exchange with the surroundings.

A wooden tank, due to its truncated cone shape, is not suitable for storing wine (this is not the case with a tun).

functional winery; fitting out a winery does not mean just filling up a building with tanks and equipment in relation to the space available. The aesthetic value does not take priority over the importance of being able to conduct vinification rationally and, anyway, functional design is in fact often aesthetic.

Tank Materials

Vinification tanks are built from three different materials: oak, cement, and steel. The cement walls are neutralized by scouring with tartaric acid or they are glass-lined or covered with a protective coating. Steel is glazed or laminated or the alloy is stainless.

The advantages and disadvantages of these materials are analyzed in the following comparative tables. Present-day tendencies appear to be going in the direction:

wood → cement → lined cement → lined steel → stainless steel

Wooden tanks are still being used in small holdings or in certain traditional

Figure 12.4. Winery in the Médoc, with oak tanks (Photo—Pierre Mackiewicz).

wineries. As they wear out, they are gradually being replaced with other materials.

So-called cement tanks are built with reinforced concrete and covered with four successive layers of a cement coating 2 cm thick. The last coating is smoothed and is pure cement. For making red wine, the walls are neutralized quite simply by scouring three times running at intervals of several days with tartaric acid (1 kg in 10 L of water). The use of fluosilicate for this purpose is forbidden since it increases the fluor in the wine.

There should never in fact be any direct contact between the wine and the cement, since, being mixed from a calcium carbonate base, it is attacked by the acidity in the wine to which it transmits high levels of calcium. In reality, the cement is quickly covered with a layer of calcium tartrate unattackable by the wine. In short, in cement tanks, wine is kept between walls of crystallized calcium tartrate, which the wine itself maintains and which get thicker with each vinification.

The products recommended for insulating cement and metal should exhibit the following characteristics:

Totally harmless from a toxicological point of view.

CEMENT TANKS

Advantages
It is thoroughly tight.
Well-scoured or covered with a protective coating, the cement is neutral.
Cement tanks may serve several purposes: vinification and storage.
The walls are easier to clean and disinfect than wood.
The simplicity of building tanks in different shapes allows better usage of the space available. (However, this convenience should not be abused by cramming the maximum volume in the minimum space, see Fig. 12.5.)

Disadvantages
If cement is badly scoured out or badly protected, it will be attacked by the wine, which will be denatured.
The tanks need supervision and upkeep: frequent descaling (at least every 3 or 4 years), fresh scouring.
If the winery is damp, the walls of the tanks get moldy. To avoid this, when building, leave a space underneath them for air to pass, do not build them against a wall, cleanse and ventilate the building.

Important remark.   Sulfur matches should not be burnt inside cement tanks. This error is often made. Fumigating empty containers only applies to wood. Indeed the acid vapors from sulfur dioxide attack the walls forming sulfite and calcium sulfate solubles, and over a period of time, disaggregate it.

Perfect chemical inertia, no influence on composition and taste.

Thoroughly impervious and perfect adherence to the walls.

Shock-resistant, scratch-resistant, elasticity.

Weak adherence of the tartaric salts on the coating, which should have a smooth, even surface.

Resistance to cleaning solutions, to disinfectant products, and to mold.

Finally the coating should be easy to put on and readily renovated.

Coatings for cement walls can be of several types: Glass or ceramic tiles, paraffin, and epoxy resin (araldite) represent the best solutions. Metal tanks can be lined with the following: glazed enamel, vinyl resin, formo-phenolic resin, and epoxy resin.

Several categories of stainless steel exist and we list those sometimes recommended for constructing tanks:

1.   Those stainless steels that are easy to weld with low carbon content stabilized with titanium or columbium (niobium). These steel compounds

Figure 12.5. An example of what not to do: cement tank installation in block form, with tanks on top of each other (Photo Institut Technique du Vin).

generally only resist average corrosion. They contain 17–19% chrome and 8–10% nickel (e.g., Z2CN 18-10).

2. Stainless steel that withstands corrosion better and contains 2–3% molybdenum, 16–18% chrome, and 10–13% nickel (e.g., Z2CND 17-12).

Preference ought to be in favor of the second group of steel, when they are intended for keeping sulfited musts or sulfited acidic white wines over a long period. For the pipes and short-term storage, for instance, for fermentation and vinification or short-term storage of a few hours prior to bottling and even for long-term storage of red wines, certain steels from the first group may be employed.

CAP MANAGEMENT

Red wine vinification may be conducted in open tanks (as it often still is in Burgundy and in the Beaujolais region) or in closed tanks (as is generally done in Bordeaux or in the south of France) with the cap floating (pushed

Advantages

Absolutely tight and round tanks even withstand slight internal pressure.

The wall does not deteriorate (with stainless steel, that is).

Cleanliness is easier to maintain and disinfecting the tanks is possible.

One of the great benefits is thermal exchange with the surrounding air. This is turned to advantage in cooling the fermentation tanks by sprinkling the outside with water.

The tanks can be moved.

Disadvantages

The life of certain interior coatings is not yet known. The exterior painting needs to be maintained.

High initial cost, in particular for stainless steel (it is competitive in large volumes).

Figure 12.6. An ideal solution: winery fitted with stainless-steel tanks (Photo Institut Technique du Vin).

OPEN TANKS

Advantages	Disadvantages
They are especially useful in hot years or for high alcoholic strengths.	The surface in contact with air promotes loss of alcohol which may be as much as 0.5%. It constitutes a danger of oxidation or acetic souring, whence the necessity to crush or punch down the pomace from time to time. This operation is only efficacious, only even possible, in small-capacity tanks.
Fermentation is made easier by better contact with the air. It is faster and goes further. It is finished off completely with higher strengths.	
Fermentation temperature is not so high because of the size of the cooling and evaporation surface.	In cold years, the tank does not "get its heat up," fermentation carries on at a low temperature and may stick.
Control is easier. You can see the tank fermenting and control the state of the pomace.	It is only suitable for short pomace contact. It must be run off before all the carbon dioxide has been given off.
It produces wines that are "made" right away, tasting better, sooner.	
	The press wine exhibits rather higher volatile acidity.
	It is an observed fact that in this kind of pomace contact, malolactic fermentation is retarded.

Conclusion. This is the type of tank best adapted to small family installations, using short pomace contact for wines with a fairly high alcoholic strength. In many regions, this system has practically disappeared in favor of closed tanks.

up and held by the carbon dioxide given off) or with the cap immersed, held down with a grid. The term cap comes from the conical shape of the heaped-up pomace emerging from the open tanks, which is collected together after it has been *pigé*, that is to say, trampled with the feet. There even exist accessories that are used to prevent the cap forming by periodically stirring and holding it in suspension.

Fermentation and extraction do not occur in the same way with different tanks and cap management techniques. The winemaker ought to know the peculiarities of each and take them into account. The tables in this chapter set out the advantages and disadvantages of various systems.

The shapes of wooden tanks vary according to the method of wine storage. In regions where the wine was kept in casks, quality wines or small-scale production areas, the fermentation tanks were of truncated cone shape, open

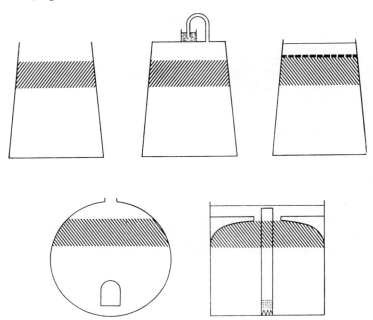

Figure 12.7. Diagrams of various systems for cap management. From top to bottom and from left to right: open tank with floating cap; closed tank with floating cap; open tank with immersed cap; tun used for vinification and for storage; tank with immersed cap using Decaillet's appliance (the central pipe raises the liquid into the small tank at the top, due to pressure exerted by carbon dioxide, but this does not mean automatic washing of the cap).

or closed (see Fig. 12.7). When wine was stored in bulk, fermentation and storage were both carried out in tuns. Today cement or steel tanks suit either use and often the distinction between the fermentation room and the storage cellar is no longer made.

The dimensions of the tanks vary widely. For economical purposes, people tend too often to increase the capacity of the fermentation tanks.

The maximum size limit depends on the uniformity of the different plots in the vineyard, the speed of picking and filling up the tanks, the cooling systems available, and the pressing apparatus. It would seem that in wine cooperatives there are drawbacks in using tanks of more than 300 hL for making red wines, since too large a capacity prevents discrimination between each member's contribution.

The ratio between the width and the height of the tanks has an important incidence on the composition of the wines obtained. This ratio effectively determines the thickness of the pomace and the surface contact with the liquid part. Old-fashioned tanks were broader than they were high and made

CLOSED TANKS

Advantages	Disadvantages
Being tight, this tank avoids any contact with the air, evaporation and acetic spoilage.	Fermentation takes place without air. There can be a risk of fermentation stoppage due to asphyxia of the yeasts.
Long pomace contact can be done with this type of tank.	
In cold years, it keeps its heat in well.	Pumping over with aeration is vital to get proper multiplication of the yeasts (besides, pumping over is beneficial from many other points of view).
It can be large-capacity, allowing considerable quantities to be vinified.	
Malolactic fermentation is easier.	
Press wine is of good quality.	Heating closed tanks is important and, for finishing fermentation, can be dangerous. Cooling systems are vital in the same way.
It is dual purpose and is often used for storage.	

Conclusion. This is a tank system for large-scale installations or for wines that require long pomace contact. This is the one being developed nowadays.

IMMERSED POMACE

Advantages	Disadvantages
There is no contact between the air and the surface of the pomace, but there is with the wine, which is constantly being renewed. In particular, by immersing the pomace, the danger of surface acetification is avoided.	Pomace is compressed under a grid or under the hatch of the tank. It is less permeable. Pockets of carbon dioxide form under the pomace.
The irksome task of crushing the pomace is avoided and open tanks with larger capacities can therefore be employed.	This packing down is contrary to good distribution of the substances in the pomace and limits extraction, whence the need to pump over more frequently to obtain sufficient color and tannin content.
Extraction is less intense if pumping over is not done.	Alcoholic fermentation is somewhat slowed.
Press wine has the same acidity as the free-run wine.	

Conclusion. Generally speaking, open tanks with immersed pomace constitute a step ahead compared with the open tanks and floating pomace. There is no point in punching down the pomace in a closed tank.

extraction easier. Vertical steel tanks raised in the shape of towers, give wines with less body and less color.

Tank fittings should be designed in such a way as to guarantee them to be airtight (upper chimney with jointed hatch and if possible a bubble system to allow the carbon dioxide to escape), to make pumping over and draining as easy as possible (protective screen fixed behind the valves), and to simplify sampling (functional unblockable faucets).

With wooden tanks, the lid can be made tight using cooper's sealing compound around the joints. As for plastering the top of the vats, this can never be more than partially effective in stopping up.

To avoid clogging the valves when pumping over, one of the most efficient methods, unless special stainless steel gratings have been fitted, consists in putting a lattice-work sieve in the form of a right angle made of white wood inside the tank, taking up the whole width of the front face of the tank, backed up with the usual vine-cuttings behind the faucets.

The ordinary tank is in point of fact badly suited to winemaking. It is only a container, whereas it ought really to be a "vinifying machine." We are a long way from the equipment used as "fermentors" in other fermentation industries, designed to allow all the necessary treatments and controls: vapor sterilization, automatic temperature control, aeration, progressive blending of cultures and nutritive factors, and so on, all of which may even be operated by means of an electronic controller.

Doubtless the reasons why vinification is behind in technical equipment can be explained by profitability. Because of the way wineries are dispersed and the seasonal nature of the trade, because too of the economic situation, the price of wine is not high enough to pay the depreciation of such installations. Nevertheless the last few years have seen great strides being made in fermentation equipment. Metal tanks have been responsible for this, because of the security they afford and their versatility.

13

Vinifying Red Wine— Conducting Fermentation

Conducting fermentation means creating those conditions that ensure the yeasts can work properly and get all the sugars completely converted. It also means controlling it by following its evolution in such a way as to be able to intervene in case of deviation. It is vital to prevent bacterial development in the presence of sugars and to have command of the temperature. Sulfiting the vintage, controlling fermentation, and neutralizing calorie output from the fermentation are the main themes in this chapter.

ADDITION OF SULFITE OR SULFUR DIOXIDE

Sulfiting the crushed vintage is a relatively recent practice which has been specially developed since the turn of the century, at first apparently as a remedy against oxidative casse. Although it has not always been used sensibly, sulfiting has marked an important step forward in conducting vinification. Its advantages are due to the many properties of sulfur dioxide set out in the table on the next page.

These numerous properties of SO_2 (when it is used in reasonable quantities) make it an indispensable product in the winemaking process; in fact, it is practically irreplaceable. The sulfiting, however, can have certain adverse consequences especially if it is practiced too lavishly. Its first drawback is doubtlessly delaying or preventing malolactic fermentation in cases when such fermentation is beneficial, thus leading to wines with too high a fixed acidity. Sulfur dioxide is known to be a fixed acid. Another drawback is that it can be the cause of the sulfide tastes that sometimes develop in young wines that

PROPERTIES OF SULFUR DIOXIDE TURNED TO ACCOUNT IN VINIFICATION

Protection against oxidation. Sulfur dioxide protects the vintage against the action of oxygen particularly by obstructing or destroying the oxidases in the grapes, the enzymatic catalysts of oxidation. It mainly concerns the polyphenoloxidases: tyrosinase of sound grapes and laccase of grapes with rot. The SO_2 thus prevents not only oxidative casse, in-depth color deterioration, and a severe form of enzymatic oxidation, but the extenuated forms as well—reduction in the air of the aromatic qualities, loss of freshness, and premature browning.

Inhibition and activation of the yeasts. Sulfur dioxide exercises a polyvalent antiseptic action on the microorganisms: yeasts, acetic bacteria, and lactic bacteria. With sufficient doses, it will inhibit them completely, but with lighter doses, it will exercise a stimulating effect on the activity of the yeasts and boost the transformation of the sugars (see Fig. 13.1).

Selective effect. It is dual. With carefully calculated doses, the SO_2 promotes selection between the different species of yeast. It hinders the multiplication of the nonalcohol-generating yeasts (apiculates, torulopsis, candida) more than the active elliptic yeasts that it tends to assist. It also promotes bacteria/yeast selection, bacteria being, in equal doses, much more sensitive than the yeasts because unlike the yeasts the bacteria are inhibited by SO_2 compounds.

Solvent powers. This term describes the increase in the extraction by the SO_2 caused by the action of this agent on the tissue of the grape cells, especially the skins. In strong doses, SO_2 undeniably makes dissolving the color and the various polyphenols easier. However, with the normal amounts used, the effect is less obvious and no significant improvement in color is observed with normal sulfiting (at least with sound grapes).

have lain too long on their lees. It is easy to avoid these accidents by using sensible doses and by keeping a check on the taste of young wines, then draining immediately with aeration.

The success of sulfiting in vinification and in storing the wines is, above all else, a question of using the right dose.

Getting the Right Dose

This is left to the winemaker's initiative and appreciation. With sulfiting, the winemaker has a means of acting radically, in whichever way he wishes, on the development of vinification and the quality of the wine obtained. The dose used should take into account several factors: the ripeness of the vintage, its state of health, its temperature, its richness in sugars, and particularly its acidity. It is obviously understandable that there are no general rules appli-

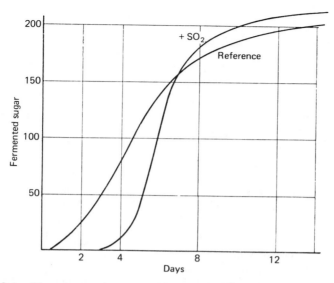

Figure 13.1. The presence of small quantities of sulfur dioxide (5–10 g/hL) delays the start of fermentation but later on speeds up the multiplication of the yeasts and the transformation of the sugars.

cable to every wine area or even within the area, to all the wineries. The table below gives an example of quantities of sulfur dioxide recommended in a temperate climate when malolactic fermentation is required.

Other factors still intervene. For instance, we recommend gradually increasing the amounts used in sulfiting during the course of vinification to compensate for the growing chance of contamination, especially by bacteria, for it is often the last tanks loaded that give finishing and deterioration problems.

AMOUNTS OF SULFUR DIOXIDE THAT SHOULD BE USED[a]

	SO$_2$ (calculated per hectoliter of finished wine)
Healthy vintage, average ripeness, strong acidity	3–5 g
Healthy vintage, very ripe, feeble acidity	5–10 g
Vintage with rot	10–15 g

[a] Red-wine vinification with malolactic fermentation in winemaking areas with temperate climate.

To a large extent, sensible sulfiting takes into account the crop's pH as well. The winemaker needs to know that in order to get the same reaction as 3 g of sulfur dioxide per hectoliter in a vintage at pH 3, he will need 10 g at pH 3.5 and 20 g at pH 3.8. The quantities of sulfiting recommended in the table correspond to vintages at pH 3.2–3.3. It can be understood that in hot regions sulfiting at 10 or 15 g of sulfur dioxide per hectoliter is recommended for healthy crops and at 20 or 25 g for vintages with rot or spoiled (sulfiting calculated on the volume of wine to be obtained).

The Practice of Sulfiting

A proper distribution of sulfur dioxide throughout the whole mass of the vintage, in such a way that every tiny part of it gets its proper dose, requires special arrangements. Too often sulfur dioxide badly distributed does not have optimum effect. Then people are forced to increase the quantities to compensate for poor mixing.

Certain essential rules must be kept in mind, for instance, always use sulfur dioxide in liquid form, not as a gas or even as metabisulfite powder. Then again sulfur dioxide should never be added to the grapes before crushing. This method of treatment causes loss due to evaporation and combination with the solid parts; also sulfur dioxide released during crushing attacks the metal and anyway distribution would be irregular.

Sulfiting should be done immediately after crushing since the first generations of bacteria start to multiply right then before the yeast begins to produce too much alcohol. One method that is currently being used consists of adding to each load as it is being put into the tank, the correct amount of sulfur solution, sprinkling the surface evenly all over. When the tank is full, the contents are pumped over to make them consistent. This method is simple but not very practical because the winemaker is constantly involved in the job and sulfiting may be irregular. When filling up the tank takes several days (this, by the way, ought to be avoided), stronger doses should be used in the beginning to prevent fermentation starting before the tank is completely full.

The most reasonable methods of sulfiting which may be recommended are as follows:

1.   The volume of sulfur solution corresponding to the whole tank is placed, slightly raised above it, in a plastic container with a faucet that allows draining to be regulated. In this way the solution flows by gravity through a flexible pipe while the tank is being filled. The flow can even be operated by the arrival of the crushed vintage itself. With this mechanism, the crush falls onto a lever arm that lets the solution run out. When pumping stops, the

lever-arm springs back squeezing the flow pipe through which the solution arrives. This practical sulfur-feed regulator ensures sulfiting is correctly distributed and is eminently suitable for medium-sized wineries.

2. The most rational method of all is injecting the diluted sulfur solution directly into the crush-pump outlet, at the base of the delivery pipe for the grapes, which may either be plastic or stainless steel. An injection-dosing pump or membrane pump is used, on which the flow rate is variable, synchronized with the movement of the crush-pump, and subject to the crushing operation being in process by means of an electric relay. In this way when the crush pump is running empty, sulfiting stops. This process is more particularly suited to bulk winemaking installations.

SUPERVISING FERMENTATION

Vinification, it must be said again, does not consist of neglecting the vintage once it is in the fermentation tank, but watching everything that happens, supervising, following the transformations through in order to be able to guide them, to anticipate their development, and to intervene immediately whenever necessary.

To be able to conduct fermentation, first of all it is necessary to control the way it works, which means constantly taking must-density and temperature readings at regular intervals. The winemaker's tool kit should include the following instruments: a Baumé aerometer from 0 to 10 degrees, another from 10 to 20 degrees, a densitometer from 0.980 to 1.130, a pocket refractometer, a mercury thermometer from 0 to 45°C, and a thermometer with a quick-reading dial (not to mention the small instruments needed to determine acidity).

Taking the Density

When the vintage arrives, the first thing to do is to check the must's richness in saccharine, either with a densitometer or a refractometer. The saccharometer or mustimeter (reading at the top of the meniscus) generally indicates on the shaft the density and the probable alcoholic strength, produced either directly or by means of a conversion table. This relation is generally only valid for white wines. For red winemaking, the assessment is overestimated. It will only be correct if the must has little sediment and mucilage. Readings obtained from the must of grapes attacked by rot are higher than normal. In fact it will only be correct if the sample taken is really representative of the load or of the tank. If these precautions are not respected, the correction made for temperature will be very subsidiary.

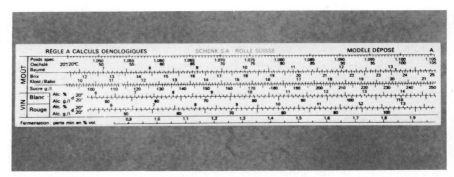

Figure 13.2. Enological slide rule. Registered model by Schenk s.a., Rolle, Switzerland.

In wine cooperatives where the grapes are taken into account in relation to their richness in sugar concentration, only density after crushing the grapes is equitable. Sampling directly from the trucking containers before crushing may give results that are below normal (case when grapes are wet) or, on the contrary, too high (the grapes with most sugar get crushed first).

For red-wine grapes, it is a coincidence that the readings on the Baumé aerometer dipped in the must correspond fairly accurately with the degree of alcohol in the finished wine, at least for the 10–12 degree readings (below 10 degrees they are too high, and above 12 degrees they are short). In any case, these degree extrapolations are only approximate. In the same way, the Oechsle degree (which is the density reading over 1000 and is used in Alsace, Germany, and Switzerland) represents fairly well the weight of alcohol contained in a liter of wine after fermentation (Fig. 13.2).

In the long run, the refractometer does constitute a simple and very practical way of measuring the richness of must. In fact, the refractometer has advantages over the densimeter in that it only needs a few drops of liquid and also it is less sensitive to nonsugar substances, which tend to distort the density readings by increasing the viscosity of the must. However, it is most important that this very restricted sample does represent a sufficient volume of homogeneous must, and every precaution must be taken in this regard. Therefore, readings taken with a refractometer berry by berry have little significance (Fig. 13.3). There are in use in certain wineries refractometers that automatically sample the must and directly indicate its strength.

In the course of fermentation, the fall in density can be followed by means of a densitometer, from a sample taken halfway up the tank from the tasting faucet, after having cleared it with a few liters. It is suggested a graph be made to show the direction in which fermentation is moving and to let the winemaker judge its regularity.

Figure 13.3. Refractometer using a few drops of must to give the projected strength of crop as a direct reading (installation at Château Latour in Pauillac, France).

Taking the Temperature

The temperature of a tank during fermentation is not uniform. It is higher in the mass of pomace and always lower at the bottom of the tank. During the first hours of fermentation, the pomace becomes the center of sudden fluctuations in temperature, sometimes very localized.

The temperature of the must in fermentation sampled from the tasting faucet, which is against the walls of the tank is always lower than in the center. The correct way to take the temperature is to dip the thermometer just under the layer of pomace. Readings taken just after having pumped over, mixing the various parts of the tank together, are bound to be the most accurate.

Controlling temperature requires frequent readings, repeated at regular intervals. These temperatures should be indicated on the same graph as the density (Fig. 13.4). Their development allows the winemaker to calculate when cooling will need to be done. Twice daily readings, morning and evening, as is normal practice, are enough when nothing is happening but do not allow anomalies to be anticipated and prevented. In hot regions, readings are made every 3 hours, night and day. The ideal solution is to have a sounding thermometer with a thermistor that stays in position permanently in the warmest part of the tank just under the layer of pomace and that can be read off any time by relay to a control panel.

THE THERMAL PROBLEM

The main difficulty to be dealt with in vinification comes from the amount of heat that fermentation releases. Overheating only occurs during vinification with a certain mass of grapes. Small volumes of vintage sometimes need to be warmed. On the other hand, more generally, during vinification in large-sized tanks it becomes indispensable to be able to absorb the calorie output

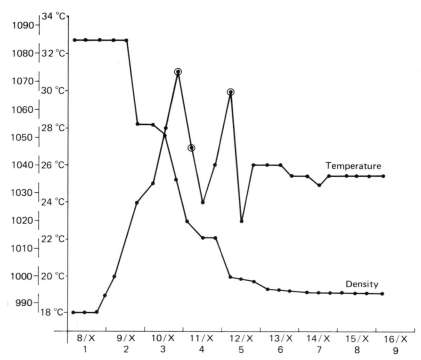

Figure 13.4.   Fermentation control of a tank achieved by taking density and temperature readings three times a day.

in order to prevent the grapes reaching the critical temperature above which fermentation cannot continue. Fermentation accidents, that is to say, stoppages leaving some sugar still in the wine, more often than not, are due to excess temperature. Mastering fermentation temperature means at the same time mastering the fermentation process.

Heat Released by Fermentation

The heat released by alcoholic fermentation of sugar has been measured by any number of research workers. It is proportionate to the amount of sugar fermented. The fermentation of 100 grams of sugar produces roughly 13 calories, that is to say, the amount of heat needed to raise the temperature of a liter of water (or approximately a liter of must) by 13°C. Obviously there can only be heating as long as sugar is being transformed.

According to this law, if some must contains 200 grams of sugar, that is, if it weighs about 11.5%, the increase in temperature during fermentation will theoretically be 26°C so that its temperature should go up, for instance, from 20 to 46°C. This rise would be observed if fermentation were instantaneous, explosive. In reality fermentation lasts several days and there is always some heat loss by diffusion and exchange with the surroundings through the walls of the tank and particularly from the surface. One of the principal ways heat escapes is through the massive emission of gases. Carbon dioxide (more than 40 L for each liter of must in the preceding example) entails the evaporation of a few grams of liquid per liter, which means using up calories. Heat loss by diffusion is difficult to quantify. It depends on several factors: volume of the tanks, what they are made of, layout, ventilation of the winery, outside temperature, length of fermentation, and so on. Wood is a poor conductor; cement and especially metal diffuse heat better.

In fermentation, the amount of heat emitted is not constant. It is particularly intense during the first 2 or 3 days of rapid fermentation. Then, as fermentation begins to slow down, the emitted heat gets lower too and is compensated by spontaneous cooling.

Generally speaking under normal working conditions, the possible increase in temperature is seen to be slightly higher than that number which would represent the strength of the fermented sugar. For instance, taking a must with a potential 10% strength, the rise in temperature will be as much as 12 or 13°C. So that if this vintage reaches the crusher at 20°C, the maximum temperature will border on 32 or 33°C, that is the critical level.

The following two practical rules may be formulated:

1. The possible increase of temperature of a medium-sized tank corresponds approximately to the alcoholic strength that will result, plus 2 or 3%.

2. Each time the temperature of a crushed vintage, having a richness of more than 10%, goes beyond 20°C in temperature, there is good reason to anticipate cooling.

These numerical relations are approximate since they depend on very variable conditions but they can guide the winemaker and allow him to foresee, as soon as the tank is filled, whether the temperature is likely to reach 30°C and whether he may expect to have to cool it down. Also if this seems necessary, cooling must be started without waiting for the temperature to reach the critical level. This means, in fact, preventing the temperature from exceeding the dangerous level instead of trying to bring it back down after it has gone beyond it. In that case a lot of yeasts will already be dead and cooling will not really be of much help.

Methods of Cooling

Briefly this involves using up calories. All-round cooling but especially using cold water or even ice are among the more or less efficacious or practical methods that can be used.

It's no use banking on pumping over with air alone to provide cooling. This is unlikely to give more than 1°C loss by the evaporation provoked by it, still it is by no means useless since it activates the yeasts by aerating them and helps make the temperature more uniform throughout the tank. The system, which consists of loading several tanks at the same time, adding fresh vintage onto the vintage that is heating up, prolongs fermentation in the tanks but is not very efficient in keeping down the maximum temperature. Thoroughly ventilating the winery and particularly trying to get the utmost benefit from the cool night air are recommended. On the contrary, sulfiting to arrest fermentation while the temperature goes down is open to criticism. However, this technique of fermenting in two stages has been practiced in certain wine areas in hot climates.

One makeshift method even consists of running out a part of a hot tank into a cistern buried in the ground or into an empty tank or again into casks. After it has cooled down, the must is pumped back into the tank, where the pomace has remained.

Another palliative is to mix into the vintage a certain percentage of wine as soon as the tank has been loaded. This wine acts by delaying the start of fermentation, by slowing it down, and by absorbing some of the calories itself.

These different procedures, easy enough to carry out in a small-sized operation, are not enough if the temperature of the vintage is high or the must is rich and in a general way when sugaring is done if the winery is sizable. Water-cooling apparatus is essential.

Rather than pipe-coils or "flags" sunk inside the tanks, exterior cooling systems through which the must to be reduced in temperature is circulated are to be preferred. There are two types: the horizontal cooler using tubes with cold water running over them (see Fig. 13.5) or a pipe system immersed in a tank of chilled water. These require a considerable volume of cold water at a maximum temperature of 15–18°C. The water can be recovered and cooled in its turn by evaporation in ventilated towers. Appliances that ensure temperature exchange and, at the same time, cool the water by ventilation can be employed.

One of the great advantages of metal tanks is that they allow cooling without moving the must by running or spraying water over the outside (see Fig. 13.6). In this second case, cooling is augmented if the tanks are situated outdoors or in a well-ventilated building. Cooling can be increased even more by improving evaporation, for instance, by covering the tank with a tarpaulin

Figure 13.5. Tubular cooler using trickling water. The fermenting must is circulated through the pipes in closed circuit with the tank during pumping over.

that is kept wet. However, all these systems based on evaporation will only be efficient in a dry climate when the hygrometry of the air is below 60%.

When ice is available, the water in the tanks can be kept at low temperatures and cooling is faster. Even ice blocks wrapped in plastic bags can be used, sinking them in the little pumping-over tank. The water is emptied out once the ice has melted. One kilogram of ice allows 1 hL of wine to be cooled by 1°C. Therefore, it requires 1 metric ton of ice to cool a 200-hL tank by 5°C.

The use of a refrigerating plant to cool the must can only be advantageous for lowering the temperature below that of the water available (low kilocalories). In vinification mostly high kilocalories are used and cooling by means of water is more rational. However, a refrigerator can allow the water to be cooled in closed circuit.

It will be seen that a number of possible solutions to the thermal problem of vinification exist. It is vital for each installation to have a sufficient means of cooling, adapted to its particular working conditions, otherwise the success of vinification can only be at best the result of a series of lucky accidents.

DEALING WITH STUCK FERMENTATION

When the temperature is not under control, cases of stuck fermentation are not unusual. If the temperature of a tank is high and aeration insufficient, the

Figure 13.6. Cooling stainless-steel tanks by letting water run over the outside casing. An electro-valve (visible on the above plate) operated by a thermometric probe permanently fixed under the pomace automatically releases the sprinkler as soon as the programmed temperature is reached. Pumping over is necessary to make the temperature uniform through the tank during cooling.

yeasts do not transform all the sugars and the wine may stay sweet. When fermentation begins to slow down, which is always a sign that yeasts are dying, this is noted on the density development chart. The winemaker has to intervene immediately and not just hope the fermentation will start again of its own accord; the chances are slim.

As soon as a tank shows signs of slowing, whatever the amount of sugar left unfermented, it must be drained. It is too dangerous to leave it on the pomace; lactic souring is the logical outcome of such a situation. It is indeed an experimental fact that fermentation restarts better once the wine is separated from the pomace. Draining will be carried out with aeration and a light sulfiting, say, 3–4 g of sulfur dioxide per hectoliter in order to delay the appearance of the malolactic bacteria. This is one of the rare cases of racking where sulfiting is recommended.

Often fermentation starts again spontaneously with the help of aeration, of slight cooling, and the stimulating effect of the sulfiting on the yeasts. The press wine often referments better than the free-run wine. These fermentations should be controlled by frequent analysis. Normally they continue until the sugar is expended. The slightest increase in volatile acidity would reveal bacterial intervention, which must be prevented at all costs.

In a few cases, there is no spontaneous revival of fermentation after draining and it is necessary to inoculate with active yeasts. A must in fermentation should never be used for this purpose since it would add yeasts not accustomed to alcohol and would increase the sugar level. Rather, a wine whose fermentation has terminated normally should be added. In such a case, press wine should be used with great prudence because of the dangers of bacterial contamination. A light addition of ammonium salts (5 g/hL) or of thiamine (50 mg/hL) makes further multiplication of the yeasts easier. The most favorable temperature is 20°C (not 25°C as it is sometimes said). In the cool season, it will be necessary to use a *Saccharomyces oviformis* culture to restart, using progressive amplification, it is a delicate task requiring patience. It is often better to wait for a spontaneous revival at the end of spring. A count of the live yeasts or bacteria as well as the development of the volatile acidity show the way to operate. Careful sulfiting will prevent any deviation.

14

Vinifying Red Wine— Conducting Extraction During Pomace Contact

Red wine is a macerated wine. It is made up of substances extracted from the juice of the grapes and also those found in the solid part, the matter from the pulp, skins and seeds. Maceration is a fractional extraction. Among the constituent parts of the grape, only those that are useful, endowed with pleasant aromas and a pleasant flavor, need to be dissolved. In the skins and the seeds, there are substances with a herbaceous taste, vegetable, pungent, bitter, substances with a leafy or greenery odor; you only need chew a few skins or seeds to prove it for yourself. These products should never be used for making good wine, so extraction needs to be gentle and must be conducted in such a way as to avoid them being dissolved.

Extraction gives red wine its specific characteristics: its color, tannins, extract constituents, and aroma. Everything that differentiates red wine from white, to the eye and on the palate, is the result of the phenomena of extraction.

LAWS OF EXTRACTION

The conversion from grape into wine is the result of a complex set of separations: excretion, dissolving, solubilization, extraction, diffusion, infusion, and expression, with the help of the mechanical operations of crushing, grinding, washing, pressing, stirring up, and the occurrence of alcoholic fermentation.

INFLUENCE OF THE FERMENTATION TEMPERATURE ON COLOR AND ON THE TANNINS

	Polyphenol Index	Color Intensity[a]
Fermentation at Constant Temperature		
20°C	44	0.71
25°C	48	0.87
30°C	52	0.96
Fermentation at Increasing Temperature		
20–37°C (average temp. 29.5°C)	52	1.21
25–37°C (average temp. 32.6°C)	60	1.43

This experiment by Sudraud shows the influence of the temperature of fermentation, in particular the maximum obtained, on the dissolving of the phenolic compounds. The rise in temperature increases the levels of total phenolic compounds and color intensity.

[a] Color intensity is the sum of the optical densities measured at 420 and 520 μm.

To study the factors of extraction, distinction should be made between those that act on the dissolving of the various extract substances and those that influence their distribution throughout the mass. To this should be added the reactions of binding, insolubilization, precipitation, crystallization, and flocculation. The first group of factors tends to increase the substances from the extraction, while the last group tends to reduce them.

Dissolving means the extraction of a solid substance from the cell, generally the vacuoles, into a liquid state. Dissolving is facilitated by the mechanical action on the grape tissues and breaking up of the solid particles according to the intensity of the crushing. Then it is assisted by the death of the tissues and the cells under the influence of anaerobiosis and the presence of alcohol. Finally temperature and the length of contact with the solid parts, that is to say, the length of pomace contact, are important factors in dissolving.

Dissolving is obviously localized around the level of the pomace and the interstitial liquid is the most highly concentrated part in all the constituents. Distribution throughout the mass is ensured by internal movement but particularly by the circulation of the fermenting wine through the layer of pomace (pumping over), which renews the liquid in contact with the skins and the seeds several times over. The operation of punching down the pomace and letting it float back up accentuates distribution.

The different factors do not act in the same way on the various substances to be dissolved, in particular on the polyphenols. The red anthocyanins are

INFLUENCE OF DESTEMMING AND THE LENGTH OF
POMACE CONTACT ON COLOR AND TANNINS

	Polyphenol Index	Color Intensity
Vintage not stemmed		
run off at 1020	54	0.74
run off at 1000	54	0.75
6 days after 1000	80	0.83
20 days after 1000	100	0.95
Destemmed vintage		
run off at 1020	35	0.83
run off at 1000	37	0.86
6 days after 1000	52	0.88
20 days after 1000	65	1.02

This experiment by Sudraud shows the tannins surrendered by the stems and the effect of the stems on the reduction in color. The presence of stems introduces into the wine colorless phenolic compounds that are different from the point of view of their makeup and flavor from those found in the skins and seeds. This experiment also shows the progression of the dissolving of the phenolic compounds when pomace contact is prolonged. The color increases proportionately less than the tannin content.

extracted rapidly, especially for certain varieties when the grape is very ripe, simply due to the crushing operation or the short extraction that takes place before the start of fermentation. The homogenizing pumping over of the tank accentuates this dissolving. The other phenolic compounds are dissolved more slowly. This is why short pomace contact for very ripe grapes gives a fairly well-colored wine but a not very astringent one with a low polyphenol index.

There is, generally speaking, an improvement in the taste of young wines by all these measures taken to help extract the color without increasing the tannin level. Aroma and fruitiness are generally in inverse proportion to the level of phenolic compounds. However, making wines for laying down, good storage, gustatory development, and color permanence requires higher concentrations of tannins. In fact, after a few months or a few years, the color of the wine no longer relates to the presence of red anthocyanins in the grape (which will have largely disappeared) but rather to the color of the tannins.

INFLUENCE OF PUMPING OVER ON COLOR AND TANNINS

	Tanks with Floating Pomace			
	Without Pumping Over		With Pumping Over[a]	
	Polyphenol Index	Color Intensity	Polyphenol Index	Color Intensity
After 3 days	39	0.83	46	0.93
After 4 days	43	0.87	48	0.98
After 10 days	45	0.89	52	1.04

This experiment by Sudraud shows the enrichment in color and in tannins provided by pumping over at the beginning of fermentation.

[a] The tank was pumped over twice, on the first and third day.

On the other hand, the anthocyanins have very little flavor. The proportion of tannins conditions the taste and the life span. For all wines that owe their quality to a certain degree of aging, successful vinification is based on trying to make a compromise between the need to ensure richness in tannins and the opposite need for a certain suppleness and a certain fruity quality.

The intensity of extraction depends on the type of wine. It also depends on the grape variety. Extraction is cut short for ordinary wines, in areas where the soil environment is not favorable. It is generally longer for the more thoroughbred varieties in quality wine areas.

All that is extracted from the skins and the seeds of the grapes is far from representing the totality of the colored pigments and tannins in them. Wine only extracts 20 or 30%. In grapes there is a large proportion of insolubles and wine can never be the whole of the grape.

With prolonged pomace contact, the color of the wine may diminish because the anthocyanins settle on the seeds, the skins, the tannins, and eventually on the stems, and color them. In addition, the yeasts absorb the anthocyanins and drag them down into the lees. Finally, the reducing reactions during fermentation diminish the coloration of the anthocyanins, at least temporarily.

Many other substances are extracted during maceration: nitrogenous substances (the total nitrogen content may double if pomace contact is prolonged), polysaccharides, pentoses, mineral matter, etc. The odorous substances from the skins are quickly distributed. In a few hours in a weak alcoholic solution, the flavor is extracted from the skins.

LENGTH OF POMACE CONTACT

The length of time pomace contact takes is one of the first factors to influence extraction. This is one of the most variable of wine characteristics between one area and another. It needs to be decided by the winemaker in relation to prevailing conditions: the quality of the grapes and the type of wine being made, and not decided once and for all. The table on pomace contact conditions may be helpful. Pomace contact exercises an influence on body, on the greater or less astringent taste, on the evolution and life of the wine, and the ease with which malolactic fermentation takes place.

As an overall framework, let us consider three possible draining times:

1. Before fermentation is over, when the wine still contains sugar.
2. Immediately after fermentation is terminated, as soon as the wine has no significant quantities of sugar left. This is called draining "hot."
3. Finally by prolonging extraction for several days after the end of fermentation. This is called draining "cold."

The first method, short pomace contact, lasting 3 or 4 days, is generally recommended for table wines, wines to be drunk young or coming from grape varieties that are rich in tannin or from crops grown in hot regions. Racking is therefore carried out at densities of 1010 or 1020. This is done when what is being looked for most of all is that supple character and lightness needed for products intended to be drunk young, when hoping to relieve the commonplace character of a grape variety.

The second method is best suited to wines for laying down or wines that, in great years, come from a very ripe vintage or wines that were made in open tanks. The third method is best for wines intended for slow aging and in years or areas of average maturity.

Exact laws are, after all, difficult to lay down within a given area. The length of pomace contact has to be adapted to the type of wine that is being sought as well as to the conditions of the particular year. Indeed, it must be admitted that in the same winery each tank-load has its own particular problem. The polyphenol index reading and constant tasting during vinification help the winemaker choose the best moment to drain (see Fig. 14.1).

DRAINING

This operation, also called racking or drawing off, consists of pumping the wine out of the fermentation tank into some other container where it will be finished or where it will be stored. The wine that runs out from the fermen-

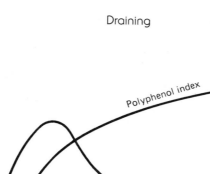

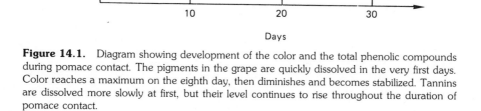

Figure 14.1. Diagram showing development of the color and the total phenolic compounds during pomace contact. The pigments in the grape are quickly dissolved in the very first days. Color reaches a maximum on the eighth day, then diminishes and becomes stabilized. Tannins are dissolved more slowly at first, but their level continues to rise throughout the duration of pomace contact.

tation tank is the free-run or free-draw wine or pull wine (*vin de goutte*). It is also called *grand vin* or *vin de fleur*. The drained pomace is taken out of the tank and pressed. The containers that receive the free-run wine can be, according to circumstances, wooden casks, tuns, or other tanks.

Since it is essential to maintain sufficient temperature in order to let fermentation terminate, it is advisable to drain into receptacles of a certain size. In point of fact when wine is drained into small-capacity casks, it quickly levels down to the surrounding temperature and biological development is interrupted: Terminating alcoholic fermentation and especially getting malolactic fermentation started are all the more difficult to achieve the lower the temperature is. Controlling the end of fermentation is easier with greater volume. Inoculating by mixing tanks in different stages of evolution is also beneficial.

CONDITIONS DETERMINING LENGTH OF POMACE CONTACT

Long Pomace Contact	Short Pomace Contact
High production yield.	Production per hectare is low.
Grapes not ripe.	Very ripe grapes.
Acidity fairly high.	Low acidity.
Grapes with little color and moderately tannic varieties.	Grapes very rich in tannin.
Sound grapes.	Grapes partly rotted or spoiled.
Normal sulfiting.	Low sulfiting or none at all.
Closed tanks.	Open tanks.
Fermentation temperature low.	Fermentation temperature high.
Type of wine for laying down, full-bodied, improves with aging in barrel or bottle.	Type of wine to be consumed quickly, supple, easy to drink, does not improve with age.

Racking into a tank gives other advantages: (1) It gives more homogeneous units, because the first casks drawn from a fermentation tank do not have the same constitution in color, in polyphenols, or in the amount of lees as the last. (2) It is easier to separate off the large lees. (3) It simplifies blending.

Naturally this way of draining supposes the tanks are full and hermetically sealed because the wine may have to stay in the tank for as long as several weeks to finish off.

Putting newly made wine into tanks, however, raises a few difficulties the winemaker needs to be aware of. First clarity is not as good as in casks because sedimentation and the movements within the wine are slower. Second, the taste is not as agreeable either: The wine stays more gaseous and is more likely to get "reduced" odors of hydrogen sulfide, lees, and so on.

Racking fermentation tanks is generally done with aeration, letting the wine run out by gravity into a small tank from which it is drained by pumping. This aeration is beneficial for the subsequent development of the wine.

Then again, generally speaking, sulfiting should not be practiced at the time of racking in order to avoid impeding the finishing fermentations. Malolactic fermentation, especially, would be jeopardized if sulfur dioxide were added and might be delayed or even prevented altogether. There are three exceptions where sulfiting may be carried out when emptying the tank: when volatile acidity is already high under the influence of a bacterial attack, when the fermentation hasn't finished, and if there is a risk of oxidative casse.

Figure 14.2. Photo of manual detanking being done from outside the tank. The pomace extraction is made easier by the tilted floor of the tank. The pomace is conveyed by worm-screw to the press cage (Photo P. Jacquet).

Testing for Oxidative Casse

If the vintage includes a certain percentage of grapes with mold, it is advisable to carry out a test for oxidative casse before draining, by exposing the wine to air to see how it reacts. Half fill a glass and leave it exposed to the air for 12 hours, from evening until morning. If during this time the wine changes color, if it goes cloudy and if it leaves a deposit in the glass, if it has lost that brightness of hue and especially if its color has taken on a brownish tint, if it exhibits on its surface an iridescent film, then it is liable to casse and it would be dangerous to handle it exposed to air. It must be treated by sulfiting. It has previously been determined that a dose of sulfuric acid from 3 to 5 g/hL, generally prevents oxidative casse in new wines. This dose can be repeated later if necessary.

There is no object in prolonging the oxidative casse tests beyond 12 or 15 hours. The changes that are wrought with exposure to air after only 24 or 48 hours would not be serious in normal working conditions where continuous aeration is avoided.

PRESSING

The fermented pomace is removed by means of a fork through the doors of the tanks or else with a conveying worm-screw (pomace-extractor). Attempts have been made to simplify this laborious manual operation by using self-

ANALYTICAL COMPOSITION OF THE FREE-RUN WINE AND ITS CORRESPONDING PRESS WINE

	Free-Run Wine	Press Wine
Alcoholic strength	12.0%	11.6%
Reducing sugars	1.9	2.6
Reduced extract	21.2	24.3
Total acidity	3.23	3.57
Volatile acidity	0.35	0.45
Total nitrogen (mg)	285	370
Polyphenol index	35	68
Anthocyanins (mg)	330	400
Tannins (g)	1.75	3.20

The press wine is richer in all the ingredients of the extract, also in colloidal substances, and in mineral matter.

emptying tanks or ones that facilitate "depomacing" by having a tilted floor and larger diameter doors (see Fig. 14.2). Pumps also exist that are capable, after the whole tank has been stirred, of transferring the mixture into a separator or even, after draining, of evacuating the solid pomace up to the press. This type of equipment gives rough handling and is not compatible with producing quality wines. If the pomace needs to be moved to a fixed press station, it is best to choose the conveyor-belt solution with a traveling apron that leaves the pomace intact and does not grind it up, rather than the worm-screw.

The pomace removed from the tank is pressed in such a way as to extract all the wine it contains. This wine is called the press wine and represents about 15% of the wine harvested. It is made up of the interstitial wine, not very different from the free-run wine (*vin de goutte*) and easy to keep apart, and the wine that has been soaked up by the tissues of the pomace, which takes longer to extract. In this way the first press wine (10% of the total volume), of higher quality, is generally separated from wine obtained from the last press (5%) after crumbling and digging over the pomace. Automatic crumbling does squeeze the pomace out dry but also promotes deleterious oxidation. Before beginning the pressing operation, mechanical draining can be used.

The different types of presses will be described in relation to vinifying white wine. They play an important part in determining the quality of the finished product. What must be avoided as much as possible is oxidation during pressing. Utmost cleanliness of the receiving tanks is vital to give protection against acetic spoilage.

It may be said of press wine that it is a concentrate of all the constituent elements, except alcohol. It is the typical extraction wine. The table on free-run and press wine gives an example of its composition. If it comes from good grape varieties used in quality wine areas, the first press wine is rich in aromatic elements and noble tannins and is therefore beneficial, even indispensable, for blending. More commonplace wines tend to give dominant herbaceous characteristics and unpleasant astringency and their press wines are discarded.

The use of press wine where quality wines are concerned is subject to an analysis of its bacterial status (volatile acidity) and its tannin composition and to a tasting test. Four possible situations may be encountered after pressing:

1. The press wine is sound, there are no excess reducing sugars, no malic acid, and the tasting is acceptable. It may be used for mixing with the free-run wine without waiting or else during blending.
2. The press wine is sound but too astringent, "rough." After being left to settle over the winter, it will be racked, fined, and filtered before being used. Its clarification is considerably eased by incorporating pectolitic enzymes called clarifying enzymes, used immediately after pressing.
3. The press wine still has some sugar left and some malic acid. It will be kept under observation until it is terminated. Blending it will only be done with reserve.
4. The press wine has high volatile acidity or an off taste. It will definitely be discarded.

TECHNICAL EVOLUTION BY AREA

Where vinification is concerned, reference is often made to what are called the traditional methods that have created the type of wine and given it its reputation. Nevertheless present-day techniques are in permanent evolution. Changes are slow even though over the last few years they have speeded up, but it is necessary to look back to see what progress has been made. It is the same in all the wine-growing areas.

The direction developments are taking in red-wine making is determined by the tendency not to crush the grapes so much, to use more hermetically sealed containers, and to reduce pomace contact time. The progress made in conducting fermentation keeps step with controlling its temperature. Finally, people are looking for red wines with lower acidity thanks to the general introduction of malolactic fermentation.

METHODS OF VINIFICATION BY WINE AREAS IN FRANCE[a]

	Beaujolais	Bordeaux	Burgundy	Côtes du Rhône	Midi Languedoc	Touraine
Crushing	At present hardly used or not at all	Generalized	Generalized	Done more or less according to method of vinification	Generalized	Not done or done very little
Destemming	Not done	Generalized	Almost completely	May or may not be practiced	More or less done but not on Aramon	Done in the vineyard by hand
Sulfiting the vintage in g/hL	Previously 5–10. Maceration carbonique O.	3–10 according to maturity and sanitary state	5–10 according to sanitary state	10–20 in classical vinification with maceration carbonique 5	10–25, tending to be reduced.	0–7 according to sanitary state
Method of fermentation	Closed tank	Closed tank, floating cap	Open tank, floating cap or sometimes submerged	More and more closed tank	Closed tank, floating cap	Open tank, floating cap covered by tarpaulin
Pumping over	Not done	Several times	Little practiced—crushing pomace	Little practiced	Once at the start and in case of stuck fermentation	In general not practiced
SCT or time of fermentation on pomace	About 1030, after 3 or 4 days SCT	Great wine 10–25 days. Medium wine 6–8 days.	About 1000 after 6 days SCT	After 4 or 5 days vatting, or 10 or 15 days extraction.	About 1010 after 3 or 4 days	After 12–20 days SCT
Malo-lactic fermentation	Always sought	Always sought	Always sought	Always sought	More and more looked for	Always sought
Storage	In tanks or "pieces"	In tanks or casks	In "pieces"	In tanks or tuns	In tanks or tuns	In casks

[a] This only shows general tendencies, since there are many exceptions.

182

The method currently being used in the Bordeaux area where great wines are concerned is as follows: Crushing is light and destemming general and total; mean sulfiting used per hectoliter of wine is about 5 g; pumping over is done several times; the ideal temperature is set around 28–30°C; pomace contact is continued beyond the end of fermentation and it is tasting that decides when the wine will be drained. This is done into tanks to control malolactic fermentation, considered indispensable. It is observed that this type of vinification can be used by the majority of vineyards throughout both hemispheres wherever top grape varieties are grown and where people are looking to make quality wines that behave well during aging.

The method used in Burgundy, perhaps a little less codified, comprises: eliminating 70 or 80% of the stems and mechanical crushing as part of the pomace contact process ; sulfiting on the order of 50 g of sulfur dioxide per ton of vintage; stirring up every day in the tanks in fermentation by means of crushing or pumping over; regulation of fermentation temperatures trying to reach an optimum between 30 and 32°C; trying to promote malolactic fermentation.

The table on the previous page compares the techniques used in the various French wine areas.

15

Vinifying Red Wine—Recent Techniques in Use

Preceding chapters have dealt with the basic phenomena and vinification techniques most commonly practiced. These are the most widely known and might be described as classical. Properly conducted these methods are sufficiently flexible to allow good wines to be made whatever style is wanted. This is the standard method. However, there are other possible vinification systems, some of only recent invention. For instance, one way is to try to rationalize industrial vinification, cutting out all the manual tasks involved, centralizing operational control, monitoring fermentation, and processing vinification in one large tank equipped to put at the winemaker's disposal all the necessary controls and means of intervention (instead of in a large number of small tanks, which would disperse supervision). This is the continuous vinification principle. There also exist individual tanks fully equipped in the same way to facilitate certain manual tasks in winemaking.

Maceration carbonique can equally well be practiced on whole grapes to obtain wines possessing special aromatic characteristics as well as greater suppleness due to a reduction in the concentrations of tannin and acidity. The winemaker can even, if he wishes, separate the vintage by heating, keeping the extraction phase apart from the fermentation phase and extracting the maximum soluble substances from the skins. But not all innovation is progress.

As soon as an original technique appears or a new piece of equipment enables some new method to be developed, some innovators try to apply it to every wine and to every case in practice. Thus it has been suggested that thermovinification ought to be generalized or that all wines should be made using maceration carbonique. In reality, certain techniques give good results

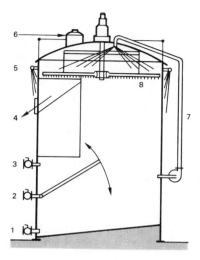

Figure 15.1. Diagram of continuous fermentation equipment: 1, seeds discharge; 2, wine outlet with adjustable level; 3, input for crushed and sulfited vintage; 4, pomace discharge; 5, water-spray cooling nozzles; 6, expansion dome for use as storage tank; 7, pumping-over column; 8, rotating rake for pomace extraction.

in one particular situation but are quite unsuitable in others. Each has its own area of application and its limits.

The recently adapted processes described in this chapter do not apply to all wines. It would be nonsense to want to base all winemaking on these principles alone. Classic winemaking remains the fundamental method but these techniques can have advantageous applications in a limited number of cases.

CONTINUOUS FERMENTATION

Continuous fermentation has arisen from research into more rational installations for the making of red wine in bulk with good work organization methodology. The winemaking industry is very different from other fermentation industries. Its seasonal character sets labor problems that are becoming increasingly difficult to solve and often makes it hard to justify all the heavy investment in the elaborate equipment necessary. In the case of "bulk wine making" applied to a single style and a single quality of wine, continuous fermentation constitutes a practical solution to these problems.

How These Installations Work

A continuous fermentor (see Fig. 15.1) generally consists of a cement tank, or better still, one of stainless steel, sometimes plastic-lined, with a capacity range between 800 and 4000 hL, set up outside the vinification cellar. An inlet nozzle situated on the lower part of the apparatus enables the vintage to be fed in. The quantities introduced each day must correspond in volume to an equal discharge of wine, pomace, and seeds. The wine runs out through an outlet adjustable for height, fixed on the upper part of the apparatus at the bottom of the pomace. A diametrical spout, a sort of grille with a large filtering surface, or else a lateral strainer, allows the wine to flow out by gravity and retains the solid matter.

The pomace is automatically extracted by means of a worm-screw fed by a revolving rake, adjustable in height, that levels the surface around its axis. The pomace falls directly into the trough of a continuous press. The shape of the bottom of the tower simplifies accumulation of a part of the seeds which are emptied out every day. That way any astringency, which over a period of time the dissolving of their tannins might impart, is avoided. A washing system that sprays the pomace is incorporated. On the outside the tower has rings of water vaporizers all round it that are used for preventing rises in temperature. The crushed vintage is sulfited as it comes out of the crusher by means of an adjustable feed-regulator pump. Just as in traditional vinification, frequent density and temperature readings at different levels allow the transformation of the sugar into alcohol to be followed. It is up to the winemaker to determine how long he wants the extraction from pomace to last by changing the input and output rates.

In spite of the restrictions imposed by the volume involved, working the installation is fairly flexible. In fact even though the fermentation is continuous, introducing the vintage and draining the wine are necessarily, more or less, discontinuous. The pomace and the wine can be withdrawn as and when the vintage arrives or, better still, a volume of wine representing a third or a quarter of the container capacity can be drained in the morning, then, at the end of the day, all the pomace that has been pushed up by the vintage pumped in and pressure from the carbonic gas, can be extracted.

Advantages of Continuous Fermentation

Continuous fermentation saves labor as the result of centralizing in a single work station operations normally spread across a large number of tanks and especially as the result of the automation and mechanization of numerous tasks, in particular extracting the pomace.

Economy in space and material is also achieved. For instance in classic vinification, about 7500 hL of tank space is required to make 5000 hL of wine because of the volume of pomace and the expansion of the fermentation. In continuous fermentation, a 5000-hL container space is enough.

Extraction of the pomace and draining the wine being done from a fixed position leads to a reduction in the number of appliances normally needed in a winery—pumps, pomace conveyors, and so forth. Moreover, the continuous fermentor is installed out of doors so it does not take up room inside the building.

A number of comparisons with fermentation temperatures taken during vinification tank by tank indicate deviations of 5–7°C in favor of continuous fermentation in a metal tank, without the cooling device even being turned on. This lower temperature arises from the continual replacement of the hot wine discharged by fresh vintage and also a better thermal exchange due to the metal.

Experience likewise shows that malolactic fermentation is facilitated and that, everything else being equal, it begins and ends more quickly with continuous fermentation than with classic vinification. The reasons for this are as follows: acid levels are made uniform; the lactic bacteria are more evenly distributed; the better species, resistant to acidity, are selected; the fact that from beginning to end some amount of the first wine remains in the apparatus; probably sulfiting in equal doses is less efficient, the sulfited vintage being immediately in contact with the must in fermentation. Disappearance of malic acid if it came about inside the system would constitute a risk of lactic souring. It is prevented by shortening the fermentation period, by sulfiting in gradually increasing doses, and by controlling the evolution of total acidity and of volatile acidity every day.

The disadvantages of this system come more from operating the apparatus incorrectly: mixing up different qualities of vintage and standardizing the wine produced; the impossibility to diversify or select; tendency to cram the apparatus so that it receives excess tonnage in vintage every day. As far as industrial vinification is concerned, it may be considered that continuous fermentors constitute a certain technical progress for operations dealing with large volumes of table wines.

VINIFICATION IN SPECIALLY EQUIPPED TANKS

Traditional vinification raises the objection that it is conducted in tanks designed simply to be storage vessels rather than to make the various operations and controls easy to carry out. Very real improvements have been made in tank equipment. Conditioned metal tanks are provided with heating systems using electric resistances or exchangers incorporated in their design plus cooling systems using cold water sprinkled over the outside, which adds evaporation to the effect of the trickling water. Thermal control may be manual or it may be automated. A thermocouple permanently fitted under the pomace in the highest temperature zone controls the opening of an electro-magnetic valve at a given temperature which sprinkles the outside of the tank casing. When the temperature returns to normal, the electromagnetic valve cuts off the water. These tanks may also include pumping-over systems that regularly spray the surface of the pomace with a special sprinkler or antisplash nozzle.

Processes that allow repeated pumping-over during fermentation, known as "vino-washers" or "autovinificators," work off the pressure inside the tank from the carbon dioxide release. By means of a valve which stops the gas from escaping until a certain pressure has built up, the must is forced up into a small tank at the top, then from there the must pours out all at once in-undating the cap as soon as the back-pressure valve opens. By the aeration it provokes, the action of this device regulates fermentation and keeps the temperature down. Wines with better color, but often with excess astringency as well, are obtained. It is true that the duration of this automatic operation can be limited to counteract this drawback.

Extracting the pomace from the fermentation tanks, a tough manual op-eration, can be made easier by using "automatic detanking" systems using so-called self-emptying tanks (see Fig. 15.2). The tilted floor of the tanks includes a wide opening blocked by a movable hatch that can be handled with complete security. A horizontal tank that can be tilted forward by jacking it from behind has also been conceived. The pomace that is still wet slides by its own weight into the press hopper placed under the tank or it is trans-ferred to the press by means of a worm-screw conveyor.

With a view to speeding up extraction, certain appliances take the pomace during the fermentation and mix it with the must by pumping it down to the bottom of the tank. This "recycling" gets the maximum coloring matter ex-tracted in a few hours. The average time in the tank is reduced by 24 hours. However, this process of accelerated extraction does not conform with usual vinification methods and calls for some reservation. Paradoxically, in recy-cling, it is, in fact, circulation of the solid matter that has been chosen which can only be done by crumbling and mixing with the liquid before pumping. The slow, gentle extraction by the washing operation is replaced by rapid mechanical extraction, which is bound to alter the ratio between the quantities of substances extracted.

Another contrivance involves a cylindrical-shaped, horizontal tank fitted at each end with a grille to retain the pomace. The tank is supported on two bearings and turns slowly lengthwise at low speed. The inside is fitted with spiral separations in the form of an Archimedes' screw, which is used to break down, split and batter the pomace, then discharge it from the front once the liquid has been drained. The tank is raised up over a drainer and a press. Experiments have also been made with vertical tanks rotating on a pivot

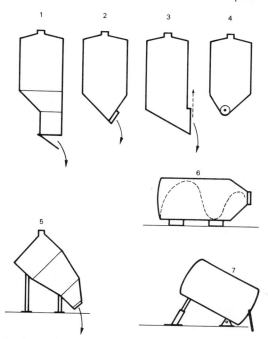

Figure 15.2.   Diagram of various tanks enabling pomace to be extracted without manual handling. 1,2,3,5, self-emptying gravity tanks; 4, tank emptied by means of a worm-screw incorporated into a channel at the bottom of the tank; 6, rotating tank giving internal mixing and pomace discharge; 7, tip-tank raised from underneath by means of a jack.

placed halfway up the cylinder which reinforce extraction and make it easier to get the pomace out.

However, it must be acknowledged that a device that increases extraction by mechanical methods applied to the pomace and that tries to speed up the transformations in vinification to a few hours, rarely leads to an improvement in quality.

VINIFICATION WITH MACERATION CARBONIQUE

This term covers techniques of vinification without crushing the grapes. It consists of putting the bunches whole into a closed tank with a carbon dioxide atmosphere. In these conditions the whole grapes undergo intracellular fermentation or autofermentation. Crushing and pressing only intervene after a period of extraction. This form of vinification without, or with only partial, crushing was in use in certain areas long ago. At a period when grapes were not processed mechanically, crushing could hardly ever be complete. Sometimes in fact the grapes were just poured straight into the fermentation tanks without either crushing or destemming.

Pasteur made the following statement on this subject in 1872: "It would be interesting to know what would be the difference in quality between two wines where the producing berries in one case were totally crushed and in the other left for the most part whole just as it happens with an ordinary vintage." Vinification with the berries whole has been the subject of important studies in recent times. Today we do have better knowledge of the phenomena involved in maceration carbonique, and we know how to utilize them in a more rational way.

Intracellular Fermentation of the Grapes

Ripe grapes put into total oxygen-free conditions, in a confined atmosphere or into carbon dioxide or nitrogen undergo complex changes. Inside the berry, fermentation is produced which, without the yeasts intervening, transforms a small amount of sugar into alcohol. It forms under these conditions some 1.5–2.5% alcohol. It is the cells themselves within the fruit which, anaerobically, provoke this transformation. It stops when the cells are killed by the alcohol and lack of oxygen. Carbon dioxide is formed as well, a little glycerol, succinic acid, and various secondary products from the sugar fermentation.

These are not the only transformations. One of the most important is the reduction of the malic acid in the grapes; half of it disappears. The acidity of the must and later that of the wine are brought down a great deal by this.

Extraction results in the dissolving of substances in the solid parts of the grape. A rise is observed in the amount of nitrogen, mineral matter, and polyphenols, particularly in the color of the juice.

The aromatic substances in the skins are distributed in the pulp. The pectins from the cellular walls are hydrolyzed, altering the consistency of the fruit.

Conducting Vinification with Maceration Carbonique

The grapes have to be transported intact to the winery and emptied carefully so as not to crush them through the upper hatch in a thoroughly airtight tank. The empty space is filled with carbon dioxide, either from a gas cylinder or else by placing at the bottom of the tank 5 or 10% of fermenting must. Anyway the grapes gradually are crushed by their own weight and normal fermentation keeps up the required carbon dioxide atmosphere. The reduction in malic acid only takes place in grapes that are intact.

ANALYSIS OF WINE[a] MADE BY MACERATION CARBONIQUE[a]

	Classic Vinification	Vinification with Maceration Carbonique
Reduced extract	24.8	18.5
Total acidity	4.31	3.43
Volatile acidity	0.30	0.42
Malic acid (g)	1.34	0.07
Color intensity	1.380	1.023
Anthocyanins (mg)	800	503
Tannins (g)	3.64	2.40
Polyphenol index	60	47

These analyses by Sudraud carried out 4 months after harvesting show that wine obtained with maceration carbonique is less rich in extracts, in acidity, in coloring matter, and in tannin. It finished malolactic fermentation earlier than the reference sample.

[a] Malbec variety, Bordeaux area.

Sulfiting is not usual but it has been recommended as an antibacterial protection as well as acidifying.

The length of extraction depends on a number of factors, particularly the temperature. The lower the temperature, the longer the fermentation has to last. Extraction, therefore, may last 8–10 days or more. The time to empty the tank is fixed by it cooling down, giving off no more gas, by the density of the free-run wine, by its color and by tasting it.

The yeasts may develop very well on the grapes during the anaerobic phase. Lactic bacteria may appear after a few days extraction, which endangers the final phase of vinification.

The volume of free-run juice varies at racking between 50 and 75% of the total volume. Its fermentation is very nearly complete. It has been calculated that 20% of the grapes are crushed and undergo alcoholic fermentation by the yeasts and that 20% of the grapes remain intact and become centers of intracellular fermentation. The remaining fraction (60%) undergoes both transformations. The press wine, still with sugar, is mixed with the free-run wine. Normally fermentation finishes in 48 hours. This renewed fermentation gives an agreeable aroma of ethereal salts. The malolactic fermentation is made easier because of the reduction in the acidity during extraction and incubation of the bacteria.

The advantages of this type of vinification lie especially in the absence of heating up and in an improvement of the organoleptic characteristics: softening due to reduction in acidity and to lesser extraction of the polyphenols, development of a characteristic and complex secondary aroma. The enhancement of the aroma, its originality, and the loss of specific varietal flavors may offend tasters accustomed to the classical styles in quality wine-growing areas. On the other hand, the improvement is very plain for certain mediocre varieties. It is also more intense in certain years. Vinification with maceration carbonique is specially suited to areas that tend to make hard, acidic wines. It is beneficial for preparing semifine wines to be drunk young. Wines made in this way keep their agreeable character during the first year but do not withstand aging well and lose their special fruity qualities.

The difficulties met with in this vinification (which are the main obstacles to its more general use) consist in the astringency imparted by the stems if held before pressing too long and especially in the danger of bacterial spoilage due either to the multiplication of acetic bacteria when the tank is not completely airtight or to the development of lactic bacteria, which takes place immediately after racking and pressing, in the presence of sugar.

THERMAL VINIFICATION

Hot extraction of red grapes, before the fermentation, is considered to be a vinification method of recent conception. Yet ever since wine has been made, it is probable that people always tried to cook grapes. The natural heat caused by fermentation and the way it looks as though it is boiling must have quickly given this idea to a keen observer. Maupin said in 1781: "Following my principles, one third of the vintage shall be boiled. . . . The quantity of boiling grapes should vary according to the difference in the years. The mild, rainy years are those which require the most; and the years when it is dry right up to vintage-time are those which need the least." Therefore, the process is not a new one. What is novel are the industrial means of heating by which considerable tonnages are quickly brought to a high temperature.

Heating Grapes

If a whole bunch of grapes is dipped into boiling water, or if steam is sent across its surface, the skins can be brought to a high temperature without the heat penetrating into the center of the pulp. The cells of the skin are killed by this cooking so that when the grapes are crushed they distribute in the juice the substances they contained: first of all, and the phenomenon is immediately apparent, the anthocyanins and the tannins and then the other

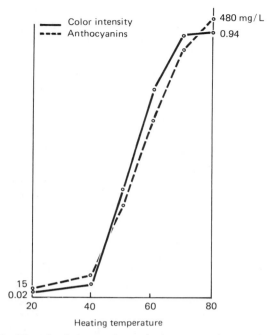

Figure 15.3.   Dissolving of red pigments by crushed grapes in relation to heating temperature.

compounds: polysaccharides, nitrogenous substances, organic acids, mineral matter, and aromatic substances. By pressing the heated grapes, a strongly colored must is obtained directly and fermentation gives a wine with a beautiful color. In the same way, when heating is applied to crushed grapes, together with their juice and the whole lot stirred up, the anthocyanins and the other constituents of the skin are spread progressively throughout the mass as its temperature gradually rises. Again, the juice obtained has an intense coloration.

With this method of vinification, the essential purpose is attempting to get the maximum extraction of the pigments. Classic vinification in fact in the best conditions only extracts 30% of the coloring matter contained in the grapes. The rest is lost in the pomace. Thermal treatment, if it is sufficiently intense and long enough, solubilizes a great deal more. Figure 15.3 shows that heating to 40°C does not bring any change. The temperature needs to reach 60°C to get any appreciable increase in color. At 80°C, most is extracted.

In the case of grapes attacked by *Botrytis cinerea*, heating stabilizes the color by destroying the oxidases and so prevents oxidative casse. But in that case the rise in temperature needs to be very rapid. In fact, the oxidases are destroyed only from 60°C up. Below this level, their activity is strengthened whereas slow heating gives the contrary effect of color loss and yellowing.

Methods of Thermal Vinification

Several ways of heating grapes and several ways of treating heated grapes have been described. It is logical that these various formulas should give different end results. Therefore, it is not possible to simply talk of "the" heating or of "the" thermovinification and generalize the results, good or bad, that these various versions may give.

The following table brings together and classifies in outline form the numerous thermal processes in use. There are in fact two main categories: those that use whole bunches and those that handle the crushed and stemmed grapes.

The heating of the grapes intact is carried out by copiously circulating steam around the bunches of grapes laid out in thin layers on a conveyor belt traveling slowly. The skins are, as it were, sealed off on the outside and raised to 75°C whereas the interior of the berry does not go beyond 30°C. After cooling and drying by ventilation, the grapes so treated can be vinified in the usual way: either by crushing, destemming, and normal pomace contact, or else by being transformed into clear must after crushing and pressing. These two processes lead to different styles of wine.

Heating the grapes after crushing is the most ancient of these processes and the most current these days. It comprises several ways of operating depending on whether it is continuous or discontinuous, whether it is applied to the whole of the crushed vintage or only to a part, more or less drained.

Heating a quantity of the crushed vintage under an open flame in pans of large capacity was one of the first methods used. Heating lasts 20 or 30 minutes or so while the mass is being continuously stirred. More functional installations consist of stainless-steel tanks with double walls heated by circulating hot water. Indirect heating prevents local overheating. The grapes are stirred to keep the temperature rise uniform and to extract the color. This simple procedure applies to small volumes, for instance, a fifth of the crop is heated, choosing the soundest and most colored of the grapes.

Continuous systems allow temperatures to rise much more quickly, and heating the whole vintage can be considered. These appliances consist of a worm-screw which draws the crushed vintage through a shaft that is heated by hot water or steam. The speed of flow and length of the shaft are calculated so that the mass comes out at the end at a sufficiently high temperature. In other continuous appliances, a pump drives the crushed vintage through a pipe heated by means of a hot water spray maintained at a temperature of

VARIOUS METHODS OF HEATING GRAPES BY
THERMOVINIFICATION

Heating Applied to	Means of Heating	Vinification Technique Used	Trying to Achieve
Whole grapes intact	Steam	Crushing, pressing, must fermentation / Crushing, stemming, pomace contact with extraction	Improvement in color, better extraction of the substances in the skins, destruction of the oxidases
Vintage crushed and destemmed (sometimes partly drained)	Direct discontinuous heating (generally partial) on sound grapes	Cooling, normal pomace contact with extraction	Immediate improvement in color, better extraction of the substances in the skins
	Continuous heating in tubular exchangers (with or without hot extraction	Pressing, cooling, fermentation in colored must / Cooling, normal fermentation on pomace	Separation of extraction from fermentation / Improvement of the extraction
	Heating the solid elements in the berries by immersion in the heated must	Draining, pressing, cooling, fermentation in colored must	Separation of extraction from fermentation, industrialization, and automation of the vinification operations

80°C in a closed circuit using an oil burner. In the immersion process where the operations are automated, the crushed vintage is first divided by draining. The must, raised to 80°C, is used to heat the pomace with which it is mixed again. Then it is moved into another drainer, then to the press. These various systems necessarily comprise a cooling device which, after the grapes have been cooked, brings the temperature back to a level likely to promote fermentation.

If we take into consideration all the multiple alternatives possible in each case: heating temperature from 50 to 80°C, hot extraction of greater or less duration, with or without mechanical mixing, fermentation developing in colored must or in the presence of heated skins, rapidity of cooling, fermentation temperature from 18 to 45°C, then we can understand that the composition of the wines obtained in anthocyanins, tannins, aromatic substances, and so on as well as their qualities in taste are going to vary a great deal and that assessment of the value of these processes is also going to differ widely.

Advantages and Disadvantages of Thermovinification

It is very difficult to make a clear-cut assessment of these processes. Without doubt, heating grapes has led in a few cases to wines with more color, better than those made by classic vinification. But other wines coming from thermovinification exhibit a vegetative aroma or a dominant fusel-oil odor, loss of freshness, bitterness, and clarification difficulties. The apparent confusion between opinions expressed on the value of these processes also comes from the fact that the results being looked for are not always the same. If some people are looking for a means of improving quality by heating, others only see it as a way of automating vinification.

If the important thing is color, immediate results are often spectacular, even though the loss of color during fermentation frequently enough makes it a disappointment. In a test, the increase in coloring matter due to heating, measured several weeks after harvesting, was 60%. The anthocyanin content went from 160 mg/L, which the classic vinification gave, to 280 mg for hot vinification. However, since the anthocyanins and the color they impart diminish in a large proportion during the first year, the benefit gained from heating becomes much less evident after a few months. It is no longer evident at all after a few years.

One argument put forward might be the advantage of separating the extraction from the fermentation phase, which overlap in normal vinification, the idea being to be able to control them better independently. The advantage is not obvious. Indeed, fermentation can be conducted by this means at a lower temperature but, on the other hand, a total loss of mastery over the extraction results. It is easier to regulate this when it lasts several days at 25 or 30°C than when the operation is all over in 20 or 30 minutes at 70°C. It is not possible to assert that quality-wise the same substances have been dissolved. Not all those that form part of the skin's composition are suitable to be extracted. Some with a vegetative odor or taste are undesirable; others should not go over a certain level of concentration. According to a formula already mentioned, wine is not all the grape.

In short, certain thermovinification techniques may be considered to be efficient ways, in exceptional cases, of improving the color and flavor of a young wine when the vintage has deficiencies in its makeup and in maturity. Trying to achieve different objectives at the expense of quality would obviously be a questionable trend.

16

Vinifying White Wine—Work with Grapes and Processing the Must

White wine is made by fermenting just the grape juice on its own, that is to say, without extraction of the solid parts from the bunch. So in the very first place the great distinction between vinifying red and vinifying white wine is this absence of any extraction. The better white wines contain none of the elements originating in the skin, the seeds, and even less from the stems. White vinification is conducted taking great care to avoid any dissolving either directly or with enzymes, of any of the constituents from the pomace.

What this means in practice is that whereas in red vinification racking and pressing are done after fermentation, white vinification requires separation by draining and pressing beforehand. There exist a few rare exceptions where white wines are extracted, fermenting with the pomace; certain modestly equipped cultivators, in order to facilitate pressing sometimes wait until the crushed vintage starts to ferment.

DIVERSITY OF TYPES OF WHITE WINE

In contrast to the relative consistency in the composition of red wines, which buyers tend to prefer when they are supple with low acidity, moderately well colored and not too astringent or bitter, we find a great variety of tastes among consumers where white wine is concerned. Types of white wine are extremely varied. They can be very aromatic or have subdued aroma, dry, medium-dry, semisweet or sweet, still, semisparkling or fully sparkling, fresh and fruity

197

or rancio and maderized, fortified with alcohol, aged in wood or stored young in airtight tanks. According to whether the grapes are picked unripe, very ripe or overripe, passerillized, according to their sanitary state and the kind of mold on them, up to noble rot, the richness of the must will vary from 10 to 20 degrees Baumé. There are excellent dry wines with strengths up to 5 or 6 g of total acidity and others no less excellent with 3.5 g at most.

These varieties of taste and composition relate to different vinification techniques. The work of getting the must ready may include successively crushing, draining, pressing, sulfiting, racking, and clarification, but none of these operations is indispensable for making wine. Every kind of vinification exists from those that use all of them and that correspond with present-day trends in the preparation of dry whites, right up to those that leave out most. The rule is anyway to get them done as fast as possible in order to keep contact with air down to a minimum. Rapidity of execution is merely a question of being properly equipped and having the work properly organized, still, some good wines of a slightly oxidized style are obtained without taking these precautions. Lastly, in certain areas, malolactic fermentation of white wines is a requisite, whereas others prefer to avoid it.

METHOD OF PICKING

This is decisive. According to the end-product being sought, the white grape's technical "maturity" may be defined in various ways. It is often said: "a white wine without aroma has nothing," it is only an acidulated alcoholic solution. And it is not even enough for white wine to have that "secondary" aroma which it gets from a good healthy fermentation, in which you can particularly pick out that note given by the higher alcohols and their esters. There has to be some "primary" aroma, one that comes from the grape. This primary aroma depends on the grape variety, its ripeness and its state of health.

The white grape's aroma, localized in the skin and the underlying cells, appears very early, long before complete maturity, so that early picking can give wines as aromatic as and often finer than late-picking (this is not the same for red wines). The evolution of aroma observed in a comparison between vinifications using Sauvignon grapes harvested at various stages of ripeness, is as follows: for grapes picked after the *véraison* (color change) the odor is strong but "green," it puts you in mind of trodden leaves or chewed grape-skin. Later it becomes more refined, fruity tones appear and it is already pleasant a fortnight before optimum strength is reached. Later still it will be more "ripe," richer in the scent of fatty acids but heavier, less vivacious.

One important fact is established: in hot areas, it is not necessary to wait for complete ripeness in order to get fruity wines. It is even ill-advised. Besides the harvest has to be got in fairly early to ensure better acid balance. Apart from its aroma, the attractiveness of a white wine has in fact a lot to do with its freshness, that is to say, sufficient acidity. Early picking also has the advantage of avoiding too much alcoholic strength. A good dry wine ought to be between 11 and 12%. Below this the wine runs the risk of being weak and small, unless it is particularly rich in aroma. Above that it is hot and too heady, its higher alcoholic content making it difficult to drink in reasonable quantities.

The best dry white wines are made from sound grapes. As soon as gray rot appears, even in small proportions, wines are of inferior quality. It is more important to make dry white wines with perfectly healthy crops than with perfectly ripe ones. In many quality wine areas, grapes are sorted by hand and those bunches or single grapes attacked by mold eliminated.

Precautions are taken not to bruise the grapes during transport, nor to crush or even pack them down in the wooden tubs. The grape needs to be brought intact to the winery. For this purpose wicker baskets are still used. This prevents any adverse effects caused by oxidation and extraction. Sulfiting the vintage should be abandoned, for it must not be imagined that putting sulfuric acid on the grapes is going to make any difference to the serious consequences of such effects. Perhaps it does counteract some of the results of oxidation but does nothing at all about extraction, on the contrary it will aggravate it. Nothing can be more detrimental to the quality of dry white wines than the practice of picking very ripe, sometimes slightly moldy grapes, crushing in the wooden tubs out in the vineyard to reduce the transport volume, spraying with sulfuric solution right away to stop fermentation then leaving it out in the sun or at high temperature, which augments the dissolving processes. Such habits, just like mechanization of the grape harvest today, tend to jeopardize the production of quality white wines.

MECHANICAL WORK WITH THE WHITE VINTAGE

Enologists are paying more and more attention to the mechanical treatment inflicted on the grapes and the reactions that take place immediately after crushing and pressing. Quality will be considerably improved if we can manage to respect certain of the fragile constituents of the grape.

Taking a close look at the evolution of winemaking in those countries that produce and consume quality white wines, what we see developing are highly sophisticated well-equipped plants capable of rapid production and clarification of the must and also for heating and cooling the wines. It is getting difficult, due to changes in taste and the increase in production volume, to make top quality dry white wine and even more so dessert wine in peasant economy conditions, in cellars that are often more wine stores than wine making plants.

Crushing

Its purpose is to provoke rupture of the skins releasing the pulp. The result ought to be enough to separate the juice, but it should not rip up or split the solid parts. Crushers with rollers are the only ones to use.

Two reasons militate against destemming a white vintage: First, it necessarily involves stirring the crushed vintage, which creates a lot of deposits, and second, it makes the separation of the must by pressing more difficult. The stems give the pomace a certain elasticity and ensure that the juice drains out well.

Whenever possible the crush-pump should be avoided. It is convenient for feeding the drainer and the press, but it does further damage to the grapes, in addition to increasing the amount of solids.

Vinification in Champagne, which is often taken as a model, does not involve crushing the grapes: They are put into the press intact and gradually compressed, which splits the skins and lets the juice escape little by little rather as though each grape were being pressed between finger and thumb. This system even allows white or only slightly colored juice to be extracted from black grapes.

The advantage of crushing lies in the speed with which the drained must is separated. It requires much less press space. The advantage of not crushing is getting a must with far less solids since it eliminates any grinding of the vintage and a must far less sensitive to oxidation since it is less rich in oxidases. This advantage only becomes obvious when pressing is correctly carried out, that is to say, gradually increasing the pressure.

It should be mentioned that screw pumps exist that allow the bunches to be transferred whole uncrushed to the press cage with a percentage deterioration of the fruit that is acceptable.

Draining

Its aim is to separate the juice freed during crushing, and this is done immediately afterward. Distinction is made between static draining, which is done by simply letting the crushed vintage lie, and mechanical or dynamic draining, which acts faster.

It could be said that draining is one of the weak points about white-wine making. It is an operation difficult to carry out correctly and which if badly done leads to loss in quality. It takes several forms according to the amount being processed, the quality being sought, and the equipment available.

The most common form of draining on a small holding consists of letting the crushed vintage fall straight from the crusher into the cage of the vertical or horizontal press. The juice runs out while the cage is getting filled and pressing only commences once the cage is full and draining is reckoned to be sufficient.

When working with large volumes of vintage in bulk winemaking processes, the irregular rate at which the grapes come in, at times more quickly than the press can accept them, means some intermediate system has to be inserted to give a primary separation of the juice between the crushing and the pressing operations.

In this case, draining chambers carry out a static separation. These consist of various shapes of open tanks, which include an open-work floor or wall. The floor, being inclined, enables the must to run out and the presses to be loaded by gravity.

Although static draining has the advantage of giving musts without too much deposits and of making pressing easier by hydrolysis of the pectins, this system should be condemned, because it gives rise to a double oxidation, once when the grapes are crushed and again when the must trickles out, and it provokes prolonged extraction. These draining chambers are to a great extent responsible for the difficulties encountered, in large-scale cellars, of making dry white wines of quality. Mechanical draining is preferable to using them.

Mechanical drainers (see Fig. 16.1) belong to several types, revolving cylinders, horizontal riddles actuated by shaking, or ones with an inclined screw-conveyor that draws the crushed vintage up into a perforated shaft. In the last case, the crushed vintage may be held down with a counterweight (hard drain) to accentuate the separation of the must. The most rationalized plants have the drainer placed under the crusher, directly fed by gravity.

Certain machines can deal with 300 kg of grapes per minute and feed two continuous presses (Fig. 16.2). The output of extracted juice is increased and amount of solids reduced by making them revolve very slowly. Another condition for ensuring that the mechanical drainers work correctly is a regular supply of fresh grapes to make sure the bottom of the hopper is always covered with a layer of crushed grapes through which the must filters and gets rid of its solids. Draining time, taking into account this brief delay, does not take more than 10 minutes and most of it is separated in the first minute. Whereas static draining renders 50% juice, mechanical draining properly conducted separates up to 75 or 80%.

The free-run must is caught in a receiving tank placed underneath the drainer. To prevent the must from trickling out, falling like rain, in cascades and from being spread in the air, a spout is used which collects the must and brings it through a delivery pipe into the bottom of the receiving tank.

Figure 16.1. Large-capacity mechanical drainer (Photo Claude O'Sughrue).

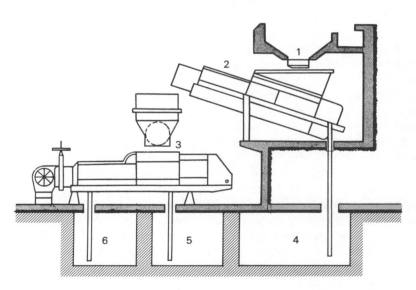

Figure 16.2. Diagram showing rationalized processing of white grapes in bulk winemaking, comprising the crusher (1), mechanical drainer (2), and continuous press (3). The juices are collected by gravity in the small tanks: (4) free-run must, (5) must from the first press, (6) must from the second press. The sulfur solution runs out at the same time as the must and immediately suppresses any tendency to oxidation.

Figure 16.3. Battery of horizontal presses (Photo Institute Technique du Vin).

Pressing

Its purpose is to extract the must under pressure exerted on the crushed and drained grapes. The pomace is dried out in this way. The extraction ought to be limited to the sweet juice of the vacuoles, excluding the vegetative saps, skins, seeds, and stems.

Different types of press are used for this task.

Vertical Presses.   Already known in ancient times, they exist in two versions, either with a screw-jack, the pressure being exerted from the top toward the bottom, or else with a hydraulic screw that raises the hopper and compresses the pomace from the bottom toward the top. Breaking up the pomace (*rebêchage*) or rehandling or crumbling, is done manually, otherwise it requires a mechanical crumbler. From three to six successive pressings are practiced.

Horizontal Screw Presses.   These presses work by rotation and by bringing together one or two mobile plates (see Fig. 16.3). The cage is made of wood, stainless steel, or plastic. They may be manually operated or automatic. Some of them are equipped with automatic control devices which alter the speed of pressing, stop it as soon as a certain pressure is reached

Figure 16.4. Pneumatic press driven by compressed air (Tankpress Wilmess).

and automatically carry out the breaking up operation on the pomace. Loading and emptying are easy. Chains inside (made of stainless steel) break up the pomace. There are models without chains called *Champenois* (Champagne-style) specially designed for pressing noncrushed grapes.

Pneumatic Presses. Also horizontal, they operate by inflating an internal bag made of thick rubber. The bag crushes the pomace against the cylindrical stainless-steel cage (see Fig. 16.4). The juice is squeezed through the cage, which acts as a sieve, or it is collected through internal draining pipes. Inflation is done by an air compressor. The breaking up is obtained by releasing pressure, which frees the layer of pomace, then rotating the cage.

Continuous Presses. Based on the principle of the endless spiral screw or Archimedes' screw, continuous presses force the pomace against a counterweighted movable stop that lets it build up a thick plug (see Fig. 16.5). Modern continuous presses have a large diameter screw, slow rotation speed,

Figure 16.5. Continuous press (Coq).

and automatic pressure adjustment. They have several must outlets enabling them to be divided into different qualities.

The table on the following page compares the advantages and disadvantages of various types of press. The evolution in equipment today is away from hydraulic presses toward the horizontal or pneumatic press.

In large wineries, the only possible solution is often the continuous press. Whatever the type of press used, results will be improved if the juice from the last pressing is eliminated. The quest for quality makes selection at every stage vital, removing damaged grapes, the last must from the press, and the lees from racking.

Generally the best wine is obtained from the free-run must to which the first press wine may be combined. The press wine has more color and is heavier. The herbaceous character of certain varieties stands out. More rarely for quality grapes in vineyards where choice wines are made, the press wine, albeit more flabby, has more body and more aroma. In other words, you find in the press wine the qualities and defects of the grapes it was made from.

The quality of a press and the way it is used can be judged by analyzing the press-must obtained. The acidity and alkalinity determination of the ash plus the potassium which represent the mineral matter, the tannins, sugars, and iron all indicate, by comparison with the free-run must, the amount of mechanical extraction of substances from the pomace. The two tables on p. 207 give examples of this.

We present a diagram of a mechanically operated winemaking plant (see Fig. 16.2). The best work lines are the shortest, those that transform grapes into must with a minimum time lag and that produce musts that are least cloudy and least sensitive to oxidation. The amount of sediment a must deposits is a conclusive test showing the quality of the treatment the grapes received, in the same way as the proof showing browning when exposed to air.

White vinification is dominated by a new concept that attempts to work with grapes and process the musts in such a way that a wine is produced straight off which will only require a minimum of finishing operations. This is what we translate by the statement: "Treat the grapes and process the must in order not to have to treat the wine."

SETTLING AND RACKING

Another way of limiting extraction consists of settling and racking the must, that is to say, either by gravity or by centrifugation to obtain a certain clarification before fermentation, by clearing the vegetative fragments and other

COMPARISON OF DIFFERENT TYPES OF PRESSES

	Advantages	Disadvantages
Vertical hydraulic press (small holding, unsophisticated wine making)	Very efficient in drying out heavy grapes for grapes with noble rot. Pressure exerted without crushing the pomace. Possible to press noncrushed grapes. Must obtained has little solids.	Pomace being very thick requires drainers being put in called *paillassons* and necessitates very great pressure. Needs a number of successive pressings, making operation last a very long time. Manual crumbling promotes injurious oxidation. These disadvantages are reduced with large-diameter presses and by dividing the must into successive pressings.
Horizontal press (medium-sized estate, quality wines)	Mechanical breaking up of pomace, facility for carrying out successive pressings. Press pressure relatively light. Pressing noncrushed grapes possible. Possible automation.	Trickling of must and much aeration. Horizontal press gives more deposits than vertical press because of a certain crumpling of the pomace by the chains during pressing and particularly at the time of breaking up.
Pneumatic press (medium-sized estate, quality wines)	Pressure light and well-distributed Pressure exerted across a thin layer of pomace whose structure is maintained. Pressure exerted by flattening without crushing the pomace.	Low work yield: The quantities of pomace processed in one press cycle are low and pressure is slow. There exist, however, new models of greater capacity. Certain heavy or overripe vintages are hard to press. The machines are costly.
Continuous press (bulk wine making)	Extraction of must very rapid High work yield, great facility in operation, labor economy.	Pomace roughly handled in press, grinding it up. These disadvantages are mitigated by the use of improved machines with large diameter screw, also by possibility of dividing up the must.

206

ANALYSIS OF MUSTS OBTAINED DURING A PRESS-CYCLE IN CHAMPAGNE[a]

	Cuvée	First Press Fraction	Second Press Fraction	Breaking up
Volumes (L)	2050	410	205	200
Total acidity (g)	8.5	7.4	6.2	about 2.1
Alkalinity of ash (meq)	44	48	54	131
pH	3.10	3.16	3.35	3.65
Tartaric acid (g)	8.3	7.6	6.9	6.2
Potassium (mg)	663	664	829	1590
Tannins (mg)	25	50	90	150
Polysaccharides (g)	1.28	1.76	2.60	3.68
Iron (mg)	2	2	4	20

[a] 4000 kg of grapes.

COMPARISON OF MUSTS FROM VARIOUS METHODS OF PROCESSING THE GRAPES[a]

	Pressing Without Crushing (Champagne-style press)	Crushed		
		Free-Run Must	Continuous Pressing	
			First Part	Second Part
Total acidity	4.22	4.51	3.83	3.14
pH	3.08	3.02	3.20	3.92
Alkalinity of ash (meq)	41	34	39	89
Tannins (mg)	50	20	100	800
Iron (mg)	2	1	3	20

[a] Mauzac grape variety.

impurities likely to cause off-tastes. For instance, must that has been pre-vented from fermenting by enough sulfur is left to settle for 12 or 24 hours in a decanting tank, then racked to eliminate the major deposits and all or part of the smaller ones. Wine made from sedimented must is fresher, more acid, and lighter. Its aroma is cleaner and better stabilized, that is to say, less sensitive to outside conditions. It has a paler more stable color, in other words, it is less sensitive to oxygen reaction due to destruction of the oxidases. The amount of iron in sedimented wine is always lower; it only represents the natural iron from the grape. It is the same for other mineral elements.

Sulfiting

Whatever the method used for settling, sulfiting the must is vital. Sulfiting and sedimentation are fundamental operations when trying to produce dry white wine by rational processes. This is present-day opinion, at least as long as malolactic fermentation is not wanted. Sulfiting ought to be done as early as possible, as soon as the must is separated by draining or pressing. On the other hand, the crushed grapes should never be sulfited. It is an inefficient operation since sulfur dioxide combines with and clings to the solid parts of the grapes and is not found in the must, so that any protection is illusory. It is an unfavorable action since it accentuates the extraction phenomena.

The sulfur solution runs down at the same time as the must into the bottom of the receiving tank by a system fixed to it. In this way any oxidation reaction is arrested right at the beginning. There is no point in waiting until the tank is full before sulfiting, damage from oxidation would have already been done. The dose of sulfur dioxide to be added depends on circumstances. This is established by a preliminary trial to discover the right amount needed to destroy the oxidases, with the help of a test to reveal these enzymes. The dose of sulfur dioxide that must be added may vary, for instance, between 6 and 12 g/hL.

Separating the Deposits

The most common separation process is sedimentation followed by racking; the quickest is centrifugation using automatic injection of the lees with a clarifying substance. The use of centrifugation in no way saves having to use sulfiting whose antioxidant role is still indispensable. Centrifugation is carried out after a short period to reduce the total amount of solids somewhat.

Because of the large amount of solids in natural must, centrifugation is far from giving such good clarification as racking after letting the must settle, and comparative tastings are in favor of static sedimentation. It is often preferable to use centrifugation for the sediment that remains after racking and on the press-must, which is always difficult to clarify correctly by sedimentation. A selection made on this basis gives, for instance: 50% free-run wine of top quality, 20% sedimented wine of secondary quality, and 30% press wine of inferior quality, which eventually requires decoloring and fining treatment.

Sedimentation is only efficient, indeed it is only possible, so long as the processes for treating the grapes do not create too great a quantity of solids. For instance, to set up equipment with a centrifugal clarifier to remove deposits from a doughy must obtained from a centrifugal stemmer-crusher would be an aberration.

Deposits are made up of soil debris, fragments from any shredding of the stems and skins, fibers from inside the grapes, pectic and viscous substances, and proteins precipitated by contact with substances localized at different spots on the grape berry. The amount and kind of deposits depend on the grape, its ripeness, the existence of mold, and the "must-producing" technique used. Grapes with mold give more solids, and these solids are brown colored, whereas from sound grapes they are greenish-gray. Pressing without crushing gives less solids except for fine deposits slow to settle, which leave the must somewhat cloudy. Mechanical crushing and draining give coarse solids that sink quickly but settle badly and remain bulky whereas the must is clear. Bulky sediment produced by rough crushing sometimes splits into two equal parts, one remaining on the bottom of the receptacle, the other floating on the surface making separation into clear juice practically impossible.

The beneficial effect of sedimentation is shown by the better taste of wines made from sedimented must. On the other hand, if sediment is extracted in an aqueousalcoholic solution, tastes of herbaceous infusions and vegetative soils are to be found in the resulting solution such as are found in ordinary wines, plus a musty taste from grapes with mold. Besides, if the wine from sediment is fermented apart, it is of mediocre quality.

Static sedimentation is only successful if it is done in containers of small volume and not too deep. Sedimentation after 24 hours settling in the cask is efficient, less so in a large tank. According to the quanitites to be processed, sedimentation-tank capacities should be limited to 50, 100, or a maximum of 200 hL. These tanks are equipped with decanting faucets, enabling racking clear to the dregs. Account should be taken of the fact that in a tank 3 m high, for example, sediment may reach a height of 80 cm.

Again attempts have been made to get better clarity by natural sedimentation alone with the help of clarifying flocculants or by filtering. Gelatin, casein, and bentonite have been recommended for this purpose; they do not completely settle by the end of a normal sedimentation period. On the other hand, the use of pectolitic enzymes is likely to improve static sedimentation. Doses of 1–2 g/hL are used. These enzymes destroy pectic matter which form part of the colloidal structure of the must and their removal facilitates flocculation, speeds up the sinking of the particles, allows more distinct separation between the clear must and the sediment area and in consequence makes possible filtration easier. This is generally difficult to do because musts rich in protective gels have a strong tendency to clog up. The best equipment for filtering musts is the circular rotary filter using vacuum suction with continuous running. The filtration surface, made of infusorial earth, is cleared by a scraper rake as it gets clogged.

The use of cold, dropping the must temperature to below 15°C, in hot areas, gives an opportunity through longer settling time to get better clarification and better separation of the deposits.

The sedimentation operation cannot afford to be slipshod. It requires perfect cleanliness of all the equipment with scrupulous daily washing down, as soon as they have been used, of the crusher, drainer, press machines, receptacles, and decanting tanks. If these are not washed immediately, after a few days, fermentation may start up due to contamination by yeasts, preventing the deposits from settling. Cleanliness of all the equipment and premises is in any case a basic requirement for good winemaking.

So long as it is done properly, sedimentation does in fact remove, together with the solids, a large part of the yeasts and delays the beginning of fermentation. Inoculation with yeasts using 10 g of *Saccharomyces oviformis* powder per hectoliter is therefore advisable.

It is important to know that removing solids modifies the ease with which the must ferments since the solids themselves are rich in biotic elements vital to the yeasts. If the must is clarified too much, fermentations become stuck, running the risk of leaving some untransformed sugars. Yeasts may also form greater volatile acidity. Therefore, it is best to leave a certain percentage of light deposits when sedimenting. It may not be prudent to try to get absolute clarity in the must at the cost of complicating the task, if at the same time this is only going to lead to further difficulties and make it necessary to add growth factors.

It is the sedimented must that any possible corrections are made to, after determining probable alcoholic strength and acidity, such as sugaring, acidification, or deacidifying. For instance, for dry wines, acidification may be imperative for musts with an acidity lower than 4 g/L (in sulfuric acid) and deacidification useful above 6 g.

TREATING MUST WITH BENTONITE

The purpose of treating with bentonite is to get rid of the natural proteins in the must. The proteins play an important part in the clarity of white wines

AMOUNTS OF SEDIMENT ACCORDING TO THE METHOD OF PROCESSING THE GRAPES

Volume of sediment in relation to total volume of must:	
Crusher with grooved rollers (without destemming), free-run must	22–45%
Centrifugal stemmer-crusher, free-run must	80–100%
Pressing without crushing (first and second press)	5–10%

since they tend to precipitate and make it go cloudy. This is known as protein casse. The best answer for stabilization of white wines in this connection is to fix their proteins on bentonite, which is a colloidal clay capable of high adsorption power. (See Chapter 29.)

Applied to must before fermentation rather than to the wine, this treatment gives several advantages combined: less handling and less tiring of the finished wine, sedimentation of the bentonite after fermentation without increasing the volume of lees, improving spontaneous clarification, partial fixation of the oxidases, slight decoloration effect, more finesse and cleanness on the palate.

The most practical way of using bentonite (as well as other corrective products) consists of adding it at the time of draining the sedimented must. It is allowed to drain by gravity into a basin from which it is pumped into the fermentation tank. During this circulation, the bentonite is sprinkled over the basin and mixed by stirring vigorously. Just flowing through the pump is all it needs to make the specks that might form disappear. The amount to be used, variable according to the musts and the quality of the bentonite, may fluctuate, say, as an indication, between 60 and 100 g/hL. These amounts are lower in the case of the base whites made for transforming into sparkling wines, in order not to diminish their capacity to become frothy.

There is good reason to put bentonite in after sedimentation, because if it is done first, it stops the solids from sinking so easily and makes them more voluminous.

17

Vinifying White Wine—
Protection from Oxidation
and Conducting Fermentation

PREVENTING THE EFFECTS OF OXIDATION

Apart from a few cases of special wines, it must be considered that air is the enemy of white wine much more so than of red wine. Oxygen harms aroma, destroys the fruitiness, and deepens color. There is no way of preventing the must and the wine from being in contact with the air, if not in a permanent way, at least on many occasions in the course of moving it or of storing it. The grape juice is subjected to action by air the moment it is crushed, it trickles down in a thin layer, in tiny drops, from the crusher into the receiving tank, where it remains exposed to air across its surface. Especially when the crushed vintage is dripping down oxygen penetration is considerable because of the large contact surface and the time this operation takes. Similarly during pressing and the handling this implies, air is always present. Its effect becomes more pronounced as the pomace dries out and the liquid phase diminishes; finally the press must trickles and drips slowly in air.

Later, during fermentation, especially when it is done in wooden casks and afterward when racking and processing the wine, oxygen dissolution is far from negligible. Its influence may be disastrous if the winemaker does not take special steps to prevent it.

Oxidations during vinification are the most serious because must is much more sensitive than wine and more difficult to protect. Oxidation of the must is of an enzymatic nature and two oxidases intervene: the tyrosinase, always present in grapes and the laccase from *Botrytis cinerea* in vintages with rot.

There are not more oxidases in the botrytized grapes but the laccase is more soluble, more resistant, and attacks the phenolic compounds more energetically than the tyrosinase. The oxidases are located on the solid parts of the grape and their getting into the must and the damage they cause there depend a lot on whether or not the grapes are roughly handled during treatment. Their proportions increase with extraction, with any mechanical grinding of the pomace, and with the pressure exerted during pressing.

Oxidation of the phenolic substances induces severe changes in color (in extreme cases, it can be oxidative casse) and the formation of acrid and bitter substances. Other constituents of the must are also oxidized, in particular the substances from the aroma. Musts consume on the average 2 milligrams of oxygen per liter per minute whereas wines take 24 hours to consume the same amount. This comparison shows the great oxidizability of musts.

What can be done during vinification to fight these injurious oxidations? One satisfactory solution has been found in the use of sulfur dioxide in sufficient doses and the speed of executing the operations of "must producing," rapidity that limits the total amounts of oxygen dissolved and combined. Sulfur dioxide acts, on the one hand, by its reducing properties and, on the other, by its antioxidasic properties. Whence its indispensable use in vinification, most particularly where the vintage has a proportion of its grapes either botrytized or spoiled. A minute or two after sulfiting the must, consumption of oxygen stops.

Other techniques for preventing oxidation have been tried, such as the use of ascorbic acid, heating the grapes or the must to destroy the oxidases, carrying out crushing and pressing operations in a carbon dioxide atmosphere, and treating musts beforehand with casein. These processes do undeniably offer certain advantages, but the sulfiting sedimentation technique remains for the time being the one that gives the simplest and surest results; it has been adopted in many areas.

Experiments with ascorbic acid in vinification have given satisfactory results and tend to keep the aroma of the grapes better. Amounts to be used are considerable, 10–20 g/hL, but it is only when combined with sulfur dioxide that protection against oxidation can be assured.

Heating the must destroys the oxidases more efficiently than sulfur dioxide but the process presents many drawbacks, even apart from the necessity of using a special apparatus: poor spontaneous clarification of the wines obtained due to neutralization of the pectolitic enzymes; sometimes deviation in the formation of the fermentation aromas, with the appearance of an ethereal character, of fusel oil odors, which dominates the primary aroma of the grape. Sulfiting is no less indispensable.

Working under a carbon dioxide atmosphere, the grapes arrive in the crusher at the same time as a jet of gas. The crushed grapes fall into the horizontal press cage, enclosed in a casing filled with gas. The must is collected in a small tank below that is filled with carbon dioxide. Experiments have led to an observable improvement in aroma, both in intensity and in finesse. However, the wine obtained in this way, often with difficulties during fermentation, is extremely sensitive to its first contact with air and quickly goes brown. Protection from oxidation is very quickly lost. In reality, what needs to be achieved is organoleptic stability in air, for it would not be realistic to contemplate keeping wine right up to bottling entirely protected from oxygen.

Finally other protection techniques may be mentioned that intervene neither on the reagent, oxygen, nor on the catalyst, the oxidase, but on the oxidizable substratum, that is to say, the polyphenols. It has been observed that adsorption of certain tannins by nylon powder (polyamide), polyvinyl polypirrolidon (PVPP), and, in a more practical way, casein in high doses (in the 50 g/hL range) gives more color stability and checks loss of freshness.

CONDUCTING FERMENTATION

Conducting fermentation is dominated, even more than with red vinification, by temperature conditions, since the level of favorable fermentation temperatures is considerably lower for white vinification. The best quality products are obtained when the temperature does not rise above 20°C. Fermentation at high temperature, in addition to the risk of stoppage, which is always detrimental to quality, is attended by considerable loss of the primary aromas. Moreover, the secondary aromas produced by yeasts at high temperature are richer in the higher alcohols and less so in esters and are therefore less agreeable.

Traditional vinification techniques in fine wine regions solved the temperature problem empirically by fermenting in small-capacity containers lying in cool cellars. Numerous highly considered wines these days are, at least in part, aged in oak casks. Some people also use tuns of anything from 9 to 15 hL.

Developments in white vinification have been imposed by concentration of production facilities and centralization of plant. This has meant moving away from casks toward large-capacity tanks for which temperature control is more difficult, without the need for cooling systems adapted to these new fermentation conditions having been properly appreciated beforehand.

Fermentation in Casks

The barrel and the "piece" with capacities of 205, 225, or 228 L placed in a temperate storage room below 20°C probably constitute ideal containers

ADVANTAGES AND DISADVANTAGES OF WOODEN CASKS FOR MAKING WHITE WINES

Advantages	Disadvantages
Favorable temperature conditions in regions with a temperate climate. Conditions of aeration favorable to the yeasts.	Great deal of manual work, controlling the casks, topping, racking. Irregularity between one cask and another in must constitution, evolution of fermentation, and so on.
Spontaneous clarification and rapid settling of the yeasts.	Storage more uncertain, risk of yeast contamination.
	In the long run, risk of losing freshness and fruitiness, aging accelerated.

for fermentation. They provide the best conditions for development of the yeasts.

First of all, the temperature cannot rise much since the cooling surface is considerable in relation to volume. Apart from the first days of the rapid fermentation phase, fermentation carries on at room temperature. The only danger is sometimes a drop in outside temperature, some wines taking 4–6 weeks to ferment, which means warming the room to prevent fermentation stoppage.

The cask still provides the best conditioning as far as the yeasts' need for air is concerned. Aeration through the bunghole and even through the wood itself is always sufficient. It is in the cask that the greatest yeast population is obtained and the highest alcohol strengths are reached. It is not unusual, with musts of Sauternes for instance, to reach 15–16% alcohol, which could never be achieved in the tank.

Ordinarily casks are not completely filled and a space of around 10-L capacity is left to avoid overspill of froth and must. It is advisable to begin topping, gradually reducing the volume of the empty space as soon as the rapid fermentation phase begins to slow down. The practice called *guillage* is no longer carried out. This was an operation for removing by overspill, rather like settling from the top, the impurities from the must, the pectic deposits that form on the surface plus a part of the yeasts. *Guillage* slows down fermentation.

Fermentation in Tanks

This is becoming the general rule with large-capacity vinification. Cement tanks are common but metal tanks, better adapted to temperature regulation, are being developed more and more.

Tank fermentation requires means of absorbing the calories released. Cooling by circulating the must in tubular coolers using running water over the outside, the only system possible with a cement tank, affords merely a partial answer since it is not possible to maintain temperature below 20°C by such means. At most, it will prevent it going beyond 30°C.

One rational method that is not always applicable, consists of chilling the sedimented must by bringing it to a temperature of 12 or 13°C using a refrigerating plant. A plant capable of 20,000 negative kilocalories per hour enables 200 hL per day to be vinified. The chilled must is seeded with 10 g of *Saccharomyces oviformis* powder per hectoliter. The start of fermentation is slow and the temperature cannot go beyond 20°C. This technique for conducting fermentation gives better results than cooling when applied to a tank whose temperature is already too high. Here again the thing is to avoid reaching a high temperature instead of, having reached or gone beyond it, having to come back down again.

Metal tanks, even of large capacity, that can be cooled by running water over the outer casing, afford far greater possibilities, particularly if, placed outside, they can be cooled by vaporization and evaporation. Experience shows that with a climate like that in the Bordeaux region, temperature can be maintained in this way at 18 or 19°C in 300–1000 hL tanks.

For this reason, strangely enough, in cooperative wineries, large-capacity storage tanks placed outside afford better fermentation conditions than batteries of tanks inside, because they are easier to cool efficiently.

Finishing Off Fermentation of Dry Wines

Although the progress of fermentation can be perfectly well defined by its density readings, the densitometer is not enough to decide when all the sugar has been transformed. Chemical determination of the reducing sugars is indispensable even if the density has fallen to 0.994 or 0.993. It is only when the level of reducing sugars is equal to or lower than 2 g that alcoholic fermentation may be considered to be over.

The way treatment is pursued depends on the option relative to malolactic fermentation as defined in Chapter 10. When this is being sought and the winemaker has avoided sulfiting the must too heavily and going too far with settling or clarification, the wine is left on its lees until the malic acid has all gone. This is the way the great wines of Burgundy are prepared. On the contrary, if this is to be avoided, racking should be done without waiting, then sulfiting at 6 or 8 g of sulfur dioxide per hectoliter in such a way that the dose of free sulfur dioxide after combination is in the order of 30–40 mg/L.

The advantage of rapidly eliminating any lees in suspension in young sulfited wines needs to be underlined. When bulk storage is used, clarification by natural settling and racking, efficient enough when wine is stored in casks, has to be replaced by mechanical operations: centrifugation and filtration. New storage procedures need to be matched by new methods of treating wines. One of the dangers of storing white wine on its lees of yeasts in large volumes is the development of sulfide odors. The technique of storing white wine on its lees, directly bottled without racking, much appreciated in certain areas, can only be done in limited quantities.

SWEET AND SEMISWEET WINES

These are wines whose fermentation has been incomplete. They are naturally sweet either because their fermentation stops of its own accord or else because a technical artifice is used to retain a certain proportion of the sugar in the grape. These wines are arbitrarily classified into semisweet (say, up to 20 g of sugar per liter), mellow (up to 36 g), and sweet. These types of wine are very widespread and respond to consumer taste over a vast population in relation to the wine region and the country. This is the case for various appellations in the Bordeaux area, among them the famous Sauternes growth, for certain wines in the Loire (*Coteaux du Layon*), the Jurançon area, the majority of German wines and the most familiar wines from California. Champagne itself is never totally dry, a brut contains 8–12 g of sugar per liter.

Although vinification of semisweet and mellow wines is close to that of dry wines, it may be said that the vinification of sweet wines (*vins liquoreux*) takes the opposite course. Indeed, harvesting is done in successive sortings, picking grapes that are very ripe, overripe, or botrytized. It is this picking technique and the late autumn season that conditions their richness and quality. The good years for sweet wines are rarely the same for dry wines since they require good weather not only during the ripening period but also during the period of overripening (*surmaturation*). It would be a mistake to try to get very rich botrytization with high concentration every year and thereby run the risk of depreciation on account of bad weather. There are a lot of disappointments with this kind of winemaking simply because people try to generalize a style of wine that is in reality an exception. Bad rot generates volatile acidity through intervention from acetic bacteria giving "fungus" tastes, moldy, "iodine," or "phenol" odors. It provokes a high rate of sulfur dioxide combination.

Preparation of the Must

Based on the same principles as any white vinification (i.e., rapid execution, protection from oxidation, and great care being taken to avoid extraction), it is conspicuous by the absence of any draining and by a reverse selection of the musts, the press must being richer and better.

Vinification from shriveled grapes, with noble rot, has little juice and separation of the must is slow and arduous. The advantages in rapidity of the horizontal press in which the vintage, whether crushed or not, is poured directly without draining, are in this case more evident than ever.

The technique of settling after sulfiting is not applicable. In order to avoid right from the outset any accumulation of sulfur dioxide compounds that would bring the margin of sulfiting during storage down to the legal limit permitted for total sulfur dioxide, the most that can be used is a sulfite treatment to 5 g/hL, enough to afford protection from weak oxidation but not enough to check fermentation for long or to destroy the oxidase. At the same time, sedimentation of the deposits by settling is slow and incomplete, the musts being viscous, thick with glucanes and other protective colloids. Centrifugation, on the condition that the oxidation it causes be perfectly compensated, could serve as a more efficient means of purifying, in the same way as refrigeration followed by a settling period at low temperature, if these processes did not compromise the ease of fermentation.

Fermentation and Mutage

The fermentability of must from botrytized grapes is very varied. Sometimes fermentation is very rapid and attains very high alcoholic strengths; this is occasionally the case with the first load of grapes outsorted. At other times, it is slow and sticks with low alcoholic levels; this is often the case with the last grapes picked. The explanation is as follows: there exists in botrytized grapes two categories of substance having opposite effects on fermentation, one activating it, the other hindering and delaying it. The discovery of a polysaccharide that inhibits yeasts links up with early observations identifying an antibiotic called "botryticine." The respective proportions of these substances decide which direction speed of fermentation of the must will take. Sulfur dioxide in small doses reduces the inhibition and then the fact can be observed, at first sight very surprising, that fermentation is faster and more complete when the affected must has been lightly sulfited.

To avoid irregularity and delay in fermentation, it is recommended adding to the must 10 g of ammonia salts to correct a fairly common nitrate deficiency, 50 g of thiamine, and 10 g of *Saccharomyces oviformis* powder, all per hectoliter.

Making semisweet (*moelleux*) and sweet (*liquoreux*) wines calls for fermentation stoppage or mutage, followed by storage in conditions where refermentation is prevented. Several means are theoretically possible to obtain mutage but only sulfiting ensures long-term stability.

1.   The best sweet wines (*liquoreux*) and the most stable of them are obtained by natural fermentation stoppage often promoted by low surrounding temperature. In the same winery the strength of some lots may be as much as 15% or more while for others fermentation stops, leaving a lot of sugar. The blending of these different lots is what gives a balanced wine. Storage is ensured by sufficient sulfiting. This technique is only possible for basic musts rich in sugars.

2.   Using artificial chilling achieves the same result. If the temperature of a must in fermentation is dropped under 10°C, the transformation of the sugar stops, but the yeasts do not die. Sulfiting needs to be done to prevent revival of fermentation when it warms up again.

3.   Heating must to 45°C kills the yeasts and checks fermentation. Here again the stabilizing role of sulfiting treatment is indispensable.

4.   Using up all the assimilable nitrate by means of successive fermentations and clarifications, utilizing centrifugation and filtration, techniques inspired from a long-standing process in making Asti Spumante, leads to an environment that is practically nonfermentable yet remains sweet.

5.   The most commonly used means of stopping fermentation, applied indifferently to musts with varying degrees of sugar content, is with a sufficient dose of sulfur dioxide.

The rule for mutage is to add at the properly chosen time, a relatively massive dose such that the remaining free sulfur dioxide content, taking the compound into account, is at least 80 mg/L. In relation to the richness of the wines, doses for mutage to be used vary between 20 and 30 g/hL. This large dose instantaneously arrests transformation of the sugar but only kills the yeasts slowly. It acts at first as a narcotic, then in the end as a poison. It requires 24 hours for practically all the yeasts to be destroyed but after several weeks a few yeasts still remain alive. Sulfur dioxide, in the doses used in practice, is not capable of completely sterilizing wine.

According to a general law on the use of antiseptics, the fewer the yeasts there are to inhibit, the less active they are, the more efficient sulfur dioxide will be. Therefore it is advisable to reduce the number of yeasts before or after halting fermentation by racking or by any other means, such as centrifugation or filtration. The object to go after to get good storage of sweet wines is to separate the yeasts as rapidly as possible. These wines have nothing at all to gain by remaining on their lees.

Sweetening Dry White Wines

Dry white wines can be sweetened either at the winery or in the merchants' cellars either using fresh musts preserved by the German technique or else by the addition of a small quantity of concentrated must.

In the first case, it is "Süssreserve" (sweetening reserve) composed of musts generally partially fermented, that is utilized. These products are preserved by dropping the temperature (5–8°C) after sterilization, filtering or under high-pressure carbon dioxide, which checks the yeasts. Blending is done just before bottling, which is carried out hot or cold in sterile conditions.

Concentrated musts are prepared from sulfited or "muted" musts that are desulfited and concentrated by heating in a vacuum at 30 or 36 degrees Baumé (630 or 800 g of sugar per liter). Enrichment is limited to a potential 2%, the strength of sweetened wines not being allowed to go beyond 12%. The use of concentrated must has a few drawbacks: If it has not been deacidified, it increases total acidity; alternatively if the must has been treated with calcium carbonate, it introduces excess calcium salts and provokes, later on, precipitations of calcium tartrate.

18

Vinifying Rosé Wines and Special Wines

DEFINITION AND PROCESSING OF ROSÉ WINES

Rosé wine cannot be defined by its color. It is an intermediate style between white wine and red wine, between wine made without extraction from pomace and wine with extraction. What it inherits from red wine is the original grape variety, the presence of a small quantity of anthocyanins. From white, it gets its general makeup, its lightness, its fruity quality, and a certain similarity in its vinification techniques.

Rosé wines exist that have more resemblance to red wines, with body and with a stronger color, their anthocyanin content varying from 60 to 120 mg/L, they are obtained with limited extraction and made more supple by malolactic fermentation. Others are more like white wines, having undergone less extraction, their anthocyanins are not more than 50 mg/L, they have less freshness and often retain their malic acid.

The technological definition of rosé wines is difficult to establish. It cannot be based solely on their origin or on their methods of vinification. Theoretically, they can be made from partial extraction of a red grape or total extraction of a gray or rosé grape. In certain areas, it is even permitted for white grape varieties to be used in part, but in no circumstances can it be made by blending red and white wine.

The majority of rosé wines are dry, but certain regions produce a semisweet (*moelleux*) type that is appreciated.

The vogue for rosé wines can be explained by their attractive appearance, a taste for refreshing drinks, seeking more fruity wines and by the fact that rosé can be drunk throughout a meal. However, it must be admitted that whereas there are great red wines and great white wines, there are very few top-class rosé wines. Perhaps because they are quite difficult to make and do not age well. Rosé is one of the wines that might benefit most from progress in enological science.

Rosé wines are obtained by two possible production methods: either by white vinification using red grapes or by a partial extraction technique.

Rosé Wines from White Vinification

These are made from red grapes processed like a white vintage using the operations of crushing, draining, and pressing but without the same precautions for limiting extraction that are generally taken in white winemaking. Besides, in order to get sufficient color intensity, it is often necessary to utilize must from the first press. Moderate sulfiting is carried out in relation to the state of the grapes, but sedimentation is not generally the rule when the crop is healthy. The processing needed after this is not particularly a problem and requires the same care used in making white wines: low fermentation temperatures and protection from oxidation. Malolactic fermentation, either total or partial, may be conducted or not, as the case may be.

Rosé Wines from Partial Maceration

These are known as clairette, café wines, or one-night wines. The beginning is the same as for red wine. A tank is loaded with crushed grapes, either stemmed or not, and sulfited. Fermentation starts after a few hours and the cap rises. At the same time, color begins to deepen through dissolution of the anthocyanins, with greater or less speed according to the variety of grape and its state of ripeness. After 12 or 24 hours, as soon as the color is considered to be sufficient, taking account of the fact that it will tend to fade during fermentation and later after sulfiting, the pomace is separated. Generally only a part of the tank is drained. The remainder goes on being vinified as red wine. Sometimes the tank is reloaded with fresh vintage on top of the pomace, but this practice is not advisable since it makes red wines that are hard.

Fermentation of the must carries on after it has been drained, slowed up a bit due to separation from the pomace. The best fermentation temperature is in the region of 20°C. Before racking, the winemaker generally tries to get malolactic fermentation.

THE WINES OF CHAMPAGNE

The demarcated area for Champagne wines includes the *départements* (counties) of Aube and Aisne. The grape varieties used in this area include two black grapes, Pinot noir and Pinot Meunier, plus the white Chardonnay. The wine of Champagne is generally a white wine made from black grapes. Only the quality called *Blanc de Blancs* (white from white) is made from Chardonnay alone. Vinification is based on a method of working that avoids any maceration, so that the anthocyanins from the grapeskins are not extracted. There is a geographical rating in growths of 100%, up to 92%, up to 86%, and so on in relation to the quality of the soil. This rating determines basic pricing of the grapes from each crop.

Vinification

Sorting to remove grapes with rot is advisable.

Grapes transported in baskets of 60–80 kg.

Uncrushed bunches pressed in the Champagne press with a wide surface area and shallow depth enabling virtually colorless juice to be obtained, with light pressure, from black grapes. Horizontal presses are also used. Dividing the must up is standardized as follows: starting with 4000 kg of grapes, 2050 L are produced for the cuvée, 410 L for the first press fraction (PF), 205 L for the second PF then 200 or 300 L of hard press, which is not used for making champagne.

Sulfiting the must to 5 or 10 g/hL, one or two settlings.

Fermentation conducted at low temperature (formerly in "pieces" of 205 L, today in up-to-date fermentation rooms equipped with circulation coolers or all-round cooling)

Malolactic fermentation is often sought.

Bottle fermentation (méthode champenoise)

Blending of the cuvée, based on tasting, including wines from various growths plus a portion of older wines.

Clarification by fining and filtration.

Addition in the form of *tirage* syrup of 24–26 g of sugar per liter, of yeasts (1 million per milliliter), of additives that help fermentation and settling of the solids, then it is drawn off (*tirage*) into bottles.

Secondary fermentation takes place at a temperature of 11–12°C; it is slow and lasts several weeks, indeed several months. The wine ages for several years on its yeast sediment.

Riddling on racks (*remuage*), an operation destined to gradually get the yeast sediment to sink onto the cork, leaving the wine clear (bottles stocked on end, *sur les pointes*, stacked in bulk).

Disgorging the sediment by opening the bottle, generally after freezing the neck (ice disgorging).

Dosage with the sweetener giving Champagne its respective degree of sweetness according to style (brut: 8–12 g of sugar; *demi-sec*: 35–45 g/L).

There are two distinct technological periods in the preparation of effer-vescent wines: making the base wine and, afterward, the secondary fermen-tation. Vinification of Champagne is based on avoiding crushing, then sep-arating the must so that the anthocyanins are not extracted and do not color the must. The *méthode Champenoise* for bottle fermentation is characterized by the fact that throughout the processing the wine never leaves the bottle.

SPARKLING WINES

Sparkling wines, produced in many wine-growing areas outside Champagne, are ranked in several categories according to the process used in making them, particularly as regards the secondary fermentation and separation of the yeast sediment:

1. Sparkling wines *méthode champenoise.*
2. Sparkling wines fermented in the bottle then transferred into a pressure tank under nitrogen or carbonic acid gas, refrigeration, filtration, and another draining into bottles.

Fermentation in the bottle
After stabilization and clarification, the cuvée is drawn off into 0.8- or 1.6-L bottles with 20–24 g of sugar per liter and 1 million active yeasts per milliliter.
Aging on the yeast sediment ought to last a minimum of 9 months for sparkling wines with an original appellation.

Transfer and filtration
With the transfer and filtration process, the operations of riddling (*remuage*), up-ending and disgorging, an essential part of the *méthode champenoise*, are avoided. Bottles are transferred into a metal tank under nitrogen pressure. The syrup is mixed in, the whole refrigerated, then filtered, still under counterpressure from the nitrogen or carbon dioxide atmosphere. Isobaric bottling is done with the sparkling wine maintained at low temperature.

Charmat process or tank fermentation
The secondary fermentation is carried out, after addition of sugar and yeast, in steel pressure tanks with several tons of hectoliters capacity. Constant temperature is maintained; sparkling quality is better when fermentation temperature is lower.
Refrigeration of the tank at −5°C allows fermentation to be stopped as soon as pressure reaches 5–6 kg, leaving the requisite amount of sugar unfermented, with-out adding the *tirage* syrup.
After a few days settling at low temperature, the wine is sulfited and filtered. This is followed by isobaric bottling.

---

3.   Sparkling wines made in a pressure tank.

4.   Gasified wines.

Base wines may belong to various different appellations. A small production of quality sparkling wines, in preparing its base wine, will follow exactly the same principles as vinification in Champagne.

Quality is directly related to that of the base wine (grape variety, vinification process) and to the method of secondary fermentation used, to be more precise, the length of time it lies on the yeast sediment.

ASTI SPUMANTE

Asti Spumante is a sparkling wine, sweet and aromatic, prepared in pressure tanks. The base wine is Moscato d'Asti made from the white Muscat grapes; its production area is situated in Piedmont in the provinces of Asti, Alessandria, and Cueno. Asti Spumante is 6–9% alcohol, contains 60–100 g of reducing sugars, with 3.0–4.8 g of fixed acidity (as sulfuric acid).

The vinification technique tends to maintain in the base wine the characteristic aroma of the Muscat in spite of stopping fermentation and stabilizing the wine with high sugar content. To control this development, the must undergoes settling, fining and filtering, repeated each time yeast development

---

Vinification technique

Crushing with roller-crushers.

Pressing in horizontal presses.

Sulfiting.

Fining with tannins and gelatin plus double sedimentation.

Filtering on linen or centrifugation.

Another addition of tannin and fining followed by filtering on linen or centrifugation each time fermentation begins again. The number of finings and clarifications vary with the crops and the composition of the raw material.

This technique for preparing the base must has been considerably simplified by storing at low temperature up to the time of secondary fermentation.

Secondary fermentation

Secondary fermentation takes place in pressure tanks, at first at a temperature of 18–20°C, later dropped to 14–15°C.

Fermentation reaches a pressure of 5 atmospheres in 2 weeks. It is chilled down to 0°C, filtered then refrigerated at −4°C for 10–15 days. It is filtered again, then bottled. Either sterilizing filtration or else pasteurization in the bottle is used.

---

and fermentation begin to speed up. In this way, the major part of the yeasts is eliminated together with the assimilated nitrate substances. Reducing the nitrogen content in forms that could be used by the yeasts is enough to give the wine biological stability. This system of vinification manages to achieve stabilization through lack of nitrogen. Present-day technology, which utilizes centrifugation and refrigeration, is more reliable.

NATURAL SWEET WINES (*vins doux naturels* = VDN)

These wines are made in the Roussillon region of France following very old time-honored customs. They are produced exclusively from the fermentation of fresh grape juice. They are sweet because by means of halting the fermentation with added alcohol they retain a large part of the sugar from the original must. The local appellation areas are Banyuls, Maury, Rivesaltes, Côtes d'Agly, Côtes du Haut-Roussillon, and Rasteau, made from crops of Grenache, Maccabéo, and Malvoisie. The Muscat growths are Rivesaltes, Frontignan, Lunel, Beaumes de Venise, Saint-Jean de Minervois, and Mireval made with crops of small-berried Muscat and Muscat of Alexandria.

Possible Methods of Vinification of VDN

Without Extraction	With Extraction		With Maceration Carbonique
Harvesting	Harvesting		Harvesting intact
Crushing	Crushing		Put into pressure tanks under carbon dioxide
(Draining)	(Destemming)		
Pressing	Sulfiting		
Sulfiting	Partial fermentation		Extraction and intracellular fermentation
(Sedimentation)	Extraction		
(Inoculation with yeasts)			
			Partial fermentation
Partial fermentation	Pressing	Stopping fermentation with alcohol	Pressing
Stopping fermentation with alcohol	Stopping fermentation with alcohol		Stopping fermentation with alcohol
		Extraction	
(Sulfiting)	(Sulfiting)	Pressing	Racking
Racking	Racking	Racking	
		(Sulfiting)	

a The operations in parentheses are optional or sometimes inadvisable.

Wines have strengths of 15–16%, 70–125 g of sugar, and total acidity of 3.0–3.5 g.

Vinification "without maceration" enables relatively light, nonoxidized VDN to be obtained, to be drunk young, say, 8–18 months after being made. This applies to white grapes. The technique "with maceration" gives Muscats that are richer in aromas and VDN reds richer in extracts, suitable for aging. Maceration carbonique produces VDN very rich in grape aroma.

The storage of VDN is carried out in full containers. The Muscats have a lot of perfume when they are drunk young. The white VDN attain optimum quality after 2 years' aging and red VDN after 3 years and more aging in wood and in bottles. The rancio of great Banyuls is acquired by keeping it in casks left out of doors that are subject to seasonal variations in temperature.

Many countries with a hot climate produce similar wines, passerillized, overripened, enriched or fortified, benefiting from prolonged oxidative aging.

PORT WINES

Port wines, generous and rich in sugar, the archetype of alcoholic dessert wines, come from the valley of the Douro River in Portugal. The original

---

Vinification technique

Fermentation and extraction.   Traditional vinification is carried out in "lagars," granite or shale containers 80 cm high, rectangular or square-shaped, in which the grapes, not destemmed, are crushed and fermentation is started. The shape of these lagars responds to the need for getting total crushing of the grapes by treading in order to get thorough extraction of the skins' constituents, especially the polyphenols. The base work includes long, tough pounding and crushing operations using a lot of knee power, continuously for several hours both before and during fermentation. The pomace is then punched down at regular intervals. Today this work is evolving toward mechanized methods, the stirring of the grapes being obtained by intensive pumping over the cap using a power pump.

Finishing and aging

Storage is carried out in "pipes" of 550 L, not completely filled. Oxidative aging therefore lasts several years, 4–5 years for the types exported youngest, at least 8 years for the "tawny" quality and often much more since these wines have great longevity. Regularity of quality is ensured by blending based on tasting. Clarification and stabilization are obtained by fining and filtering.

The years of top quality can be bottled after 2 years' storage in casks completely full of the "vintage" type, in which aging is accomplished in airtight conditions. This method of aging is very similar to the customary aging of fine red wines.

---

grape varieties are numerous (there are more than 15 different red varieties and 6 white varieties). Port is obtained by stopping fermentation of the fermenting must with spirits.

Ports are divided into extra dry, dry (generally white), *demi-sec*, and sweet (generally red). Their color range is varied: deep red, ruby red (these are the "fulls"), golden blonde, onion skin (these are the "tawnies"), pale white, straw, or golden. A good port is recognized first by its aroma; tasters judge, in fact, almost exclusively by odor.

SHERRY WINES

The wines from Jerez (once called Xeres) are wines with high vinosity obtained by adding alcohol, and they have great delicacy. They owe their special

---

Vinification

Harvesting of the grapes is done in baskets of 11.5 kg. Traditionally the cut grapes are exposed to the sun for one day on esparto mats (*soleo*). Then they are crushed, pressed at low pressure in thin layers. The must is separated and only the wine from the first press is kept; the other lots are distilled. Rectification of the musts includes acidification with a view to lowering the pH, previously by plastering, and light sulfiting. Fermentation is done in oak "botas" of 500–600 L with 40–50 L of head space.

Biological aging

The new wines chosen by the taster to be given biological aging are alcoholized to 15 or 15.5%. On the surface of the wine, a film of yeasts is formed. The transformations that they generate, formation of acetaldehyde, of acetal, and of aromatic substances, give to the wine its special aging character. During storage under this film of *flor* (flower), the wine undergoes numerous rackings and partial movements, with blending, making the lots uniform, in accordance with the "solera" system, which allows great homogeneity to be obtained both in average aging and the organoleptic characteristics of bottled wines. These wines are called fino, manzanilla, or amontillado.

Nonbiological aging

For another category of wines, the alcoholic strength is raised to 18 or 19%. Aging in "botas," which are not completely filled is carried out by slow oxidation in absence of the film, following the system of "soleras." The wines obtained, more colored and more powerful, often sweetened by the base wine (mistelle), are called olorosos.

Remarks. In the Château-Chalon region in France, the yellow wine of the Jura is harvested, aged in a rather similar way for several years in small casks under an intermittent flor film.

---

characteristics and their specificity to the various ways of storing them, differentiated by the relation of the wine with oxygen. In "biological" aging, the wine is protected from oxidation by the reducing action of the yeasts that cover it while in another type of aging, wines are kept in a permanent state of oxidation. The production area is southern Spain in the region of Jerez de la Frontera, with an Atlantic influence. The basic grape varieties are Palomino and Pedro Ximenez.

BRANDY

The vinification of white grapes for the production of Cognac and Armagnac is generally reduced to its elementary operations. Nonetheless, precautions do need to be taken to produce quality brandy.

The grapes are crushed, then pressed in vertical or horizontal presses. The musts obtained are fermented without settling and without addition of sulfur dioxide, which would denature their taste. It will be understood that in such conditions, maintenance and cleanliness of the winemaking vessels are of prime importance. Fermentation is most frequently done in cement tanks without any cooling system. This is promoted by the low alcoholic strength of the must.

The wine is not racked off its lees but distilled directly with the light lees of yeasts, the heavy murky lees being discarded. Distillation is begun as soon as fermentation has finished and goes on until spring. Malolactic fermentation is general. In years of great ripeness, acidification of the musts with tartaric acid allows better storage.

Cognac Distillation

In the Cognac area, the varieties used are Saint Emilion des Charentes (Trebbiano or Ugni Blanc) and French Colombard. Distillation in the Charentes region uses the simple copper pot-still with an open flame and it is obtained by two distillations. A first distillation produces the main fraction, the *brouillis*, at around 28%. It is taken through again by another distillation, which gives hearts at 70%. The heads are eliminated and distillate collected until 50% is reached; that is to say, as soon as the alcohol is running at 50%, it is switched into another container until the alcoholometer registers zero. These are the "seconds" or *repasse*, which will be redistilled with the wine. Distillation is conducted very slowly.

As Lafon expressed it: "The quality of Cognac is suspended by a multi-link chain: growths (nature of the soil and subsoil), grape varieties, pruning and load not to be exceeded, sufficient ripeness for minimum strength, vinification, storage of the wine, distillation, storage of the spirits. However, a chain is only as strong as its weakest link. If one of the links is unsound, the chain will break and quality drops."

Armagnac Distillation

The main varieties in the Armagnac area are the Baco 22 A, Ugni Blanc (Trebbiano), Jurançon and French Colombard. Armagnac brandy is distilled very slowly, in a single stream, in one operation in a copper still that does not include any rectification column. The Armagnac apparatus is a continuous-feed still with two or three boilers superposed. The distillation of the spirit hearts is continued until strength declines to 24%. The final blend gives 52 or 53 proof.

Finesse and clarity are basic qualities for young brandies, but it is aging in oak casks that plays the fundamental role. The wood ensures slow transformation by oxidation and brings specific aromatic elements that are called wood-*rancio*. Quality increases for several decades with the length of aging in cooperage. Once in the bottle, however, brandy does not develop anymore.

PART 5

Storage and Aging

19

Cellar Work—Cleanliness and Hygiene Measures for Wine Containers

Wine is a food product. As such it needs to be prepared, handled and stored with as many precautions as any other drink, for instance, milk or beer. Because of its alcohol and its acidity, also because of the alleged purifying action of fermentation, a certain self-preserving, even antibacterial property, wine gives a false notion of security and cleanliness. In reality, it is extremely sensitive, both in taste and in its sanitary state, to any contamination or impurities. It easily "catches" off-tastes and off-odors from the premises and containers. Yeast or bacterial disturbances are transmitted by the wine vessels and by the equipment. Therefore, inside the cellars, veritable epidemics due to infection do occur.

Measures for cleanliness begin with vinification and go on until bottling. This applies to the vinification and the storage premises as well as to the containers and equipment. Cleanliness is a basic condition for quality. The whole of enological science would be to no avail if the work itself were done in places that were dirty.

CLEANLINESS OF THE PREMISES

Wineries must be adapted to the special work of vinification and storage. Wineries should be spacious and well-aired, even ventilated; in certain regions sophisticated large-scale installations protected only from the sun are set up out of doors. Vinification cannot be done properly in a confined atmosphere.

Figure 19.1. View of a storage cellar in the Médoc. The new wine is put into 50-gal Bordeaux château barrels of new oak in the bung-on-top position. The barrel is stoppered with a glass bung (Photo Pierre Mackiewicz).

Where the wine is made needs to be dry and washable, therefore tiled or cemented. Storage cellars must conform to the same standards. Tanks should never be constructed in old cellars.

The storage conditions needed for casks are opposite to those for tanks. Cellars containing casks need to be of small size, they should be closed to avoid aeration and temperature variations (Fig. 19.1). The wine in cooperage maintains the humidity of the atmosphere. However, damp, moldy cellars with saltpetrous walls need to be converted or abandoned; beaten-earth floors should be replaced with concrete floors. Alcohol vapors that escape from the casks by evaporation feed the mildew which covers the walls of old cellars. This mildew has the advantage of deodorizing the atmosphere, but the disadvantage of maintaining undesirable microflora.

To be able to keep them in good conditions of cleanliness, walls should be smooth or rough-rendered. Washable paints with a chloride-rubber base containing an antifungal substance are the most efficient formula rather than whitewashing the walls. Tiling the walls and the face of the tanks need not be looked on as a superfluous luxury just for appearance.

The cleanliness of all the wine material used for transporting, picking, pressing, and stocking is equally imperative. Cleanliness means everything. Trying to keep equipment clean in a dirty cellar is impossible. The cellarman must understand the necessity of washing everything every evening, when work is over; baskets, hods, tubs, bins, hoppers, presses, troughs, basins, and so forth. Large cellars ought to be installed with equipment designed with this in mind. Every fermentation room and cellar must be provided with running water and good drainage for the dirty water. The rule is very ancient: "Making good wine requires a great deal of water."

Another rule of cleanliness concerns the fight against insects. You can get rid of the vinegar-fly (drosophila), an acetic-bacteria carrier that invades wineries at the time of fermentation and draining, with the help of an appliance that permanently diffuses a volatile insecticide. The same appliances used in the bottling rooms two or three times a year destroy both the larval and adult cork worms.

CLEANLINESS OF WINE CONTAINERS

"It is forbidden to use, for storage of food-associated products, any recipient which has not been washed and dried immediately before use." Cleanliness is a legal obligation.

Upkeep of Tanks

Wooden or concrete tanks require constant maintenance and periodical overhaul. A wooden tank when empty only keeps provided it is dry (Fig. 19.2); if wet, it soon starts to get moldy. When wood is very old, it deteriorates in depth and can often be the cause of off-tastes.

Concrete tanks (Fig. 19.3), if badly maintained, can also be a source of trouble. Maintenance consists of ensuring that, on the one hand, the concrete is protected and the coating adhering correctly and, on the other hand, making sure the layer of tartar does not get too thick. The lees and organic matter become sealed up by the annual layer of tartar and are centers of adulteration that give rise to off-tastes and bacterial spoilage.

Descaling is done by scraping, brushing, and, when the tartar is thick, by cracking it off or even using a blow-lamp, which makes it flake off. Chemical descaling is very efficient. It is based on the principle of spraying continuously the whole surface of the tank to be treated with an alkaline solution. Potassium bitartrate, which constitutes the major part of the tartar in vinification tanks, is made soluble in a base medium. The apparatus sprays the walls by pumping through the solution in a continuous circuit. The same system can be used for cleaning the tank walls by scouring with tartaric acid. In this connection, it is worth repeating that trying to clean concrete with silicates does not provide sufficient protection and that fluorides or fluosilicates are forbidden since they transmit fluorine to the wine.

Figure 19.2. View of a storage cellar using wooden tuns (Photo Pierre Mackiewicz).

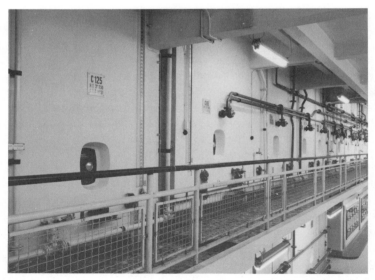

Figure 19.3. View of a storage winery fitted with cement tanks (Photo Pierre Mackiewicz).

CLEANING PRODUCTS

Products recommended for cleaning and aseptic treatment of wine containers and
  apparatus:

Alkaline carbonates

Alkaline phosphates

Alkaline polyphosphates

Caustic soda and potassium lye

Calcium chloride

Permanganate of potash

Sulfur dioxide and alkaline bisulfites

Nonfrothing quaternary ammonium

Formol

Alkaline hypochlorites

Iodofores

The condition of tanks lined with glass needs to be checked and broken
or loose tiles replaced. Plastified coatings also require overhaul in case they
need to be rejointed.

Wooden tanks when empty and dry need to be preserved with sulfurous
gas obtained by burning sulfur. Remember that, on the other hand, concrete
tanks should never be sulfured.

Hygiene of Wine Cooperage

Casks of new wood have to be specially treated before use. The wood used
in cooperage contains astringent tannic matter and ingredients with strong
odors. In order not to transmit foreign tastes to the wine, the cask is "neutralized" either by using boiling water or steaming the wood or by soaking
it for some time in lightly sulfited water. If the cask is intended to be used
for storing mature wines, it should be seasoned beforehand for a few days
with a good wine of medium quality).

When the cask is built from sawn wood, it is usually sized on the inside
to block the pores of the wood. This is done with sodium silicate or a geletin
mixture—potassium bichromate. Casks that have been sized are not recommended for maturing quality wines.

To keep properly, empty casks must be clean, dry, asepticized with sulfur
dioxide, thoroughly stoppered, and stored, insulated from the floor in
a place that is neither damp nor too dry. When a cask has just been emptied
of the wine it contained, it must be cleaned immediately by rinsing out abundantly under pressure. Then it is briefly drained with the bunghole downwards
and asepticized with a sulfur candle. After being sulfured, the cask is left to
drain for 5 or 6 days. When it is quite dry, another sulfur candle is burnt in
it and the bunghole hermetically sealed. The cask can be kept in this fashion
for about 2 months before needing to be sulfured again (see Fig. 19.4).

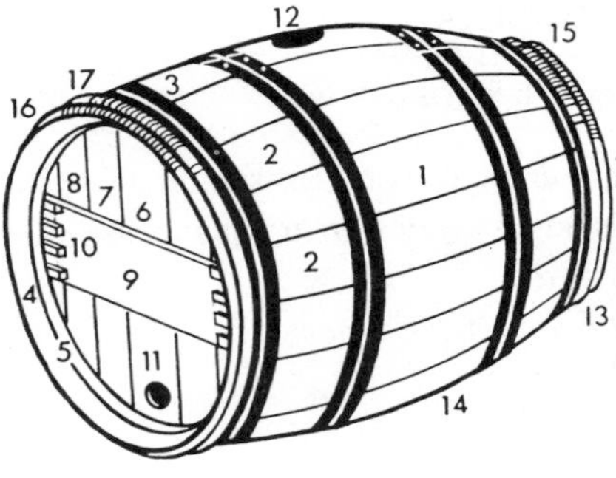

Figure 19.4. Fifty-gallon Bordeaux château barrel. 1, bilge; 2, staves; 3, bunghole stave; 4, chimb; 5, croze; 6, headpiece; 7, *aiselière*; 8, *chanteau*; 9, cross-board; 10, wedges; 11, racking hole; 12, bunghole; 13, wooden hoops; 14, iron hoops; 15, the rush; 16, head hoop; 17, collar hoop.

When a cask has remained empty for several months, it needs to be refreshed by filling it with lightly sulfited water. The wood of an empty cask is, in point of fact, impregnated with sulfuric acid from the fumigation and often with acetic acid due to souring of the wine absorbed by it. It must be realized that the wood in an empty, rinsed 50-gal (225-L) cask still contains over a gallon (5 L) of wine. Without this scouring with water, the acidity in the wine put into it would increase to the detriment of quality.

THE PRACTICE OF RACKING

Racking is the term used for transferring wine from one cask to another or from one tank to another taking every precaution necessary to ensure the liquid is separated in the best way possible from its sediment. Racking is not a simple transfer; it is decanting. The sediment separated constitutes the lees.

Racking is the first treatment a wine should be given, the most elementary, but without doubt the most important too. Setbacks during storage of the wine are likely to be caused by lack of racking or by badly executed racking. The effects of racking are multipurpose and are summed up in the table on p. 239.

Racking is also the usual way of separating, after fining and allowing sufficient time to settle, the clear wine from its fining lees. This is then known as "finings-racking" or "raising the whisk."

Period of and Number of Rackings

At what periods should racking be done and how many times a year? On this subject cellarmen should not bind themselves with overrigorous rules. Wine should be racked whenever it needs to be and that is precisely where the cellar master's skill and experience come in. However, in normal circum-

THE BENEFICIAL EFFECTS OF RACKING

Decanting
Its first role is to separate the dregs from the wine. Sediment that forms in young wines is made up of yeast cells, bacteria cells, and foreign organic substances that need to be removed from the wine. This avoids all the putrid, reduced and hydrogen sulfide tastes a young wine contracts after being left too long on its lees. To some extent, by removing microorganisms, their revived activity is prevented. There is good reason also to take out the different sediments of precipitation—tartar, coloring matter and possibly deposits from casse—in order to prevent them from redissolving, for instance, when the temperature rises again.

Aeration
The racking operation entails contact with the air and dissolution of oxygen on the order of 2–3 mL/L. This aeration facilitates the eventual completion of yeast transformations and plays a useful part in the evolution and stabilization of wine. Young red wines should be racked open to air.

Evaporation
New wine is saturated with carbon dioxide. It loses any excess by means of racking and at the same time certain volatile products responsible for fermentation aroma. Evaporation of alcohol by racking is negligible.

Homogenization
Racking makes the wine in the cask or the tank uniform. During a long settling period, within large-capacity containers, different areas of sedimentation or even areas indicating free sulfur dioxide levels tend to form. They may be insufficient in certain spots, on the surface or near the lees. Racking mixes the different layers.

Sulfiting
Racking allows readjustment of the free sulfur dioxide content, either by fumigating with a sulfur match or by adding a sulfur solution.

Cleaning wine containers
When racking, casks are checked, overhauled, and cleaned by vigorous rinsing. Similarly tanks are brushed down, the walls washed and descaled.

---

stances, for wines that are intended to mature, some general guidance may be given.

Frequency between rackings is not the same for wine stored in tanks as it is for wine in casks. In large-capacity tanks, wine has to be racked more often, for instance, every 2 months, whereas in casks four rackings in the first year is current practice. In this connection, habits may be different in different areas according to the temperature in the cellars and the type of wine. Certain aromatic white wines, light and fresh, are racked only rarely. Wines filtered young and separated in this fashion from their lees very early, only need to be racked at very long intervals. When malolactic fermentation is sought, wine is only racked after this has finished.

As far as dates for racking are concerned, we will as a practical example refer to the methods of maturing wine in the Bordeaux area where great claret is kept in 50-gal oak casks. The first racking called *débourrbage* (clearing the worst murk) is done lot by lot when malolactic fermentation is over, that is, during November or December. The wine is then racked from the tank into the barrels. For sweet and semisweet (mellow) white wines, the first racking is done a fortnight or 3 weeks after fermentation has been stopped.

The second racking is carried out in March at the end of winter and the cold season, before the temperature begins to rise in the cellars. This removes the tartrate which precipitated in winter. By sulfuring with a match, the wine is protected during the spring season. The third racking in June coincides with the period when the vine is in flower. Sulfuring that is done at this time too should ensure storage through the critical summer spell. Casks that have been kept in the "bung on top" position for topping are hermetically stoppered and "laid down," that is to say put in the "bung on the side" position where topping is no longer necessary.

Finally, in the beginning of September, before harvesting, the fourth racking is carried out. Often the wine is then transferred to the cellar used to store mature wines in order to make room for the new wines from the upcoming crop.

The second year wine is racked three times, in February when it is fined, in March when it is "raised from the finings," then in June, a few weeks before bottling.

Method of Racking

We have seen that the essential purpose of racking is to separate the wine from its lees. Lees are created by the mechanical operation of racking, which disturbs the sediment of solid matter deposited against the wood putting it back into suspension. In a barrel or tun, this deposit is not gathered in the bottom, but is spread over a wide surface and is stuck to the walls.

It is instructive to follow the racking operation in barrels that have the underside made of glass and allow the interior to be observed. When the wine is drained from the racking hole, the opening placed a few centimeters above the deposit, no movement of liquid rising from the bottom is observed but on the contrary, sucking action from the top. On their way down, the surface streams carry with them particles from the walls that become detached

Figure 19.5. Working site with racking, barrels stacked three high.

and converge on the outlet. Draining of the wine should be stopped as soon as it starts to come out cloudy, not because of the lees deposited on the bottom of the cask starting to rise but because the particles detached from the walls are brought down with the surface. The form of barrels and tuns does not make decanting easy and produces a large amount of lees. Racking with flat-bottomed tanks is more rational since it gives proportionately less volume of lees.

Racking barrels in the Bordeaux area is generally carried out in two ways: through the racking hole for wines stored with the top bung on the side, or with the help of a vertical plunger for those placed with the bung on top.

To rack via the header bung, this is removed carefully without disturbing the top bung and a faucet is driven in. The wine is drained by gravity into another cask placed at a lower level (see Fig. 19.5). There are several ways of operating. Racking with basins or churns, wooden containers that are filled and then poured into the receiving barrel using a wide funnel, ensures thorough aeration. More often, *cuirs de soutirage* are used. These are short wooden or cloth-covered rubber tubes fixed to the racking-hole faucet. The drawer lets the wine run out, then raises the barrel with a lever hooked into the rear croze, which allows it to be tilted forward. Glass in hand, the drawer inspects the clarity of the wine draining out by the feeble glow of an electric lamp. As soon as the lees appear, and this generally happens very suddenly, he shuts off the faucet.

With the plunger system of racking, the drawer inserts, vertically through the bunghole, a tube made of uncorrodible metal or plastic that is supported on an adjustable screw. In this way, the height of the side openings on the plunger can be set according to the estimated volume of lees.

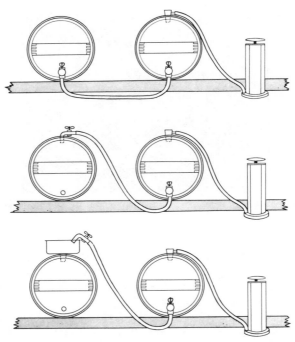

Figure 19.6. Racking cask to cask with the help of a hand pump; a compressor may also be used. *Above*, with aeration; *middle*, with moderate aeration; *below*, with aeration by running into a wide funnel.

Racking should be done by natural drainage, or for barrels on the ground, by displacement using a hand bellows or light compressor (Fig. 19.6). The duration of racking a 50-gal cask should be at least 5 or 6 minutes; going faster makes the lees rise. Racking systems using pumps to draw the wine should be condemned. They suck up the deposits from wines with heavy lees, so that racking becomes a mere transfer.

TOPPING

It has been said of topping up the casks periodically as the headspace above the wine drops through absorption or shrinkage, that it is the weak spot in storage. It is a simple enough operation but requires a great deal of care and cleanliness. Its purpose is to prevent or, at the very least, reduce the formation of an immobile wine surface in contact with air and consequently the danger of oxidation or acetic deterioration that this presents.

The frequency of topping depends on circumstances: speed of creation of the headspace, temperature, type of container. Barrels are topped twice a week; tanks, once a week.

Attention should be paid to the kind of wine used for topping (TP) and on the way the casks and tanks are bunged. Topping should indeed never be an opportunity to get rid of inferior wines. TP wines must be of at least equal quality, clear and stable. Bad TP wine can contaminate large volumes. Between toppings, TP wine should itself be kept in topped-up containers or under nitrogen atmosphere.

The best methods for making sure containers are tight are not always applied. Casks with the bung on top should never be stoppered with a piece of cloth, which often acts like a wick attracting acetic bacteria and letting them develop. A hardwood bung or better still a glass plug, easy to clean, is advisable on the condition that it is pushed in lightly then hammered home. For casks with the bung at the side, clean bung cloths are used, sometimes lightly paraffined. The tissues of plastic materials are not supple enough and do not seal up properly.

For tanks, the flat lids made of concrete or cast iron, immersed in the wine, have been replaced by plastic lids surmounted by an aseptic bung. Certain designs with a visible wine level that considerably facilitates inspection are tending to become popular.

In very large tank rooms there even exist installations with automatic TP.

STORAGE UNDER NITROGEN

Storing wines in containers that are not completely full, yet avoiding oxidation or acetic spoilage, is a problem the cellar master is often confronted with. It can arise from bad work organization where an installation does not have small capacity containers to fraction out a large tank. Sometimes wine is drawn off from a tank, from day to day as needed, in which case spoilage is promoted by constantly renewing the air.

To avoid this drawback, a device consisting of a tight float inserted into a cylindrical tank with no cover has been invented. The float covers the whole surface and moves down with the level of the wine. This is called a *garde-vin* (wine-keeper). But the most efficient method is keeping wine under nitrogen cover, this being an absolutely insoluble, inert gas. Besides, the wine is already saturated with it.

Several types of nitrogen-protected installations exist, some more sophisticated than others. The best is the one that consumes the least gas. The process can only be applied in thoroughly airtight tanks, able to withstand slight internal pressure (Fig. 19.7). Metal tanks are very suitable, also tanks

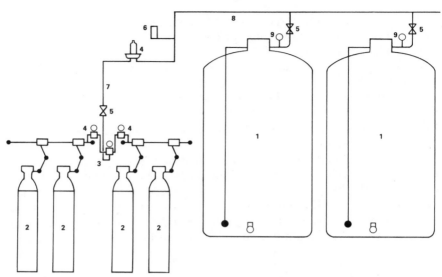

Figure 19.7. Diagram showing the principles of a wine-storage installation under inert gas atmosphere (from an Air Liquide technical handbook): 1, tanks; 2, compressed air cylinders; 3, automatic reverser; 4, pressure reducers; 5, valves; 6, over/under pressure valve; 7, average pressure circuit; 8, low-pressure circuit; 9, pressure gauges.

made of polyester and fiberglass, provided all the joints and tappings for pipes, valves, and fittings are perfectly tight. With concrete tanks lined with glass or coated with epoxy-resin, it is advisable to work practically without pressure, but under such conditions, do not expect first-rate results. Wooden tuns and concrete tanks merely acid-cleaned should not be used.

Pure nitrogen is delivered compressed in steel 20–50-L cylinders containing 3 and $7\frac{1}{2}m^3$, respectively. For large-scale use and for flow rates of 10 m^3/hour, it is advisable to stock nitrogen in liquid form in containers placed outside the buildings.

Carbon dioxide is sold in light alloy cylinders of 3.6–18 m^3 liquefied under pressure. Its great solubility in wine stops it from being used pure in tanks that are not full. Sometimes it is used mixed with nitrogen (85% N_2 + 15% CO_2) in order to avoid any loss of carbon dioxide from certain wines.

Let us take, for example, a storage cellar where the battery of tanks is fitted with a nitrogen feed released at low pressure. In the static position, each tank is isolated by shutting off the valve and the nitrogen circuit is broken. In this way the tightness of the tanks can be checked directly on the pressure gauges. At the start of the operation, the tank is completely filled with wine flush to the top opening and the sealing bung battened into place. Next a certain volume of wine is forced out through the lower faucet by gas pressure in such a way as to create a cushion of nitrogen atmosphere. Then internal pressure is set at 50 or 100 g/cm^2 (or millibars). The tank is then ready for storage. To draw the wine, merely open successively: the nitrogen cylinder tap, the gas delivery valve on the tank, the lower faucet. Perfectly clear, stabilized wines placed in the tanks can be stored for several months without mishap in conditions where oxidation and evaporation are nonexistent and with extremely limited nitrogen consumption. The wine develops in the same way as in a perfectly full tank. Several years' practice has proved this to be a highly successful process.

The use of inert gases is not only limited to keeping wines in partly full containers. Manipulating wines under a flow of nitrogen may also be contemplated, for instance, using nitrogen injected into the pipe system during displacement by pumping, temporary protection by carbonification, bottling in a neutral atmosphere, air in the empty bottle being displaced with nitrogen before being filled, or again degassing or even deodorizing operations by flushing out. Finally, adjusting the level of carbon dioxide in wines by being able to add or extract has a very important influence on taste.

BLENDING WINES

Distinction should be made in cellar work between the various mixing operations: equaling up different tanks from the same harvest within the same winery; blends made from mixing wines of the same origin or same appellation; the cuvée which is a mixture of wines from various wine-growing localities within an appellation to give generic wine (a typical example is champagne, where the cuvée is assembled with wines from black grapes as well as white, from different harvests and from the pressed wine); finally the word *coupage* is specifically reserved for blending wines from different wine areas and different years.

Blending is a natural procedure, honest, necessary, and in accordance with historical events. It is a delicate operation that requires a great deal of experience and skill and the application of concepts that can only be acquired by long practice. Moreover, each time the blending must be carefully controlled with in-depth tasting and analytical examination. The exigencies of the wine trade, which has to create vast volumes of commercially valid wines and make sure of a "back-up" all through the year in spite of the different ages of the wines and in succeeding years too, can only be satisfied by blending. Although occasionally people abuse the privilege by using blending as an opportunity to get rid of spoilt wine, this gambit is not commercially viable because it needs a lot of good wine to improve a bad one.

It is generally advisable to carry out stabilization and clarification treatment after blending rather than assembling stabilized wines.

20

Maturing and Aging
Wines

During the aging process, wines undergo a series of fundamental changes. With red wines, the effect of aging is first observed on the color, which loses its vividness, its purple and violet tints becoming progressively lighter and more and more orangey, recalling the color of bricks or tiles. It is said of old wines they have a tile color (*tuilé*). At the same time, the wine begins altering in intensity. The bouquet and the taste of the wine are thoroughly transformed. The aroma of a young wine gradually dissipates and its nose becomes more intense, more subtle and pleasing. The wine obtained after 2 years' cask life plus several more years in the bottle has nothing whatever in common with young wine, which can be rough and astringent in its first year.

With white wines, taste aging follows a similar pattern. Kept in the cask for a year or two, white wine loses the simple taste of the grape and acquires a different bouquet, a rather rancid flavor, very agreeable at first, even extremely agreeable in a great wine, but unfavorable if too pronounced. At the same time, its color deepens going first golden then browning markedly if allowed to age for too long. In this case, the wine is said to be maderizing. While it is kept in the tank, its evolution slows down. The fragrance of certain quality white wines grows rich after 2 or 3 years, or more, in the bottle. Conversely, aging white wines from those grape varieties rich in primary aromas but whose fragrance is fragile and disappears is not recommended.

There are two distinct phases in aging. The period of maturation or finishing during which the wine develops its particular flavor and achieves clarity and stability, relates to its tank or barrel life. Aging proper is carried out in the bottle and brings the wine to optimum quality.

During the maturation phase, wine maintains a certain moderate intermittent contact with air. It is aerated during racking and whenever handled or treated. The traditional container, the wooden cask, is not absolutely airtight. Oxygen does have an effect while the wine is kept in the wood even if every precaution is taken to limit its influence (sulfiting especially) and it is necessary for it to be so. On the contrary, during the second part of the aging process, penetration of air into the bottle may be ruled out, so that wine ages in the bottle in a total absence of air. This, too, is essential.

The pace at which these transformations take place, the time wine takes to develop and remain pleasant to drink, characterizes its longevity, which varies according to its style, origin, and the nature of the harvest. Wines do not all evolve and develop in the same way. Their richness in phenolic compounds, particularly the tannins, give red wines a greater life span but this is not the only factor.

The overall transformations during maturation and aging can be broken down into several phenomena: the wine's interaction with oxygen, changes in the constitution of its coloring matter, and changes in the elements of its aroma.

ROLE OF OXYGEN

Whether they are considered useful or detrimental, the interactions of wine with oxygen are very complex. They have interested great chemists like Berthelot and Pasteur. The key to aging has always been looked for here, but the problem was distorted at the beginning by a confusion. People have said; "It is oxygen which makes wine" and "oxygen is the enemy of wine," because these assertions apply to different types of wine with opposing methods of aging.

Indeed, there does exist oxidative aging obtained by irreversible oxidations. This is used to get *rancio* style wines, certain French natural sweet wines (VDN) and also styles such as port, oloroso sherry, and madeira made in hot climates, wines that are generally fortified with spirits and submitted to prolonged contact with air. But the most general case is aging with relative protection from air, the method used for the majority of premium wines, kept very carefully to prevent as much as possible any dissolution of oxygen and, what is more, always protected with a light sulfiting as soon as they are handled in air.

In the first case, wine ages in a state of oxygen saturation with high redox potential; it develops and becomes stable in taste in contact with air. In the second case, oxidations are weak and far apart; the wine ages at low redox level, prolonged contact with air is detrimental to it.

Dissolution of Oxygen

Neither new nor old wines contain oxygen in solution when they have been laid down for some time away from air. If, due to handling in air, oxygen enters into solution, it quickly combines with the wine and disappears. Wine absorbs oxygen because it contains substances that are easily oxidizable. Two classes of phenomena need to be considered: the dissolution of oxygen in wine, a physical phenomenon, and reaction with the wine's constituents, a chemical phenomenon.

It is instructive to know the amounts of oxygen that are dissolved during the various circumstances of aeration which can occur in practice in the cellar. In practice, it is difficult to realize the intensity of some of the aerations.

First of all, how can wine be handled without being aerated? When wine is transferred quickly without disturbing it, from tank to tank or from barrel to barrel, the wine being introduced from the bottom so that, immersed in the liquid being transferred, contact with the air can only take place on the surface, it does not undergo any perceptible enrichment in oxygen.

On the other hand, how can a wine manage to be saturated with oxygen? When a small volume of wine is shaken up vigorously with an equal amount of air in such a way as to emulsify it, it becomes saturated in 30 seconds. The solubility of oxygen differs with alcoholic concentration, wines with higher alcohol dissolving more, but it varies even more with the temperature. It decreases when temperature rises. It is on the order of 6 mL/L at 20°C and 8 mL/L at 0°C.

When wine is kept in contact with air, in containers not completely full, oxygen enters into solution via the still surface and diffuses into the mass. The amount dissolved is on the order of 1.5 mL/L in 1 hour for a surface area of 100 cm^2. In 4 hours, the upper layer is saturated.

In the case of barrel storage, contact with air and oxygen uptake occur in three different ways: through the wood, via the wine's surface due to the slight headspace that is always allowed in barrels, and finally during racking.

Oxygen penetration through the wood of sound oak casks is insignificant: It has been measured as 2–5 mL/L per year. It depends on the thickness and the type of wood; it is certainly greater with less close-grained wood and in smaller casks. In tuns where the staves are 5 cm thick, it is virtually nil. Account should be taken too of the quantity of oxygen surrendered by dry wood as it becomes impregnated during filling.

Uptake of oxygen via the surface is on the order of 15–20 mL/L per year, whether the cask is put in the bung-on-top position with topping at regular intervals or with the bung on the side.

Finally, each racking leads to a certain oxygen uptake, variable according to conditions, which may be as much as 3–4 mL/L, altogether some 15 mL over the four annual rackings.

Thus wine in the cask receives annually about 30 mL of oxygen. Stored in tuns or tanks, oxygen uptake is much less. It is limited to that caused by racking and uptake from the headspace via the surface between toppings.

Especially during pumping, filtering, stirring, and draining from the tank into barrels, operations that are often done consecutively at short intervals, oxygen uptake and the oxidation of the wine it causes are considerable. At the time of bottling the causes of oxygen increase are multiple. This is one of the toughest oxidation tests wine has to go through (see Chapter 30, under Filling the Bottles).

Oxygen Combination

A wine containing dissolved oxygen consumes it more or less quickly when shut off from air once more. Wine is a complex system of more or less oxidizable substances. The free sulfur dioxide content is a prime factor. For instance, combination with oxygen occurs twice as fast in a white wine containing 100 mg of free sulfur dioxide as it does in a wine containing only 40 mg. The speed at which dissolved oxygen dissipates also depends a lot on the storage temperature: the totality of the oxygen is exhausted in 3 months at 3°C, in 25 days at 13°C, in 18 days at 17°C, in 14 days at 20°C, and in 3 days at 30°C. Wine is said to be more sensitive to oxidation when cold. This is true because its state of oxidation is prolonged. The dissolution of oxygen is somewhat greater at low temperature, and its combination is slowed down considerably.

Oxygen combines in wine with various so-called oxidizable or reducing substances. Oxidation being slow and moderate only the most reducing substances are oxidized and therefore protect the others. Oxidation can be reversible and constitutes a redox situation. Thus the determination of a wine's redox potential is a measure which shows its immediate and temporary state of oxidation.

Dissolved oxygen does not combine directly with the reducing substances of the wine, among which the phenolic compounds react most rapidly. It can only do so with the help of certain catalysts, such as iron salts. Traces of copper considerably increase the catalytic effect of iron. Without iron and copper, the oxygen in the air is not very active and is incapable of combining with a lot of reducing substances in the wine.

Sulfur dioxide plays an irreversible antioxidant role by seizing the dissolved oxygen for itself, so that it is no longer available to the wine's own constituents.

Sulfur dioxide is, on the whole, more reactive than the wine's reducing substances, so it protects them from oxidation. Ascorbic acid acts in the same way, but more quickly. When the level of free sulfur dioxide is on the order of 100 mg/L, practically the totality of the dissolved oxygen fixes onto the sulfur dioxide and the wine is completely protected. If levels are only 30–40 mg, about half the oxygen fixes on the sulfur dioxide and the other half on the wine's own elements; the wine is only half protected.

What is the role attributed to oxygen in aging wines? Undeniably, it has an effect on the color of red wines; it helps finish young wine and stabilizes it to some extent but by itself it does not give aged wine all its characteristics, especially its bouquet.

CHANGES IN THE COLOR

The color of red wine changes during aging and gives an idea of its age. These transformations are complex, because many substances participate in the color of wine. There is not, as was held for a long time, a change in only one coloring matter, which would also be that of the grapes and which would change under the influence of prolonged oxidation, from the ruby red of young wine to the hue, more or less tile-colored, of aged wines. But the red coloring matter, the anthocyanins, are replaced by other brownish-red coloring agents, created from anthocyanin-tannin compounds and from their condensation. This combination is accelerated by oxidation. It has been observed that the size of a tannin molecule varies from a molecular weight of 700 for young wines to a molecular weight of 4000 for aged wines. The explanation for this color change is as follows: anthocyanins and tannins participate simultaneously in the vivid red coloring of young wines during storage, the free anthocyanins dissipate and the condensed tannins-anthocyanins complexes bestow on aged wines their characteristic tile-colored tints. Oxygen is necessary for this transformation.

This explanation also enables us to interpret observations made in practice that at first seem paradoxical. Highly colored wines can lose a great part of their color in a few months while others with little color after fermentation "gain color with age." The first, made for instance with short pomace contact time, was rich in anthocyanins and low in tannins. The second conversely had few anthocyanins and a lot of tannin. It can also be understood why sulfur dioxide decolorizes young wines and not aged wines, since only the free anthocyanins are sensitive to it.

A clear young red wine put into sealed and therefore totally airtight bottles precipitates a deposit of coloring matter within a few months. This insolubilization is not caused by oxidation, but is the result of a continuous phenomenon that also carries on without air and is particularly dependent on the temperature. It is explained by the phenomena of polymerization indicated; the molecules of the pigments tend to bond together gradually building up larger molecules. They pass like this from a soluble state to a colloidal state, then finally to an insoluble state and it is by this process, which does not need oxygen, that deposits are formed in bottles of aged wines.

Polymerization of the molecules of phenolic compounds is quicker at high temperatures, in summer, for instance. Precipitation or formation of the deposit is, on the contrary, better at low temperatures; it happens more in winter.

CHANGES IN THE BOUQUET

Just as there are two sorts of aging, there are two types of bouquet: the oxidative bouquet for special wines aged by indepth oxidation based on acetaldehyde and its derivatives and the bouquet of reduction found in premium wines that develops when the wine is kept away from air.

During the course of the first summer while the wine is still in the wood or in the tank, the aroma begins to alter and become bouquet. It intensifies as time goes on and reaches its optimum after several years in the bottle. It has its origin in the essences localized in the skins of premium variety grapes and undoubtedly again in the phenolic compounds. The fruity character of the former participate during the early stages, then give way to tannic odors, recalling bark, wood, spices, and so on.

The development of the bouquet is not only linked to the presence of particularly odorous substances, but also to the decrease of redox potential which carries on after oxygen has all gone. The intensity of bouquet appears to be related to the potential limit attained, which depends on the nature of the wine and the efficiency of corking and also on the temperature. In practice, the development of a bouquet can be speeded up with great wines in bottles, white or red, by keeping them at around 18–19°C and avoiding any temperature drop in winter.

Role of Esterification

As described by Berthelot, the formation of esters was for a long time considered important in the aging process. Esters are formed by reaction of acids with alcohols. In wine, in a diluted medium, the reaction of esterification is slow and incomplete.

Esters in wine have three different origins: a minute quantity forms part of the constituents of the odorous essences in the grape; another fraction is formed during fermentation by the yeasts; a third part arises from a chemical reaction of acids in the wine on the alcohol in the wine. Thus, after fermentation, 2–3 milliequivalents of total esters per liter may be determined, after 2 or 3 years, 6–7 milliequivalents and after 20 years, 9–10 milliequivalents. Esterification is most pronounced during the first 2 years in the cellar, it slows down after this, and becomes almost imperceptible from one year to another.

Although esters participate in the primary and secondary aromas, slow chemical esterification has practically no part in the development of bouquet. On the contrary, with time, certain esters formed by the yeasts are hydrolized. There is no relation either between the amount of total esters and the quality of wine. These phenomena occur just as much in ordinary wines, which decrease in quality as they get older, as in premium wines, which improve. Certain acetate esters, such as ethyl acetate, formed by bacteria, exercise a noxious function.

CONDITIONS FOR BARREL AGING

People have often compared aging wines in wooden barrels with the evolution of wines in large-capacity tuns or in concrete or metal tanks. First of all, wine in the barrel shows and tastes better. Young wine develops more rapidly in small volume. Tanks delay aging and do not let it achieve top-quality rating. But after 2 years, taste advantage may veer in favor of wine kept in the tank, which is cooler. This may be attributed to the fact that the uptake of oxygen in the wine in the tank is proportionately slower than in the barrel. There are other reasons for these differences.

It has been ascertained that young wine remains cloudy longer in the tank than in the barrel. Spontaneous clarification does not take place so well in large volumes. Evaporation being less and in an airtight tank practically nil, carbon dioxide remains in the wine, which therefore keeps its appearance of youth much longer. The wood of a cask plays an important part. Because of the substances it imparts, it contributes to the complexity of taste and bouquet of mature wines. Overtones of vanilla and delicately wooded flavors that are much appreciated can be found in the bouquet of wines kept in new casks from their early age. The quantity of tannins dissolved during the course of storage is not negligible. It is calculated that 200 mg of tannin per liter are imparted by new wood in the first year.

A certain permeability of the wooden cask is revealed by evaporation of liquid, resulting in what is called shrinkage. It is not the "pores" of the wood that allow this exchange with the surroundings. Wood is not porous: On one side, it absorbs liquid and swells up, and on the other it dries out through the surface in contact with air.

Shrinkage varies in relation to a number of factors, representing 1% per year in damp cellars, 4–5% in good wine stores, and more in premises that are too hot or too aerated. Shrinkage depends on the nature and the quality of the wood and on its thickness too. Starting with 100 liters of new wine, only 90 are left 2 years later when bottling begins (not counting losses from wine lees).

Evaporation through the staves of the casks involves water and alcohol. On the one hand, alcohol is more volatile than water, but on the other its molecule is larger and has more difficulty seeping through the semipermeable membranes of the wood. In fact, alcoholic strength diminishes during cask-life. However, contrary to what might be expected, it is in good damp cellars that strength diminishes the most, humidity opposing the evaporation of water, but not of alcohol.

CONDITIONS FOR BOTTLE AGING

On this subject, there are a lot of mistaken ideas. Aging in the bottle has been attributed to oxygen penetrating the wine through the corks, the cork itself allowing the wine to "breathe." Some people even go so far as to pierce a hole in metal capsules to facilitate bottle aging!

In fact, the quantity of oxygen that normally penetrates bottles corked and laid down, a position in which the cork is soaked and swollen, is negligible, if not entirely nonexistent.

In the first months, a few tenths of a cubic centimeter of oxygen come from air contained in the cork, which being made up of hollow cells slowly releases a little air when it is compressed into the bottleneck. Afterwards the amount of oxygen that filters in every year is insignificant and may represent a few hundredths of a cubic centimeter. Therefore, oxygen could never be an agent in bottle aging. What is more, when an insufficiently flexible cork is accidentally bent by the jaws of the bottling machine, we know the wine spoils quickly through oxidation due to a process that has nothing to do with normal aging. Wine kept in bottles that leak or have too large a headspace never taste well and are markedly depreciated.

Thus wines do not age in the bottle with the help of oxygen. Rather, since oxygen penetration spoils wines, they obviously age in glass due to the absence of it. You only need to open a bottle of vintage wine to appreciate this. If you leave the bottle open from morning till evening or from one day to the next, the delicacy of its bouquet evaporates and the wine loses its quality. In this context, the advice about decanting vintage wines several hours before consuming them actually leads to degradation.

It is the opposite of oxidation, a process of reduction or asphyxia, by which wine develops in the bottle. Again what demonstrates this especially is the measure of redox potential, which reaches its minimum level after several months in the bottle. The bouquet of wines only appears at low potentials. This is due to odorous substances whose agreeable odor is of a reduced form.

ACCELERATED AGING

People are always trying to age wines more quickly to reduce their storage time. But the cellarman can take action to try to direct aging in various ways. He can confine himself to securing the best conditions in terms of temperature, aeration, and storage in order to facilitate natural transformations. He can try by other processes to simulate certain effects of aging. However, despite the use of processes that bring into action various waves, ultraviolet rays, infrared rays, ultrasonics, and so on, processes to which people give all the more credit, the less they understand how they work, often only a caricature of the effects of natural aging can be achieved.

The best processes so far conceived to try to carry out induced aging, are those that bring into action intense oxidation with important variations in temperature. They consist in creating, consecutively, fairly wide temperature deviations while oxygenating the wine. The leading idea is to reproduce and then to alternate by artificial means, summer conditions, which age wines, followed by winter conditions, which stabilize them. This rough treatment is not suitable for premium wines. It only concerns the presentation; taste does not evolve by this means.

To tell the truth, the most rational way of accelerating aging, that is to say, bringing forward the time when red wine can be put on the market and drunk, has its point of departure in the vinification. The winemaker tries to obtain in the young wine a harmonious balance of flavors, particularly in the tannins. Moreover, it is incorrect that really astringent wines become more supple with time. Wine should be born supple, because supple wine matures more quickly and better. Then it can be bottled as early as is reasonably possible to do so, when it still has prime qualities of body, fat, and freshness, on the condition of course that it has been satisfactorily stabilized. The best way of growing old, which also holds true for wine, is to keep one's qualities of youth for a long time.

21

Microbial Spoilage

During its preparation and storage, wine is always prone to microbial contamination, which can depreciate it and even, in extreme cases, make it unfit for consumption. Various microorganisms can develop in wine at the expense of its essential ingredients. By destroying these constituents and also by formation of undesirable substances, the composition of wine and its taste are fundamentally changed, the wine goes cloudy because it contains microorganisms in suspension. It becomes gassy and its color is sometimes affected. The wine is said to be "sick" or spoiled.

Spoilage of wine can be classified into several categories. In common parlance, we speak of acescence, of *tourne*, or of casse. Acescence, which has various causes, is characterized by volatile acidity increase, especially the formation of acetic acid. *Tourne* indicates decomposition in the wine, in its appearance as well as its taste; it is accompanied by sourness. The various forms of casse that we shall examine later are not of microbial origin; they correspond to fundamental changes in color and clarity.

The various microorganisms of wine sickness can be divided into two categories, according to whether they need a lot of oxygen, or not, to develop:

1. Those that multiply on the wine's surface exposed to air, which are called aerobic. They are the agents of acetic acid production or of film production.

2. Those that thrive in the mass of the wine itself, cut off from air. They are called micro-aerophiles, or optional anaerobia; they may attack either the sugars, the most common form of sickness, or else the tartaric acid or the glycerol, less frequent sicknesses but more serious, possibly leading to total loss of the wine.

ACETIC SPOILAGE OR ACESCENCE

Production of acetic acid or acescence or souring is brought on by acetic bacteria or vinegar ferments. Pasteur gave them the name of *Mycoderma aceti*, which was accepted for a long time but which is incorrect. They belong to the *Acetobacter* species.

Under the microscope, acetic bacteria look rather like little cylindrical cells, very short, lined up in small chains but very often grouped in twos in the form of a figure eight. Their diameter is less than a micron (one thousandth of a millimeter).

Acetic bacteria form a film on the wine's surface that quickly covers it and exhibits various aspects: either thin and white, growing quickly, or else fat and of slow formation, or again in a thick layer, viscous and difficult to tear, commonly called "mother of vinegar." There exist several species of acetic bacteria in wine: *Acetobacter rancens*, *Acetobacter ascendens*, *Acetobacter xylinum*, and so forth.

These bacteria live by their breathing. It is the alcohol in the wine that suffers oxidation; it is transformed into acetic acid:

$$\text{alcohol } + \text{ oxygen } \rightarrow \text{ acetic acid } + \text{ water}$$

Bacteria need a great deal of air to multiply and accomplish this oxidation. For a rise in volatile acidity of 0.40 g. in sulfuric acid, they need to fix onto a liter of wine all the oxygen from a liter of air. This great need for oxygen means the acetobacters can only develop on the surface with wine-to-air contact, on the condition, moreover, that it does not move.

Formation of Ethyl Acetate

The formation of acetic acid is always accompanied by some formation of ethyl acetate, a volatile ester whose burning taste and penetrating odor depreciate wine. Contrary to what was believed for a long time, it is not acetic acid that is, at least on the nose, the body responsible for the acescent character, but ethyl acetate.

Acetic acid acts above all on taste and gives an acrid, bitter aftertaste, distinctly perceptible from 0.75 g. of volatile acidity upward although at this level it does not have a noticeable odor. However, it is from only 120 mg up that ethyl acetate, without being perceived by smell, has an influence on aftertaste and strengthens the disagreeable impression of hardness and burning. Above 160–180 mg/L, according to the wine and the taster, ethyl acetate has an effect on smell as well. It must be reckoned a factor of poor quality. It is the trace left behind by intervention of the acetobacters. The care taken in keeping wines during their cellar life can be judged by their ethyl acetate content.

These observations enable us to understand why the odor of a wine may give an appearance of deterioration with only 0.60 g of volatile acidity and why another may tolerate 1.20 g without having a smell of acescence, since the ethyl acetate content is not necessarily proportionate to that of the acetic acid.

Factors of Acetic Spoilage

Acescence is connected with conditions of topping tanks and casks, also with conditions of stoppering. It is indispensable for good storage that the bungs be hermetically sealed. Sometimes certain developments can be seen in spring and summer around the bungs of badly stoppered casks and can be detected by smell. This can be avoided by laying them with the bung on the side.

Acetic bacteria are to be found everywhere, on the grapes, in the cellar, on the walls and floors, even inside the wood of the storage containers. Wines only slightly sulfited retain some right through their evolution. When a red wine is exposed to air, at a favorable temperature, if it is young, more often than not it starts to have a film, then becomes acescent. If it is aged, it becomes acescent directly.

The real acidity of a wine, represented by its pH is a prime factor: at pH 3.0, acescence can be considered impossible, whereas it could happen at pH 3.2 and at pH 3.4 it easily comes about. Temperature is another important factor: Spoilage is twice as fast at 28°C as at 23°C and again twice as fast at 23°C as at 18°C. Resistance tests are carried out in a drying oven.

If the cellar master is obliged to store wine in containers that are not completely full, which is never advisable, he should choose the formula of protecting it under an inert gas rather than injection of sulfur gas into the empty part. Aseptic bungs protected with sulfur solution shield the surface of the wine by diffusing sulfur dioxide and not, as is thought, by sterilizing the air which penetrates through. Contamination of wine through the air in the cellars is a fallacy because ferments carried by the air are few compared to those that exist in the wine itself and its containers.

Infection of the containers is the most commonly found. It also happens that the empty cooperage, without actually smelling of the sharpness of acetic acid, does contain some acetic acid, formed in the thickness of the wood from the wine soaked into it.

Acescence, a serious accident since acescent wine quickly becomes unfit for consumption, is the sickness of wines stored carelessly in containers that are not full or are badly stoppered. It is easy to avoid with a modicum of care and attention and proper cleanliness of the equipment.

FILM YEAST (FLOR)

This type of yeast on the surface of wine is not a very dangerous disease, but is sometimes a nuisance. It is provoked by mycodermic yeasts known for a long time as *Mycoderma vini*. They belong mostly to the *Candida mycoderma* species. These yeasts can be recognized under the microscope by their ramifications and by the fatty inclusions that appear as one or two bright spots (see Fig. 21.1). Other species belonging to the genera *Pichia, Hansenula,* and *Brettanomyces* may also grow on the surface of wine.

Candida mycoderma is a yeast with intense respiration whose fermentary action on sugar is practically nil. It oxidizes alcohol into acetaldehyde and also other constituents of wine, particularly the organic acids. Fixed acidity always weakens during development of the film of yeasts and even volatile acidity may diminish.

When the film is large and when it is thick, the wine appears to be overaired and is dominated by the odor of acetaldehyde. It gets a flat, aqueous taste due to loss of acidity and alcohol. It generally goes cloudy. In this form, flor can only intervene in practice on wines that have been left for a long time without attention.

But without producing any indepth changes, the sickness called flor or film yeast is sometimes exhibited during storage of wines with low strength. Its development is frequent with young wines at 9 or 10% kept in tanks, inside the lids and the overflow ducts, on the surface of wine in contact with air, or even around the cask-bung. The bulk of the wine is not necessarily spoiled,

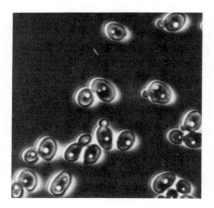

Figure 21.1. Mycodermic yeasts capable of forming a film on the surface of wine.

but it is advisable to avoid this superficial vegetation by having properly adapted stoppering systems.

Development of flor is more troublesome when it occurs, during the summer, in table wines kept in liter bottles stopped with a crown cork. The bottles have a considerable "cavity" and are handled in cases in an upright position. Patches of flor appear in the neck. This means insufficient clarification and stabilization. The dangers of film formation are reduced by fine filtering, adding 30 milligrams of free sulfur dioxide (although mycodermic yeasts are fairly resistant to sulfiting), and stoppering them hermetically, leaving only a small space in bottles. It can be completely avoided by hot-bottling.

LACTIC SPOILAGE

More serious in one sense than surface diseases, but easy to avoid, another form of spoilage is due to lactic bacteria, which multiply in-depth inside the mass of wine. In fact, they affect wines that appear to have been properly looked after, which tends to baffle the cellar master. The wine is topped up, racked, it may have been fined and filtered yet during the summer, between two tastings and in the space of two or three weeks, there is an abrupt change for the worse: Suddenly it appears dry, meager with a whiff of volatile acidity, sometimes it simply loses its freshness and its taste deteriorates or else it becomes gassy, flat, and dull-colored with the disagreeable odor of sick wine.

Old manuals took up the nomenclature for these disorders that Pasteur used with the names *tourne*, *pousse*, bitterness, ropiness or *graisse*, and mannitic fermentation. Modern classification of lactic spoilage, based on the constituents attacked, is as follows:

Fermentation of tartaric acid or *tourne*.

Fermentation of glycerol, with possible formation of acrolein, or bitterness.

Lactic fermentation of the sugars in the must, or lactic spoilage.

Lactic fermentation of traces of sugar and pentose.

Graisse or the disease of ropy wines, occurring at the same time as malolactic fermentation.

TOURNE

This sickness is defined by the occasionally total fermentation of the tartaric acid in wine. This transformation is fundamental and makes wine undrinkable. It is caused by lactic bacteria belonging to several species which in certain conditions, especially when acidity is low, attack the tartaric acid forming lactic acid, acetic acid, and carbon dioxide.

Under the microscope, the bacteria that cause *tourne* appear as bacilli and are difficult to distinguish at first from certain of the malolactic bacteria. If they are longer and thicker, it is often because their development is greater. Cocci may also attack tartaric acid. When the sickness is acute, the bacteria group together into a voluminous sticky deposit, in which case, under the microscope, they look like sinuous filaments that resemble shorthand signs.

Wine that has turned (*tourne*) loses fixed acidity and gains volatile acidity. The wine's essential acid, the one that conditions its acid powers, its taste, and its resistance disappears and the wine seems flat and flabby. The pH increases. The color of red wine loses its vivacity, becomes dull and goes brownish. Microbial development makes the wine go cloudy and sometimes silky waves can be seen when the wine is shaken up in a glass. Wine becomes gassy due to the carbon dioxide released. A special bouquet is formed at the same time. When the disease is advanced, the odor becomes disagreeable and the flavor is sometimes referred to as "mousy taste." This character does not only have *tourne* as its sole cause.

Bacteria that attack tartaric acid only develop in a medium with low acidity, generally from pH 3.5 up. *Tourne* is the disease of wines with little acid. Fear of it has made some people consider, wrongly of course, that any reduction in acidity particularly in malolactic fermentation is very bad.

Fortunately, bacteria that attack tartaric acid do not occur as frequently as the malolactic fermentation bacteria. They are very sensitive to sulfur dioxide even in compound form so that this disorder has become very rare in good vinifications and wines correctly stored. With the progress accomplished in this area, it may be confidently declared that *tourne* is on its way to have disappeared altogether. However, it would be quite common if wines were made and kept without any sulfur dioxide being used at all.

FERMENTATION OF GLYCEROL

This disease would perhaps correspond to what was called bitterness, known best of all for the havoc it caused in the Burgundy wines toward the end of the last century. These days, thanks to better vinification conditions, it has become exceedingly rare. However, it is sometimes come across in bad years when the grapes lack maturity yet nevertheless go moldy and spoil on the vinestock. It affects wines with low acid strength, particularly press wine and lees wine. Lactic acid and acetic acid plus other fatty acids, undoubtedly form. There may be production of acrolein, which gives the bitter taste. This substance is discernible by distillation, affected wines give a distillate that has a pungent odor. Acrolein is encountered in spirits made from badly preserved lees and ensilaged pomace.

LACTIC SOURING

This is an innocuous fermentation accident, spoiling wines that have retained sugar. The majority of lactic bacteria, including those from malolactic fermentation, are capable of attacking sugar with the formation of lactic acid and acetic acid. Certain bacteria, helpful when they make malic acid ferment and make the wines supple, are dangerous if they develop in a wine in which alcoholic fermentation has stopped.

Lactic spoilage generally takes place in the following way. After an excessive rise in temperature during fermentation, development of the yeasts slows down, then stops, and the wine still has sugar. If alcoholic fermentation does not start up again quickly, it is not unusual to see total and volatile acidity rise. This is precisely the danger of such fermentation stoppages, by playing into the hands of the lactic bacteria attacking the sugar. The spoiled wine exhibits a taste at once acetic and sweet; it is sweet and sour.

This disease has also been called mannitic fermentation since it is sometimes accompanied by the formation of mannitol, discernible by letting a few cubic centimeters of wine evaporate in a watch glass. The mannitol crystallizes in 48 hours in the shape of silky needles that are visible as transparencies. The mannitol comes from lactic fermentation of fructose.

This accident is not often found these days in any serious form thanks to the rational use of sulfur dioxide in vinification, and the presence of mannitol has become exceptional. However, milder forms of the disease leaving the wine with 0.7–0.8 g of volatile acidity after running off are still unfortunately encountered. They most readily affect press wines.

We have seen in Chapter 13 recommended ways of intervening in cases of fermentation stoppage.

LACTIC FERMENTATION OF SMALL QUANTITIES OF SUGAR

After complete alcoholic fermentation, all red wines retain a few traces of reducing sugars, on the order of 1.5–2 g/L. These sugars are made up of an unfermentable fraction, the pentoses, arabinose, and xylose plus a residue of fermentable sugars, a mixture of glucose and a trace quantity of fructose. Glucose even increases in the first months of storage through hydrolysis of glucosides. The lactic bacteria at the time of malolactic fermentation generally use a few decigrams of these sugars. They may continue a limited attack once the malic acid has disappeared and sometimes start it again a few months later. So frequently a slight bacterial evolution, particularly with wine in the cask, makes it more acid, more "dry," more thin. Fixed acidity rises slightly due to a small formation of lactic acid at the same time that volatile acidity is increased.

Some wines during the first or second summer undergo a slight bacterial attack which in very short time raises the volatile acidity by 0.2 or 0.3 g. This accident may pass unnoticed, at least as long as no analysis is done, since the wine remains clear. Volatile acidity passes from 0.30 after malolactic fermentation to 0.50 or 0.60 g and sometimes more; after this the wine seems to be stable and does not develop anymore.

In present-day conditions of storage of premium red wines, it is seen that these rises in volatile acidity concern quite a number of cases. It is not true spoilage, the bouquet is not spoiled, not at least in the beginning, but the wine has dried out and lost some of its flow and fat. People do not realize the nature of the transformation it has undergone and content themselves with saying that the wine has not lived up to its expectations. This evolution is often irregular from one cask to another, as is indeed the case every time a wine evolves, since in fact the slightest thing can either facilitate or arrest spoilage. Loss of quality is always substantial.

To get an idea how common this disease is, you only need to look at volatile acidity levels in various premium wines kept until bottling. Volatile acidity over 0.40 g (in sulfuric acid) is the sign of bacterial evolution that will certainly make wine lose its freshness and delicacy. In fact, red wines can frequently be found showing at the time of bottling, more than 0.40 g of volatile acidity.

The bacteria concerned are those that remain alive long after malolactic fermentation is terminated. Except when fine filtering is done early, wines remain spontaneously bacterial for a long time, sedimentation of the bacteria being slow and imperfect.

Most of the bacteria are incapable of developing below pH 3.3. They are helped by a high pH, but the production of acid that results from it lowers pH and makes the environment less favorable. Bacteria are hindered by the acidity they produce. Because of this acidification, evolution is arrested and the ailment is in a certain manner restricted by its own presence.

How can such deviations be avoided? Is it possible to bring red wine right up to bottling after 15 or 20 months storage with only 0.40 g of volatile acidity? This can, in fact, be achieved, thanks to appropriate storage facilities, thanks to all the customary treatments, judiciously applied: early clarification, racking, and rational fumigating adapted to the wine's needs and the circumstances of the season (see Chapter 22).

ROPINESS (*GRAISSE*)

Ropiness or *graisse*, the sickness called ropy wine (*vins filants*), is becoming less frequent in most wine areas due to the progress of vinification. It is still encountered in wines destined to be made into spirits that cannot be sulfited. Besides, this is not always spoilage; it is a very special occurrence of malolactic fermentation. In certain conditions which are not exactly defined (e.g., large quantities of malic acid transferred or absence of sulfiting during vinification) certain *Leuconostoc* from malolactic fermentation surround themselves with a mucilaginous substance, a polysaccharide of the glucane type that connects bacteria one to another and makes wine look oily. The wine is heavy, it ropes when poured, and flows without any noise. Volatile acidity is not necessarily high; certain ropy wines only show 0.40 g. The danger of ropiness is that it prepares the ground for serious spoilage.

Preventive measures include the judicious use of sulfur dioxide in quantities that do not prevent malolactic fermentation but that stop mucilage from forming. The curative treatment is sulfiting at 6–8 g/hL followed by a violent mechanical churning of the wine. This churning breaks the thread that is making the wine ropy and almost immediately stops it looking this way. Ropiness is produced in red wines as well as white. Adding tannin does nothing to prevent it.

MICROBIOLOGICAL CONTROL

It was held, that every wine disease had its specific microbe. In reality, there is no such thing. Wine bacteria are the result of adaptation by a large number of species to this environment, which is in the first instance unfavorable to them. A few cells of each species have been able, with time, either by mutation or by adaptation, to attack the wine's substrata (tartaric acid and glycerol) and have changed into spoilage bacteria.

From the foregoing, although microscopic examination of wines gives useful indications on the presence and development of bacteria, it does not always enable their nature to be determined at a time when this would be of most avail, at the beginning of their evolution. Bacteria with different physiological properties can look alike.

The most rapid development of bacteria in wines generally takes place at about 25°C, but it can already be fairly fast at a lower temperature, even below 15°C. Faced with a given wine, how can you know if it will keep well, what its resistance is likely to be?

An analysis, particularly of its volatile acidity, its malic acid content, gives information that can complement the microscopic examination. Resistance tests are conclusive.

SUMMARY TABLE OF BACTERIAL SPOILAGE IN WINE—IN-DEPTH DEVELOPMENTS

Spoilage	Symptoms Appearance of Spoiled Wine	Transformations	Bacteria Responsible for the Spoilage
Fermentation of tartaric acid (tourne)	Diminution of acidity. The wine becomes flabby and flat, cloudy and gassy. Disagreeable odor. Color loses its vivacity.	Tartaric acid disappears. There is formation of lactic acid, acetic acid, and carbon dioxide.	Mutant lactic bacteria: *Lactobacillus brevis*, *Streptobacterium sp.*, *Leuconostoc oinos*.
Fermentation of glycerol (bitterness)	Increase in acidity. The wine gets a butyric, putrid odor, it turns sour, and has a strong bitter taste.	The glycerol partly disappears. There is formation of lactic acid, acetic acid, and acrolein.	Lactic bacteria of various species. Other bacterial groups may intervene.
Lactic fermentation of sugars — Serious form (lactic spoilage, mannitic fermentation)	Bittersweet wines. The sugar masks the beginning of spoilage. The taste becomes acetic; it is more affected than odor. Spoilage takes place during vinification. Certain wines of the sweet type are subject to it.	From glucose, lactic acid and acetic acid form. From fructose, lactic acid, acetic acid, and mannitol are formed.	Lactic bacteria of every species including malolactic bacteria, more generally bacilli but also, at higher pH, *Leuconostoc*
Lactic fermentation of sugars — Mild form	Slight increase in fixed acidity (0.2–0.4g) and volatile acidity (0.2–0.3 g). The wine loses its suppleness and tends to dry. Marked decrease in quality.	From pentoses, the formation of volatile acidity is superior to the formation of lactic acid. From hexoses, it is above all the reverse.	Same lactic bacteria as above, among those capable of surviving for a long time in the wine.
Ropiness (graisse)	Wines oily and ropy, generally gassy.	Malolactic fermentation.	*Leuconostoc* forming polysaccharides; the cocci remain connected to each other by a thread of glucanes.

264

The open-to-air test (acetic spoilage) is carried out in a drying oven at 25°C in half-filled bottles. If the film develops in 48 hours, the wine will not resist well. If it remains 5 or 6 days without getting spoiled, it will definitely perform well during storage.

The away-from-air test (all bacterial evolutions, including malolactic fermentation) should last several weeks in a full, stoppered bottle. After this lapse of time, increase in volatile acidity and evolution of total acidity are determined. These experiments in a drying oven can be practiced at 25°C at the beginning of winter. In this way, it will be known before spring comes, by having detected them early enough in advance, the storage problems a particular wine is likely to have.

Microbial Counts

The purpose of a microbial count is to determine within a given volume of wine, the population of live yeasts (considered in this case as agents of cloudiness or refermentation) as well as of lactic or acetic bacteria. These techniques enable a count to be made of the reproducible cells, also called viable cells. A microscopic examination alone is not enough to forecast the way a wine will keep. These counts give a measurement of its "microbiological clarity." They enable the efficiency of a clarifying process, fining or filtering, to be appreciated, the preparation of wines destined for bottling to be checked out, the most suitable filtering process to be chosen, or, after bottling, the "practical sterility" to be controlled, that is to say, a sufficient lack of germs to guarantee the wine will keep well in the bottle without any risk of sedimentary deposits or new microbial developments.

Relatively simple techniques for counting, for isolating, and for identifying germs exist that are within the scope of enological laboratories. Their systematic use brings information helpful in interpreting and solving the microbial problems met in practice in wineries.

22

The Use of Sulfur Dioxide in the Storage of Wines

The rational use of sulfur dioxide, also called sulfurous acid or SO_2 is the very basis for storing wines. Sulfur dioxide is a gas that forms when sulfur is burnt. It is a very old preserving product, but the generalization of its use in wines and the correct rules for its application are more recent.

It may be positively stated that fumigating casks and sulfiting the vintage have enabled the various types of wines familiar to us today to be developed. The storage technique creates the wine style. Wine does not keep on its own, left to its own devices, it soon starts to spoil and at best becomes vinegar. It cannot withstand the handling and shipping vital to its distribution and export without the help of a preserving agent. It is sulfur dioxide that has allowed long storage in wood, then bottle aging and even more recently the maintaining of its fruity flavors and freshness.

The metering of sulfur dioxide into wines ought to be arithmetical. Two errors easily committed in practice in this connection have prompted the saying that sulfur dioxide is the best thing there is and the worst! If the amount added is too potent, be it by only about 10 mg, wine gets the piquant odor of the product plus a disagreeable aftertaste, this is the "sulfur taste" professionals complain about. On the other hand, if the quantity added is too weak, again by some 10 mg, dry wine is not protected from oxidation nor sweet wine from refermentation.

To reply to objections regarding hygiene raised by the addition to the wine of a foreign product, it must be granted that sulfur dioxide has the advantage of being of ancient usage. Nevertheless it is true that the amounts put in should be limited as much as possible. Progress in enological technique has enabled doses to be gradually reduced. Different limits are set by the regu-

PROPERTIES OF SULFUR DIOXIDE MADE USE OF IN WINE STORAGE

Antiyeast

The fraction found in a state of dissolved SO_2 gas has the power to inhibit yeasts strongly; the fraction in the form of bisulfite, exercises a much weaker inhibition.

Antibacteria

Lactic bacteria are sensitive not only to the titratable free SO_2 but also, although with less intensity, to the SO_2 compound, even to the one in the form of sulfurous aldehyde acid.

Antioxidant

The antioxidant powers of sulfur dioxide are due to its reducing properties. It hoards the oxygen, which oxidizes it into sulfuric acid. It is the totality of titratable free SO_2 that has a reducing effect. Thus it prevents yellowing and maderization.

Antienzymatic

We have already seen in relation to vinification that sulfur dioxide destroys oxidases, enzymatic catalysts of oxidation, and that in this way it prevents oxidasic casse as well as its milder forms.

Taste improvement

By reacting with acetaldehyde and blocking this substance in the form of a stable sulfitic compound, sulfur dioxide improves a wine's taste and retains its freshness of aroma. Sulfur dioxide clears away fatigue, flatness, and the temporary oxidative characteristics of a wine. It enables it to attain a favorable redox potential.

lations in force in wine-producing countries. For member countries of the EEC, the 1981 amounts of total sulfur dioxide (in mg/L) not to be exceeded were:

Red wines	Sugar lower than 5 g: 175; above this: 225
Rosé and white wines	Sugar lower than 5 g: 225; above this: 275
Appellation controlled (AOC) white wines	300 or 400 according to type and appellation. The amount of free sulfur dioxide is not covered by the regulations.

FORMS OF SULFUR DIOXIDE IN WINES

As Figure 22.1 shows, sulfur dioxide is found in wines in two main forms: in free form and in the form of organic compounds with certain other constituents of wine. Total sulfur dioxide or total SO_2, corresponds to the sum of the free SO_2 plus the SO_2 compound.

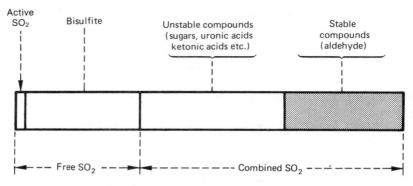

Figure 22.1

Free Sulfur Dioxide

This is the fraction directly determinable by the iodine in the acidified wine. The major part of the free sulfur dioxide is found in the wine in a protonated state, in the form of acid or bisulfite salts. In this form, free sulfur dioxide has a mild antiseptic power on the yeasts; it has no odor.

The part that is to be found in the form of free SO_2 gas is the most active from the antiseptic viewpoint. It is this form that gives the unpleasant odor of "sulfur." At equal doses of free sulfur dioxide, the proportion of dissolved SO_2 and consequently the antimicrobial efficiency and the odor the wine shows, depend on the real acidity of the wine, on its pH.

For a wine to contain 2.0 mg of active SO_2 per liter, a dose that seems to be enough for the storage of a sweet white wine, it must possess approximately, according to its pH, the following quantities of free sulfur dioxide:

at pH 2.8	20 mg
3.0	29 mg
3.2	43 mg
3.4	61 mg
3.6	81 mg
3.8	100 mg

These levels have been calculated taking account of a certain antiyeast power of salified sulfuric acid.

Sulfur Dioxide Compounds

Sulfur dioxide combines with many substances belonging to the chemical group of the aldehydes and ketones. With them, it gives two types of compounds of different stability.

Sulfur dioxide forms with acetaldehyde produced by the yeasts, a very stable definitive compound (with a weak chemical dissociation constant), called bisulfite addition product. Acetaldehyde is an intermediary substance from the fermentation of sugar. The sulfiting of the must blocks it in the form of a sulfitic compound. Similarly, the refermentation of a sweet wine followed by sulfiting raises considerably the level of sulfur dioxide combined with acetaldehyde. It is in this way that sulfur dioxide compounds accumulate in certain wines.

Sulfur dioxide forms, together with other constituents, incomplete combinations, reversible (with strong dissociation constants). The question is one of balancing reactions, which depend on the one hand, on the amounts of substances that fix the sulfur dioxide and on the other, the levels of total sulfur dioxide; balance also depends on temperature. To satisfy this balance, the amount of sulfur dioxide compound rises when sulfur dioxide is added to the wine and decreases when the free sulfur dioxide subsides; it rises when the wine is cooled and goes down again when it is warmed up; a white wine in which, for instance, 85 mg of free sulfur dioxide is determined at 15°C will show 68 mg at 0°C and 100 mg at 30°C. Combined sulfur dioxide in unstable form constitutes a sort of reserve that comes to feed the free sulfur dioxide as and when it subsides through oxidation. The substances in wine that fix the sulfur dioxide in this unstable form (some fifteen are known) have several origins:

1. Substances existing in sound grapes and must, such as glucose, arabinose, galacturonic acid, the polysaccharides, the polyphenols.

2. Substances formed in botrytized grapes or those attacked by a bacterial microflora that oxidizes the sugar, such as diketogluconic acid and ketofructose.

3. Substances formed by the yeasts under normal conditions or accumulated in the fermentation of musts from moldy grapes such as pyruvic acid and α-ketoglutaric acid.

Therefore distinction is made between cases of normal, limited combinations that arise generally in wines made from sound grapes and cases of abnormal combinations that intervene in wines coming from moldy, spoiled grapes and that are likewise due to a deficiency of vitamins for the yeasts.

STATE OF SULFUR DIOXIDE IN A DRY WHITE WINE[a]

Analytical composition: acetaldehyde 72, pyruvic acid 132, α-ketoglutaric acid 85, uronic acids 124, diketogluconic acid 50, ketofructose 32, xylosone 78.

Total SO_2	231
Free SO_2	25
Combined SO_2	206
with acetaldehyde	105
with ketonic acids	78
with uronic acids	1
with diketogluconic acid	8
with ketofructose	6
with the xylosone	8

[a] Content throughout in milligrams per liter.

The big disadvantage of sulfur dioxide as a preserving product is in connection with its chemical reactivity, which makes the greater part of it inactive. To maintain in the wine a sufficient proportion of active SO_2, it has to accumulate several tens of milligrams in its free state and several hundred milligrams in total.

COMBINATION RATE OF ADDED SULFUR DIOXIDE

What happens when sulfur dioxide is added to a white wine which already has some in it, when racking, for instance? Every new addition has as a consequence the combination of a part of the dose added with certain of the constituents. A few hours after adding it, the total amount expected is no longer found. Take, for example, a dessert wine with 40 mg free sulfur dioxide to which 60 mg is added. After 3 or 4 days, it is not 100 mg (40 + 60) of free sulfur dioxide that is found but a noticeably lower amount, say 80 mg; a certain quantity, in this case, 20 mg, has combined.

In practice it is important to take into account the fraction that may combine when trying to adjust accurately, to the level chosen, the free sulfur dioxide content. The rate of combination is variable according to the wines (according to the nature and the quantity of substances that combine with it); it varies also according to the amounts of free sulfur dioxide already contained in the wines.

In practice, the following rule can be accepted, as a rough guide in order to be able to calculate the addition to be made to a normal wine: "When sulfur dioxide is added to wine, two-thirds of the dose added remains in free form and one-third combines.'' So, if the winemaker wants to bring the free sulfur dioxide content up to 40 mg, in a wine that only has 16 mg, he needs to add: 40 − 16 = 24 plus half of 24, that is to say, in reality 36 mg, 24 in fact represents two-thirds of the dose to be added. Without being strictly accurate, this way of calculating in practice in the winery allows the amount of free SO_2 in a wine to be brought to the required level. In certain cases, however, the combination rates are higher.

DOSES OF SULFUR DIOXIDE TO BE USED

To ensure preservation, it is generally considered inadvisable to let sulfur dioxide content fall below 10 mg for a red wine, 15–20 mg for a dry white, and below 40–50 mg/L for a semisweet (moelleux).

Indeed the free SO_2 content does not remain constant. It steadily goes down during the course of storage because of progressive oxidation. This shrinkage is just the sign of the sulfur dioxide's efficacity, since the oxygen which oxidizes it is separated from the wine in this way. The reduction depends on storage conditions. In 50-gal casks the average loss in free SO_2 is about 10 mg per month, total SO_2 drops by 15 mg, which corresponds to the yearly loss of 180 mg/L. The formation of the corresponding sulfuric acid (275 mg) is one of the reasons why the taste of wines in the wood gets thinner in the long term. When stored in large-capacity tanks, the reduction in SO_2 is two to three times less. In the bottle, it does not amount to more than a few milligrams per year.

The doses for storage indicated in the following table may seem high. It is certain that at such levels white wines smell of sulfur dioxide. But these are not doses for consumption. They are calculated fairly generously so that wines can remain 4 to 6 months between two rackings without dropping to an inadequate level. These amounts have been fixed from long experience. They could be appreciably reduced for wines with a lower pH or stored in colder climates and also at the winery, where they escape all the shipping and handling distribution imposes. Recommended doses for shipping are the result of prolonged observation. They will be higher for extended trips and for smaller casks.

The free sulfur dioxide content necessary to prevent fermentation of a semisweet wine (moelleux) is independent of its richness in sugar. Fermentation will set in just as easily with 5 g as for 50 g of reducing sugars per liter. The resistance of these wines is more related to alcoholic strength. It needs more sulfur dioxide to prevent refermentation of a wine at 10% than one at 13%.

**LEVELS OF FREE SULFUR DIOXIDE TO BE MAINTAINED IN WINES,
ACCORDING TO DIFFERENT PRACTICAL CIRCUMSTANCES**[a]

Doses for storage	Premium reds	10–20
	Ordinary reds	20–30
	Dry white	30–40
	Semisweet white	80–100
Doses for consumption (or for bottling)	Red wines	10–20
	Dry white	20–30
	Semisweet white	50–60
Doses for bulk shipping	Red wines	20–30
	Dry white	30–40
	Semisweet white	60–80

[a] In milligrams per liter.

INSTRUCTIONS FOR USE OF SULFUR DIOXIDE

Not the least of this product's advantages lies in the various forms it takes, as a gas, a liquid, a solid, at the user's convenience, easy to measure in volume or in weight. The following table summarizes these forms of utilization. The efficiency of the different sulfitic products is exactly the same in equal doses of free sulfur dioxide because these products do not stay in the wine in the same form they had at the time of being added; they get into salification and combination balance in exactly the same way.

Fumigating

Sulfiting by using a sulfur match to fumigate individual casks is acidifying, limited and irregular from one cask to another. It is not suitable for a large volume.

Theoretically the sulfur burns giving twice its weight in sulfur dioxide: 32 grams of sulfur combines with 32 grams of oxygen to make 64 grams of sulfurous gas. In point of fact, this efficiency is not achieved and in best conditions 10 grams of sulfur burnt in a cask only gives 13–14 grams of SO_2, in other words, a loss of 30% on the theoretical efficiency. This shortfall is due to the formation of sulfur trioxide. When sulfur is burnt, one-third gives sulfuric acid, a potent acid without any antiseptic power and two-thirds give sulfur dioxide. So it is understandable that there is a sulfiting shortfall and acidification of the wine by repeatedly burning matches.

The quantity of sulfur that can be burnt in a cask is limited by the difficulty of combustion. In a 50-gal cask, the combustion of sulfur does not go beyond

FORMS IN WHICH SULFUR DIOXIDE MAY BE USED

Liquid sulfur dioxide

Sulfur gas liquefies at −15°C or under 3 bars pressure. It is sold in metal cylinders of 10–50 kg. In this form, it is used for large additions, measured by weighing, putting the cylinder directly on the scales. Sulfidoseurs, with a set of valves, enable a graduated tube to be filled with direct addition of small doses into the cask. Liquefied SO_2 is also found in siphons of thick glass, which are handy to use.

Standard sulfur solutions

For accurate additions and for smaller volumes, SO_2 is used in water solution, generally at 6 percent. The strength must be checked or guaranteed before using. Because of high evaporation, the handling of these solutions is unpleasant.

Concentrated solutions

These are solutions of potassium bisulfite, stable, with hardly any smell and easily handled. They are found in concentrations of 10% and of 18–20%. They are less acidifying than the preceding ones.

Potassium bisulfite

They are found in crystal or powder form, easy to dissolve. It is advisable to make it into a solution before use. Bisulfite can also be bought in tablet form standardized at 5 or 10 grams of SO_2, which is convenient for introducing small amounts into casks.

Burning sulfur

Fumigating with a match is the oldest form of use. The match consists of sulfur run onto a cloth wick. It is cut, suspended on a hook, and burnt in the cask. Part of the sulfur may melt and drop to the bottom of the container. Sulfur tablets ensure a more regular release of SO_2 since they do not melt and they burn completely. It is a mixture of sulfur and an incombustible excipient to be kept in a dry place. A match is used for racking and for storing empty casks.

20 g, for a maximum production of sulfur dioxide of 30 g. This comes from the property of sulfur gas obstructing combustion. As soon as it reaches a concentration of 5% in the atmosphere, it stops the combustion of the sulfur. Also when a 36–40-g sulfur-match is burnt in a cask, do not imagine that all the sulfur is consumed; even if only the charred wick is left, half of the sulfur has sunk to the bottom of the barrel.

Sulfiting wine with a match is not very accurate or regular. Depending on the cask, the quantity of SO_2 produced and its dissolution in the wine at the time of racking may vary considerably. The combustion of sulfur is different from one cask to another and is obstructed in damp casks, but the dissolution

DENSITY OF SULFUROUS SOLUTIONS (PREPARED BY DISSOLUTION OF SULFUR GAS IN WATER)

SO$_2$ Percentage	Density at 15°C	SO$_2$ Percentage	Density at 15°C
3.0	1017	6.5	1035
4.0	1022	7.0	1038
5.0	1027	7.5	1040
5.5	1030	8.0	1043
6.0	1033		

of sulfur dioxide in the wine which, at racking, flows into the cask, is even more irregular. According to the speed of filling and the force of the fall, the loss of sulfur gas through the bunghole may be anything from 10 to 50%.

Lastly, after racking fumigated casks, an uneven distribution of sulfur dioxide in the mass of wine is found. The first wine that flows absorbs the highest proportion while the last is not sulfited. The distribution of sulfur dioxide in the cask by simple circulation then requires some 10 days. There is advantage in making the sulfur dioxide content uniform by rolling the barrel.

For the same reason, with more than 6–9 hL capacity, fumigating wine containers is not a good way of sulfiting.

Practical instructions for sulfiting by fumigation are as follows:

Change matches for sulfur tablets.

Only use fumigation for wines kept in small-capacity casks.

For large volume containers, replace fumigation by a precise addition to the wine of known quantities of sulfur dioxide using a sulfur solution.

OTHER PRESERVATIVES USED WITH SULFUR DIOXIDE

Research into methods or products to replace sulfur dioxide in order to reduce the amounts used has led to the development of means for reinforcing its action: sorbic acid exercises a complementary action on the yeasts, ascorbic acid reinforces the antioxidant protection. But these preservatives are only efficient as long as they are used in conjunction with sulfur dioxide.

Use of Sorbic Acid

Sorbic acid was introduced in the 1950s for use in preserving certain food products, taking advantage of its antifungal properties.

Sorbic acid is a fatty acid, unsaturated, nontoxic, perfectly assimilable. It possesses a specific antiyeast action. It is a stable fungistatic. It opposes the multiplication of the wine yeasts more efficiently away from air and their power of making the sugars ferment without destroying them.

Its use is authorized in France since 1959 and for other EEC countries since 1979 at a maximum dose of 200 mg/L. Analytical methods enable its presence in wine to be discerned and the amount added determined. Certain countries do not accept imports of wines treated with sorbic acid. Sorbic acid's action against yeasts is strongly reinforced by the presence of alcohol. The following doses are recommended, considered efficient for wines correctly cleared of yeasts:

Wine at 10%	150 mg/L
Wine at 11%	125
Wine at 12%	100
Wine at 13%	75
Wine at 14%	50

In cases of possible contamination, these doses should be slightly increased.

Sorbic acid activity depends again on pH; it declines by approximately half when going from pH 3.1 to pH 3.5. Above pH 3.5, the maximum dose of 200 mg/L may be inadequate. Finally, the action of sorbic acid on the yeasts is considerably strengthened by the presence of small quantities of free sulfur dioxide.

In the doses indicated, sorbic acid has no antibacterial properties. Although it avoids refermentations in sweet wines, it does not prevent either acetic spoilage nor the various lactic attacks. Bacterial danger doubles when there is dissipation of the sorbic acid with the appearance of a disagreeable odor, recalling that of geraniums, due to formation of hexanedienol.

Sorbic acid only presents satisfactory practical efficiency in association, on the one hand, with a certain alcoholic strength and, on the other hand, with a certain sulfur dioxide content. It reinforces the action of the latter, but could never replace it.

Sorbic acid not being very soluble in water, the more soluble form potassium sorbate is preferred. A solution of potassium sorbate at 270 g/L contains 200 g of sorbic acid. Because of the low solubility of sorbic acid, precautions need to be taken when introducing it or mixing it in the wine. It needs to be added slowly, stirring vigorously; better still, a feed regulator can be used enabling the potassium sorbate solution to be injected during racking.

Finally, sorbic acid helps in yeast stabilization of wines under the following conditions.

Sufficient quantity is used, taking the wine's strength and acidity into account.

The wines in which it is used have been carefully clarified (yeast population, e.g., below 100 per milliliter).

Mixing is rapid and perfect.

Treated wines that are stored have a free sulfur dioxide content sufficient to prevent oxidation and bacterial developments.

Red wines or dry whites are not used.

Use of Ascorbic Acid

This exists in small amounts in grapes (about 50 mg/L of juice), but it disappears during fermentation or the first aerations, and generally wines are devoid of it.

Asorbic acid, or vitamin C, has a reducing character, which signifies that it opposes oxidations. In the wine, it quickly fixes the dissolved oxygen and turns into dehydroascorbic acid. Fifty milligrams of ascorbic acid consume about 3.5 mL of oxygen. The use of ascorbic acid is permitted by EEC regulations at a maximum dose of 150 mg/L. Practical doses are between 50 and 100 mg.

Ascorbic acid can be expected to be effective for two purposes: on the one hand to prevent iron oxidation and consequently ferric casse; and on the other hand, by exhausting the oxygen in a wine, to avoid oxidation of the fragrant ingredients and maintain a fresh, fruity aroma.

When a wine that has just had ascorbic acid added is aerated, it will be ascertained that the iron in it, whatever the level, stays entirely in its ferrous state, contrary to what happens in the reference wine in which formation of several milligrams of ferric iron will be observed. A wine with casse treated in this way stays clear. If ascorbic acid is added after aeration and it is done at a time when the wine already shows ferric iron, the iron will be seen to return to its ferrous state. In this way, ferric casse can be turned back at the start and wine showing an onset of cloudiness can be cleared.

This reducing effect of ascorbic acid can be applied in practice. Addition of ascorbic acid protects a wine rich in iron from ferric casse, which could come about by handling it in air, for instance, during pumping or filtering or bottling. Thus a wine showing excess iron can be bottled without any other treatment. The great susceptibility of ascorbic acid to oxidation only ensures efficiency in practice when contact with air is limited. It offers thorough protection against slight temporary aeration, but not against a lot of or continuous oxidation.

Its practical purpose is limited to protecting wine from aeration subsequent to bottling. It offers no advantages for cask storage.

In the case of dry white wines coming from aromatic grape varieties and bottled young, an addition of ascorbic acid helps preserve the fruity or flowery dominance in its aroma. For red wines, the length of time bottle-sickness lasts (period during which the wine shows badly at tasting) is shortened. Good results are obtained in the taste of sparkling wines by incorporating ascorbic acid into the shipping syrup.

Ascorbic acid only exercises its reducing properties fully if the wine contains sufficient free sulfur dioxide and can only act in conjunction with it. Finally, ascorbic acid is more efficient as a preventive, to avoid the annoying consequences on taste of aeration, rather than as a curative, to arrest the effects of oxidation already induced.

PART 6

Clarification of Wines

23

Concept of Clarity

Clarity, or brilliant appearance, is a quality that the consumer demands wine should exhibit. He can see right away when a wine is cloudy or has deposited some sign of spoilage and he feels ill-disposed toward it even if its taste is actually quite wholesome. It is not enough for the wine to be good, it must also be clear and not have any deposit. People are even more severe with white wines, stored in transparent bottles, which show up the slightest sediment if the bottle is upturned. Sometimes this goes too far, a few potassium bitartrate crystals, for instance, do not diminish a wine's organoleptic qualities in the slightest, but it is impossible not to heed this customer requirement in the trade.

Moreover, it must be admitted that a cloudy wine does have some reason to show an inferior taste. First, the particles that it contains in suspension interfere with tasting, but often they may also be a sign of storage deviation, chemical casse or microbial spoilage.

Clarity should be a permanent quality. It is not enough that a wine be clear at a given moment by applying some appropriate clarification procedure such as it is always possible to do. It should stay that way whatever the conditions of temperature, aeration, or light it may be subjected to, which is much harder to achieve. In practice, not only should you obtain clarity, but fixation of this clarity.

As for fairly old red wines in the bottle, the situation is rather different because in the long run the formation of a deposit of coloring matter is normal and in certain wines practically inevitable. Still, these deposits should not be too plentiful and should not appear until the bottles have 4 or 5 years cellarage. They should sink rapidly when the bottle is put upright, be easy to separate by decanting and should leave the wine clear. They ought to be composed of coloring matter excluding any yeast or bacteria cells, tartar, or other precipitates.

There are two distinct problems in cellarage that should not be confused: a clarification problem, achieving clarity and a stabilization problem, preserving clarity, avoiding any deposits. These problems are different since a clarification process is not necessarily a stabilizing process. Filtration, when it is appropriately applied, enables a cloudy wine to become instantaneously perfectly clear, but it does not stabilize it: after filtration, the wine may well go cloudy again, sometimes within a few hours if, for example, it is suffering from ferric casse.

At the same time a product that stabilizes wine does not necessarily clarify it. Citric acid and gum arabic are not clarifying agents but stabilizers. Bentonite removes proteins but does not always give enough clarity.

Everyone has experienced what it is to have a clear liquid and a cloudy liquid. It can be understood that an appearance of turbidity relates to the existence of particles in suspension. A wine appears cloudy because the light rays that pass through it meet these particles, which reduce its intensity and diffuse light, giving a blurred impression.

A series of terms are used to describe clarity. Wine that is limpid, brilliant, clear, "fine," "crystalline" is contrasted with wine that is cloudy, turbid, milky, opalescent, "white," "red," veiled.

EXAMINING CLARITY

How is clarity in a wine examined? This is a problem which is more delicate than it would at first appear. Whether the wine is in the wood or in the tank, the sample must be taken without getting it dirty. Precautions need to be taken. The glass pipette, dipped into the bunghole, the hole drilled in the wooden cask-head, risk soiling the sample, so for this purpose a plastic siphon is recommended. The tasting faucet on tanks has to be cleared by draining for some time.

Examining clarity is practiced in two ways: by direct transparency or by side-angle lighting (see Fig. 23.1). In the first of these, the glass or bottle is placed so that the light source can be seen directly through the wine. In this manner all the coarser, more intense deposits can be examined, sometimes even the very elements of turbidity can be seen, little particles apart from each other appearing as bright spots. In this way, however, a light haze (i.e., cloudiness made up of very fine particles) cannot be seen. For a better scrutiny, it is preferable to make the examination by indirect lighting in such a way as to pass light through the wine without the light source having direct

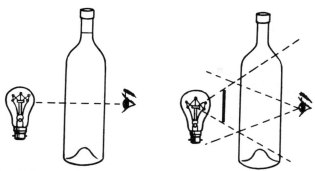

Figure 23.1. *Left:* examining clarity by direct transparency. *Right:* examining clarity by side-angle lighting, the light source being masked.

impact on the eye. Side-angle lighting gives a lot more sensitivity to the examination.

In practice in the cellar, a candle is used to examine the wine in a glass against a dark background, or else with a light bulb of weak intensity: 15 W for white wines, 25 W for red wines. The light source should not dazzle or tire the eye. Instruments called nephelometers allow much more accurate examinations to be made. In general they define the clarity of a wine in relation to the turbidity of a silica suspension, so that it is said a wine has a turbidity of x milligrams of silica per liter. Below 3 mg, a white wine appears clear, between 5 and 15 mg it lacks clarity, and above this it becomes more or less cloudy. In another field, electronic counters are capable of counting the particles in suspension in a wine, distributed according to their dimensions.

PARTICLES IN SUSPENSION IN WINE

Even if the wine is quite clear, it ought to be considered as a liquid phase having in suspension a large number of highly resistant solid particles. These particles are very varied in both their nature and size. When they are relatively numerous and relatively large, they constitute cloudiness. The best means of clarification still leave a considerable number. Wine can never be made "optically clear." Even if the winemaker gets rid of the maximum of visible particles in suspension, it still exhibits the characteristics of a colloidal solution, especially the Tyndall effect. Thus when a bottle of clear wine is illuminated crosswise by a strong light beam, the beam going through it creates an opalescent zone limited by the beam lighting up the colloidal particles. The light beam reveals the colloids in the wine just as the sun rays reveal dust in a dark room.

SAMPLE PARTICLE COUNT OBTAINED BY MEANS OF AN ELECTRONIC COUNTER FOR A CLEAR WHITE WINE AFTER A FILTRATION

Diameter of the Particles (μm)	Number of Particles (per mL)
7 and over	100
6 and over	224
5 and over	484
3.5 and over	1,180
3.0 and over	2,172
2.5 and over	2,990
2.0 and over	5,494
1.5 and over	15,012

The particles responsible for cloudiness in wine, either suspensoids or colloids, are not passive. A number of reactions relating to clarity in wine and their clarification are based on the way the particles are charged electrically. It has been established that most of the substances in suspension in a wine and on the walls of containers it is kept in are negatively charged. This is the case with condensed tannins, coloring matter, yeasts, bacteria, bentonite, infusorial earth, carbon, and so on. Only the cellulose fibers used in filtration and the proteins, nitrogenous substances responsible for cloudiness or used in fining, have a positive electric charge.

The stability of a suspension and of a colloidal solution is in fact due to the existence of these charges which repel the particles, since particles charged with like signs repel each other. Therefore, they stay apart from each other without coming together again. But if for whatever reason this charge lessens or is cancelled out, the particles that are no longer subject to reciprocal repellence start to cluster. The internal circulation in the liquid brings them into contact with each other and due to gravity they tend to sink to the bottom of the container.

Another important principle that controls these clarification reactions is the notion of protective colloids. Certain stable colloids hinder the flocculation of other colloids by enveloping them and preventing them from gathering together. When they react on colloidal particles that are fine enough to allow wines to remain clear, the protecting colloids stabilize this clarity. When the particles are bigger and make the wine cloudy, this cloudiness is made more stable and clarification becomes even more difficult.

PARTICLES IN SUSPENSION IN WINES

	Diameter of the Particles (μm)	Nature of These Particles
Particles visible under an ordinary microscope, producing cloudiness in wine, arrested by the filters.	5–10	Yeasts, various fragments, microbial aggregates, flocculants, crystals of tartaric salts.
	0.5–1.5	Acetic bacteria and lactic bacteria, amorphous particles, various precipitates.
	0.2–0.5	Amorphous particles (at the limit of ordinary microscopic observation).
Colloidal particles invisible by microscopic examination, leaving wine clear under visual examination, passing all the usual filters.	0.01 and under	Gums, mucilages, polysaccharides, proteins, coloring matter, tannins, etc.

Protective colloids exist naturally in the wine. They are the polysaccharides, gums, or glucanes. It is legal to increase protective colloid content by adding gum arabic.

SPONTANEOUS CLARIFICATION

After fermentation, wine contains in suspension yeasts, bacteria, fragments of cells from the grapes themselves, amorphous particles, colloids, and fine crystals. Young wine is always very cloudy. It tends to clarify when left to settle. Spontaneous clarification or sedimentation consists in the gradual sinking of the particles in suspension by gravity. Little by little the fairly large, fairly heavy particles fall to the bottom of the container from which they are removed by decanting or racking.

The speed of spontaneous clarification of wines depends on their richness in protective colloids. The dextrans in the wines coming especially from moldy grapes delay clearing the wines. In a general way, spontaneous clarification comes about more easily the smaller the containers are and the more shallow the tank. In large wine vessels, the convection movements also interfere with the fall of the particles. Clarity achieved spontaneously is never sufficient to be able to bottle a wine directly and some method of clarification such as fining or filtering is always necessary.

What are the laws that govern spontaneous clarification? Let us imagine a tiny isolated sphere falling in a liquid, representing a particle of turbidity. It falls with a certain speed governed by the density and the resistance the liquid offers to it. Resistance depends on the surface friction in relation to the volume displaced. From this, it results that the smaller the sphere, the more slowly it will sink since its surface friction with the liquid is proportionately greater in relation to its volume. Consequently, the settling of particles causing cloudiness in a wine generally adopts the following aspect: The coarser elements fall first while the finer elements fall slowly. The particles sort themselves by size, which results in a stratification into successive zones of sedimentation getting more and more clear the closer it is to the surface, each zone corresponding to particles of similar diameter.

In practice in the cellar it is therefore by means of successive sinking that a young wine gradually gets rid of foreign particles held in suspension. These deposits, which constantly build up, are removed by racking.

It can be calculated that when the diameter of the particles varies between 1 and 10, their speed of fall varies roughly from 1 to 100. The fall of a yeast cell is 25 times faster than the fall of a bacterium. It is reckoned that below 0.1 μm, particles practically no longer settle in a wine. From these calculations, it should be kept in mind particularly that bacteria settle slowly and generally speaking so do very fine particles, especially when there are no protective colloids present. It is not surprising that certain wines remain cloudy for several months. The necessity of putting wines into use rapidly added to the tendency to utilize large-capacity containers becoming more and more widespread make it necessary to turn to more efficient methods of clarification.

24

Clarification by Fining

Fining consists of adding to a wine a clarifying product capable of coagulating and making large particles which precipitate in the form of floccules that carry down the particles of cloudiness and clarify the wine. Clarifying products called fining agents in common parlance are generally proteins; their coagulation is carried out under the influence of the tannins and sometimes solely by the wine's acidity.

Fining wines has been practiced for a very long time. In olden times they used natural products like milk, egg-white, and ox blood, whose clarifying properties had been observed empirically. The most commonly used finings these days are gelatins, albumins, and casein; clay and bentonite are also used.

When a solution of fining agents is mixed into a white wine, a clear gelatin solution, for instance, after a few minutes cloudiness is seen to appear which gradually becomes more intense. The cloudiness next resolves into floccules, which coagulate and sink slowly, leaving the wine more and more clear.

In red wines the appearance of cloudiness is immediate and floccules begin to form in a few minutes. They grow rapidly and appear more and more colored; they form a meshwork that shrinks and falls to the bottom of the container. This first fall still leaves the wine cloudy with little floccules that gather together in their turn less quickly than the first and fall more slowly leaving the wine a little less cloudy with even smaller floccules and so on until total precipitation and clarification is achieved. After a few days, the wine becomes clear. Thus fining is a means of carrying down the particles in suspension which would require much longer to settle or never would settle. This is only one aspect of its function: It also fixes the colloidal coloring matter and carries away the tannins, which are more or less polymerized and cause astringency.

MECHANISM OF FINING

Two stages in fining may be distinguished: the reaction of the fining agent, generally with the tannins in the wine that coagulate it and make it insoluble, and the precipitation of the finings or flocculate carrying down the impurities with them as they sink.

Reaction of Tannin and the Finings

Instructions like these can be read in certain manuals: "It needs 0.8 g of tannin to precipitate 1 g of gelatin." In reality such numerical relationships are inaccurate since it is not a chemical reaction associating constant weight of the reagents, but a colloidal reaction with each carrying the other down. The composition of the deposit of finings is variable. There is no proportionality between the doses of finings and the quantity of tannin carried down. Thus by experiment it can be shown that a fining treatment four times stronger only entangles twice as much tannin.

Again, as an example, in wines with low tannin content, the quantity fixed may represent the fifth of the weight of the finings, whereas in tannic wines it may attain double this weight. The polyphenols of acidic wines with low pH are less easily carried down. The temperature of the wine at the time of fining also has an influence: Lowering it greatly increases the efficiency of fining and the quantity of tannin that accompanies the deposit of finings.

The mechanism of fining can be explained in a simplified way by the opposite charges of the particles present (see Fig. 24.1). The proteins utilized in fining are colloids which in the wine are positively charged. On the other hand, the tannins, of which one part is found in the colloidal state, and the particles that constitute the turbidity both have a negative charge. When they are brought together, they are attracted to each other, which is the starting point of flocculation.

The turbid particles are not passive in the fining process. They react with and accelerate the fall of the floccules. The finings fall more quickly in cloudy wines. It is to this interaction of cloudiness that the advantage should be attributed of incorporating inert substances into the wines to be fined: kieselgur and various earths. Certain complex clarifying products thus contain charges that accelerate the fining process.

The mechanism of fining is explained by saying that the tannin "denatures" the proteins, that it transforms them from lyophilic colloids into lyophobic colloids, which are coagulated by the salts in the wine. Fining can only function effectively in the presence of mineral matter, calcium, magnesium, potassium salts, and ferric salts.

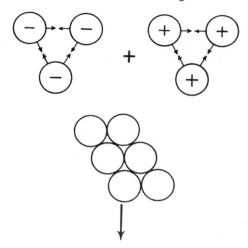

Figure 24.1. Mechanism of fining: the particles in suspension with a negative electric charge (particles of cloudiness) and those having a positive electric charge (organic finings) are attracted to each other; the charges are cancelled out and the particles that have come together precipitate (flocculation).

Role of Salts in Fining

This action of salts has been known for a very long time since the use of sodium chloride or common salt is an ancient practice. Adding it directly to the wine is not permitted.

There is good reason to underline the role of ferric salts when clarifying with certain finings, much more important in fact than that of other salts. When using gelatin for fining a white wine free of ferric iron (which has remained for instance for a long time undisturbed away from air), flocculation and clarification are considerably delayed or even impeded. All that is needed is to aerate the wine, which forms ferric salts, so that the clarification can be improved. Fining succeeds better on aerated wines. Besides, it has always been recommended to carry out fining after racking and to churn it up vigorously.

Effect of Temperature

Fining with proteins does not succeed so well when the temperature is higher (it is not the same with bentonite). The difference in the result is considerable between fining carried out for instance at 10°C in winter and at 25°C in summer. The difference comes from the speed of fall of the floccules and from the clarity obtained. Again, when there is the choice, fining is an operation that is best practiced in winter.

Overfining

It is vital to make sure the proteins added to the wine to fine it are completely coagulated and that they do not remain in a solution in the wine. The clarity of overfined wine is not stable. It goes cloudy again if it is cooled down or warmed up, or if it is blended with another wine or if, over a period of time, it is in contact with the tannin in the wood, even the minute quantity the cork may impart.

The coagulation of fining agents is complete when the wine contains sufficient excess tannin. This is generally the case with red wines. On the contrary, overfining is quite possible with white wines and is common when gelatin is used. A white wine overfined in this way includes in solution at the same time both tannin and gelatin. Other finings have less tendency to overfine.

To detect overfining all that is needed is to add to a sample of the wine 0.5 g of commercial tannin per liter. After 24 hours, cloudiness more or less intense in proportion to the amount of overfining, is seen to appear.

Addition of Tannins

Special virtues ensuring that wine is easily preserved have been attributed to enological tannins. In reality, the tannin extracted from wood has no similarity either in its composition or its qualities to grape tannins. It has neither the same taste nor the same properties.

Until such time as a true grape tannin can be prepared from the seeds, which should be feasible, addition of tannin to white wines should be reserved for cases where it is absolutely indispensable, that is to say to fining with gelatin. Tannin needs to be added at 10 grams per hectoliter for fining with 5–6 grams of gelatin per hectoliter.

In other fining treatments, the use of tannin is not necessary. Fining with fish glue (isinglass) clarifies even less after adding tannin. Casein coagulates without tannin. Besides, tannin hardens white wines and tends to make the color go leaden. As for red wines, they have enough tannins to ensure coagulation of the fining. Moreover, it is always possible to use a fining product requiring little tannin.

FINING TESTS

There is a great deal of trial and error before getting fining right for a particular wine. There are several clarifying products and each of them reacts differently in relation to conditions that are difficult to define concerning the wine's composition, its colloidal structure, and the nature of the particles in suspension. Each wine has a different coagulation power and each fining has coagulant and clarifying properties which are also different. It is often impossible to anticipate how certain wines will behave when they are difficult to clarify and are, as it were, rebellious towards flocculation. Only previous fining tests allow the best formula and the right dosage to be determined.

Fining tests can be practiced in white 75-L bottles or better still in vertical glass tubes 80 cm long and 3–4 cm in diameter. However, fining in small volumes can never exactly reproduce conditions prevailing in practice. In the bottle, the mixing of the finings is easier, the speed of fall of the floccules faster. The tube gives a better idea of the time sedimentation takes.

From fining tests, the cellar master can ascertain:

1. The time the floccules take to appear, which corresponds to the speed of coagulation of the fining.
2. The speed of fall (some finings give light floccules that may clarify well enough but do not fall easily).
3. The degree of clarity obtained after it has sufficiently settled.
4. The height of the lees and their tendency to pack down. He will then choose the finings that clarify best, fall fastest, and leave least volume of lees.

FINING AGENTS

The products suitable for fining are numerous. They are generally animal proteins: albumins, globulins, caseins, or again proteins transformed by boiling animal tissues, such as gelatins.

To this list should be added certain enological specialities which are mixtures of different finings with other substances. Certain preparations have very real advantages in relation to rapidity of flocculation and sedimentation. These are generally mixtures with bentonite, dried ox-blood, even powdered gelatin in certain proportions.

Bentonite, a clay flocculable in wine is endowed with high adsorbant and stabilizing properties. Its clarifying power may be insufficient for some wines. The use of bentonite will be dealt with in Chapter 28.

Gelatin

It is obtained by prolonged cooking in a vacuum pan of collagenous substances: ossein, tendons, gristle, and skin. Bone glue is the most common.

LIST OF RECOMMENDED CLARIFYING PRODUCTS

White Wines	Doses to Be Used (g/hL)	Red Wines	Doses to Be Used (g/hL)
Isinglass	1.0 to 2.5	Gelatin	6–15
Powdered ox blood	10 to 15	Powdered ox blood	15–25
Casein	10 to 100	Egg albumin	6–10
Bentonite	25 to 50 and more	Bentonite	25–40

Gelatin destined for fining wines must have little color and a neutral odor. It must undergo a degradation process (strong heating, sometimes in the presence of acid, or enzymatic action) the purpose of this being to break down the large molecules. Thus it loses the property of gelling but gains in clarifying power.

The preparation of a gelatin suitable for fining takes account of its flocculant properties and also of its adsorbant properties. These are defined by physicochemical measurements in relation to the average length of the macromolecules: gelling power expressed in Bloom units (100–200) and viscosity expressed in millipoises (30–60). The molecular weight of the fractions that compose them varies between 15,000 and 140,000

Gelatin is sold in slabs, pearls, or as a powder. It is dissolved in hot water before being used. Preference should be given to gelatin in its solid form as opposed to concentrated solutions, which are less pure and very degraded.

Combined *Kieselsol*-Gelatin Fining

Kieselsol is a colloidal solution of silica or gel in water at 30%. It is used to advantage instead of tannin for fining white wines. Its use is current in Germany

As a fining with 5 g of gelatin per hectoliter, 25–50 mL of *kieselsol* solution is used. The most judicious quantities are determined case by case after testing. The racking after fining is carried out 2 weeks later and it is filtered.

Combined *kieselsol*-gelatin fining gives excellent clarity, particularly in the case of wines rich in mucilaginous colloids, which are difficult to clarify, for instance botrytized dessert wines. There is no fear of overfining, the *kieselsol* carrying away the totality of the gelatin.

PREPARATION OF ISINGLASS

One kilogram of isinglass chips or "vermicelli" is weighed out and poured into 100 liters of water diluted with 100 grams of tartaric acid and 20 grams of sulfur dioxide as a preservative. The glue swells up rapidly and in a few hours forms a jelly. It is made uniform by constantly stirring it. After a few days, the clots are crushed with a brush and it is poured through a hair sieve.

The jelly obtained, thinned out at the time of use, is applied in the proportion of 1 L for two to four 50-gal casks (that is about 1–2 grams of dry glue per hectoliter), solely in white wines.

Isinglass

As opposed to gelatin, isinglass is used just as it occurs in the animal tissue. It is removed from the air bladder of certain fish. It occurs in the form of chips that are practically transparent when they are of good quality or cut into the shape of "vermicelli" which is easier to prepare. Isinglass is used in the form of a jelly obtained by making it swell up cold through the action of a small quantity of acid. It should never be heated.

Isinglass has certain advantages over gelatin for fining white wines: it clarifies much better in smaller doses, it gives greater brilliance, there is no overfining, and it requires less tannin to coagulate. In any case it does have one drawback: Because of the low density of its floccules, it gives voluminous lees, which settle badly and cling to the walls of the casks. Two rackings are needed to get rid of them. These floccules tend to clog the filters.

Egg Albumin

Egg-white contains albumin and globulin. Albumin is soluble in cold water, globulin is only soluble when salts are present. When egg-white is mixed with water, a cloudy solution is obtained. It becomes clear if the mixture is salted. The use of cooking salt is justified in preparing the solution of egg-white for fining.

Egg-white contains 12% proteinaceous substances suitable for fining. Each white corresponds to 3 or 4 g of active product. Generally speaking red wines are fined with between 5 and 8 egg-whites per 50-gal cask. The albumin from eggs can be bought in the form of a dried powder or flakes (dose for use, 8–15 g/L) or as frozen egg-white.

Egg albumin is not suitable for white wines. On the other hand, it is the best fining for premium red wines. It makes them supple without making them thin. It respects their delicacy.

When preparing egg-white for fining, avoid making it foam before incorporating it into the wine. In fact, coagulated foam floats on the surface of the wine and takes no part in the fining process. It compromises clarification. This recommendation concerns all finings that foam.

Powdered Blood

Ox blood contains 70 g/L of proteins active in fining. The form to be used is defibrinated ox blood, dehydrated at low temperature and reduced to a fine powder. This brownish colored powder contains albumins from the serum and red corpuscles, that is to say 75% proteins, of which the largest proportion is active in fining. Blood powder is a rapid, energetic fining agent very suitable for young wines. It is capable of making red wines that are a little astringent more supple.

To fine with blood powder, mix first in a small quantity of cold water. Results will be better if it is left to swell for a short time. Dissolution of the albumins from the serum will be helped by adding a little potassium bicarbonate.

Casein

A liter of milk contains 30 g of casein and 10–15 g of albumin. Fining with whole milk is an ancient process that had several decoloration and deodorizing advantages. European regulations have forbidden its use in the treatment of wines.

Powdered casein is a choice product for fining white wine. The product on the market contains a small quantity of potassium bicarbonate necessary to help it dissolve (potassium caseinate). The powder is mixed in cold water shortly before use.

When clarification is all that is desired, the amounts to be used vary between 15 and 30 g/hL. For some treatments, a higher quantity can be used, for example, 50 or 100 g/hL since it precipitates under the effect of acidity alone and does not overfine. Therefore, it bleaches white wines that have undergone browning and oxidization and gives them a little more freshness in the taste once again. It fixes a small quantity of ferric salts in aerated wines. Applied preventively, it can prevent maderization by drawing off in advance the polyphenols responsible for browning.

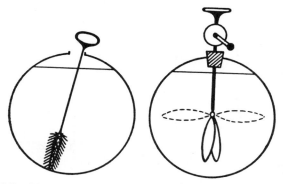

Figure 24.2. Methods of "whisking" a barrel to mix the fining (or other product).

METHOD OF USING FINING AGENTS

In fining, mixing the agent into the wine is more difficult to do rapidly the larger the volumes to be treated. Because certain fining agents coagulate fast, it is essential for them to be diffused throughout the mass of the wine without delay. If it takes too long to make the mixture homogeneous, coagulation of the finings is likely to be complete before the mixing has been properly finished. In these conditions, parts of the wine will receive finings that have already lost their clarifying powers.

Therefore to get good clarification it is essential to produce quickly, almost instantaneously even, uniform diffusion of the finings. First of all, make sure to use solutions that are sufficiently diluted, easy to mix, and that react more slowly. Dilute the product in water, adding about a quarter of a liter per hectoliter of wine to be fined. Never dilute the clarifier directly with the wine: This would introduce into the wine to be clarified a fining agent already partly coagulated.

The ideal way of fining in small quantities consists of squirting the fining agent under slight pressure into the wine, which is set in motion by stirring or rocking it. In the barrel the fining agent is injected with a syringe after having set the wine in motion by a preliminary whisking. The mixture is then obtained by stirring using a hair-whisk or a mechanical twist-whisk (see Fig. 24.2).

When large volumes, several hundreds of hectoliters for instance, need to be fined in tanks, several methods may be used according to the equipment at the winemaker's disposal. These techniques for mixing are shown in Figure 24.3.

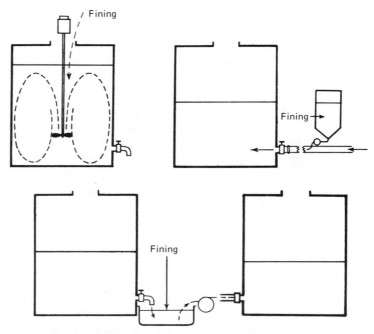

Figure 24.3. Various methods of mixing the finings into a wine in the tank. *Below,* adding during transfer from tank to tank. *Above left,* stirring by means of rotators that can be displaced and that stir the finings in little by little. *Above right,* introducing the finings by means of a dosage pump directly into the pipe system through which the wine is transferred.

During the course of a transfer the fining agent is incorporated in small aliquots stirred into an intermediary small-sized tank. The sprinkling of the agent continues to be diffused right throughout the wine's transfer. Certain tanks are equipped with mixing systems: either broad paddles that turn slowly or small fast-moving propellers. The fining agent is circulated under pressure into the wine in movement. Lastly, injecting the agent by means of a dosage pump into the pipe system through which the wine is being transferred, constitutes the recommended process. The pump is set in such a way as to synchronize the injection of the product with the circulation of the wine so that each volume of wine receives the same amount of finings instantaneously mixed in. The same systems for mixing are suitable for incorporating products for other treatments.

STABILIZING EFFECT OF FINING

In the preceding chapter, we made the distinction between clarification and the stabilization of clarity. Correctly utilized, fining is in many cases both a clarifying as well as a stabilizing treatment. It not only carries down the particles of the haze in suspension in the wine, it also carries down certain colloidal particles that could give rise to cloudiness. It removes not only the visible turbidity but also potential turbidity.

Let us take the case of a young red wine, not fined but perfectly clear. It always contains a fraction of its coloring matter in a colloidal state. If it is not removed before bottling, the wine becomes cloudy during the winter, it deposits an abundant sediment, sometimes covering the walls of the bottle with an adhesive crust. Fining carried out with sufficient doses of albumin or gelatin carries down the colloidal coloring matter in its totality; afterwards the wine does not go cloudy and no longer settles a deposit when it gets cooler. Fining is indispensable for red wines destined to be bottled.

Fining with organic fining agents is a long way from having the same efficacity in the stabilization of white wines. More often than not, it can be dispensed with. As a means of clarification it is slow and not very efficient. It is only used in special cases, for instance, to flocculate stabilizing products, like ferric ferrocyanide or bentonite. Apart from such cases, it can be replaced by an appropriate filtration.

25

Clarification by Filtering

Filtering is a general clarifying technique that consists of passing a cloudy liquid through a filter bed of very fine ducts or pores. Particles and impurities in suspension are retained by various processes. The practical operation of filtering is called filtration. Like every mechanical process, it sets a problem of quality and a problem of quantity: quality of the operation first which relates to the clarity obtained, next the quantity of wine filtered in relation to the filtration surface or the efficiency ratio of the filtering.

The flow rate from a filter is the volume run through per unit of time. It diminishes progressively as the impurities build up in the filter bed producing a gradual stoppage or clogging up. The efficiency of a filter is the volume of wine filtered during the course of a filtration cycle until such time as it is completely clogged. In practice, good quality filtration together with satisfactory quantitative filtering are the primary requirements.

Various Filter Beds

These are made of various types and forms of material, of very fine structure, fibrous or powdered, irregularly piled up in layers that are more or less thick, more or less compact, more or less permeable; or again made of thin membranes whose exceedingly small pores are of the same gauge.

The main materials used to make filter beds are: cellulose fibers (linen, cotton, pulp, cellulose powders), diatoms (synonyms: infusorial earth, fossilized silica, kieselguhr), and perlites. The filter beds can be prepared and used in different ways: by precoating, continuous feed, or in the form of filter pads.

Precoating consists of laying a filter bed onto some support backing. The most common example is a cloth filter covered or smeared with diatoms. The turbid particles are arrested on the surface of the bed prepared in this way.

298

The process, which is not very efficient, is no longer used in modern filtering. It has been replaced by the continuous feed method, which consists of mixing the filtering product into the wine to be filtered in such a way that the particles of deposit are dispersed among the filter bed itself, which in this fashion gradually settles onto the support backing. Prepared filter pads are cellulose sheets of varying porosities with cellulose fibers treated in various ways; they occasionally contain diatoms.

Asbestos fibers (magnesium silicate of the chrysolite type) have been used for this purpose for a very long time. They made it possible to get filter beds of more tightly knit texture. The use of asbestos for filtering drinks became suspect, because of carcinogenicity, then forbidden. Nevertheless, it has never been proved that the possible release of asbestos from the filter pads might be a menace to health.

The membranes are made of similar cellulose esters or polymers with calibrated pores whose diameter might be, for example, 1.2 or 0.65 μm.

MECHANISM OF FILTRATION

Filter beds are broadly classified into two categories: those that work, in particular, more by adsorption, and those that use the sifting principle membrane, which has an efficiency that is a function of its pore size (see Fig. 25.1).

The Adsorbant Filter

Suppose we have a thick layer of very loose cellulose fibers, only lightly compressed. Through it is passed a cloudy wine under light pressure containing, say, yeast cells in suspension. The filtered wine is collected in successive lots. It will be observed that the first lot that passes through the filter is brilliant. Clarity persists for a certain time, then the following lots become less clear. As the filtering goes on, the wine gets more and more cloudy until it finally comes out of the filter almost as murky as it was going in.

This is a good example of a filter working by adsorption. Adsorption is a superficial phenomenon of attraction and adhesion that takes place in the layer separating the solid from the liquid. The filter ducts are of a larger diameter than the yeast cells since these are no longer withheld after a certain time. The fibers of cellulose, positively charged, attract and retain the yeast cells, negatively charged, until the moment when their power of attraction becomes saturated. It is not the width of the ducts that matters but the bulk, the kind and the surface area of the fibers. Examples of filters working only by the adsorbant principle are rarely found in practice, the majority of filter

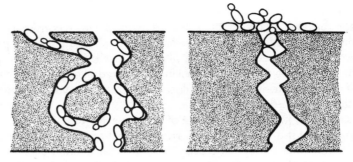

Figure 25.1. Diagram of the filtration mechanism. *Left*, stopping yeast cells by adsorption; *right*, stopping by sifting (according to Filtrox).

pads working at the same time on both the adsorption and the sifting principles, in varying proportions.

The Membrane Filter

Let us take the preceding example this time using a porous membrane made of cellulose esters at 1.2 μm (Millipore, Sartorius, Pall). We then can observe that with this filter the yeast cells are always withheld and the wine always comes out clear. Here the ducts of the filter bed are smaller than the yeast cells, which cannot get through and block up the inlet. In this case, the suspended material is arrested by the action of entrapment. But it is also seen that the output flow diminishes and clogging soon sets in.

FILTERING USING FILTER PADS

The mixture of cellulose fibers (see Fig. 25.2) variously treated beforehand, sometimes containing diatomaceous earth powder, enables filter pads to be made having a wide range of porosities and capable of being used in a large number of cases and different conditions in practice. The loosest of these plates are composed of large, long cellulose fibers, the tightest knit, used for sterile filtering, are of cellulose fibers chopped up, thinned, and compressed. When the texture of the filter pad is "tightened," the sieving action is increased to the detriment of the adsorptive action, a larger proportion of fine particles in suspension is withheld, flow is reduced and clogging occurs earlier.

Filter pads are classed in three categories as high throughput, clarifying, and sterile pads. High throughout pads are generally thick and work by indepth action. They often contain diatoms, which loosen the contexture and

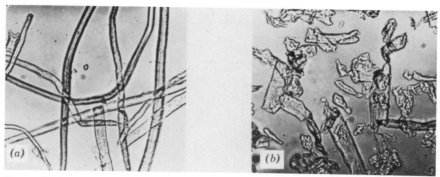

Figure 25.2. (a) Cellulose fibers (enlarged 200 times) and (b) cellulose fibers cut and chopped up (enlarged 200 times).

increase the internal surface of the filter bed. They have high filtration flow, low clogging tendencies, and good retaining power for the particles. They are used as a first filtration of wines thick with colloids. They prepare the way for clarifying filter pads.

Clarifying filter pads have 3 to 5 mm thickness and exist in several porosities, indicated by numbers, for instance from 3 to 10. The higher figures refer to tighter packed filter pads. The table on the following page gives a comparison between the performance of various plates from the same manufacturer. It is observed that different brands give a very different throughput, which can be as much as double for pads bearing a similar reference. Thus the same number does not mean that pads of different brands are exactly interchangeable. The clarifying effect is not just a question of the size of the ducts but also of the kind of fibers used and their surface properties.

Sterile filters, which also exist in several porosities, are obtained, in the absence of asbestos, by new forms of manufacture of cellulose fibers specially treated and more densely packed.

The fineness of the pores and ducts on these filter pads and their rapid clogging only allow them to filter wines that are already very clear, having been prepared by passing through clarifying pads first to clear them of all the clogging colloids as well. Sterile filtration is applied at the time of bottling. It requires special equipment to ensure sterility of all the material (filter, bottle-filling machine, corking machine, pipe work), the premises, the bottles, and the corks.

Filter pads start working by adsorption, then the particles withheld close up the ducts and they work more by the action of sieving, their flow is therefore abruptly reduced and finally stopped. Good filtering action is obtained when clogging occurs after passing 2–4 hL of wine per 40 × 40 cm^2 pad. For

PERFORMANCE OF VARIOUS FILTER PADS[a]

Filtered on:	Flow	Turbidity	Number of Yeasts
High throughput pad			
SSK	3300	2.6	0
Clarifying pad			
K3	4000	3.2	300
K5	2588	3.0	100
K7	1951	2.0	20
K10	1178	1.8	0
Sterile pad			
EK	720	1.8	0
EKS	307	1.8	0

[a] Flow is expressed in liters of water per hour per milliliter at a pressure of 0.2 bars. Turbidity of nonfiltered white wine: 4.3 mg of silica per liter; yeast count: 37,000 per liter.

larger volumes, filtration is not sufficiently tight and for smaller ones cost is too high.

The particularity of filter pads is that they are especially suitable for wines that are already relatively clear. They do the polishing filter and are not adapted for clarifying slightly murky wines. Possessing adsorbant qualities, they do not retain the totality but only a large percentage of the particles present. The following example gives a clear idea of the way they work. A slightly cloudy white wine has a yeast count of 102,000 per milliliter, it is filtered the first time on No. 5 pads. The filtered wine is almost clear but it still has 18,300 yeasts per milliliter. After passing it a second time through No. 5 pads, the yeast count drops to 900 per milliliter. Thus filtering with pads only retains each time a fraction of the particles from the turbidity (see Fig. 25.3).

Several precautions need to be taken when using prefabricated pads; it will be advisable to recall them:

1.   The materials used in the manufacture of pads gradually release foreign substances but they may communicate a paper taste to the first wines to flow through them. It is advisable to run water through the filter after setting up and to put the first liters of wine to one side.

2.   Filter pads must be used under constant pressure. They give better performance when filter pressure is obtained by working at different levels using gravity rather than by means of a pump. At too high a pressure certain qualities of pad tend to give way slightly, leaving fibers visible in the wine.

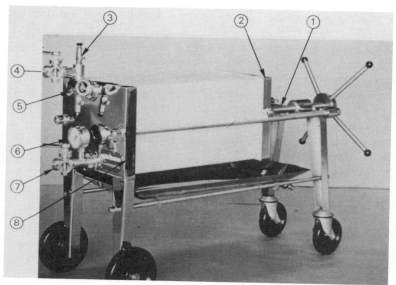

Figure 25.3. Pad and frame filter. 1, screw for tightening plates; 2, movable end-plate; 3, air-cock; 4, filtered wine outlet; 5, see-through wine clarity check; 6, pressure gauge; 7, inlet for wine to be filtered; 8, fixed end-plate (Seitz).

3. The two sides of the pad are not identical. They must be used the right way round for filtering. The side on which the texture is more tightly packed, where the checker pattern of the filter has been stamped, has been specially treated. This is the side the filtered wine should come out. The other side is less regular and this is where the wine should go in. Fibers would flake off if the pad were put on the wrong way round.

MEMBRANE FILTERING

Thin filtering membranes are made of cellulose esters and other polymers (see Fig. 25.4). They act like extremely fine sieves. They exist in several porosities according to their usage. The two sizes most commonly used for

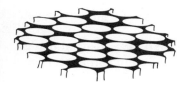

Figure 25.4. Cross-sectional diagram of a membrane enlarged 6000 times shows large volume of the pores (80%) in relation to solid matter (20%) (Millipore).

sterile filtering of wines are 1.2 μm for removing yeast cells and 0.65 μm for retaining lactic and acetic bacteria. The thickness of the membranes is 150 μm. The membrane arrests on its surface all particles whose size is greater than the diameter of its pores. It only works by sieving.

Despite the fineness of their pores, membranes do have high through-flow, for instance, 40 times greater at equal pressure and surface area than thick pads made of fibers. The pores, in fact, take up 80% of the total volume of the membrane.

Even though they are very thin, they have very good mechanical or heat resistance. Recommended pressure is 3–5 bars and they can withstand 85°C sterilization temperature.

There are several models of membrane filters: with horizontal end-plates or with vertical tubular cartridges, the filter elements being housed in hermetically sealed stainless steel tubes or bells.

Membrane filters are used as sterile filters just prior to bottling. They can only be applied to very clear wines, cleared of their colloids and already put through tight pads. It is a supplementary filtering additional to the usual filtering and which therefore gives greater security in the removal of microorganisms.

FILTERING THROUGH DIATOMACEOUS EARTH

Diatomite is a rock of the siliceous type composed of an accumulation of fossilized shells from microscopic algae or diatoms. After treating the friable rock, a highly porous powder is obtained whose weight per liter is on the order of 100–250 g according to the quality. The result is that in a filter bed, the ducts occupy 80% of the total bulk, a characteristic particularly helpful in filtration. It has been calculated that 1 g of diatoms represents a surface of 20–25 m^2.

There are a large number of different qualities of diatoms also called kieselguhr in the trade, which offer a whole range of porosities and allow filtering to be tighter or looser. Microscopic examination gives a rough idea of their filtering power (see Fig. 25-5). Filter throughput can vary from one to three with the most commonly used products.

A quality should be chosen that does not give the wine any off tastes or foreign substances. This can be checked by taking a pinch of diatoms in a glass of wine. Sometimes the thinning and tiring of a wine are due to bad quality filter products.

Diatomaceous earth-beds operate by sieving but their adsorbant properties linked to their considerable surface-area play an important part also in clarification.

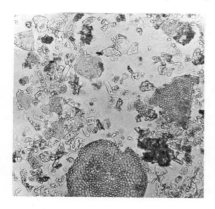

Figure 25.5. Infusorial earth examined under a microscope, enlarged 200 times.

Perlites, other filtration supports obtained by heat treatment on volcanic rock, have a much lower density than diatoms and give beds with an even finer structure.

Continuous Dosing Earth Filters

Flannel pouches were the first known filters. The idea was to spread on this backing a layer of infusorial earth (or asbestos-cellulos) that constituted the filter bed. This was the first application of smearing or precoating, which for a long time was the only filtering system in use. The big drawbacks with sleeve filters were as follows: folded pouches lacked rigidity, the material lacked resistance, irregularity in thickness and insufficient adherence of the filter bed, low efficiency with rapid clogging, difficulty in cleaning. These filters have been replaced over the last 20 years by those called: "continuous dosing earth filters" (see Fig. 25.6). These belong to two different types: filters that can be dismantled with vertical end-plates fixed to a framework, and tank-filters containing plate-supports.

The backing for a diatomaceous earth filter bed can be made of porous cardboard or of an extremely fine-woven stainless steel strainer. In the latter case, filtering begins by covering it with a first layer of cellulose onto which the primary layer of infusorial earth is deposited, carried down by clear wine or even by water.

Filters are preceded by or equipped with a device for automatic smearing or a dosimeter for infusorial earth, producing a mixture of the filtration catalyst with the wine to be filtered. Forty to 120 g of diatoms per hectoliter of wine are used according to the intensity of the turbidity and its clogging power. The cloudiest wines or those that are richest in clogging colloids need more plentiful smearing.

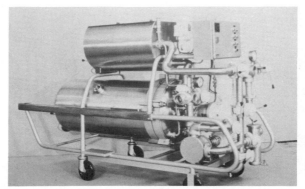

Figure 25.6.   Continuous dosing filter for infusorial earth (Seitz).

For the same surface area, continuous dosing earth filters ensure high throughput and deal with volumes ten times greater than sleeve filters. They avoid formation of a superficial layer of particles of cloudiness and retained mucilage responsible for rapid clogging in filters with direct smearing. With the continuous dosing earth technique, impurities are dispersed in the thickness of the filter bed and do not create an impermeable film on the surface.

Clogging Power of Wines

It is observed in practice that different wines do not behave in the same way in relation to the same filter surface. Some wines have very little tendency to clog. For example, several hundreds of hectoliters may be filtered through 5 m^2 of surface area using continuous dosing filtering. Other wines, on the contrary, clog very rapidly and they are not always the most cloudy ones. The same filter will then be blocked up with only a few hectoliters of wine.

A lot of clogging is always linked to the presence in wine of certain colloids, mucilaginous matter, or glucanes. Again interference from the protective colloids is to be found in this case. Wines from moldy grapes are the ones that clog most. Clogging matter is stopped, at least in part by the filter bed and anyone who has carried out the operation will have observed their presence on the surface of the plates or the filter tissues, which are sticky to the touch.

When wines rich in clogging colloids are filtered the first time over diatoms, they clog the polishing filters much less afterward. These colloids with a high molecular weight occur in the form of chains or constitute a screen whose elements can have up to 8 μm in size. Clogging can be lessened by reducing these macromolecular fabrics into smaller particles. Good results have been obtained in this direction, especially with press wines, by the action of pectolitic enzymes. Doses for use are from 1 to 2 g/hL. A mechanical action (ultrad-ispersion) can also break up the mucilage.

In fact, the elements of turbidity visible under a microscope take a greater or lesser part in clogging. Yeasts clog very little; bacteria, especially the cocci, clog more. Certain elements of turbidity clog less when they are flocculated by fining. On the contrary, the lees of certain finings, especially bentonite, quickly stop up the filters.

Another practical piece of information concerns the filterability of wines (i.e., their ease of clarification by filtering). It depends on the kind of turbidity. Wines with high concentration of yeast cells clarify easily. Bacterial wines that have undergone malolactic fermentation are more difficult to make clear. Lastly there are opalescent conditions due to fairly fine colloidal suspension which filters do not manage to catch on to and which can only be removed after flocculation caused by precipitation or fining.

THE SENSORY CONSEQUENCES OF FILTERING

Filtering has only become common practice over the last 30 or 40 years. It gradually spread throughout all the winemaking areas as technical know-how and market requirements moved forward. The marketing of younger wines and the development of bottling have made filtering an obligation.

Resistance to the practice of filtering arose from the reproach made that it tended to thin down and emaciate the wines. Nevertheless, if every pre-caution is taken to prevent accidental off tastes due to the use of filter products and the dissolving of oxygen, it may be stated that the mechanical action of filtering has never had a negative influence on quality. To suggest the contrary would mean conceding that the foreign substances in suspension and the impurities that form the lees, which filtration is precisely designed to remove, have a favorable taste function.

In point of fact, the taste of cloudy wines is always purified by filtration. A clear wine always tastes better than the same wine when it is turbid even if the turbidity is only slight. And, careful tastings have always proved it, the finer the filtration, over sterile pads or over membranes, the more the wine is improved.

FINING OR FILTRATION?

One question that constantly crops up in practice on the subject of clarification of a wine is this: should it be fined or should it be filtered?

The great advantage that filtering has over fining is that it clarifies wines more swiftly and more surely: It allows you to clarify immediately young wines that are very cloudy, sometimes rich in mucilaginous matter. On the other hand, as far as stability is concerned, the future clarity, fining is superior; it enables you to go further than filtering in the separation of certain very fine elements which are carried down by the floccules of finings whereas they pass through the filters. This is the case, for instance, with colloidal coloring matter in red wines or the hazes beginning to develop whose particles are still slender enough to squeeze through the filter beds.

In the conditions in which commercial firms are obliged to work and each time bottling is carried out, there is good reason to execute both operations, fining and filtering, on the same wine; in this way the advantages can be drawn from both. They are complementary.

Fining preceding filtration increases the efficiency of the filters by flocculating the particles in suspension, which become therefore less clogging. Conversely, filtering a cloudy wine even very roughly enables it to be fined earlier. A wine "takes" the fining better when filtration has removed a part of the large colloids and matter in suspension.

CLARIFICATION BY CENTRIFUGATION

The use of centrifugal clarifiers for the clarification treatment of musts and wines has been developed a great deal in installations that finish or treat large volumes.

We have seen that the natural separation of the particles in suspension in a wine occur spontaneously by sedimentation. The purpose of centrifugal clarification is to accelerate the fall of the deposits and enable the wine to be decanted rapidly. We know that if we make a body spin at high speed round an axis, a force is created called centrifugal force, which tends to push the body away from the center of rotation. Gravity is multiplied by the speed of rotation to a very high degree since it grows with the square of the speed, this being directly proportional to the turning circle. Centrifugal clarifiers generally spin at 4000 or 5000 rpm. Recent models spin at more than 10,000 rpm.

Applied to a turbid wine, centrifugal force achieves sedimentation of the inert or microbial substances in a few minutes. Equipment is designed to execute decanting in the same operation. The wine goes into the clarifier murky and comes out cleared of most of the impurities in suspension, at least all the heaviest.

There exist various models of centrifugal separators which can be applied for different purposes. Distinction can be made between clarifiers with deposit

Figure 25.7.   Centrifugal clarifier with automatic evacuation of lees (Westphalia).

chambers, self-decanting clarifiers, and hermetic clarifiers. The first need the bowl to be opened and cleaned out each time the chambers get clogged up. Self-decanting clarifiers (see Fig. 25.7) with automatic evacuation of the sludge are the most frequently used; they work without interruption. The evacuation of the lees is programmed at given intervals or automatically set off in relation to the clarity of the wine as it comes out or according to the accumulation of deposits in the bowl. Hermetic clarifiers, perfectly sealed, are very suitable for sparkling wines.

Centrifugation is used for the following practical purposes:

1. Rapid sedimentation of the musts immediately after draining or pressing. Sulfiting remains necessary. However, the totality of the fresh must can be treated, after a short settling period to allow removal of heavy parts which might be abrasive. Also only the lees from sedimentation can be treated after drawing off the clear must.

2.   Clarification of the young wine shortly after fermentation in order to
     remove the yeast cells. After this, the wine can be stored with less chance
     of mishap.

     Centrifugal clarifiers separate the lees out well. In one example, the yeast
population went from 15 million per milliliter to 21,000 with a clarifier with
a flow of 50 hL/hr. Therefore, 99.8% of the yeast cells were removed. Ordinary centrifugation is less efficient for separating very tiny particles. Under
the conditions described above, it left 80% of the bacteria cells. On the other
hand, high-speed machines would be capable of removing particles with a
diameter less than 1 µm; 99.6% of the lactic bacteria would be separated.
But filtration remains the surest way of arresting colloidal clusters.

PART 7

Stabilizing Processes
for Wines

CLARIFICATION AND STABILIZATION

We have seen from the preceding chapters that the clarification of a wine and its stabilization stem from two distinct methods of treatment. A wine correctly clarified by filtration or by fining is liable to go cloudy again and a deposit will settle if, for instance, the wine contains an excess of certain metals or simply potassium bitartrate. If this precipitation occurs during storage, it results in spontaneous stabilization. But if it occurs after clarification, particularly if it happens when the wine is ready for shipping or is already bottled, the accident is always serious because it stops it from being sold.

In this way wines are genuinely liable to spoilage of appearance. The forming of the cloudiness may stem from several causes: development of a microbial infection (from yeasts or from bacteria), or the formation of chemical precipitations, that is to say, insolubilization of excess substances. These second forms of cloudiness are known in practice by the name of casses.

The seventh part of this book deals with the various causes of cloudiness in wines, it studies how they come about, the conditions in which they appear, the measures to be taken to avoid them, the way of treating them and thereby stabilizing clarity in wines in a systematic way.

First the term "stabilization" needs to be defined. Stabilizing a wine does not mean fixing it in the state in which it is found and arresting its evolution, it just means avoiding any hazards or deviations during storage. It does not mean preventing a wine from aging, but giving it a stable color and clarity throughout its life, what is called good resistance. A wine should be made stable in terms of the extremes of storage conditions, as far as aeration, exposure to light, or to low and high temperatures are concerned. It is precisely when it is stable that the evolution in its taste can be most normal and most favorable.

In this introduction it might also be advisable to make the comparison between "preventive" enology and "corrective" enology. The first gives ways of preventing the roots of future clarity troubles right from the start, in vinification and during storage. Corrective enology allows excess constituents, very often foreign to grapes and dangerous for clarity, to be eliminated. It constituted the first form of intervention for limiting the consequences of faulty vinification. Corrective enology which calls on chemistry for its remedies, has been criticized in its principles but it was a first step, inevitable given the conditions under which work had to be carried out at the time. It is, in fact, the progress made by corrective enology that paved the way for preventive enology to come into being. Today's motto: "Treat the vintage and the must, in order not to have to treat the wine" was only able to reach its full significance once the causes of these different kinds of turbidity had been perfectly mastered.

26

Basic Principles of Stabilizing Processes

CLOUDINESS

These disorders occur in wines that are relatively clarified, when they go cloudy again or deposit a sediment. They effect clarity and color. The wine maker must not confuse these abnormal forms of turbidity with the usual absence of clarity in young wines that have not been clarified.

Three categories of clarity spoilage may be considered: oxidative turbidity, microbiological turbidity, and turbidity of chemical origin.

We have seen that oxidative casse is due to the presence of a polyphenoloxidase, laccase, in the grapes attacked by rot and in the wines made from them. Oxygen in the air, activated by the oxidizing enzyme reacts with constituents of the wine, particularly the polyphenols. White wines deepen in color, go cloudy, and take on a "coffee" hue. Red wines lose the red anthocyanins and become "chocolate" colored. In Chapter 14, we explained methods of testing for casse to be carried out before detanking or racking. Oxidative casse is a disease of young wines that appears during the first weeks of cellar storage. It generally disappears after a sufficient addition of sulfur dioxide to the first racking (3–5 g/hL). It is repeated if necessary.

In exceptional cases, oxidative casse may occur in aged wines even after several years storage in the bottle. *Tourne* is accompanied by a similar color transformation in air.

As for microbial cloudiness, see Chapter 21. Turbidity due to the yeasts is possible in dry wines and in semisweet (*moelleux*) wines, even without sugar fermentation. It comes as a sequel to aerating the wine. The appearance of the deposit formed varies: sometimes it is powdery and light, sometimes

315

THE VARIOUS FORMS OF CLARITY SPOILAGE IN WINES[a]

Oxidative turbidity (oxidative casse)

Microbial turbidity:
Yeasts, bacteria, particularly lactic bacteria

Chemical Turbidity:

White Wines	Red Wines
Ferric casse	Ferric casse
Cupric casse	Precipitations of coloring matter
Protein casse	Tartaric precipitations
Tartaric precipitations	

[a] Rosé wines are susceptible to the same forms of turbidity as white wines. The behavior of natural sweet wines (VDN), dessert wines, and aperitif wines is generally allied to that of red wines.

flocculent looking like protein deposit, or at other times heavy like a tartar deposit. It is detected in advance by microscopic examination, yeast, or bacteria count or by a development test in a drying oven at 25°C for an adequate time. It is prevented by sterile filtering, by appropriate sulfiting, or, again, by heating.

Turbidity of Chemical Origin

The above table gives an exhaustive list of these. Ferric casse appears after an aeration and is due to an *excess of iron*. Cupric casse appears in the absence of air and is due to an *excess of copper*. Protein casse is a flocculation simply due to settling of the natural proteins in white wines. Precipitations of coloring matter are part of the normal evolution of these substances. Finally, the crystalline precipitations of potassium bitartrate and neutral calcium tartrate appear after cooling or sometimes simply in the long term when wines are bottled young.

There are, in point of fact, only four kinds of precipitation affecting white wines and three concerning red wines. The position is therefore fairly simple: There are no unexplained forms of turbidity nor, for that matter, any unknown remedy. Wines may be accidentally contaminated by aluminum, tin, lead or zinc salts. Their turbidity may be included with those due to iron or copper. It should be added that *every colloidal precipitation is accompanied by a precipitation of polysaccharides.*

Determination of a Turbidity or a Deposit

This is a question the enologist is commonly faced with: in the presence of a wine that has deposited a sediment, define the nature and cause of the turbidity. The circumstances of the appearance of the deposit can give on-the-spot help in identifying it. A brief analysis, microscopic examination, and a few reactions enable the enologist to formulate a diagnosis. Observation of the deposit under a microscope, if necessary after centrifugation, determines one of three categories: organized deposit (yeasts, bacteria), crystalline deposit (tartar), amorphous deposit in the shape of particles with indeterminate outlines or irregular lumps (various precipitations). The table on p. 318 defines the characteristics that allow various chemical turbidities to be identified.

RATIONAL BASES FOR STABILIZING PROCESSES

The system that is applied for stabilizing clarity in wines and that is appropriate for every case in practice, is based on the following operations:

1. Resistance or detection tests, helped by analysis, which consist in placing the wine in extreme storage conditions, in order to make every possibility of turbidity appear.
2. Knowing by this means the defects of the wine to be treated, the treatment or treatments best adapted to its particular case can then be applied.
3. New resistance or control tests are carried out to check the efficiency of the treatments used.

It is only when the wine keeps its clarity throughout the control tests that its shipping or bottling can be contemplated.

Where business undertakings, always dealing with the same type of wines, are concerned, generally speaking, blended wines or tank-mixed wines, this system tends to be reduced to its simplest terms. The wines are treated for certain metallic casses according to the results of analysis and other treatments are routine. But stability tests after treatment still remain indispensable.

Stability Tests

Preferably, these tests are applied to a wine that is clear. If the wine is cloudy, a sample if filtered over cellulose in the laboratory. For white wines, avoid asbestos or infusorial earth, liable to fix the proteins.

IDENTIFICATION TESTS OF A TURBIDITY OR A DEPOSIT IN A WINE

Kind of Turbidity	Characteristics of the Turbidity
Ferric casse	Soluble when cold in diluted hydrochloric acid, more quickly when hot. Immediately soluble by addition of sodium dithionite (reaction specific to ferric casse). Red coloration by addition of hydrochloric acid and sulfocyanide to the centrifugated and washed deposit.
Cupric casse	Soluble when cold in diluted hydrochloric acid, more quickly when hot. Soluble by exposing the wine to air for 24 or 48 hours; the wine becomes clear again (reaction specific to cupric casse). Reaction of copper to di-quinolyle applied to the deposit dissolved by acidification and oxidation.
Proteinaceous casse	Insoluble in diluted hydrochloric acid. Generally soluble by simple heating to 80°C.
Precipitations of coloring matter	Soluble at 40°C or in alcohol. Characteristic microscopic appearance: granules, lumps, colored slabs.
Tartar	Potassium bitartrate (see Fig. 26.1): soluble in hot water, acid reaction sensitive to taste when the crystals are bitten. Neutral calcium tartrate: insoluble in hot water; reaction on calcium oxalate applied after dissolution of the crystals in a slightly acid medium.

Ferric Casse. A sample of the wine to be examined is placed in a white-colored bottle, half-filled. An oxygen atmosphere is created above the wine by spraying this gas onto it. The bottle is stoppered and shaken for 30 seconds in order to saturate the wine with oxygen. Then the bottle is upturned, neck downwards, and placed in the dark at cellar temperature. Wines very prone to casse go turbid in 48 hours. If a wine remains clear for more than a week, it means it is not liable to casse under practical conditions.

Remaining at 0°C for a whole week also makes ferric casse apparent, especially for red wines.

Cupric Casse. The white wine is put into a white bottle, full up and mechanically corked. The bottle is laid down exposed to indirect sunlight, for instance, in the shade out of doors or inside behind a window. The lapse of

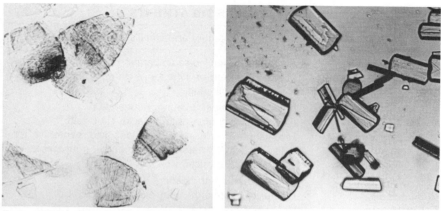

Figure 26.1. Potassium bitartrate crystals. *Left*, collected from a red wine; *right*, after being dissolved in hot water and new crystallization. The different shapes of the crystals show there are inhibition factors in the wine that upset the regularity of the crystallization (Seitz-Werke collection).

time of this exposure should be 7 days. A wine that remains clear in these conditions will not go cloudy during storage in the bottle.

Again the wine may be exposed to ultraviolet rays for a few hours in a flat flask. Cupric casse also appears after three to four weeks in a drying oven at 30°C in well-stoppered flasks.

Proteinaceous Casse. Wine is heated in a water-bath for 30 minutes at 80°C. Generally, it will stay clear during heating, then become cloudy when cooled if it contains precipitable proteins. Clarity is examined after 24 hours.

STABILITY TESTS

Clarity Spoilage	Corresponding Resistance-Test Experiments
Ferric casse	Oxygenation or strong aeration Storage at 0°C (7 days)
Cupric casse	Exposure to light Oven heating at 30°C
Proteinaceous casse	Heating at 80°C Adding tannins
Precipitations of coloring matter	Storage at 0°C (24 hours)
Tartaric precipitations	Storage at 0°C or below (several weeks)

LIST OF WINE TREATMENTS

Purpose	Category and Details of Treatment
Clarification	*Treatment based on sedimentation:* fining, centrifugation. *Treatment based on filtration:* sieving, adsorbant or sterilization filtering.
Stabilization of clarity	*Physical treatment:* heating, refrigeration. *Chemical treatment:* ascorbic acid, citric acid,[a] metatartaric acid, racemic tartaric acid, bentonite, ion-exchangers,[b] potassium ferrocyanide, gum arabic, oxygenation, calcium phytate.
Microbiological stabilization	*Physical treatment:* heating. *Chemical treatment:* sulfur dioxide, sorbic acid[a]
Color improvement	Decolorization of wines stained with carbon, wines maderized with casein.

[a] These treatments are not permitted in any country.

[b] These treatments are not permitted in EEC member countries.

The addition of 0.5 g of tannin per liter also reveals the presence of proteins.

Other tests have been suggested, such as, prolonged heating at 40°C or addition of reactive phosphotungstate.

Precipitations of Coloring Matter. Keeping a red wine in the refrigerator at 0 or 4°C for 12 hours, say from evening till morning, makes the colloidal coloring matter precipitate. The turbidity produced dissolves again as it warms up.

Tartaric Precipitations. Keeping a fairly large volume of wine (75 cL) for a long time below 0°C, inseminated with tartaric crystals, enables these precipitations to be detected to a certain extent. The test, however, is not very reliable, crystallization being sometimes extremely slow. Partial freezing of the wine should be avoided as it would lead to wrong conclusions.

LIST OF TREATMENTS

The above table sets out all the different treatments applicable to wines. It concerns the operations possible, not just those recommended. Of course the wine should only be subjected to the one therapy required to stabilize it. It is found in practice in certain large-scale production working methods that a

EXAMPLES OF TREATMENT IN DIFFERENT PRACTICAL SITUATIONS[a]

Red wines	Slow stabilization (where grown)	Storage in tanks or casks, racking, sulfiting, fining (with a protein fining), possibly filtering. According to the type of wine, bottling in the same year as harvesting or after 18 to 24 months.
	Rapid stabilization (in the merchant's cellars)	*Physical treatment:* refrigeration, hot-bottling. *Chemical treatment:* fining (protein or bentonite fining), metatartaric acid, or for wines to be drunk quickly: gum arabic. The two kinds of treatment may be combined. If the wine shows excess iron, use a calcium phytate iron-removing treatment.
White wines	Stabilization during vinification (where grown)	Sedimentation of the musts, treating with bentonite, taking precautions to avoid contact with metals. Early clarification by filtering with perhaps contributary fining.
	Rapid stabilization (in the merchant's cellars)	*Physical treatment:* heating, refrigeration. *Chemical treatment:* ferrocyanide, bentonite, metatartaric acid. The two kinds of treatment may be combined. Treatment with ferrocyanide is only advisable if the wine shows an excess of copper or iron.

[a] This is in reality just a summary outline. The following chapters are dedicated to a detailed study of the various forms of treatment and their practical application.

lot of errors of this kind are committed, wines being made to undergo a whole series of processes, some of which are quite unnecessary. It should be made quite clear that a treatment is only rational so long as it is essential and the less a wine is treated the better it will prove to be. The ideal is to vinify in such a way that afterwards the wine will only need straightforward clarification, but working methods differ in relation to various finishing and marketing requirements.

Different Practical Cases

The "traditional" method, which is the one that relates more specifically to the wine producers can be contrasted with the "industrial" method, which is more generally practiced by wine merchants. In the first instance, vinification conditions are theoretically under the winemaker's control, the wine does not have to undergo bulk shipping and the moment for bottling can be chosen in relation to the wine's development, the one thing the winemaker does precisely have time to wait for.

   In the second instance, more often than not, stabilization has to be carried out quickly on a wine which is in itself a blend of various wines that have been purchased. The wines have to be pumped, shipped, blended, stirred; bottling or shipping closely follows the stabilization and clarification treatments. The enologist has at his disposal a whole range of processes for treating them which apply to every different situation encountered in practice, according to type, age, and quality of the wines, the size of the installation and the degree of modernization of the equipment, and marketing requirements. It is up to the enologist to choose those best adapted to the working conditions.

27

Stabilization in Regard to Metallic Casse

DESCRIPTION OF FERRIC CASSE

Ferric casse was undoubtedly the most dreaded accident that might spoil clarity since, until quite recently, it was the most frequently found, especially in white wines. The measures taken during vinification together with the doing away with any equipment made of corrodible metal, have largely reduced its seriousness and treatment has become easy and efficient.

Here are a few examples of the appearance of this sickness. After assembling wines in the tank, perhaps followed by fining, filtering and running off into casks, a wine goes cloudy in a few days. Another instance: a perfectly clear wine is shipped during winter and arrives at the purchaser's turbid. Or again a more serious case: a wine is bottled by means of an installation where the tank is at a higher level, there is a plate-filter and a bottling machine; it is brilliantly clear when bottled but after 3 or 4 days it begins to form a haze and cloudiness gradually builds up subsequently in the bottle. In all these various situations, one condition appears in common: during handling the wine has been exposed to air and has dissolved a lot of oxygen.

Ferric casse is the sickness of aerated wines showing high iron content.

The small amount of ferric salts found in wines may come from three sources. A fraction barely exceeding 2–3 mg/L constitutes the normal or biological iron from the grape itself. A portion again comes from the soil or soil dusts that may get onto the surface of the grape. In white vinification, rapidity of pressing limits the dissolution of the iron they carry and at the same time it may be removed with the murk after primary sedimentation as we saw in Chapter 16. Lastly, another portion may come from corrosion of

323

metal equipment or, accidentally, the containers, or during transport. The amounts of iron content met with today in various samples taken from wines vary from 4 to 20 mg/L with average content from 6 to 12 mg.

Iron salts exist in wines in two states of oxidation: in its ferrous state, represented by Fe II, and in its ferric state, represented by Fe III. The oxygen dissolved in the wine at each aeration makes a certain proportion of ferrous salts change to a ferric state and each time wine is handled in contact with air, its ferric salts content rises. Conversely, when aerated wine is again allowed to stand, away from air, the oxygen dissolved is consumed, the ferric salts are reduced and change back into a ferrous state. The iron in wines switches constantly in this way between its reduced state and its oxidized state.

MECHANISM OF FERRIC CASSE

Ferrous salts are all soluble and leave wine clear. On the contrary, certain ferric salts are insoluble or colored. This is the case with ferric phosphate, a whitish salt which is the source of white casse, otherwise called phosphato-ferric casse. At the same time the compounds of iron with the polyphenols of a dark blue color give rise to blue casse. White wines are more subject to the first; on the other hand, red wines rich in tannin deposit a bluish or blackish sediment. But all the ferric compounds do not precipitate and there exist in wines substances that join the ferric salts to make soluble complexes and therefore oppose its precipitation. The table below gives a diagram of the mechanism of the appearance of cloudiness due to ferric casse.

Wines will be more or less liable to casse depending on their composition; some go cloudy with 6–8 mg/L of iron while others remain clear with 25 mg. It is not possible to predetermine a wine's resistance to air solely by its iron content, the test for casse is necessary.

Certain factors considerably facilitate cloudiness, the wine's level in phosphoric acid, for instance. Ferric casse is again linked to the presence of oxidation catalysts so that in an indirect way copper also shows a casse phenomenon.

Temperature conditions play an important part in changing the solubility of ferric phosphate. Ferric casse is an accident that occurs mostly in winter. For example a wine may resist aeration at a temperature of 20°C without going cloudy but slight casse may occur at 15°C and heavy casse at 10°C.

Acidity has a complex incidence on ferric casse since it is less the acid content itself that is important but the kind of acid.

Wines do not get casse because they lack acidity as is commonly believed since in fact deacidification may prevent casse. Moreover, phosphato-ferric

DIAGRAM OF THE MECHANISM OF FERRIC CASSE

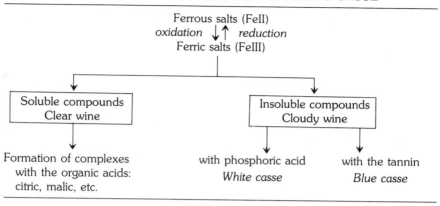

casse is only possible below pH 3.5. For this reason, it is unknown in certain areas.

PROCESSES FOR TREATING FERRIC CASSE

The cellar master has several methods at his disposal for stabilizing a wine liable to ferric casse. Certain treatments diminish total iron content in such a way that the proportion of ferric salts formed never reaches the insolubilization threshold; others prevent the formation of ferric salts or yet again solubilize the iron by complexing it. It is also possible to check ferric precipitation by using colloid protectors. The table below gives a list of possible treatments for ferric casse.

Oxygenation

This treatment cures casse by inducing it. This was the usual method of treatment in the 1930s and 1940s. The operation was performed in the following way: First, tannin was added to the wine at the rate of 10–15 g/hL; after settling, it was saturated with oxygen by circulating it through an apparatus creating a gaseous wine-oxygen emulsion; ferric casse was started in a few days appearing in particular by the color going leaden; fining was added to eliminate the iron precipitated either with gelatin or better with casein; filtering gave clarity more quickly; sometimes stabilization was made complete by adding citric acid.

LIST OF POSSIBLE TREATMENTS FOR
FERRIC CASSE

Treatments reducing iron content	Oxygenation
	Calcium phytate
	Potassium ferrocyanide
	Ion exchangers[a]
Antioxidant treatment	Ascorbic acid
Solubilizing treatments	Citric acid
	Sodium tripolyphosphate[a]
Protector treatment	Gum arabic

[a] These treatments are not permitted within the EEC.

The efficiency of the treatment was better in winter than in summer. The drawback lay in loss of aroma and of character. Very young wines stood up to the treatment better. Nowadays treatment by oxygenation is no longer practiced or only exceptionally.

Calcium Phytate

The preceding process in fact caused blue casse. The elimination of iron goes much further if phytate is added to the wine and if phytato-ferric casse is started off by aeration. Ferric phytate is indeed particularly insoluble.

Phytic acid is the form the phosphorus reserves take in the berries; it is found especially in the outer cover or husk. Calcium phytate, a commercial form used in enology, is close to the "phytin" used by pharmacists. To precipitate 1 mg of iron, about 5 mg of calcium phytate are needed. To avoid using excess phytate which would remain in solution in the wine, the amount of the product to be used is calculated in the following way. The wine to be treated is aerated or better still oxygenated. After 3 or 4 days, the iron content in its ferric state or precipitable iron is determined, say, at 16 mg/L. To precipitate these 16 mg, you need to add: 16×5, making 80 mg of calcium phytate. A certain margin is kept back for security and only 70 mg are used (i.e. 7g/hL).

The phytate in the form of a white powder is diluted and dissolved hot in a sufficiently concentrated solution of citric acid, then thoroughly mixed into the aerated wine. Casse is set off rapidly. After 3 or 4 days, it is clarified by fining and filtering.

The process suits red wines very well. It is, in fact, the only one permitted in France to remove iron from them.

Potassium Ferrocyanide

Much more radical than the preceding treatments is the use of ferrocyanide. First put to use in Germany as early as 1918 and called blue fining, it has been authorized in France for the treatment of white and rosé wines since 1955; certain·EEC countries also use it to treat red wines.

Ferrocyanic acid has the property of combining with metals and giving with them salts that are totally insoluble and variously colored. Iron in its ferric state gives a precipitate having a deep blue color, Prussian blue; ferrous iron gives a whitish salt; copper, a brown salt. Lead, zinc, and manganese are also precipitated. Theoretically, it is calculated that 5.65 mg of potassium ferrocyanide are needed to precipitate 1 mg of iron in its ferric state. In reality, in wine, a fixed numerical relation cannot be applied for three good reasons:

1. Commercial potassium ferrocyanide is not absolutely pure.

2. The proportions of precipitation of iron in its ferrous state is different and can be as much as double the amount, from 3.78 mg to 7.56 mg for 1 mg of iron according to the composition of the ferrous ferrocyanide formed.

3. Furthermore, ferrocyanide is used up by the precipitation of other metals present in the wine, particularly by copper.

In practice, when using this treatment, it is seen that 1 mg of iron is precipitated per 6–9 mg of potassium ferrocyanide, depending on the wine. Because, on the one hand, there is this irregularity in the reaction and, on the other, since all the iron in a wine is not found in its immediately precipitable state, the recommended method of determining the dosage of ferrocyanide to use is not a simple calculation but requires tests to be carried out beforehand in the laboratory.

These tests are the job, in France, at least, of the enologist charged with carrying out and responsible for this treatment. He must prescribe the required dose according to the sample given and check the way treatment is executed. The enologist gives the user the prescription which authorizes purchase of the potassium cyanide and delivers the availability order without which wine that has been treated cannot be sold. The various procedures for analytical control of treatments are detailed in the text of the official analysis procedures manual. The user must fill in a declaration in advance and is obliged to have the treatment done by an enologist.

The practical operating method for ferrocyanide includes primarily making the product into a solution with cold water. Mixing it into the wine should be done with great care to ensure that the product is completely spread throughout but also in such a way as to avoid any isolated contact between the wine and an excess of ferrocyanide. It is vital to follow up the mixing with a fining operation using a proteinaceous fining agent, powdered blood, for instance, with the object of speeding up flocculation and the fall of the ferric ferrocyanide and also to facilitate clarification. Treating with ferrocyanide always requires filtering over infusorial earth or cellulose pads. It is advisable to filter 4 days after the addition since with shorter settling-time clarification becomes more difficult, but a longer settling time, leaving the wine for a greater length of time in contact with ferric ferrocyanide, may have an unfavorable effect on taste.

Undeniably ferrocyanide is extremely efficient not only for ferric casse but for cupric casse as well since it removes copper from the wine at the same time. Indeed, this is one of the big advantages of the process since it treats both types of metal casse. It stabilizes as it were automatically white (or rosé) wines and in the end considerably simplifies treatment techniques, resistance tests, and control tests.

However, this product should not be looked upon as a cure-all, nor should people be led into thinking that a wine treated with ferrocyanide is from then on, by definition, protected from any form of deposit. It only acts on metal casse. As far as premium wines are concerned, one reproach that can be made against it is changing the evolution of bottle-aging. Interference in the wine's bouquet may be observed which is explained by the very low level of oxydo-reduction reached in the absence of metals.

Besides this, it is not necessary to treat all wines. We consider that this treatment should only be used as an exceptional measure. The tendency to bring iron content in wines down to 2–3 mg/L is going too far; such iron purging serves no useful purpose. Ferrocyanide ought only to be used on wines that cannot be treated in any other way, particularly by addition of citric or ascorbic acid.

Citric Acid

This acid does not act on ferric casse by raising acidity, there are other stronger acids which do not in fact have the same properties, but as a chelating agent, a solubilizer, of iron by formation of a soluble ferrocitric acid. Most EEC countries permit addition of citric acid subject to keeping the final content of the wine treated below 1 g/L; certain countries do not allow this treatment (Germany, Austria).

Citric acid addition is reserved for wines with little tendency to casse not having more than 15 mg of iron per liter and whose taste is capable of tolerating this acidification. However, maximum addition is not always required. An addition of 20–30 g/hL, as prior tests for casse may show, is often enough. Authorization to use potassium citrate, which is nonacidifying, would be desirable.

Please refer to Chapter 22 for details of the use of ascorbic acid at the time of bottling wines rich in iron and to Chapter 29 for the contribution to stabilization that gum arabic affords.

There are therefore many different solutions to the problem of stabilizing wines liable to casse due to excess iron. However although efficient remedies do exist the best thing is not having to use them thanks to the preventive measures taken at the time of vinification to avoid any accidental dissolution of iron salts.

DESCRIPTION OF CUPRIC CASSE

Cupric casse (sometimes called cuprous casse) is a cloudiness occurring with bottled white wines due to the presence of excess copper. This defect is serious because it happens just at the time when the wine is finally ready for sale and for consumption. All that can be done is to reopen the defective bottles and treat the wine once more.

The deposit from white wines in the bottle may show three possible aspects: dusty, made up of very fine elements and colored a reddish brown; flocculent in the form of whitish streaming particles; or else flocculent and colored brown. The first one is a manifestation of cupric casse, the second is protein casse, and the third means both forms of haze superimposed.

This is how cupric casse generally appears. A clear wine is bottled and after a few months, often during the first summer, it is seen to be going cloudy. At first some bottles appear more cloudy than others. It is a generally observed fact that when wines go cloudy whatever the nature of the accident they behave differently in different storage volume units. There only need to be slight variances in conditions regarding temperature, lighting or copper content for the bottles to show differently. When these cloudy bottles continue to be kept laid down in the cellar, a deposit gradually forms, first of all a small patch on the shoulder of the bottle, then a brownish trace right down its length. This deposit contains copper. The characteristics of this turbidity is that it disappears when the bottle is opened and the wine aerated. Clarity returns after 24 hours.

A fairly fine quantity analysis shows that all wines contain a little copper. All fruits and vegetables normally contain trace amounts, but the grape can be covered with it when the crop is gathered on account of treatment with Bordeaux mixture or some organocupric products. It is not unusual to find 5 mg of copper per liter of must or even more. However, new wine only retains 0.1–0.2 mg/L. Copper from the grape is eliminated during fermentation by fixation on the yeasts and by precipitation in an insoluble sulfur state thanks to hydrogen sulfite formed in small amounts.

The few tens of milligrams of copper which normally remain in the wine are not capable of causing cupric casse. But during storage and shipping there are numerous occasions when the wine can become enriched with copper. Above 0.5–0.6 mg/L, cupric casse becomes possible in the bottle; at 1.5 or 2 mg, cloudiness and deposits become abundant.

So long as in all the equipment likely to come into contact with the wine, even for a short time, the tiniest unprotected bronze or copper surface has not been eliminated (valves, faucets, pipes, joints, pump housing, nozzles on bottling machines and all the small utensils in the winery: buckets, funnels, ullers, plungers, siphons, etc.), there is considerable risk of copper-enrichment. Again, enameling the inside of the pipes, or silver-plating, which only give illusory protection, must be avoided.

Here is an example of cupric casse accident after bottling. A wine with 0.2 mg of copper per liter is drawn off into bottles by means of a bottling machine with six silver-plated bronze nozzles. These nozzles have been in use for several weeks and the silver-plating on the outside appears to be in good order. The first 50 bottles from this run were however, starting to show signs of turbidity from cupric casse afterward. Their copper levels varied from 4.0 to 0.6 mg. It is the inside of the nozzles where the layer of silver has worn which is responsible for this accident.

All the copper-based metals need to be completely replaced by noncorrodible material such as plastic or stainless-steel.

MECHANISM OF CUPRIC CASSE

Cupric casse can only happen to white wines showing excess copper and in highly reduced conditions (the opposite of oxidation), that is, at low redox potential, reached in bottles after a certain period of storage in the presence of free sulfur dioxide. It can happen to rosé wines, but not reds.

Light plays an important part and especially the color of the bottles and their permeability to light at most wavelengths. With equal copper content and for the same wine, cupric casse is common in white bottles and rare in bottles made of colored glass. It happens in a few days when there is indirect sunlight but requires several months when stored in cases or dark cellars. Cupric casse is of a photochemical nature.

Copper normally exists in wines in the oxidized form of cupric salts leaving the wine clear. The change to the cuprous state that gives rise to the deposit can only occur in strictly airtight conditions. Reddish brown-colored hydrosulfide derivatives of insoluble copper are formed. Several mechanisms have

LIST OF STABILIZATION PROCESSES FOR CUPRIC CASSE

Treatments that reduce copper content	Heating
	Potassium ferrocyanide
Treatments that obstruct the flocculation of the precipitate	Bentonite
	Gum arabic

been suggested. The proteins and certain amino acids play an essential part in the formation and flocculation of the cuprous salts. In the absence of a protein colloidal medium, the cloudiness and the deposit have difficulty in forming.

TREATMENTS FOR CUPRIC CASSE

These treatments belong to two categories according to whether they avoid formation of the cuprous derivatives or whether they only resist flocculation. Heating is dealt with in Chapter 28, bentonite and gum arabic in Chapter 29. We have seen previously that treatment with ferrocyanide brings copper content automatically down to 0.1–0.2 mg/L, that is, very much below the dangerous level. It is the most efficient way of removing copper from wines.

In this case once again we believe the true enological solution for achieving stability in white wines in the bottle does not consist in the various curative means detailed but in preventive measures within everyone's scope, avoiding accidental dissolution of copper in the wines.

28

Physical Treatments Applied to Wines

Physical processes make use of natural energy sources such as cold, heat, or infrared rays. It is futile trying to compare them with treatments based on chemical methods that consist of adding products. The first, it is true, raise no objections of a hygienic nature. In their industrial dimension, they symbolize technical progress. Automation of the apparatus used avoids constantly calling on the cellar master's attention. They do not give any serious consequences if they are implemented without their application being really necessary. Nevertheless they do have drawbacks: They require costly equipment, only relative efficiency not covering every risk of turbidity, rough handling involving the destruction of certain fragile constituents, and loss of quality in delicate wines. In fact, they are only beneficial for young wines during a fairly brief period.

Chemical processes of stabilization, much more widespread, have the double advantage of being easy to apply and efficient at the same time. They involve putting into suspension, in solution or mixing. Correctly implemented they do not affect either taste or the food value of the wine. However, the insertion of foreign substances does call for some reserve, these treatments need to be limited and controlled to keep the wine's hygienic qualities.

In reality, physical treatment and chemical treatment are complementary. It is a good thing to have in this way several possible solutions to a stabilization problem. Without systematically adopting a position on principle, the technician can choose the most appropriate treatment in relation to the means at his disposal. The most common physical processes in use are thermal treatments, which by exposing the wine to extreme temperatures achieve stabilization in the natural conditions of cold and heat.

STABILIZING WINES BY HEATING

The effects of heating are not limited to sterilization only. They are more complex than were supposed and the possible applications of heating, more far-reaching.

Various Effects of Heating on Wines

1.   Young wines consist of solutions supersaturated with potassium bitartrate and calcium tartrate. The crystallization of these salts is not only slow, it is only possible if the wine contains submicroscopic crystals or crystallization nucleii, which constitute the starting point for the construction of the crystals. By destroying these nucleii, heating allows this state of supersaturation to be maintained for a very long time and obstructs crystallization. By this artifice, when a wine is warmed in the bottle, the tartaric deposits have more difficulty in forming.

2.   If a white wine containing proteins is heated up, cloudiness appears when it cools down again. "Denatured" by the heat that transforms the lyophilic colloids into lyophobic colloids (flocculable), the proteins precipitate. For certain wines, the cloudiness remains stable and the deposit does not settle spontaneously. With others, richer in proteins, it flocculates and the deposit sinks. The experiment shows that in practice white wines treated in this way, heated say for 10 minutes at 80°C or for 30 minutes at 60°C then clarified 24 hours after cooling, remain perfectly clear in the bottle whatever the storage temperature afterwards. A slight loss of aroma and of character is observed but, commercially speaking, the difference is considered insignificant. Heating wine also causes the colloidal particles to swell, a reaction that stops the sediment from settling and from flocculating and increases its froth capacity.

3.   Heating acts on the redox phenomena. Through prolonged heating in the presence of free sulfur dioxide, the excess copper in white wines is reduced and changed into colloidal form, separable by fining.

Heating aerated wines for several weeks at low temperature, gives a certain aging effect. This is not comparable to that of quality wines but rather comes closer to that of certain dessert wines whose rancio characteristic is obtained by a process of oxidation. Indeed, a traditional process consists of heating fortified wines in contact with air at a temperature of 30°C, then gradually raising it for a period of one to three months with the object of getting the color and taste of a mature wine; or again of leaving it out in the sun in demijohns not completely filled. At the same time, it is well known that slight heating away from air (19–22°C), shortens the period of "bottle sickness" and accentuates the reduced bouquet. Bottled wines develop more quickly in warm cellars, but keep longer in cool ones.

4.   A lot of importance is attached to the enzymatic stabilization of wine. It is usually achieved by sulfiting. Heating is another way of obtaining it. Young wines after fermentation contain various enzymes from the grapes or from the yeasts. Most of them have little enological importance but it is not the same for oxydases. It is known that wines from moldy grapes are rich in laccase and susceptible to oxidative casse. Even wines from healthy grapes contain enough tyrosinase to amplify the process of oxidation 10 times. To destroy enzymes, a few minutes heating at 75°C or a few seconds at 90°C (flash-pasteurization) is utilized.

5.   After having shown that the deterioration of wines was due to the proliferation of ferments, Pasteur found a remedy for it in heating. Following this, heating was used as an antiyeast treatment for keeping wines of the semisweet (*moelleux*) or sweet types. The minimum temperature to be reached and the length of time it should last depend on a number of factors, some related to the wines treated, some related to the microorganisms to be destroyed. Higher alcoholic strength, lower pH and greater free sulfur dioxide content reinforce the efficiency of heating.

The resistance of each microorganism is determined by two values: the growth-limit temperature above which microorganisms cannot multiply and the cellular destruction temperature at which they are killed. There is about 10°C between these two values. In wine, the majority of yeasts and several bacteria are killed in a few seconds of heating, but their total destruction requires several minutes.

The mortality or lethality of microorganisms in a given medium is related to a dual parameter: the temperature level and the length of time this temperature is maintained. The higher the temperature, the shorter the time required to destroy the cells and vice versa. The "mortality heating time" is the number of minutes required to completely destroy at a given temperature a given concentration of germs. This value represents what is also called the thermoresistance of a microorganism. Again the amount of heat required to produce sterilization of a medium may be expressed in terms of pasteurization units. One unit corresponds to heating at a temperature of 60°C for one minute.

Heating is efficient on the condition that it is not followed up by another contamination. Consequently, the only process which is absolutely sure is heating the wines in corked bottles, this is in point of fact how all the heating experiments were carried out at the beginning and, in the very first instance, those done by Pasteur. Bulk pasteurization has never been developed since it calls for difficult aseptic precautions to be taken for the containers the treated

Figure 28.1.   Plate heat-exchanger used for hot-bottling (Padovan).

wine is put into. Sterilization of the containers is only possible when using metal tanks. On the other hand, present-day vinification and storage methods and better controlled use of sulfur dioxide make it possible to ensure the wines keep well.

Heating in the bottle requires sophisticated equipment and has the disadvantage of leaving an empty space in the neck of the bottles after they have cooled down. Hot-bottling has solved the practical problem of heating. Also used for fruit juices and beer, this process consists of heating the wine to 45 or 48°C and bottling at this temperature. The bottles cool down afterward on their own. This process is particularly suitable for young red wines and semisweet white wines of average quality and ensures they keep perfectly. Sufficient free sulfur dioxide at bottling prevents the oxidative shock this treatment gives. Filling bottles under inert gas is recommended.

Techniques for Heating Wines

In the first pasteurizers, the wine flowed through tubular calefactors in the form of coils immersed in a water bath. Modern heating apparatus consists of honeycomb plate-exchangers (see Fig. 28.1) in which the wine circulates in thin layers. Hot water is run over the other side of the plates in the opposite direction. This apparatus allows the regulation of the wine's output temperature, which can, by means of a cold water circuit, be brought back to normal temperature.

Some models use infrared radiation to raise the wine to the chosen temperature. Infrared rays do not exert any particular chemical action but ensure uniform penetration of heat into the stream of wine circulating in transparent tubes.

HEATING LEVELS FOR THERMAL TREATMENT OF WINES

Treatments	Purpose	Temperature and Length of Heating
Pasteurization	Sterilization of the wine	A few minutes at 55, 60, or 65°C
Flash-pasteurization	Sterilization, enzymatic stabilization	A few seconds at 90 or 100°C
Hot-bottling	Sterilization of the wine	Heating at 45 or 48°C with spontaneous cooling in the bottle
Thermal stabilization	Elimination of the proteins from white wines	15 minutes at 75°C or 30 minutes at 60°C
	Elimination of excess copper	15 minutes to 1 hour at 75°C
Air-conditioned storage	Aging of certain types of wine	Several days at a temperature of 30–45°C with or without aeration
	Aging in the bottle	Several weeks of storage at a temperature of 19–22°C according to the type of wine

REFRIGERATION OF WINES

Refrigeration or treatment by chilling consists of cooling wines down to below 0°C in the neighborhood of freezing point, letting them settle deposits at this temperature for a while then clarifying by filtration. In this way, young red wines destined for rapid bottling are stripped and their color and clarity stabilized. Substances precipitated and separated by filtering do not create deposits in the bottom of the bottle afterwards. This treatment is just as efficient for white wines, VDN, and dessert wines.

It has been known for a long time that cooling has a beneficial effect on new wines. Letting wines undergo the action of winter cold has always been recommended. Carrying out refrigeration enables extreme winter conditions to be simulated artificially in a few days.

Refrigerating wines only produces physical changes and, in particular, causes insolubilizations. The precipitations it causes can be divided into two categories: precipitation of crystals (tartaric salts of potassium and of calcium) and colloidal precipitations (coloring matter from red wines, ferric complexes,

SOLUBILITY OF POTASSIUM
BITARTRATE[a]

Temperature (°C)	Soluble Potassium Bitartrate (g/L)
30	4.60
25	3.72
20	3.05
15	2.53
10	2.12
5	1.75
0	1.41
−4	1.21

[a] Solution with alcohol at 10°C.

partial protein precipitations); the polysaccharides are carried down. With young wines, these precipitations are abundant.

Furthermore, chilling has no chemical action and the decline in microbial activity is only temporary. Yeasts or bacteria momentarily paralyzed become active again as the wine warms up. Do not therefore count on chilling to give a wine lasting microbial stability. On the other hand this treatment facilitates all the clarification processes.

Tartaric Precipitations

It is known that the solubility of tartaric salts diminishes during fermentation on account of the formation of alcohol. For this reason, wine contains only half as much tartaric acid as the must does. But crystallization is slow, retarded in comparison with what it would be in a model solution without colloids.

At the same time, the solubility of potassium bitartrate is considerably reduced when temperature is lowered whereas that of calcium tartrate is less sensitive to temperature conditions. Refrigeration allows a new solubility balance to be achieved, permanent for potassium bitartrate (unless the wine should happen to be reduced later to a temperature lower than that of the treatment) but incomplete and temporary for calcium tartrate if it is in excess. The guarantee of stability offered by refrigeration, often put forward as a selling argument, is never in reality total.

When a wine is chilled, the following observations can be made: If chilling is slow and progressive, there will be formation of large tartar crystals, but precipitation will be incomplete; if, on the other hand, chilling is rapid, there will be formation of very fine crystals difficult to separate and precipitation will be complete up to the solubility threshold.

Crystallization is easier when crystalline nucleii are added (in the form of bitartrate powder from a little of the lees from a previous treatment), when it is constantly stirred, when ultra-sounds are used, and also when it is filtered or centrifugated beforehand.

Precipitation of Coloring Matter

Young red wines possess a fraction of their coloring matter in a colloidal state. In this form, the coloring matter is soluble at normal temperatures and the wine is clear, and insoluble when cold and the wine goes cloudy. Therefore, all red wines with enough color lose their clarity when cooled down to around 0°C, when a bottle is put in the freezer, for instance.

It is the colloidal fraction of coloring matter that becomes insoluble during storage. It forms a part of the lees in young wines especially in winter and the usual deposit of mature wines in the bottle. Fining with gelatin, albumin, or bentonite carries down the colloidal coloring. Wines that have been fined remain clear when cold and only settle a deposit slowly in the bottle. Refrigerated wine stays clear when it is chilled a second time.

Stabilization achieved in this way by fining or refrigeration is, moreover, temporary with wines to be laid down, since the colloidal coloring forms again in a few months, less abundantly however; but in practical terms such treatment is sufficient for several years.

Other Precipitations

In a general way, being kept in a cold state creates flocculations and gives rise to colloidal precipitations of several kinds. Filtration, which completes the treatment, is made a lot easier because of it. Chilling distinctly improves the filtration cycle of wines that tend to clog. Fining carried out at low temperature is also more efficient, but permanent colloidal stability is not always achieved for all that.

Although low temperatures emphasize the insolubilization of ferric phosphate and iron complexes with the polyphenols, the proportion of iron removed by refrigeration remains low and generally insufficient to guarantee cure of a wine with casse. In the same way, refrigeration does not clear white wine of its excess proteins or guarantee protein stability.

Taste Improvement

Refrigeration of young wines always distinctly improves their taste and the younger the wine, the greater the taste improvement. Applied a few days after fermentation has finished, the new wine is completely transformed, not aged, but as it were purged of all its pristine impurities. If it is done later, after winter, the difference is not so marked. After a year's storage the treatment even makes the wine, especially quality wine, lose bouquet and character and anyway, in this case, it is bound to be less beneficial.

For young wines, improving taste is linked to the precipitation of potassium bitartrate; the sour taste is reduced. Refrigeration, therefore, makes a wine more supple but conversely has little effect on substances with a bitter or astringent taste. The polyphenol index is not reduced by this treatment any more than by fining.

Conducting Refrigeration

The efficiency of the treatment depends in the first instance on the level of cooling (i.e., on the minimum temperature the wine is brought down to). To get maximum effectiveness from refrigeration, the temperature of the wine needs to be taken as low as possible, down close to freezing point. This point depends on the alcoholic strength and to a lesser extent on the amount of extract. For dry wines, this comes very close to the negative value of half the alcoholic strength (a wine at 10% strength freezes at $-5°C$; a wine at 12%, at $-6°C$).

The operating conditions differ according to the length of time the chilling lasts. Up until now static processes have been used consisting of a period more or less prolonged under refrigeration. New processes under study at the moment are attempting to initiate crystallization in order to complete the operation in a single day. In the "contact" process, this activation is obtained by seeding with 4 g of potassium bitartrate per liter of wine to be treated, shaking it throughout. In another "continuous" process, the wine, instantaneously refrigerated, goes through a "crystallizer" element.

Refrigeration equipment using the classic already old-fashioned process consists of insulated tanks in which the chilled wine remains for a given time (see Fig. 28.2). If all that is required is the precipitation of the pigment from red wines, 24–48 hours may suffice, followed by clarification. On the other hand, if the cellar master wants to be sure of removing all the tartaric salts, he may need to leave it a lot longer. The 5 or 6 days normally recommended will not always be enough, and it is advisable to allow 10 days or a fortnight. Final filtering is carried out at minimum temperature (Fig. 28.3).

Over the last few years there has been a tendency to use another method of chilling made possible by storage in metal tanks: maintaining them for a long period in a cold chamber kept at a temperature close to 0°C. Young wines, preferably filtered beforehand, are kept in this way for a month or two months at low temperature. They are filtered again when taken out of the

Figure 28.2. Apparatus for treating wines by chilling (Gasquet). The following elements can be seen: ultrarefrigerator, control panel, exchanger, insulated filter, isothermal tanks.

cold chamber. The same refrigerated tank can be used for fermenting white wines at 15 or 16°C for white vinification.

All-round chilling forms part of recent techniques for better control of storage temperatures, each stage of the wine's evolution needing to take place at a particular level of temperature. What can be imagined is a storage complex made up of various independent cellars each at a given constant temperature: 18°C for finishing young wines, especially for completing malolactic fermentation; 0°C or below for all-round chilling; another at 10–12°C, say, for storing white wines in bulk or in the bottle or at 15–18°C for storing red wines.

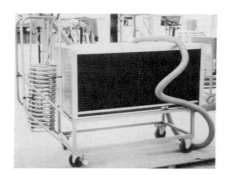

Figure 28.3. Mobile chilling apparatus (Edscheid) enabling on-site refrigeration of the wine. The refrigerating coil is immersed in the wine via the upper lid on the tank.

MODIFICATION OF A WINE'S COMPOSITION BY CONCENTRATION[a]

	Before Concentration	After Concentration[b]
Alcoholic strength (%)	8.8	10.8
Dry extract (g/L)	21.0	23.8
Total acidity (g of sulfuric acid/L)	4.40	4.68
Volatile acidity (g of sulfuric acid/L)	0.27	0.34
Alkalinity of ash (meq)	20.2	18.0
Tartaric acid (g/L)	2.80	2.22
Lactic acid (g/L)	2.05	2.55
Polyphenol index (meq)	36	43
Suppleness index	2.9	4.4

[a] Malolactic fermentation of the wine was complete. Reduction in volume was about 24%.
[b] All of the analytical values, except tartaric acid, alkalinity of ash and total acidity, rose in proportion to the concentration. Suppleness index and taste were improved.

Concentration of Wines by Partial Freezing

When a wine is chilled to below freezing, ice crystals form in the mass of wine. They are composed of water since alcohol does not solidify at this temperature. Stirring it up all the time prevents the ice crystals from gathering. When enough water has frozen in this way, it is separated with a drying machine which extracts a sort of snow that does not show more than 0.5% alcohol. By this method, a certain amount of water is withdrawn and most of the constituents will be concentrated, in relation to the reduction in volume. On the other hand, tartaric acid and potassium diminish. Fixed acidity does not rise proportionately. To improve the quality of red wines, concentration should be applied to wines without taste defects that have finished their malolactic fermentation. Concentration brings out any astringency or acidity defects.

Concentration of wines by chilling is used to increase the strength of wines that are too weak and to ensure proper storage and marketing. In this case, concentration must not exceed 25% of volume and 2% increase in alcoholic strength. Greater concentration applies to special cases (base wines for aperitifs, concentrated wines in cans).

29

Other Treatments Applied to Wine

Under the term physicochemical treatment, it is convenient from a didactic viewpoint to include a few enological practices which treat certain colloidal phenomena, using adsorption, protection, or inhibition. The adsorbant treatment with bentonite, the protective treatment with gum arabic, and the use of metatartaric acid as a crystallization inhibitor all belong to this category.

USE OF BENTONITE

The clarification of wines with certain clays is a very old process. It continues to be used empirically in some countries with special earths (Spanish earth). As a result of studies carried out by J. Ribéreau-Gayon, the first rationalized treatment for stabilizing white wines against protein cloudiness used kaolin. As a result, it became possible during the thirties to go ahead with the first early bottlings without risk of sediment. Bentonite, tried out later, was to offer the advantages of being more efficient and easier to use as well. Its use spread rapidly after 1945 for the treatment of white wines. Later on, its capacity for fining red wines also became recognized. Finally its use during white vinification developed more recently.

Properties of Bentonite

Bentonite comes in powder form, greasy to the touch, or else in granulated form, more convenient for use. It is a natural mineral substance of the clay family, a hydrated aluminum silicate.

342

Different clays are ranked in two categories: those which like kaolin are made of kaolinite and those like bentonite, which are made of montmorillonite. Kaolin has a crystalline structure, does not swell up in contact with water, and its adsorption properties are weak. Bentonite, on the other hand, swells up considerably and fixes as much as 10 times its weight of water, which allows gelatinous pastes or slurries to be prepared. Its colloidal character and the electronegative charge its particles possess afford it potent adsorbant power. These are the adsorption and flocculation properties, which are made use of in treating wines.

There are a large number of qualities of bentonite from various origins that have different industrial applications but not all of them are suitable for the treatment of wines. Some would impart off tastes or would introduce foreign substances, others, although neutral, have no clarifying or adsorbant power and, included in recipes for enological products, are mere make-weights of no interest.

For enological purposes, it is mostly sodium bentonite that is used activated by sodium carbonate. It has an alkaline reaction. Nonflocculent calcium bentonite is less active and not to be recommended. The best-known bentonites come from Wyoming; certain deposits in North Africa or Europe also give enological bentonite.

It is not the chemical composition of the bentonites, in any case highly variable (silicon content fluctuates between 48 and 60%, aluminum from 18 to 25%) which explains their properties, but their colloidal structure. It has been calculated that a gram of bentonite in suspension in water presents a surface of 5 m^2. This combination of a large surface with a permeable texture gives bentonite its remarkable adsorbant properties.

Stabilizing Power of Bentonite

Bentonite treatment is the specific remedy for protein casse and the very basis of the stabilization of clarity in white wines.

We have seen that young white wines contain various proteins liable to precipitate with heat, or over a period, giving rise to cloudiness and a flocculate deposit. The macromolecules of these proteins have a positive electric charge. Bentonite, with a negative charge, fixes them by means of attraction or adsorption and in this way allows them to be removed.

A white wine treated with bentonite does not go cloudy afterwards when warmed up. Total nitrogen content diminishes from between 20 and 50 mg/L in the course of treatment.

At the same time, bentonite transmits to the wine treated, better powers of resistance against cupric casse. When this accident occurs, the presence of small quantities of proteins is necessary to ensure precipitation of the cupric colloids. Bentonite treatment removes, as it were, the backing on which the cloudiness forms. Whereas a white wine containing 0.8 mg of copper per liter would normally go cloudy in the bottle, it can tolerate up to 1.5 mg when treated by a sufficient dose of bentonite.

Furthermore, bentonite ensures removal of the colloidal fraction of the pigments from red wines and dessert wines, often better moreover (thanks to the large amounts that can be used) than the usual finings with gelatin or albumin do. That could not have been assumed, starting with the electrostatic theory of adsorption. Wines fined with bentonite remain clear when cold and no longer settle a sediment in the bottle. Bentonite fixes the anthocyanins and therefore discolors young wines, rosé wines, and patchy wines. The bentonite lees from white wines made from black grapes are always pink-colored.

Fining red wines and special wines with bentonite can therefore be recommended on the same grounds as classic fining. Besides, it is better to use both.

Clarifying Power of Bentonite

When bentonite is introduced into the wine, the acidity and the salts make it flocculate; the appearance of the flocculate is rather similar to the one caused by protein fining. Nevertheless the clarifying power of bentonite is irregular and depends on the wine's composition. Sometimes as good as proteinaceous fining, often it proves to be distinctly inferior. The only wines which can be properly cleared with bentonite are whites or reds free of mucilaginous protective colloids.

To ensure better clarification of difficult wines, bentonite needs to be put in suspension in water; if it is prepared directly in the wine, flocculation, sedimentation, and clarification generally are not so good.

As a general rule, it is preferable to try to stabilize the wine first by means of bentonite treatment and only then ensure clarification by fining or filtering. Good results are obtained, for instance, by associating with the bentonite a fining with gelatin or blood-powder. Filtration throughput is doubled with bentonited wines if this kind of fining is done first.

Method of Use

Many different situations can occur. Treatment may be carried out in the winery on a settled must (this was seen in Chapter 16), on a young wine at its first racking, or again in the merchant's cellars on a wine which is much further developed. Early treatment is always preferable.

When it is used in powder form, bentonite can be used with or without making it swell up in advance. Swelling, which is recommended when clarification is required, can be done either with water or with the wine. In preparing suspension of the bentonite, to prevent it from curdling, the powder should be poured onto the surface of the liquid little by little and mixed in as it sinks and not the liquid poured over the powder. When it is used in granulated form, it always has to be swollen first, but it is much easier to put in suspension. The preparation of a bentonite milk with wine makes it coagulate and diminishes its clarifying properties. Swelling it with hot water (50°C) is faster. Injection with a pump is the best way of breaking up the tiny specks.

Doses to be used vary with the wines and the quality of the bentonite, say, for instance, in normal situations between 40 and 100 g/hL.

Merging it into the wine is done by vigorous churning, still taking the same care to make sure the mixture is homogeneous as with any ordinary fining. Perfect clarification is obtained after settling, racking, and filtering.

USE OF GUM ARABIC

Gum arabic is the typical protective colloid. A stable colloid, it resists flocculation of unstable colloids. It prevents, therefore, the formation of cloudiness and deposits in a clarified wine by stopping the colloidal particles from agglomerating. But it also stabilizes the colloidal cloudiness in a wine, slows down its sedimentation, and hampers clarification. Thus it can only be used in clear wines.

Wine naturally contains protective colloids: various polysaccharides, sometimes glucane. Very old references to the use of gum arabic in wine can be found.

Gum arabic is exuded from the trunk of various African acacias. It appears in tears, in lumps, or else in powder. For enological purposes, a pure white gum is used in conformity with the pharmacopoeia standards.

Gum arabic is used in solution. There are solutions at 150 or 200 g/L to be found on the market. They can be made up by dissolving powdered gum in hot water or soaking gum in tear form in a little linen bag such as those used for infusions. Solutions are opalescent and it is better to let them clarify by settling before use, or to filter them. They are preserved by adding 0.5 g of sulfur dioxide per liter.

Doses for use are from 10 to 15 g/hL as a security treatment against cupric casse for white wines and from 20 to 25 g to prevent ferric casse (generally in conjunction with citric acid) or to ensure stabilization of colloidal coloring matter in red wines. Gum arabic is incorporated into wine before the polishing filtration.

It should not be used for red wines or special wines likely to be laid down for long storage. Stopping the natural formation of deposits in aged wines, in the long run, would give them an opalescent appearance and a dull color.

USE OF METATARTARIC ACID

The problems of stabilizing wines with metallic and protein casse were the first to be solved. Without doubt, the accident that has become the most frequent after bottling is precipitation of tartaric crystals. It is all the more worrying since delivery in bottles or liter flagons is being developed and also since, for investment reasons together with changes in consumer tastes, wines are being put on the market younger.

We have seen in the previous chapter the efficiency of treating by chilling in this context and we defined its limits. A radical process would be to use cation exchangers, a technique which, however, is unlikely ever to be authorized.

The use of DL-tartaric acid (the racemic mixture of tartaric acid) has been recommended in Italy to remove excess calcium. The calcium racemate is not in fact very soluble (32 mg/L in water as opposed to 266 mg for the L-tartrate). It is performed on wines cleared of their heavy colloids by treating with bentonite and a fine filtration. The dose of racemic acid to be added is calculated by multiplying the calcium content by 3 (which corresponds to three quarters of the dose needed theoretically to precipitate all the calcium). Calcium racemate has a strong tendency to produce supersaturated solutions so that it is advisable to keep the wine in movement by continuous churning. The racemic mixture of acid can be added during refrigeration to take advantage of the insolubilizing action of chilling. Precipitation lasts one week. Treatment succeeds best on wines with little acid. Previous laboratory tests with quantitive analysis of the calcium precipitated are recommended.

One original way of preventing crystallization was discovered around 1955: adding to the wine small quantities of a crystal inhibitor, metatartaric acid. This produce is obtained by transforming tartaric acid, heated for a sufficient time at its fusion point, 170°C. Its use is permitted in doses limited to 10 g/hL.

This product is not new, its preparation has been known for a hundred years, but it is only recently that its advantageous properties have been discovered. From the chemical point of view it is allied to the internal lactides or esters which are formed by reaction of the acid and alcohol functions in the same body; it is the hemipolylactide of tartaric acid.

Manufacture of Metatartaric Acid

A certain weight of tartaric acid in a fine powder is heated to high temperature in a vessel made of an incorrodible material. Tartaric acid melts at 170°C. The mass is shaken up continuously and the temperature maintained for some 20 or 30 minutes or more. As the liquid boils, steam is given off and at the same time a sort of caramelization takes place with coloration and browning. Direct heating at 170°C and over in fact produces secondary reactions, especially formation of small quantities of pyruvic acid. If heating is continued, a large amount of gaseous substance is seen to be released, the mass increases in volume and froths copiously. Heating is then stopped and the vessel allowed to cool, leaving a solid product more or less vitreous and compact, more or less spongy and friable.

Parasitic reactions can be avoided to a large extent by carrying out the operation in a vacuum. With this method, reactions begin at a lower level, 150–160°C. The products obtained from it are whiter, more soluble, and more neutral in odor.

Metatartaric acid is hygroscopic; it congeals into a mass and becomes deliquescent by absorbing humidity from the air. It must be kept away from humidity in hermetically sealed plastic bags.

Anticrystallizing Efficiency of Metatartaric Acid

This product constitutes a remarkable inhibitor for the crystallization of tartaric salts. Introduced into young wines in doses of 100 mg/L, formation of crystals is rendered impossible for several months on the condition that a properly prepared and correctly dosed product is used. It acts by coating the crystalline tartar nucleii and thereby prevents them from growing any bigger.

The efficiency of metatartaric acid depends on the amount of active hemipolylactide it contains and its degree of condensation. Control of the quality of metatartaric acid preparations is based on measuring their esterification index or percentage of the esterified functions in relation to the totality of the tartaric acid put to use.

The most active products have an esterification index of 38–40%; it requires twice as much of the product at 30% to obtain the same protection.

When added to the wine, metatartaric acid is slowly hydrolyzed, transforming itself back into tartaric acid so that it gradually loses its activity. The length of time metatartaric acid remains efficient depends a great deal on the storage temperature of the wine being treated. At 0°C in a refrigerator, the inhibition lasts several years; at 10–12°C it lasts more than 18 months; at 12–18°C certain wines begin to settle a deposit at the end of a year; in a drying over at 25°C, metatartaric acid disappears after a month or two. In short, the product is most stable in conditions of greatest utility, that is to say, in winter. But a wine treated and bottled before summer may not be protected throughout the following winter. This treatment is especially suitable for wines that are only destined to remain in bottles for a limited time. This is the case with table wines sold by the liter and a great many appellation wines, particularly whites. Wines that have been treated ought to be kept in cool cellars.

Method of Use

Just before adding it to the wine, the product is dissolved in cold water, say at about 200 g/L. Hot water, which activates hydrolysis, should be avoided. Concentrated solutions lose some of their strength (1%/day) and need to be used as soon as they are ready.

Metatartaric acid is used for preference after the wine has been treated and fined and before filtering. Indeed certain flocculations carry it down partially; this is particularly the case with bentonite and potassium ferrocyanide; even straightforward fining with gelatin or albumin fixes some 10–25% of it. Metatartaric acid is incompatible with calcium phytate. On the other hand, certain preparations with a high esterification index, added to clear wines, can cause slight opalescence, so it is better to merge them in before final clarification. If the cellar master is obliged to treat a clarified wine, say at the time of bottling, he can avoid any formation of matter in suspension by preparing the metatartaric acid solution, exceptionally, 24 hours in advance.

The use of metatartaric acid ought to be applied in higher doses to wines that are more acid. It is unwise to use it to treat wines that are too rich in calcium or wines kept in concrete tanks that have been badly scoured out or again in containers that are heavily coated with tartar.

PART 8

Bottling Wines

30

Bottles and Bottling

Bottling is the logical end-process and the ultimate form of storage for wines. A bottle enables a wine to be presented correctly, but it is not just a convenient method of distribution. It should be considered the best way of developing and preserving over the longest period the taste qualities of a great wine.

Bottling is a very stressful operation for a wine and the enological problems it causes are numerous: considerable oxygen uptake, keeping out microorganisms and particles in suspension by filtering, constant struggle to prevent any contamination of yeasts by the apparatus itself, cleanliness of the glass, efficiency of closure, etc. The organizational and engineering problems themselves (setting up bottling plants, choosing machines, wine and accessories supply, method of bottle-filling, stoppering process) must be resolved in accordance with enological requirements and with deference to quality.

This cellaring operation has been transformed considerably over the last few decades with the growth in the volume being bottled and the size of work units. The speed of bottling achieved with manual or small-scale processes as well as their work-quality were soon seen to be inadequate. Bottling plants with a high production rate (1500–6000 bottles an hour or more) have been perfected. It is in this sector that the most spectacular advances in equipment improvement have been made. Active input by enologists is here becoming more and more important. One of their functions is to ensure correct presentation of the wine in the bottle while at the same time respecting and, if possible, intensifying potential quality.

GLASS: ITS NATURE AND COMPOSITION

Glass is a substance that is amorphous, noncrystalline, transparent, insoluble, acid- and alkali-resistant, obtained by fusion at 1500°C of matter rich in silica, soda, lime, alumina, and magnesium plus other metal oxides used as coloring.

COMPOSITION OF
BOTTLE GLASS

Silica	68–71%
Soda	14.5–15.5%
Lime	7–10%
Magnesium	1–3%
Alumina	1–2%

Actually, bottle glass is not absolutely neutral from a chemical point of view. It is alkaline and has a tendency to become hydrolyzed on the surface. The surface layer of new glass is charged with Na+ ions; it can be treated and charged with K+ ions, for instance. The surface of glass is not neutral and passive. In relation to its hydrolytic resistance, reactions with acid liquids and certain limited cation exchanges may be observed. The bottle glass made in the eighteenth century was too soft, so that wine corroded it, and this caused the wine to become spoiled. Used bottles were preferred to new glass. Today, due to surface treatments, glass is harder and more resistant, which has enabled the thickness and weight of bottles to be reduced.

Color of Bottle Glass

Glass is more or less colored by various iron oxides (FeO: blue tints, Fe_2O_3: yellow tints). Semiwhite glass used for white wines contains 0.08–0.15% of iron oxides; light green glass contains 0.8–1.2%; dark green glass, 2–2.5%. To get a tint that is less green, manganese bioxide is added (glass tinted by iron-manganese). The dead-leaf tint is given by ferric peroxide. Chromium oxide gives a lovely emerald green color which is masked with nickel oxide (glass tinted by chrome-nickel).

The color of glass can protect wine from action by light rays. According to its shade and intensity, a bottle will allow penetration by a greater or less radiation from the spectrum range (see Fig. 30.1). White glass stops ultraviolet and partially stops violet rays but lets all other radiations through. Green glass impedes ultraviolet and violet better, lets a little blue and a lot of yellow pass through, and keeps out a higher proportion of other radiations. The wine is better protected.

It is an observed fact that white wine ages more quickly in white bottles than in colored bottles. The redox potential declines more quickly and reaches a lower level in clear glass. This is an advantage for types of white wine that take on a pleasant reduced bouquet in the bottle. It is a disadvantage for

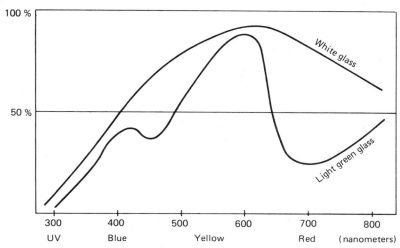

Figure 30.1. Transparency to various radiations from the spectrum for two qualities of bottle glass. The curves express the percentage of light that passes through the glass in relation to the wavelength.

those that are made, say, from aromatic grape varieties and that need to keep their freshness and fruity flavor.

Another disadvantage of colorless bottles is that the decline in redox potential they cause, ends by reducing the cupric salts. This may give rise to cupric casse, which is practically never encountered in white wines kept in tinted bottles. Even red wines, although they are less permeable and less sensitive to light, develop more harmoniously in the darkest colored bottles.

Manufacture of Bottles

The main stages are as follows:

1.   Fusion of raw materials for making the glass is executed in a furnace at 1500°C working continuously; salvaged glass is recycled.

2.   Making the actual bottle is done by molding and by glass blowing. The quantity of molten glass required to make one bottle, called a parison, is automatically delivered to the molds at a temperature of 1000 to 1100°C. The molding operation is done in two parts: first the neck and the collar, then the bottle itself is brought to its final shape by blowing in a second mold.

3.   The third stage is annealing; the bottle leaves the mold at 500°C. If it were left to cool at the surrounding temperature, it would break due to internal tensions. The purpose of annealing, which is carried out in a tunnel

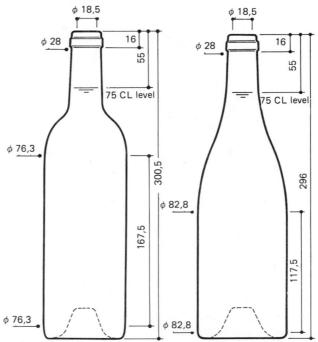

Figure 30.2. Traditional Bordeaux bottle: capacity to brim of neck, 76.7 cL; effective capacity, 75 cL at 55 mm from top; weight, 550 g; tint, semiwhite champagne. *Right:* Traditional Burgundy bottle: capacity to brim of neck, 76.7 cL; effective capacity, 75 cL at 55 mm from top; weight, 608 g; tint, dead-leaf champagne.

furnace called a calcar, is to counteract these tensions. To improve the mechanical resistance of glass, harden its surface, and avoid it being scored by impact or abrasion, various treatments are applied to the outside surface of the bottle during annealing. The most common consists of burning sulfur in the calcar; in this way, a layer of sodium sulfate is formed on the surface of the glass. Titanium salts are used for the same purpose.

4.   Production control operations are carried out at the end of the calcar, as the bottle emerges. All bottles undergo automatic dimension control, and any which do not conform to the standards for shape, height, weight, regularity of thickness and the neck sizes are rejected (see Fig. 30.2). A second series of statistical controls test resistance against impact, pressure, and temperature variations.

CLEANLINESS OF BOTTLES

Impurities of New Bottles

On emergence from the calcar where it is annealed and then cooled, bottles are sterile but not necessarily clean. Anyway, sterility is only provisory since handling and storage lead to contamination. One-third of new bottles when they arrive at the winery contain microorganisms, especially molds.

Depending on the annealing process, new bottles may contain chemical impurities, such as whitish traces of sodium sulfate, called calcar mist, on the outside surface and sometimes inside the neck. New bottles may exhibit dust and glass particles, but also accidental stains: traces of soot due to bad combustion of the oil used in the calcar's burners, spots of graphite grease coming from lubrication of the molds. Finally dirt-marks attributable to conditions of storage and transport (either direct-loaded or palleted) dust, insects, rainwater, or condensation drops may be found.

Bottle Washing

Some wineries have thought they could get away without having to rinse new bottles. Nevertheless, to avoid leaving themselves open to complaints from their customers, they must clean the bottles before filling them. A simple jet of hot water would seem to be sufficient for this purpose. On the other hand, dust removal using compressed air is definitely not effective enough. Anyway, washing bottles is a legal obligation, clearly set out in France in a circular dated 1962 (see Chapter 19, Cleanliness of the Wine Containers).

As for bottles that have already been used, known as returned empties or returnables (frequently the case with the trade in table wines in liter bottles), they exhibit numerous dirt-marks: On the inside, the remains of liquid rich in molds, yeasts, bacteria, especially acetic bacteria, pellicles from microorganisms dried onto the walls, various forms of dirt and dust; on the outside, labels, traces of glue, salts from the capsules over the stoppers, and so forth. These bottles need a very thorough wash capable of removing all the visible stains plus all the microorganisms that could be detrimental to the wine's stability in the bottle.

Mechanical processes are used for these washing procedures (see Fig. 30.3), very often combined with chemical methods using an appropriate detergent. The mechanical processes are based on the absorptive and dissolving power of hot water under pressure together with brushing. For washing throughput of lower than 600 bottles an hour, the most common process consists of soaking in hot water followed by brushing and pressure rinsing.

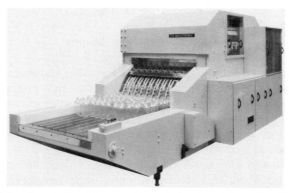

Figure 30.3.   New-bottle rinsing machine with loading platform (La Girondine).

In the case of high throughput, in addition to mechanical cleaning, various products with a chemical action are used which, what is more, destroy all the microorganisms as well. It is difficult to propose a polyvalent detergent. The user would do best to accept the mixtures prepared by specialized manufacturers.

Visual cleanliness of the bottles can be checked by directly viewing them against a light when there are not too many. Electronic inspection is better suited to high-speed operations. Microbiological control tests on washed bottles are highly recommended. These are carried out in the following way. A bottle is rinsed with a small volume of sterile water and this liquid is then passed through a membrane filter 5 cm in diameter (Millipore type) with very fine pores. Then the membrane is deposited in aseptic conditions on a solid nutritive medium. Each living microorganism retained by the membrane, after several days, gives birth to a visible colony. Counting the colonies indicates the number of germs per bottle.

FILLING THE BOTTLES

Filling or bottling (or *tirage* or *mise*) consists of filling bottles having the correct capacity in compliance with regulations with an exact volume of wine, leaving the required headspace for corking and possibly room for a certain expansion. Among all the various filling systems that exist, we will only deal with those that are in most widespread use for wines.

Machines Used for Bottling

Drawing off the wine into the bottle by means of a faucet, directly from the cask, is never recommended and anyway is hardly ever done anymore for wines sold commercially. Performance is inefficient and work quality inadequate. Specially designed machines are used called fillers (in French, *soutireuses* or simply *tireuses*). Their output can be very variable and they may, in fact, be adapted to any kind of situation in practice. A large number of models exist on the market. Some are semiautomatic, the empty bottles being fed in by hand, for an output up to 800–1000 bottles per hour. Automatic models are mechanically fed with a traveling apron and provide much higher output.

Bottling machines used in the wine trade belong to the "constant level" system. Among the large number of variants of this type of apparatus, we will describe briefly those that operate by siphoning, isothermic bottlers, and those that work on differential pressures.

Filling by Siphoning

All siphon bottling machines work on the principle of communicating vessels. There is no sealing ring between the filling spout and the neck of the bottle, flow is free, and the air displaced escapes through the neck. The tip of the flow spout is on a lower level than the liquid plane in the feed tank. A tubular clapper valve blocking the tip of the spout is raised by the bottle. When the level of wine in the bottle reaches the level in the tank, flow stops. Speed of filling slows down as the wine rises in the bottle. When the full bottle is withdrawn, the clapper drops back into place, blocking the spout again.

With automatic machines, the filling spouts are placed in line with the necks of the bottles in two different ways according to the model: either the siphons are fixed and the bottles raised up onto them or else it is the siphons that are mobile and are inserted into the bottles. In the first case, the level of wine is the same in all the bottle-necks; in the second case the bottom of the bottle is leveled up and any disparity in the height of the bottle (with returned bottles) leads to differences in the level of filling.

The siphon system of bottling is limited to models used for small-scale output. The advantage of this system lies in the simplicity of design of the spouts. The siphons do, however, have disadvantages: They have to be primed, bulky spouts dipped in the wine causes differences in the level of filling, cracked bottles are filled up just the same. However, some machines using the mobile spout principle have automatic priming; others are equipped with a system for equalizing filling levels.

Isobarometric Filling

With this process, the neck of the bottle is fitted with a hermetic sealing ring and the atmosphere in the bottles is directly connected to the atmosphere in the wine supply tank; pressure is therefore the same throughout the circuit

Figure 30.4. Bottling machine with spouts under slight pressure (Chelle).

(see Fig. 30.4). Again it may be the same as, less than, or greater than atmospheric pressure. This pressure has no effect on the speed of flow, which remains constant throughout the filling operation. The spouts comprise an air-return tube whose depth of immersion determines the height of the wine in the neck of the bottle.

When operating at atmospheric pressure, these machines have the disadvantage of also filling up leaking or broken bottles. They also require that the joints between the necks and the spouts are perfectly tight. On the other hand, when filling is done under depression, defective bottles are not filled but the wine's loss in carbon dioxide is appreciable, especially when hotbottling. Counterpressure bottling machines suit wines that are more or less effervescent. To avoid outgassing the wine, pressure above it needs to be greater than that of the dissolved gas; this may reach, in relation with the type of wine, anything from 0.2 bars for still wines to 7 bars for sparkling wines. Counterpressure bottling machines have numerous advantages. If bottles are cracked or shatter when put under pressure, the flow valve cannot open and there is no loss of wine.

Filling by Differential Pressure

With this system, the bottles are subjected to depression, whereas the supply tank is kept at atmospheric pressure, whence the term "differential pressure." Machines that work on this principle are called "vacuum" machines (see Fig. 30.5). The depression realized represents 10–30% of atmospheric pressure.

These machines operate either on the siphon principle or by gravity. The depression created in a vacuum chamber is transmitted to the interior of the bottle by an air suction tube. The speed of flow of the wine is of course all the faster the greater the depression, but it is limited by any emulsion or frothing of the wine. When the level reaches the opening in the suction tube, excess wine is drawn up into the vacuum chamber and the bottle is detached from the spout. Depression prevents the spouts from dripping.

The thing users complain about with these systems is that they are difficult to clean and to sterilize. Filling bottles is only properly done provided the sealing between bottle necks and the spouts is perfect. Loss of carbon dioxide is considerable.

Oxygen Uptake Due to Bottling

Oxygen has the opportunity to penetrate into the wine at every stage of handling during bottling. Indeed the different volumes of oxygen dissolved all add up in the end by the time the wine has gone through the supply tank, inside the machine, in the bottle plus the actual headspace remaining in the neck and even the amount locked in the hollow air pockets in the cork, which often proves to be the most significant. It is this accumulation of oxygen merging into the wine which reduces the amount of free sulfur dioxide and causes more or less acute flatness known by the name of bottle sickness.

Enrichment in oxygen as the wine is being fed into the bottling unit should be restricted to the barest minimum. Proper precautions involve circulating the wine via the bottom of the tanks, in pipes kept full, frequently purging the air from the filter pads and injecting an inert gas into the empty parts of the tanks and the reservoir of the bottling unit.

While filling the bottles, contact with air is very short-lived, but it occurs over a relatively large surface and in certain cases with turbulence. Oxygen

Figure 30.5. Bottling machine working under slight vacuum (Stone).

dissolved in this way may vary between 0.5 and 2 mg/L. Depression bottlers are the ones which cause least oxygen uptake. The amount of oxygen dissolved also depends on the length of the spouts as well as the shape and force of the jet of wine.

Certain spouts make the wine aerate considerably so that it retains tiny air bubbles for quite some time. However, counterpressure bottling machines exist that enable the air in the bottle to be driven out by a stream of nitrogen, which diminishes the oxygen uptake a great deal.

According to the headspace left under the stoppering device, the amount of oxygen finally dissolved can be extremely variable. When the bottle is stoppered with a cork, if the headspace is only a few millimeters, uptake will be slight. On the other hand, when closing with a crown cap and tear-off capsule, the usual method for wines sold by the liter, or when the stopper is a screw cap, the headspace may be as much as 20 mL per bottle, containing 4 mL of oxygen. To limit this oxidation, one of the most important the wine is likely to have to undergo, manufacturers propose bottling machines which, after filling, force out the air from the neck with a jet of inert gas (often carbon dioxide). This operation is done just before closing.

31

Corks and Closures

TECHNOLOGY OF CORK

Closing with corks must have origins as old as storing wine in bottles since this cannot be imagined without a tight stopper. Even today cork has maintained its superiority and its prestige and constitutes the only method of closure capable of ensuring long-term storage of quality wines.

All the same, the fact that cork is not above reproach is due as much to the technological progress made in bottling processes as to the quality of cork being collected these days. Proper use of corks stems from a better knowledge of this natural product, its physical, mechanical, and chemical attributes as well as the machining and treatment it has to undergo to be made into a stopper.

Structure and Properties of Cork

Cork represents the bark of a particular variety of cork oak, the *Quercus suber*, a tree that has the faculty of renewing its bark indefinitely. Cork used for the manufacture of bottle closures is a reproduction cork that is formed again after several barkings. Some 10 years are needed between each harvest of cork boards.

Cork appears as a cortical alveolate fabric. It has a hollow structure rather like foam rubber. It is made up of tiny hexagonal cells some 40 μm across. The thickness of the walls of each cell is on the order of 1 μm. It is estimated that 1 cm^3 of cork numbers 15–40 million cells. Therefore, the gases (nitrogen and oxygen) that fill the cells of the cork occupy more than 85% of its volume. It is this finely compartmented structure, putting you in mind of some kind of wooden moss, which accounts for the mechanical and physical qualities of cork.

The suberous texture is not perfectly uniform; it is crisscrossed within its thickness by pores or ducts with walls more or less lignified, the lenticels. They are filled with powder of a reddish-brown color, rich in tannin. This cork powder, of which a small amount may fall into the wine during the corking operation, is one of the disadvantages of cork stoppers. The lenticels are permeable to gases and liquids. They are often invaded by molds and other microorganisms. The best cork is one that has least of these. Trade ranking of cork in board form or machined corks is based, in fact, on the number of lenticels and their size.

On account of its low density, compressibility, impermeability, preservation over long periods in contact with liquids and the structure of its surface when polished, cork constitutes a matter that is unique for closing bottles.

The extreme lightness of cork is due to its gaseous volume; its density is very low, 0.20 on the average. But its most characteristic properties lie in its great suppleness, combined with its exceptional elasticity that enable it to rapidly recover its original dimensions after any deformation. Cork possesses the compressibility of its important gaseous zone. It shrinks considerably under the action of compression. In one instance the contraction was 25, 65, and 85% for pressures of 5, 10, and 15 kg/cm^2, respectively.

These considerable distortions are not permanent. Cork returns to its original shape in two stages: As soon as compression is released, a cork will spring back almost instantaneously to four-fifths of its original diameter; the second stage of elastic recovery is much slower; it requires 24 hours for it to retrieve practically its full volume.

With Trescases, we observe that suppleness or compressibility and elasticity or resilience are different notions and are often confused. Cork that is supple may be soft and nonelastic; it can easily be compressed, but does not expand back much. However, its inertia is less pronounced than that of more rigid qualities of cork and the first stage of redistension may be more rapid with soft cork than with hard cork. On the other hand, the second stage will be better with firm cork. Over the years of being compressed in the neck of the bottle the elastic powers and therefore the security of stoppering diminish more quickly with soft cork having few veins than with slow-growing cork in which the annual layers are tighter knit.

As users know, the suppleness of cork also depends on its moisture content. Moistened cork (8% water) is very supple and difficult to break by hand, whereas in a dry state cork is brittle.

Cork possesses a high friction coefficient, it does not slide well on a surface and is nonslip. This is an explanation of its adherence to glass and its power of stoppering, which adds to the action of pressure it exerts on the smooth inner surface of the bottle neck. These properties are attributed to the little cups created by the cells being sliced through when the cork is cut out, which form so many microscopic suckers.

Cork is practically impermeable to liquids and to gases or at any rate the osmosis of liquids and the diffusion of gases through the walls of the cellular membranes are extremely slow. A thickness of 1 millimeter of cork, built up from some 30 layers of cells, ensures almost perfect impermeability.

It is its chemical composition that gives cork the property of repelling moisture, as well as its impermeability and its imputrescibility. The waxy or ceroid part (about 5% of the weight of cork) is soluble in organic solvents. Suberin (about 45%), which is the main portion, resists solvents and can only be rendered soluble after polymerization. This compound, formed by the condensation of various acid-alcohols, has a high molecular weight and it can be hydrolized.

The walls of the cells also contain cellulose and polysaccharides (about 12%), lignin (about 27%), which is a constituent of wood, phenolic compounds (about 6%), mineral matter, and so forth. Cork contains the same catechin tannins as oak but in a smaller amount. It happens that turbidity in bottles of white wine rich in proteins starts in the proximity of the cork; this means coagulation has been set off by the tannin imparted by the cork.

MANUFACTURE OF CORKS

Barking the cork oak or *démasclage*, strips the bark into boards of varying thickness (2–6 cm). The boards are allowed to weather and are subjected to external conditions for two or three years with alternating rain and sun. Cork needs to age just like oak for staves before being shaped and assembled by the cooper. It loses its sap and its odor of green wood, its polyphenols oxidize, and its texture contracts.

Cork boards are then put through a boiling process. They are scalded to disinfect them and rid them of their impurities, the cork swells and acquires its definitive elasticity. Left in a cool cellar it gets a level of humidity that makes the work of the cutting tools easier. Then the boards are recut and ranked into seven categories of thickness and six categories of quality.

The cork boards are next sawn into strips, the thickness corresponding to the future cork length. Shaping the corks into cylinders is done by chopping the strips into tubes with a punch. The cylinders obtained are retooled by grinding to give them their final length and diameter. Polishing ensures a very smooth surface, like "rollers." The ends are cut and rubbed down until they are perpendicular to the cork's axis.

A great deal of rough cork is needed to make good cork stoppers. Machining 100 kg of cork produces 30 kg of finished corks (on average, so sometimes less) and 70 kg of waste; from this some 2000 to 20,000 corks are extracted according to their quality.

After manufacture, corks are washed to clear dust and disinfect them. For this purpose, they are put through the following operations: rinsed in clear water, soaked in lightly chlorinated water, then passed through an oxalic acid solution (these two baths having a sterilizing and blanching action), possibly coloration, then they are dried.

Corks are ranked in six classes of quality from the "extra superior" or superfine quality down to the sixth and last category. These qualities do not relate to mensurable and codifiable standards, but are based on the sorter's evaluation of the visible pinholes and lenticels.

A large proportion of the cost of a cork comprises labor costs, a great many operations only being possible manually, but also successive sortings must be very exacting. Cork is a natural product that is particularly inconsistent. It involves matter that is very irregular in structure, appearance and composition. It is chosen for production in relation to the dimensions and quality of the corks. Finally, it could be said that no two corks are exactly identical. Sorting into categories, which is an entirely visual operation, is a difficult and important task.

Corks may be given other treatments to make them look better. Plugging consists of removing dust from the lenticels and refilling the pores and cracks with a very fine cork powder mixed with a glue; a final rubbing down gives a smooth appearance.

Paraffining cold is carried out by putting the corks into a drum together with pieces of paraffin and slowly turning it over on its own axis. By wearing down the lumps of paraffin, the surface of the corks gets covered with thin scales which give them a glazed appearance. Paraffined corks are used dry since the coating helps them slide into the jaws of the corking machine and into the bottleneck. Paraffining can also be done hot (the case with champagne corks). In order to ensure the same form of lubrication, corks can be sprinkled with soapstone or treated with wax emulsion, synthetic resin or silicone oil; these treatments replace paraffining advantageously.

Corks can undergo other forms of preparation: outsorting those which exhibit one or two "mirror" ends (i.e., those that are without lenticels) or preparing "clean ends" by making incisions to empty out the contents of the open lenticels at top and bottom (in this way the dust from them cannot drop into the wine). Chamfering, a less justifiable operation, consists of rounding the ends of the cork to facilitate penetration into the bottle neck, but this has the disadvantage of shortening the effective length of the stoppering.

DIMENSIONS OF CORKS

	Length	
	In Rows	In Millimeters
(1 row = 2.256 mm)		
	15	34
	17	38
	20	45
	22	50
	24	54
Champagne cork		53
Diameter of corks for bottles:		24 ± 0.5
halves:		22 ± 0.5
for champagne:		31.5 ± 0.5

For bottling with sterile filtration, germ-free corks, called sterile corks, need to be used. They are prepared by patent sterilizing processes generally using formaldehyde. Hydrated by steam (humidity at 8–12%), they are put under sulfur dioxide atmosphere into airtight polythene bags.

CORKING BOTTLES

This mechanical operation brings in several factors: the shape of the bottle neck, the characteristics of the bottling machine, and the preparation of the corks.

Shape of the Bottle Neck

The necks of the different bottles have been standardized for several reasons: to make the exterior section on which the outer capsule is placed uniform; to choose an internal diameter suitable for the spouts on the bottling machines and an internal section in compliance with conditions of closing with corks.

The *Cetie* standard ensures regularity of the outside of the bottle neck and its collar, which are produced in a mold. The internal section has the following dimensions: diameter of 18.5 ± 0.5 mm at "uncorking" and a maximum of 21 mm at 45 mm from the top. These dimensions result in a certain conicity. Cork manufacturers consider that to obtain good sealing the cork needs to be subjected in the bottle neck to compression corresponding to a reduction of one quarter of its diameter, that is, 6 mm. Therefore, corks 24 mm in diameter before use are brought down in the bottle neck to 55% of their initial volume. This reduction in its diameter has to be greater still for effervescent wines to compensate for the pressure of the carbon dioxide: for instance, 7 mm for "pearl" wines (1 kg of pressure), 12 mm for sparkling wines (5–6 kg of pressure).

Corking Equipment

The mechanical operation of stoppering is carried out in two stages. First of all, the cork is squeezed to reduce it to a smaller size than the inside of the neck of the bottle, then it is abruptly thrust inside the neck. This compression is obtained by the "chops" or "jaws," which bring it down to 14 or 15 mm in diameter. Quick penetration of the cork duly compressed in this way into the bottle is done by a vertical piston.

Modern corking machines are fitted with jaws made up of various moving parts, perfectly fitted. They use triple or quadruple compression so as to exercise uniform pressure along all its surface, without any friction, pinching, or puckering.

These various types of compressors are mounted on either manual, semiautomatic, or automatic machines. With these latter ones, cork feed creates problems that are difficult to overcome adequately, especially at high throughput speed.

Preparing the Corks

If dry corks are used placed in an upper storage hopper, they slide down well through the feed chute, but they tend to dissipate a lot of cork dust and can be crumpled by the chops of the corking equipment due to lack of suppleness. On the other hand, if corks that are too wet are used, they cling to each other and slide badly into the head of the corking equipment.

However, the mechanical properties of moist cork (8–12%) are far superior; it can be shown to be more supple and more elastic by simply pressing it with the fingers or by trying to break it.

For great wines, the best stoppering is obtained with long corks (54 mm), made of what is known as natural cork, untreated, simply made dust-free and moistened by means of a quick rinse and thoroughly drained before use.

Efficacy of Closure and Height of Filling

When closing, the stroke of the piston on the corking apparatus (see Fig. 31.1) should be adjusted in such a way that the upper end of the cork is just flush with the upper part of the neck. Corks pushed in too far do not stopper well.

368 Corks and Closures

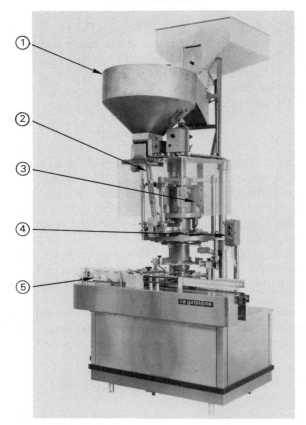

Figure 31.1. Automatic corking machine (La Girondine): 1, cork hopper; 2, cork-feed chute; 3, cork-insertion piston; 4, electric controls; 5, delivery conveyor for bottles.

The level to which the bottle should be filled depends on the bottling temperature of the wine, but also takes into account the time of packaging (capping and labeling) and the expected length of aging. For instance, when using hot-bottling (at 45 or 50°C), the corking should be done "touching the wine"; after cooling, the headspace may attain 30 mm below the cork. Stoppering allows a small space, for wines known as "bottled and corked" then binned in the cellar, which are not going to be sold for several months. There will be time for the reactions of contraction and expansion to take place, the pressure to balance out, and the corks to settle into place. This would not be the same for great wines. Stoppered with long corks, these are going to have to endure 10 or 20 years or more storage without getting too "low."

CORK DEFECTS

Leaking bottles (lack of tightness)

Corks puckered, pinched and deformed by the chops of the corking equipment.

Bottles having irregular or oversize necks.

Cork with diameter below standard size.

Cork too soft, out of round.

Cork material of low quality, porous, cut too close to the bark crust.

Result of wine expanding: filling at low temperature or accidental exposure to high storage temperature.

Old corks having lost their impermeability through time.

Cork-worm

Lepidoptera (tinea) contaminate the bottle-store and lay their eggs on top of the corks; the larva dig galleries into the corks.

Measures to be taken: combat the lepidoptera moths by repeated spraying with insecticide (from June to October) or use capsules over the corks; temporary plastic capsules can be used.

Corky taste

This defect is well known but its definition is not explicit, any more than its origin:

Mold from the cork board.

Specific taste of cork tannins.

Contact of the wine after decorking with the superficial layer polluted by a moldy adulterated cork.

Certain faulty tastes in wines are wrongly attributed to the cork; in this case it is the complete lot of wine put into bottles that is at fault.

When stoppering leaving 1 or 2 cm headspace, the cork compresses the air under it and internal pressure after stoppering may reach 3 kg/cm^2. If bottles are capsuled and laid down immediately, this will result in wine seeping through the gap between the cork and the neck of the bottle; the capsule, sometimes the label and the back label, are stained. Another disadvantage of this kind of stoppering: It locks in a larger quantity of air. A headspace of 1.5 cm under the cork represents 20 mL of air compressed at 3 kg/cm^2.

To cope with this difficulty, it is advisable to replace the air found in the neck of the bottle above the wine, before closure, with carbon dioxide. Bottles get a jet of this gas before going into the corking machine. This tiny quantity of carbon dioxide, dissolving into the wine, creates a depression which prevents the phenomenon of bottles leaking due to the wine expanding.

It should be remembered that to get good tight bottles during cellar life, they must be laid down horizontally in palettes or cases or even neck down in cartons so that the corks remain constantly in contact with the wine.

Closing with Screw Caps

Because of the difficulty in procuring good quality cork, other closing techniques have been sought. In spite of a certain reticence on the part of users to abandon corks, these other techniques have occasionally begun to be applied. This is the case particularly for closing with a metal screwcap crimped directly onto the neck of the bottle. Tightness of sealing is ensured by clamping a sealing ring over the top edge of the bottle neck made of a neutral and impermeable substance that is incorrodible in contact with the wine. This form of closing demands very high precision in the molding of the bottle necks as well as in the way the clamping machine works. In today's conditions, this system of closing, which is suited more particularly to wines to be drunk young, can only offer, in the best of circumstances, security of storage for a limited period of time.

Index

Page numbers in **bold** type indicate more important references, paragraph headings, illustrations, diagrams, etc.

Accelerated aging, defects of, 254
Accident, microbial, 84, 133
  avoiding, 160
Acescence, 19, 22, 26, 33
  lactic, 124, 128, **256**
Acetaldehydes, 93, 94, 251
  odor of, 258
  SO_2, 269
Acetamide, 23
Acetic bacteria, 192
Acetic deterioration, 242
Acetic odor, 21
Acetic souring, 155
Acetic spoilage, when topping, 181, **257**
Acetobacter, 256. *See also* Acids, acetic;
    Acids, volatile acidity; Bacteria;
    Vinegar, odor
Acetol, 22
Acids, 50, 63
  acetic, 19, 30, 31, 33, 39, **42,** 54, 74, 93,
    94, 125
    spoilage, 255
    see also Casse; Spoilage
  acid balance, on white wine, 199
  acidification, 85, **89**
    by burning sulfur, 272
  acidity, 16, 27, 33, 39
    definition of, 54, 64, 66, 69, 74, 79, 85,
      86, 89, 104

    incidence on casse, 324
    influence of, 119, 121, 123, 145, 160,
      192
  acidity/alcohol balance, white wine, 123.
    See also Malolactic fermentation
  acid taste, 25, 28, 30
  amino, 43
    tables, 49, 62, 65, 117, 134, 135, 331
  ascorbic (vitamin C), 213, 250, 276, 328
  aspartic, 49, 63
  benzoic, 46
  butyric, 31
  carbonic, 54, 122
  cinnamic, 46
  citramalic, 39, 94
  citric, 30, 33, 39, **41,** 89, 122, 282, 325,
    326, **328**
  dehydroascorbic, 276
  diketogluconic, 269
  dimethylglyceric, 39
  enanthic, 49
  ferrocitric, 328
  ferrocyanic, 327
  fixed acidity, 18, 39
    deacidification, 88, 122, 133, 341
    definition, 54, 86
    distinction between fixed and volatile,
      42
  galacturonic, 39, 48, 269

371

Acids (*Continued*)
  gluconic, 39, 74
  glucuronic, 39
  glutamic, 48, 49, 63, 117
  ketoglutaric, 39, 119
  α ketoglutaric, 94, 269
  ketonic, 119
  lactic, 30, 31, 33, 39, **42,** 93, 94, 121,
    122, 123, 132
  malic, 30, 33, 39, **41,** 61, 63, 64
    graphs, 66, 67, 69, 70, 74, 102, 103,
      104, 120, 122, 123, 130, 132, 134,
      190
  metatartic:
    manufacture, **347**
    use of, **346**
  mucic, 39
  organic, 33, 43, 53, 62, 65, 193
  oxalic, 39
  pantothenic, 52, 118, 119
  pectic, 48
  phosphopyruvic, 63
  phosphoric, 40, 325
  phytic, 39, 63, 93, 94, 119, 269, 346
  racemic, 346
  sorbic, odor, 21, 54, **274**
  succinic, 30, 31, 33, 39, **42,** 93, 94, 190
  sulfuric, odor, 22, 54, 122, 130, 132
  tartaric, 25, 27, 28, 30, 31, 33, 39, **40,**
    41, 54, 64
    adding, 83, 85, 87, 88, 89, 127, 128
    brandy, 229
    chilling, 341
    graphs, 67, 69, 74
    scouring, 150
    spoilage, 255
  uronic, 270
  volatile acidity, 39, **42**
    definition, 54, 90, 119, 122, 123, 124,
      127, 134, 155, 170, 171, 178, 180,
      187, 257, 262
Acrid (bitter)-tasting substances, 213
Acrolein, 260
Adjusting vintage, **83**
Adsorbant filters, **299**
Adsorption:
  powers, 211, 301
  properties, 343
Aeration, 39, 110
  beneficial effect when racking, 239
  influence of, 111, 112, 113

  influence on malolactic fermentation, **134**
  objections and answers, **116,** 131
  when draining, 178, 188, 234
Aerobiosis, 112
African acacias, gum arabic, 345
After-taste, 7
  astringent, 23, 256
Ageusia, 24
Aging, 246
  accelerated, **254**
  effect through heating, 333
  extraction, 175
  Port, 227
Air:
  casse, 323
  enemy of white wine, 212
Alanine, 63
Albuminous material, *see* Proteins
Albumins, 287
  egg, 293, 297
Alcohol, 15, 19–20
  sweet taste, **28, 38,** 50, 92, 94
  yeast sensitivity to, 99
  yeasts resistant to, 100, 101, 125, 127,
    131, 173, 275
Alcoholic fermentation, 36, 93
  acetic acid, 43, 86, 92, 131, 132, 143
  lactic acid, 42
Alcoholic strength, 52, 86
  after aging, 253
  heating, 334
  influence on malolactic fermentation, 135,
    180
  refrigeration, 339, 341
  SO₂ doses, 271
  white wine, 199
Alcoholometric strength, definition, 53
Aldehydes, 22, 37, 269
Alessandria, 224
Algae, 298, 300, **305**
Alkaline:
  salts, 44
  solution, 235, 343
  see also Lye, taste
Alkalinity of ash, 39
  CO₃, 45
Alsace, 164
Aluminum, in glass, 351
Aluminum silicate, *see* Bentonite
American vines, 23
Amino nitrate, 49

Ammoniacal nitrogen, 117, 118, 119
Ammonia cations, 47, 49, 53
Ammonium nitrate, 49, 117
Ammonium phosphate, 90
  graph, 118
Ammonium salts, **117,** 171, 218
Ammonium sulfate, 117
Amontillado, sherry, 229
Anaerobia, 134, 255
Anaerobiosis, fermentation in, 112, 173
Analysis:
  for bacterial intervention, 170
  champagne musts, 207
  free-run and press-wine, 180
  after malolactic fermentation, 123
  press-wine, 205
  white wine, 40, 122
  wine from maceration carbonique, 191
Analytical definitions, 52
  control-spoilage, 263, 327
  examination, 245
Annealing, glass, 353
Anosmia, 24
Anthocyanins, 45, 46, 47, 65, 70, 71, 72,
    81, 116, 173, 175, 180, 192, 193
  aging, 250, 344
  Champagne, 223
  rosé, 221
Antibacterial, 233, 267
Antibiotic, botrycine, 218
Anticrystallizing, efficiency, of metatartaric
    acid, **347**
Antienzymatic, property of SO_2, 267
Antifungal products, 81, 97, 105
  painting cellars, 234
Antioxidant, sulfiting, 249, 267
Antioxidasic, property of SO_2, in vinification,
    213
Antiseptic, sulfuric acid, 22, 103, 135, 219
Antiyeast, 267, 275, 334
Appelation wines, 12, 348
Aqueous taste, 258
  alcoholic solution, 209
Arabinose, sweet taste, 37, 38, 261, 269
Arabitol, sweet taste, 37
Archimedes' screw, 188, 204
Argentine, 82
Arginine, 49
Armagnac, 228, **230**
Aroma:
  alcohol, 38

bouquet, 20
  after malolactic fermentation, 123, 172,
    174
  press-wine, 205
  primary, 213, 252
  secondary, 252
  smell, 4
  in white wine, 198
Aromatic substances, 81, 193
Asbestos, in filters, 299, 305
Asci, 96
Ash, 43
  analysis table, 45
  definition, 53
Aspergillus, 80
Asphyxia, 22, 111, 113, 119, 157
  bottle aging, 353
Asti Spumante, 219, **223**
Astringence, 19, 28, 181
  astringent wines, 254
Astringency, 192, 287
  chilling, 341
Astringent taste, 23, **44**
Attack, tasting, 7, 25, 27, 32
Australia, 103
Austria, 123
Autofermentation, maceration carbonique,
    189
Automation, 186, 332
Autovinificator, 188
Auxoautotrophia, 134

Bacilli, 124, **125,** 133, 250
Back-pressure valve, 188
Bacteria, 45, 50, **92,** 120, **126,** 127, 130
  acetic bacteria, 96, 243
  bacteria counts, 171, **265,** 316
  bacterial cultures, 121
  bacterial spoilage, 192, 235, 263
    table, **264**
  disease bacteria, in low acidity, 119, 133
  fall during clarification, 286
  lactic bacteria, definition of wine, 35, 41,
    43, 96, 102, 120, 124, 125, 191,
    192, 259
  malolactic bacteria, 90, 121, **124,**
    129
Balloon glass, 26
Banyuls, **225–226**
Bark, odor, 251
Barking, oak, 362, 364

Barrel:
  Bordeaux château, 238
  cask pieces, 109, 214
Barrel-aging, conditions for, 252
Barrel-life, 246
Bars, pressure, 304
  millibars, 244
Base-wine, for sparkling, 211, 223
Baumé aerometer, 163
Baumé degrees:
  conversion table, xvii, 74, 85
  white wine, 198, 220
Beaujolais, open tanks, 153
Bentonite, 88, 90, 209
  treating must, **210,** 282, 287, 291, 331
  use of, 342, 348
Berry, grape:
  composition, 59
  cross-section, 58
Berthelot, 247, 251
Biochemical deacidification, malolactic
    fermentation, 120, 122
Biological aging, sherry, 228
Biological stability, 120
Biotic elements, 50
Biotin, 52, 118, 119
Bisulfite, see Sulfur dioxide
Bitter taste:
  and astringent, 44
  balance equation, **15,** 25, **29**
Bitterness, acescence, 260
Blanc-de-blanc, 223
Blending:
  in casks, 178
  press-wine, 181
  to promote malolactic fermentation, 137
  rosé, 221, **245**
  sweet wines, 220
Blood, ox-blood, for fining, 287, 291, **294**
Bloom, grape-, 96, 117
Bloom units, gelling power of finings, 292
Blue casse, 324
Blue fining, 327
Body:
  full-bodied, 16
  after malolactic fermentation, 123
  press-wine, 205
  rosé, 221, 254
Boiling grapes, Maupin, 192
Bone-glue, gelatin, 291

Bordeaux, area, 88, 135, 148
  Bordeaux mixture, 329
  bottle, **354**
  closed tanks, 153, 183, 216, 217
  racking, 239
Boron, 44
Botas, sherry, 229
Botryticine, 74
Botrytis cinerea (gray-rot), 49, 59, 73, 74,
    80, 81
  heating, 193
  laccase, 212
Botrytized grapes, 39, 79, 213, 217, 218,
  269
Bottle, secondary fermentation, 101,
  106
  méthode champenoise, 225
Bottle-aging, 100, 246
  conditions for, 253
  in white bottles, 352
Bottle-glass, table, 352
Bottleneck, 253
  shape, standards, 366
Bottle-rinsing machine, 356
Bottles and bottling, 351
Bottle-sickness, 277, 333, 359
Bottling, 100, 101, 102, 130
  hot bottling, 259
  apparatus, 335
  corking, 368
  loss of CO_2, 359
  sterile filtration, 301
Bottling plants, 102
Bottling-machines, 102, 253, **356, 358,**
  360, 361
Bottling-room, 234
Bouquet:
  aging, 264
  aroma, 20, 38
  changes in, **251**
  volatile acidity
Brandy, 228
Breathing, 94
Breeding, 21
Breweries, 102
Brix, conversion table, *xvii*
Bromine, 44
Bronze (copper), 330
Brouillis (cognac), 230
Browning, 205, 214, 246

Brownish tint:
  cupric casse, 329
  oxidative casse
Brut (champagne), 217
Bubble system, 112
  on tanks, 158
Budding, yeasts, 95, 107, 111
Bulk winemaking, 163
  diagram, white, 202
Bulyleneglycol, 37, 39, 93, 94
Bungs, 102
  acetic spoilage, 257
  cloth stopper, 243
Bung-on-top/on-the-side, 240, 241, 248
Burgundy, 123
  bottle, 354
  open tanks, 153, 183, 216
Butyric, odor, 21

Café (or one-night) wines, 222
Calcar, tunnel-furnace, 354
Calcar-mist, sodium sulfate, 355
Calcium, 43
  analysis of ash, 45, 86, 88
Calcium carbonate, 86, 87, 133
  cement-tanks, 151, 220
Calcium phytate, **326,** 348
Calcium racemate, 346
Calcium salts, 40, 87, 220
Calcium tartrate, 40, 87
  cement tanks, 151, 220, 330, 337
Calefactors, heating wines, 335
Calendar, phenelogical, table, 77
California, 103, 217
Caloric output, 85, 110, 159, 166
Camphor, oil, 46
Candle, for examining limpidity, 283
Cap management, **153**
Cap of pomace, 114
Capsule, 369
Captan, 97
Carbon, 53
Carbon dioxide (CO_2), 22, 54, 62, 92, 94,
  112, 122, 125, 155, 158, 167, 188,
  190, 244, 252, 357
  corking, 369
Carbonic acid gas, 223
Carbonic maceration, *see* Maceration
  carbonique
Carbonification, 245

Carbonyle components, 50
Carcinogenicity, of asbestos, 299
Cardboard, for filter beds, 305
Casein, 209, 213, 287, **294**
Cask, barrel:
  faulty, 23, 100, 102, 109, 112
  settling in, 209
  for white wines, 215
Casse, 22, 90, 255
  cupric, 329
    colorless bottles, 353
    treatment, 331
  ferric, 318
    description, 323
    treatments, table, 326
  limpidity, 312, 316
  metallic, 323
  oxidative, sulfiting, 159, 178, 193, 315
  phosphato-ferric, 324
  phytato-ferric, 326
  protein, 210
    tests, 319, 329, 343
Catalysts, 214, 249
Catechin tannins, from cork, 364
Cation-exchangers, 346
Cellarage, 281, 282
Cellular destruction, 334
Cellulose, 57
  corks, 364
  esters, 303
  fibers, 298, 301
  paper, 100
Cellar-work, **233**
Cement (concrete) tanks, advantages and
    disadvantages, 152
Centrifugal clarifiers, 308, **309**
Centrifugal crushers, 148
Centrifugal crusher-stemmers, 145
Centrifugal force, 308
Centrifugal stemmer, 147
Centrifugation:
  clearing yeasts, 100, 105
  settling, 205, 208, 217, 218, 219
Cetie-standard, *see* Bottleneck
Chains, for crumbling pomace, 204
Chamfering, corks, 365
Champagne:
  adding tannin, 90, 105, 123, 200, 217,
    222, 224
  corks, 365

Champenois press, 204
Chaptel, 83
Chaptalizing (sugaring):
　detecting fraudulent, 38, **83**
　during pumping-over, 155
Character, in wines, 21, 339
Charmat-process, tank fermentation for
　sparkling, 225
Chelating agent, 328
Chemical deacidification, 86, 123, 133
Cherries, flavor, 72
Chilling, 40, 216, 219, 337. *See also*
　Refrigeration
Chloride anion, 45
Chloroform, 36
Chlorophyll, 58, 62, 70
Chocolate-colored, red wine, 315
Chrome-nickel, glass, 352
Chromotography, **50**
　chromatogram, 52
　malic acid, 130
Churning, 263
　bentonite, 345
　finings, 289
Clairette, 222
Clamping machine, for screw-caps, 370
Clapper-valve, 357
Claret, in oak casks, 240
Clarification, 130, 181, 205, 210,
　279
　centrifugation, 308
　by filtering, **298**
　by fining, **287**
　products, table, **292**
　stabilization, 312
Clarifiers, types of, 308
Clarifying pads, 301
Clarifying power, of bentonite, 344
Clarity:
　brandy, 230
　concept of, **281**
　failures, **315**
　spoilage, table, **316**
Clay, 287
Cleanliness (hygiene), 100, 101, 210,
　233
　of bottles, 351, **355**
　cleaning products, list, **237**
Climate, 81, 83
Climatic conditions, 76, 78, 82

Clogging:
　filters, 301
　power, 306
Cloudiness, **315**
Coating, concrete tanks, 150–151, 235
Cobalt, 44
Cocci, 122, 124
　shapes, **125,** 132
Coffee hue, 315
Cognac, **228**
Cold, *see* Refrigeration
Cold-chamber, 340
Colloidal particles, 333, 345
Colloidal precipitations, 316, 336, 338
Colloidal stability, 338
Colloidal structure, bentonite, 343
Colloids, 218
　gum arabic, 345
　protective, 284, 301, 306
Color, 4, 79
　aging, 250
　effect of rot, 81
　extraction, 172
　glass, 330, 352
　graph, 353
　graph-heating, 193
　pomace contact, 174
　rosé, 221
　temperature, 173
　thermovinification, 196, 198
Color change (véraison), graph, 64
Coloring matter, 44
　cloudiness, 282
　colloidal, 345
　precipitation, **320, 338**
　see also Phenolic compounds
Columbium (steel), 152
Combustion, 67
Comportes (grape baskets), 79, 144
Compressibility, of corks, 363, 367
Concentration, by freezing, table-
　composition, 340
Conducting:
　alcoholic fermentation, **107, 159,**
　214
　extraction, **172**
　malolactic fermentation, **129**
　refrigeration, **339**
　vinification, with maceration carbonique,
　190

Containers, 79
  cleanliness, **234**
  tanks, 148, 177
  for transport, **144**
Controlling fermentation, 187
Controlling temperature, 181
Control-tests, 317, 328
Cooking grapes, *see* Thermal vinification
Cooling, 40, 110, 149
  metal tanks, 154
  taking temperature, 165, 167, 187, 216, 336
Cooling apparatus:
  device, for heated grapes, 195
  water, 168, **169**
Cooling methods, **168**
Cooling systems, 156, **185**
Cooperage:
  brandy, 230, 234
  hygiene, **236**
  see also Barrel; Cask (barrel)
Cooperatives, 144, 156, 164, 216
Copper (bronze), 23, 86, 249, 328–330.
  See also Casse
Cork boards, 364
Cork defects, table, **369**
Corking machines, 102
  equipment, **367, 368**
Cork-oak, 362
Corks and closures, **362**
Cork worm, 234
  insecticides, 369
Coste system, categories of wine, 13
Counters, electronic, for examining clarity, 283
Coupage, 245
Cremant, 22
Crown caps, 361
Crumbling pomace, 180
  vertical-press, 203
Crushers, types, 147
Crushing grapes, 35, 143, 145, 146
  advantages and disadvantages for taste, 149, 172, 173
  heating, 194
  white, 200
Crystallization, 173, 320, 330, 337
  inhibitors, 342
  metatartaric, 347
Cueno, 224

Cupric (cuprous) casse, *see* Casse
Cuvée (champagne), 207, 224, 245

Deacidification, 33, 83, **86**
  using yeasts, 103, 115, 133
    table, **104**
  white musts, 88
Débourbage, 240
Decanting, *see* Racking (sedimentation)
Densitometer, 163–164, 216
Density:
  of must, 145
  taking, **163**
  of wine, 85
Depomacing, 180
Deposits:
  in bottles, 251, 281
  determination, **317, 329**, 338
    table, **318**
  racking from lees, 238
  sediments, yeasts, 100, 137, 205
  volume, table, **211**
Descaling, cement tasks, cleanliness, 235
Dessert wines, 105, 117
  fining with kieselsol, 292
  malolactic fermentation, 124, 135
  Port, 227
  refrigeration, 336
Destemming, 58, 90, 143, 145
  advantages and disadvantages, table, **146**
  Burgundy, 183
  influence of, table, **174**
  white, 200
Detanking, **179,** 188
Deviation, 159, 213
Dextran, 49, 285
Diacetyl, 90
Diammonium phosphate, 117
Diatomaceous earth, 300, **304**
Diatomite, 304
Diatoms, 298, 300, **305**
Dichlofluanide, 97
Difulatan (captan), 97
Diglucoside, 45
Dimensions, of corks, table, **366**
Disease bacteria, *see* Bacteria
Disgorging champagne, 224
Distillate, **15,** 29, 30, 42
  Cognac, 230

Dosage:
  champagne, 224
  sparkling, 84
Dosage pump, 163
  finings, 296
Dosimeter, for infusorial earths, 305
Douro, 227
Drainer, mechanical, 195, **202**
Draining:
  chaptalizing, 85, 143, 158
  time of, **176,** 195
  white, 200
Draining chambers for white, 201
Drosophila (vinegar fly), 234
Dry extract, definition, 53
Drying oven, 257, 265, 316, 319, 348
Ducts, for filtering, 298, 301, 304

Earthiness, 23
Earths, for fining, 288
E.E.C., 35, 43, 84, 86, 89, 117, 267, 276,
  320, 327, 328
Efficiency, of filter, 298
Egg albumin, *see* Albumins
Egg-white, for fining, 287
Elasticity, of corks, 363
Electric charge, particles in suspension, 284,
  289
Electro-magnetic valve, 188
Electro-static theory of adsorption, 344
Emulsion, in bottling, 359
Enological bentonite, 343
Enologist, *viii*, 100, 130
  tests by, 327
  white, 199
Enology, 92
  preventive and corrective, 312
  yeasts, 98
Enzymes, 94, 197, 208
  pectolitic, 181, 209, 307
Epidemics, infection, 101, 102, 233
Epoxy resin (eraldite), 152
Erythritol, 37
Essence, from skins, 72, 251
Esterification:
  metatartic acid, index, 347
  role of, 251
Esters, 17
  analytical tasting, 25, 50
  white wine, 198, 252
Ethanol, 38

Ethereal salts, aroma of, 191
Ethyl acetate, 17, 19, 34, 94, 105, 252,
  256
Ethyl enanthate, 17
Ethylic alcohol, 37, 53
Evaporation:
  cooling by, 216
  during racking, 239
Evolution:
  in tasting, 7, 25, 27, 32
  technical, 181
Examining clarity, **282**
  diagram, 283
  see also Clarity
Extract, refrigeration, 339
Extraction, (maceration), 116, 143, **172**
  VDN, with or without, 226–227
  white wine, absence of, 197
  wicker baskets, 199

Fatness, 16, 36, 38, 89, 254
Faucet:
  bronze, 23
  decanting, 209
Fe II, Fe III, 324
Feed-regulator:
  pump, 186
  sorbic acid, 275
  sulfiting, 163
Feed-tank, bottling, 357
Fe_2O_3 (yellow-tinted glass), 352
"Ferment," 83, 257
Fermentation, **91**
  aeration, 112, 115
  products formed, table, **94**
  supervising, 163
  temperature, table, **108–110**
Fermentation tanks, **148**
  apparatus, **143**
  shapes of, 156
Fermentors, 158
  continuous, champagne, 185
Ferric casse, *see* Casse
Ferric iron, 42, 276, 289
Ferric peroxide, glass, 352
Ferric phosphate, 324
Ferric phytate, 325
Ferric salts, 289
  from casein, 294, 324
Filling, bottles, 356

Film (flor):
    sherry, 229
    spoilage, **258**
    of yeasts, 101, 102
Filterability, of wines, 307
    fining or filtering, 307
Filtering, 87, 100, 101, 130, 137, 209
    Asti Spumante, 224, 325, 328
Filtration, 217, 219, **298**
    filter pads, table, **302**
    mechanism, **299**
Finale, 7
Finesse:
    bentonite, 211
    brandy, 230
    character, 21
    degrees of, 72
    odor, 20
    SO₂, 34
Fine wines, see Premium (fine or quality)
        wines
Fining, 45, 100, 130, 132
    Asti, 224, **287**
    mechanism, **288**
    tests, **290,** 325
Finings-racking, raising whisk, 238
Finish, 25, 27, 28, 32. See also Finale
Finishing operations, 246
    Port, 228
Fino (sherry), 229
Fish glue (isinglass), 290
Flabby wines, 19, 123
    press-wine, 205
    tourne, 260
Flannel pouches, for filtering, 305
Flat wines, 19, 20, 21
Flavone, 46
Flavor:
    balance, 14
    by extraction, 175, 254
Float (garde-vin), 243
Flocculants, 209
Flocculate, deposit, 343, 344
Flocculation, 173, 209
    bentonite, 343
    fining, 291
Floccules, 287
Flow, filtering speed, 302
Flowery, aroma, 277
Fluor, 151
Fluorine, 44

Fluosilicates, 151, 235
Folin's index, 16, 34, 45. See also
        Polyphenol index
Folpe, 97
Food value, chemical treatment, 332
Formaldehyde, 366
Formo-phenolic resin, metal tanks, 152
Fortified wines, 226
Foxy odor, 23
Free-run must, 201, 205
Free-run wine, 84
    analytical composition, table, **180**
    draining, **177**
    maceration carbonique, 191
    refermentation, 170
Freezing, see Refrigeration
Friction coefficient, of cork, 363
Froth capacity, 333
Frothy bottling, 359
Frothy carbon dioxide, 22
Fructose, 30, 36, 37, 38, 60, 63, 85, 261
Fruit-stone flavor, 72
Fruity aroma, 72, 123, 277
Fruity odor, 21
Fulls (Port), 227
Fumigating casks, 266, **272**
Fungistatic, 275
Fungus, 73
    tastes, 217
Fusel-oil, odor, 196, 213

Galactose, 38, 49
Gas, in tanks, 178
Gaseous malolactic fermentation,
        121–122
Gaseous yeasts, 100
Gasified wines, sparkling, 223
Gassy CO₂, 22
Gassy spoilage, 255
Gay-Lussac, equation, 93
Gayon, 121
Gelatin, 209
    mixture, 236, 287, 289, **291,** 297
Gels, see Colloids
Generic wine, 245
Genus (genera), 95
    bacteria, 124
    yeasts, 97
Geraniums, odor, 21, 275
German technique, sweetening dry wine,
        219

Germany, 123, 164, 217
  kieselsol, 292
  potassium ferrocyanide, 327
Germination, of yeasts, 95
Germs, lack of, 265
Glass, **351**
Glasses, shapes, **26**
Glass-lined tanks, 150, 152
Glucanes, 218, 263, 284, 306, 345
Glucosamine, oseaminate nitrate, 49
Glucose, 30, 36, 37, 38, 49, 60, 61, 63, 85
  fixing SO$_2$, 269
Glucosides, 38, 45
Glycerine, 38
Glycerol, 19, 30, 32, 37, 38, 42, 74, 93, 94,
      125, 127, 190, 255
  fermentation of, 260
Glycine, 63
Golden (color), 246
Graisse, 263
Grand vin, 84
Grape, description, 57, **58**
Grape varieties, 66
  Baco, Z2A, armagnac, 230
  Cabernet-franc, 69, 76
  Cabernet-Sauvignon, 59, 60, 64, 68, 69
  Chardonnay, 76, 124
    champagne, 223
  Colombard, French:
    armagnac, 230
    cognac, 229
  different maturity, 76, 77, 79
  Gamay, 76
  Grenache, 225
  Jurançon, armagnac, 230
  Maccabee, 225
  Malbec, 60, 69
  Malvoisie, 225
  Merlot, 60, 69, 72, 76, 77
  Muscat, 223, 226
  Muscat of Alexander, 226
  Muscatel, 69
  Palomino, sherry, 228
  Pedro Ximenez, 228
  Pinot noir, 76, 77
    Champagne, 223
  Pinot meunier, Champagne, 223
  Petit verdot, 69
  preventing malolactic fermentation, 123
  Saint Macaire, 69

  Sauvignon, 69, 198
  Semillon, 59, 69
  Ugniblanc (Trebbiano), 69
    cognac, 229
    armagnac, 230
  Verdot-colon, 69
Grating:
  destemming, 145
  to prevent clogging, 158
Gravity:
  delivery,144
  settling, 205
Green wines, odor, 198
Grille, to retain pomace, 186, 188
Grinding, mechanical operation, 172
Gristle, for gelatin, 291
Growth (nutritive) factors, for yeasts, 114,
      118
Growth limit, heating, 334. *See also*
      Multiplication
Guillage, 215
Gum arabic, 282, 329, 331
  use of, 345
Gums, **48,** 284
Gustation, 3. *See also* Tasting
Gustatory sensations, 27. *See also* Taste

Hardness, in wines, 48, 89, 256
Harmony, of flavors, 14–15
Harvesting, **75**
  machines, 80
  for white, 199
Harvest work, **79**
Haze, examining, 282, 308
Header-bung, 238, 241
Heads, cognac, 230
Headspace:
  botas (sherry), 229
  bottles, 361, 369
  oxygen, 248
  topping, 242
Healthy, *see* Hygiene; Sanitary state
Hearts, cognac and armagnac, 230
Heat:
  exchangers, 134
  from fermentation, 166
  physical treatments, 332
Heating must, 85
  mutage, 219
  preventing oxidation, 213

Heating wines:
    concentration, 37, 130
    cupric casse, 331
    stabilization, **333**
Hemipolylactide, of tartaric acid, 346, 347
Herbaceous (leafy) aroma, 72
Herbaceous (leafy) taste, 172, 181, 205
Hexanedienol, 275
Hexoses, 37
H+ ions, 40, 54
Homofermentary strains, 124
Homogenization:
    by pumping over, 115
    racking, 239
Honeycomb plate-exchangers, 335
Hormones, 111
Hot-bottling, see Bottling
Hot regions, 89, 110
Hydrogen sulfide, 22, 105, 178, 330
Hydrolysis:
    metatartaric acid, 348
    of sucrose, 38, 85
Hygiene, 127, **233**
Hygrometry, for cooling systems, 169
Hygroscopic, 347

INAO, 77
Industrial vinification, 148, 184, 187
Inert gas:
    for bottling, 335, 359
    diagram of installation, 244
Infrared rays, 254, 332
    heating wines, 335
Infusorial earth, 100
Inhibition:
    botrytized grapes, 218
    to seeding, 138
Injection, of finings, bentonite,
        345
Inocular cultures, use of, 136
Inoculation (seeding), 102–103
    with bacterial cultures, 137
    stuck fermentation, 171, 177
    techniques, 105, 108, 131–135
Inositol, 30, 37, 39
Insecticides, 81
    cellars, 234
Intensity, of wines, 4, 47
Intracellular fermentation, 190
Iodine, odor, 217, 268

Iron, 42, 45, 86, 208
    oxidation, ferric casse, 276, 323, 328
    salts, 299, 324
Iron manganese, glass tinted by, 352
Isinglass (fish glue), preparation, 293
Isobaric bottling, sparkling wine, 225
Isobarometric filling, 357
Isoleucine, 49
Italy, adding calcium racemate, 346

Jeres, Xeres, 227
Jura, yellow wine, 229
Jurançon, sweet wines, 217

Kaolin, 342
Kaolinate, 343
Katabolism, 94
Ketone:
    functions, 37
    SO₂ compounds, 269
Kieselgur, 288
Kieselsol, **292**
Kilo-calories, 169, 216
K+ ions, glass, 352

Labor:
    problems, 185
    saving, 186
Laccase (polyphenoloxidase), 160, 212, 213,
        315, 334
Lactic fermentation, see Malolactic
        fermentation; Souring (lactic)
Lactic souring, 261
Lactic spoilage, 259
Lactobacillus, disease bacteria, 125, 128,
        137
Lafon, 230
Lagars, Port, 228
Lead, salts, 44
Leaden, color, 325
Leaven, see Inoculation (seeding)
Lees:
    cement tanks, 235
    finings tests, 291
    isinglass, 293
    odor, 22
    racking, 238, 240
    yeasts, 96, 102, 137, 175, 178, 217
Lenticels, in cork, 363, 365
Leucine, 49

Leuco-anthocyanins, 34, 46, 71
Leuconostoc (bacteria), 125
    gracile, 134, 263
Levels of perceptual acuteness, *see*
    Thresholds
Life-span, *see* Aging
Lignin, cork, 364
Lime, glass, 351
Limpidity spoilage, *see* Clarity
Linalool, 31
Logarithmic growth, 114, 132. *See also*
    Multiplication
Lye, taste, 19
Lyophilic, lyophobic colloids, 288, 333
Lyophilized yeasts, 105

Maceration, *see* Extraction (maceration)
Maceration carbonique:
    deacidification, 86, **189**
    VDN, 226
Maçon, 123
Macromolecules, 292, 343
Maderization, 22
    aging, 246
"Made" wines, 82, **221**
Magnesium, 43, 45, 135, 351
Malate, 87
Malolactic fermentation, 41
    brandy, 229
    lactic acid, 42
    before racking, 239
    rosé, 221
    volatile acidity, 43, 86, 89, **120**
        graph, conditions, **131,** 143
Maltose, 38
Malvidol, 45
Manebe, 97
Manganese, 44, 135
    bioxide, 352
Mannitic fermentation, 261
Mannitol, 30, 37, 53, 125, 261
Mannose, dextran, 49
Manzanilla (sherry), 229
Marteau, 62
Match, sulfiting when racking, 240
Maturation:
    finishing (aging), 246
    period of, 59
Maturity index, 69
    table, **71**
Maturing wines, **246**

Maupan, 192
Maury, 225
Meagerness, 84
Mechanical operations, 143, **144**
    white, **199**
Mechanization, on quality, 199
Median turbinates:
    sense of smell, 8
    vinegar odor, 34
Mediterranean, 81, 82
Melibiose, 38
Mellowness, 36, 120, 123
Mellow wines, *see* Semi-sweet wines
    (moelleux)
Membrane-pump, 163
Membranes, *see* Filtration
Mercaptans (thiols), off-taste, 22
Mesoinositol, *see* Vitamins
Metal:
    astringent taste, 22
    tanks, **154**
Metallic casse, *see* Casse
Metal oxides, coloring glass, 351
Methanol, 48
Méthode champenoise, see Bottle, secondary
    fermentation
Microaerophil species, 134, 263
Microbes, 263
Microbiological control, **263**
Microbiological spoilage, *see* Spoilage
Microbiology, *vii,* **91**
Microflora, *see* Yeasts
Microscope, 95, 96, 100, 121, 124, 129,
    260
Microscopic examination, 263, 265, 304,
    316, 317
Migration (translocation), 61
    overripening, 72
    table, **62**
Mildew, in cellars, 234
Milk:
    bentonite, 345
    for fining, 287
Mullipoises, gelatin viscosity, 292
Millipore, membrane filters, 300, 356
Mineral matter:
    concentration, 85
    extraction, 175, 190
    for finings, 288
    grape-nourishment, 65
    yeasts, 107, 117

Mirror-ends, on corks, 365
Mistelle (base-wine), 38
  sherry, 229
Mixed finings, diagram, **296**
Mold:
  white, 79, 80, 96, 179, 199
  wood, 23, 75
  see also Rot
Moldy grapes, 23, 118, 119, 269, 285. See
    also Botrytized grapes
Molecular fission, breathing, 94
Molecular weight:
  suberin, 364
  of tannin, 250
Molybdenum, 153
Monoglucoside, 45
Montmorillonite, bentonite, 343
Morphological classification, lactic bacteria,
    124, **125**
Mortality heating times, germs, 334
Moscato d'Asti, 223
Mother of vinegar, 256
Mousy acetamide:
  flavor, 101
  odor, 21, 23
  tourne, 260
Mucilage, 48, 263, 306
Mucous membrane, smell, 8
Multiplication:
  of bacteria, 131, 132
  presence of alcohol, 135
  of yeasts
Muscovado taste, 84
Must:
  concentrate, 85, 220
  density of, 163
Mustimeter, 77, 163
Mutage, 218
Muté, 101
Muted must, 85, 220
Mycelium powders, 119
Mycrodermic yeasts, see Yeasts
Myricetine, 46

Na + ions, 352
Napa, 82
Natural sweet wines, see VDN (natural sweet
    wine)
Nephalometers, 283
Neutralizing tanks, 150
Nicotinamide PP, see Vitamins

Nitrate, **47,** 49
  sweet wines, 219
Nitrogen, 47, 49, 117, 180, 190
  Asti Spumante, 225
  bentonite, 343
  bottling, 361
  cork, 362
  storage under, **243**
Nitrogenous substances, 107, 109, 117, 175,
    193
North Africa, 343
Nouaison, **58**
Nozzles:
  ajutage, 114
  causing cupric casse, 330
Nucleic nitrate, see Nitrate
Nucleii, of crystals, 333, 338, 347
Nutrition:
  bacteria, 134
  yeasts, **117**
Nutritive factors, 114, 118

Oak-gall tannin, 25, 90
Oak tanks, table, **150**
Odor, 4, 14
  balance, 17, 20, 38
  Port, 227
  sulfide, 217
  see also Off-odors
Oechsle degrees, 164
  table, xvii
Off-odors, 26, 233
Off-tastes, 22
  from filters, bentonite, 304
  oak, 150
  press wine, 181, 205, 233, 235
  rot, 81, 84
Olfaction, see Smell
Oloroso (sherry), 229
Optically clear, 283
Optic density, table, **47**
Organic matter, 85
  concrete tanks, 235
Organocupric product, 329
Organoleptic examination, see Taste
Osmosis, of liquids, 364
Ossein (gelatin), 291
Outgassing, wine, 359
Overfining, **290**
Overripening (surmaturation), 59, **72**
  good years, 217

Overripening (surmaturation) (*Continued*)
    harvesting, 79
    VDN, 226
Oxidases:
    heating, 193
    SO₂, 160
    stabilization by heating, 334
    sulfiting, 208
Oxidation, 4, 80
    ascorbic acid, 276
    crumbling pomace, 180
    ferric casse, catalysts, 324
    open tanks, 155·
    protection from, **212**
    sherry, 228
    SO₂, 160
    topping, 242
    white, 199
Oxidative casse, *see* Casse
Oxidative spoilage, *see* Casse
Oxydo, reduction, 328
Oxygen, 21, 94, 111, 112, 114, 134, 190,
    247
    combination, **249**
    in cork, 362
    ferric case, 323
Oxygen uptake, due to bottling, 351, **359**
Oxygenation, treatment, **325**

Pads, for filtering, **300, 303**
    table, **302**
Palate, 27. *See also* Taste
Paper taste, 302
Papillae (taste buds), 7
    malolactic fermentation, 122
    taste, 6
Paraffining, corks, 353
Particle count, table, **284**
Particles in suspension, 240, 281, **283**
    table, **285**
Passerilage, 73, 198
    VDN, 226
Pasteur, 84, 92, 93, 94, 111, 120, 128, 190,
    247, 259, 334
Pasteurization, 108
    flash, 334
    units, 334
Pearl wines, 367
    pearled, 22
Pectic matter, 57

Pectins, 48
    draining, 201
    maceration carbonique, 190
Pediococcus, 125
Pellicles, *see* Skins
Penicillium, 80
Pentosanes, 38
Pentoses, 37, 38, 43, 125, 127, 175, 261
Perlites, 298, 305
Permanganate index, *see* Folin's index
Pétillant, 22
Petri-dish, 100
pH, 19, 30, 40
    deacidification, 87, 89, 119, 124
    definition, **54**
    heating, 334
    sorbic acid, 275
    sulfiting, 135, 145, 162, 257, 268
    threshold, 132
Pharmacopeia standards, 345
Phenol:
    odor, 217
    taste, 80
Phenolic compounds:
    bouquet, 251
    characteristics, 19, 25
    color, 44, 116
    extraction, 174
    life-span, 247
    oxidation, 213
Phosphate:
    anion, 45, 117
    feeding yeasts, 117
Phosphato-ferric casse, 326
Photosynthesis, 60, 62
    table, **63**
Physical treatments, **332**
Phytate, 326
Phytato-ferric casse, 326
Phytin, 326
Picking, 77
    for white wine, **198**
Pieces, 109, 214
Piedmont, 224
Pigmentation, 70, 90. *See also* Anthocyanins
Pipes:
    under inert gas, 245
    of Port, 228
Pips, *see* Seeds, pips
Piquant, taste, 22, 266

Plastering, musts, 86
Plugging corks, 365
Plunger, for racking, 241
Polarimeter, 38
Polishing filter, 302
Polyalcohols, 25, 36, 38, 125
Polyamide (nylon powder), 214
Polymerization, 34, 251
Polypeptides, 47
  nitrate, 49
Polyphenol index, 16, 34
  explanation, Folin, 45, 47, 72, 174, 176,
    177, 180, 339
Polyphenol oxidases, see Laccase
    (polyphenoloxidase); Tyrosinase
    (polyphenoloxidase)
Polyphenols, 71, 173, 190, 192, 214
  Port, 228, 269
Polysaccharides, 48, 175, 193, 218, 263,
    269, 285, 316, 337, 345
  cork, 364
Pomace, 58
  aroma, 72, 85, 113, 116
  immersed, 157
  stuck fermentation, 170
  temperature, 165
  white, 197
Pomace contact, 140, 149, 173
  conditions, 178
  length, table, **174**
Population, yeasts, 100, 102, 112, 115
Pores, 298, 301, 304
Porosities, of filters, 303
Portugal, 227
Port wines, 227
  table, **228**
Potassium, 43, 45, 86, 88, 89, 135
  chilling, 341
Potassium bicarbonate, 86, 87, 294
Potassium bichromate, sizing wood, 236
Potassium bitartrate, 40, 43, 85, 87, 235
  crystals, 281, 312, **319**
  heating, 333, 339
  table, **337**
Potassium caseinate, 294
Potassium citrate, 329
Potassium ferrocyanide, **327,** 348
Potassium sorbate, 275
Potassium sulfate, 53
Potassium tartrate, 86, 87

Pot-still, cognac, 230
"Pousse," 121
Precipitation, 173
  chemical, 312
  clarification, 287
  of crystals, 336
Precoating, filtrating, 298, 305
Premium (fine or quality) wines, odor, 20,
    82, 130, 180, 183, 247, 251, 252,
    254, 262
Presses:
  continuous, 186, **204**
  hydraulic, pneumatic, 205
  table, **206**
Pressing, 143, 172, **179**
  white, **203**
Pressure tanks, see Tanks, for fermentation
Press-wine, 84, 155, 170
  analytical composition, 191, 205
  table, **180**
Processing must, **197**
Production control, of bottles, 354
Prolin, 49
Protective colloids, see Colloids
Proteins, 45, 47, 210, 287, 288,
    291
  cloudiness, 316
  stability, 338
Puckering, astringence, 19
Pulp, of grape, 57, 59, 62, 71
Pumping-over, 84
  bubble-system, 158
  cooling, 168
  deacidification, 88
  dissolving, 174
  extraction, 173
  influence, table, **175**
  Port, 228
  stirring, 108, **113, 115**
  technique, 85
Punching down, 113, 115
  extraction, 173
  open tanks, 155
  Port, 228
Pyridoxin, 52, 118
Pyrogallic tannin, 46

Quality wines, see Premium (fine or quality)
    wines, odor
Quercitin, 46

Quercus suber, 362
Quinine sulfate, bitter taste, 25, 27, 29, 31

Racking (sedimentation), 72
  beneficial effects, table, **239**
  by centrifugation, 308
  clarification, 286
  deacidification, 87
  deposits, **208, 238**
  diagram, **242**
  draining, 176, **205**
  lees, 137
  malolactic fermentation, 130
  method, **240**
  oxygen, 248
  stuck fermentation, 170
Raffinose, 38, 63
Rainfall, 75, 77
Raisins, odor, 22
Rake, for pomace-extraction, 185, 186
Rancio:
  Banyuls, 226
  brandy, 230
  heating, 333
  oxygen, 247
  taste, 22
Ranking, 12, 13, 32, 33
  corks, 363, 364, 365
  see also Rating
Rating, 34
  champagne areas, 223
  pH threshold, malolactic fermentation, 133
Recycling, pomace, 188
Redox potential, 247, 249, 251, 253, 330, 352
Reduced bouquet, 334, 352
Reduced extract, 86, 180
Reduced odors, 22, 178
Reducing sugars, 33, 38, 61, 63, 69, 74, 100, 128, 180
  chemical determination, 216
Red wine:
  analysis table, **36**
  principles for making, 130
  sulfiting, 135
Refermentation accident, 101, 266, 269
Refractometer, 62, 77, 163, 164
Refrigeration, 222, **336**
  refrigerating plant, 169, 216, **340**
Relative density, 52

Repassing, cognac, 230
Residue, **15,** 29, 30, 42
Resiny taste, 23
Returnables (empty bottles), 355
Rhamnose, 49
Ribéreau-Gayon, 63, 71, 342
Riboflavin B2, *see* Vitamins
Ripening, **57,** 77
  table, **64, 77**
Ripening period (*véraison*), 58, 70, 76, 78
Rivesaltes, 225
Robe, 4
Rollers, on crushers, 147, **148**
Ropiness, **263**
Rosé wine:
  malolactic fermentation, 124, **221**
  temperature, 110
Rot, 90, 117, 315
  gray rot (bad rot), 23, 80, 199
  green rot, 79
  noble rot, 39, **73**
    table, **74**
    see also Botrytized grapes
  see also Mold
Rotary filters, 210
Roussillon, 225
Ruby Port, 227

Saccharine, 36, 163
Saccharomyces, 95, 98, 171, 218
Saccharose, *see* Chaptalizing (sugaring)
Salts:
  used in finings, **289**
  in wine, table, **44**
  see also Sodium chloride (common salt)
Salty taste, 25
  substances, 43
Sampling techniques, grapes, 78
Sanitary state, 21, 75, 79, 80
  cellar work, 233
  picking, 198
Sap, 121
  cork-boards, 364
Sapid, taste, 25
Sartorius, 300
Sauternes, 215, 217
Scoring, 12
  table, **13**
  see also Rating
Scouring, cement tanks, 150

Screw-cap, 361, **370**
Screw-conveyor, *see* Worm-screw feed
Sealing ring, in bottling, 357
Secondary fermentation, *see* Bottle,
    secondary fermentation
Security, 89
  cleanliness, 233
  screw-caps, storage, 370
Sediment, *see* Deposits
Sedimentation, *see* Racking (sedimentation);
    Settling
Seeding, *see* Inoculation (seeding)
Seeds, pips, 57, 59, 60, 140, 147, 172
Semifine wines, 192
Semi-sweet wines (*moelleux*), 217
  rosé, 221
Sensory analysis, *see* Tasting
Sensory consequence, of filtering, 307
Serine, 49, 63
Serum, 294
Settling, **205,** 208
  Asti Spumante, 224
Séve, 21
Sherry, **227**
Shipping syrup, 277
Shrinkage, 252
  of SO₂, 271
Sick-wines, 42, 255, 259. *See also* Casse
Sieve, filter, 303
Sifting, 299
Silica:
  glass, 351
  kieselsol, 292
  suspension, 283
Silicates, 235
Silicone, 44
Silver-plating, 330
Siphoning, filling bottles, **357**
Skin contact, 121. *See also* Pomace contact
Skins, 57, 59, 71, 140, 146, 172
Sleeve-filters, 305
Slide-rule, enological, **164**
Smell, 4, 8
  olfactory examination, 21, 26
  senses, 31
Soap-stone, 365
Soda, 351
Sodium, 43, 45
Sodium bentonite, 343
Sodium carbonate, 343

Sodium chloride (common salt), 25, 31, 289
  cooking salt, 293
Sodium silicate, 236
Sodium sulfate, 354
Softness, 19, 36, 38, 89
Solar energy, 62, 70. *See also*
    Photosynthesis
Soleo (esparto mats), sherry, 229
Solera system, sherry, 229
Sonoma, 82
Sorbitol, 37
Sorting, 224
Souring (lactic), 85, 135, 170, 187, **261**
Sour taste:
  equation, 15
  flavor, 14
  table, **39**
South Africa, 103
Spain, 99, 228
Spanish earth, 342
Sparkling wine, 22, 84, 101, **223**
Special (made) wines, 82, **221**
Species:
  bacteria, 124, **127**
  yeasts, 95, 97, **98**
Specific gravity, 52
Spectrophometer, **44**
Spectrum (range), 352
Spices, bouquet, 251
Spoilage:
  acetic, 256
  bacteria, 128
  bacterial, 43
  cloudiness, 281
  identification, 101
  malolactic fermentation, 124
  microbial, **255**
  yeasts, 100
Spontaneous clarification (sedimentation),
    252, **285**
Spores, 95
Stabilization:
  of clarity, 282
  by fining, **296, 311**
  processes, **315**
  treatment for, 130
Stachyose, 38, 63
Stalks, 59, 71, 175
Starch, 61
Starter culture, 104

Steam, for heating grapes, 192, 194
Steel tanks, 153
  stainless, **154**
Stemmer-crusher, 144, **147**
Stems, 59, 71, 175
Sterile corks, 366
Sterile filtering, 300
Sterility, 301
  of bottles, 355
Sterilization:
  containers, 335
  by heating, 108
  pure fermentation, 102
Sterols, 109, 111, 118
Stoppage (stuck fermentation), 105, 107,
      110, 117, 119
  Asti Spumante, 224
  lactic souring, 261
  stuck, **169,** 210, 214
  temperature, 133, 166
Stopper, 362
Stoppering:
  acescence, 257
  headspace, 361
Storage, 92, 125, 132, 133
  cellular, **235, 266**
Straw wine, see Passerilage
Stuck fermentation, see Stoppage (stuck
      fermentation)
Suberin (cork), 364
Sucrose, 25, 28, 30, 38, 61, 63, 85
Sugar, 15, 33, 36, 42
  brown sugar, cane/beet, 84
  fermentation, 107
  in grape, **60**
    table, **62**
  lactic fermentation of, **261**
  malolactic fermentation, 130, 170
  nourishment, **65,** 66
  yeasts, 117
Sugaring, see Chaptalizing (sugaring)
Sulfide, odors, 217
Sulfiting, 39
  aromas, 72, 80, 102, 103, 104, 124
  clarity failures, 316
  cooling, 168, 170, 171
  when draining, 178
  maceration carbonique, 191
  malolactic fermentation, 130, 132, 138,
      159
    table, **136**

oxygen, 247, 263
  practice of, **162**
  racking, **239**
  vintage, 199
  white wine, 208
Sulfur:
  burning in calcar, 354
  odor, 268
  off-taste, 22
  taste, 266
Sulfur anhydride, 41, 54
Sulfur candle, match, 152, 237, 272
Sulfur dioxide:
  addition of, **159**
    properties of, **160**
  bottle-sickness, 359
  color, 250
  cooperage-hygiene, 236
  forms, 315
    table, **273**
  free and combined diagram, **268**
  gustatory role, 34, 37, 90
  malolactic fermentation, 136, 140
  noxious yeasts, 100, 101, 104, 105, 119,
      135
  oxidation, 213
  oxygen combination, 249
  properties, table, **267**
  tourne, 260, **266**
  yeasts, 99
Sulfur tablets, 274
Supple, 41, 89
  egg albumin, 94
  malolactic fermentation, 120
  pomace contact, 176
  refrigeration, 339
  rosé, 221
Suppleness, 18, 122
  of corks, 363
  index, **16,** 29, 30, 32
Surmaturation, see Overripening
      (surmaturation)
Suspensoids, 284
Süssreserve, 220
Sweetening, dry wines, 219
Sweet-tasting substances:
  alcohol, **28,** 29, **30,** 33, **36**
Sweet wine, 105, **217**
  racking, 240
Swelling, finings, 295
Switzerland, 123, 164

Syringe, for injecting finings, 295
Syrup, for chaptalizing, 84

Table wine, 259
Tank life, 100
    finishing, 246
Tanks, for fermentation, **148**
    cement, **237**
    closed, 157
    fermentation in, **215**
    open, 155
    pressure, sparkling, 223, 225
    sedimentation in, 209
    shapes, **156**
    specially equipped, **187**
    upkeep, **234**
Tannins, 16, 19, 27, 29
    adding tannin, **90**
        ferric casse, 325
        fining, 290
        see also Phenolic compounds
    barrel-aging, 252
    casks, 34
    extraction, 116, 172
    finings, **288**
    heating, 192
    phenolic compounds, 47
    temperature, 180
        table, 173–174
    in wine, 46
Tannins–anthocyanins complex, color, 250
Tartar:
    descaling, 235
    malolactic fermentation, 121
    metatartaric acid, 346
Tartar crystals:
    metatartaric acid, 346
    precipitation, 40
Tartaric precipitations, **320**
    refrigeration, **337**
Taste, **3,** 4, 14
    filtering, 307, 332
    improvement, **338**
    microorganisms, 92
    SO₂, 267
Taste buds, see Papillae (taste buds)
Tasting, **1**
    analytical, 6
    exercises, training, **24**
    group, **11**
    hedonic, 5

    methods, **11**
    sensory analysis, 3
    vocabulary, **17**
Tasting faucet, 165
Tasting room, **10**
Tawnies, Port, 227
Tear-off capsule, 361
Tears, of gum arabic, 345
Temperate region, 86, 110, 125
Temperature:
    on color and tannins, table, **173**
    cooling, 167
    effect on fining, **289**
    fermentation, table, **109**
    malolactic fermentation, 121
        influence of, **133**
    pumping over, 115
    SO₂ balance, 269
    spoilage, 257
    supervising fermentation, 163, **165**
    tasting, 10
    yeasts, **107**
Terpineol, 50
Tests:
    acetic spoilage, 265
    fining, **290**
    stability, **317**
        table, **318–319**
Thermal exchange:
    casks, 150
    metal tanks, 154, 187
Thermal problem, **165**
Thermal treatments, 332
    table, **336**
Thermal vinification, **192**
    methods, **194**
    table, **195–196**
Thermistor, 165
Thermocouple, 187
Thermometer, 163
Thiamine, B1, see Vitamins
Threonin, Acids, amino
Thresholds:
    insolubilization casse, 325
    sensitivity, 17, 25, 31
    solubility of crystals, chilling, 338
    yeasts, 97
Tile color (tuilé), 246, 250
Tired wine, 21
    tiring, 304
Tirage syrup, Champagne, 224

Titanium:
  salts, 354
  steel, 152
Tongue, **7**
Topping, **242**
Touch, 5
Tourne, 21, 40, 255, **259**, 315
Translocation, *see* Migration (translocation)
Transport, *see* Containers
Treatments:
  examples, table, **321**
  list of, **320**
Trehalose, 38
Trescases, on corks, 363
Tulip glass, 26
Tunnel furnace, 354
Turbidity, *see* Deposits; Particles-in-
  suspension
Turbinates, *see* Median turbinates
Tyndall effect, 283
Tyrosinase (polyphenoloxidase), 160, 212,
  213, 334

Ultra dispersion, 307
Ultra-sounds:
  physical treatment, 338
  ultrasonics, 254
Ultraviolet rays, 254, 319, 352

Vacuoles, in grape berry, 140, 147, 173
Vacuum dehydrates, *see* Yeasts
Vacuum machines, for bottling, 359,
  360
Valin, *see* Acids, amino
Vanilla flavor, from wood, 252
Vaporization, cooling by, 216
Varietal flavors, 72, 192
Variety, *see* Grape varieties
VDN (natural sweet wine), **225**
  refrigeration, 336
VDQS (*vins de qualité produits dans une
  région déterminée*), 86
Vegetable taste, 172, 181, 205
Vegetative aroma, 196
Vegetative cycle, 75
Vegetative period (*nouaison*), 58
Véraison, 64
Vinegar, odor, 34
Vinification, 92, 113, 130, **139**
  definition, **140**
  methods, table, **182**

Vinifying:
  red wine, **143, 159, 172, 184**
  rosé and special wines, **221**
  white wine, **197, 212**
Vinifying machine, *see* Fermentors
Vin nouveau, 22
Vinous spirits, 32
Vintage:
  adjusting, **83**
  delaying, 66
  quality of, 61
  setting date, **75**
Vintage years, quality of, 81
Vinyl resin, lining tanks, 152
Viscosity, 292
Vitamin C (ascorbic acid), 276
Vitamins, **50**
  growth factors, 118
  list of, **52**
  sterols, 111
Vitis vinifera (European vines), 45
Vocabulary, **14**
  gustatory, **17**
Volatile substances, **49**
  chromatogram, **52**
  list, **51**
Voluminal mass, 52

Washing:
  bottles, **355**
  cleanliness, 234
  pomace, 172
Water, incidence of, **67**
Wavelengths, color of bottles, 330
Waxy (ceroid) part, cork, 364
Weather forecasts, 75
Whisks, **295**
White wine:
  clarity, 281
  cupric casse, 329
  malolactic fermentation, 123–124
    types of, **197**
  overfining, 290
  refrigeration, 336
  temperature, 110
  testing for casse, 318
  see also Vinifying
Wicker baskets, picking white grapes, 199
Wine:
  composition, **35**
  definition, **35**

Winery:
  cleanliness, space, 233
  fitting out, 150
  yeasts in, 96
Wine trade, blending wines, 245
Wood, oxygen uptake, 248
Woody (or bark) taste, 21, 72, 251
Worm-screw feed, 144, 194, 201
  pomace extractor, 179, 186, 188
Wyoming, bentonite, 343

Xylose, 37, 38, 261

Yeasts:
  clarity spoilage, 316

count, 100
distribution table, **97**
lactic acid, 42, **93**
mycodermic, **258**
need for air, **111**
noxious, 101
populations, **96**
shapes, **95**
smell, 21
species, **99**
  table, **98**
variety, 97
yeast-count, filtering, 302

Zinc, 44